Japanese Eyes
American Heart

Dedication

In World War II we trained and played together, worked side by side with each other, and fought and grieved together—on the battlefields of Europe, in the deep and dark jungles of Asia and the Pacific islands, and here at home in Hawaii. Close to eight hundred of our buddies never lived to see the headlines proclaim "Peace at Last!" or to bask in the warm sunlight of the island home we helped change for all of Hawaii's people. To you, our comrades in arms who made the supreme sacrifice for America, we dedicate *Japanese Eyes . . . American Heart*.

Japanese Eyes

Personal Reflections of Hawaii's World War II Nisei Soldiers

American Heart

Compiled by the Hawaii Nikkei History Editorial Board

Tendai Educational Foundation • Honolulu

ISBN 0-8248-2144-0 (paper)
ISBN 0-8248-2162-9 (cloth)

This book is printed on acid-free paper and meets the
guidelines for permanence and durability of the
Council on Library Resources.

Book design by Nina Lisowski

Distributed by
University of Hawai'i Press
2840 Kolowalu Street
Honolulu, Hawai'i 96822

Contents

FOREWORD *by U.S. Senator Daniel K. Inouye*   *ix*
INTRODUCTION *by Hideto Kono*   *xiii*

Chapter 1

Hawaii's Nisei Soldiers: Who Were They?

100th Infantry Battalion (Separate)   *3*
442nd Regimental Combat Team   *5*
Military Intelligence Service   *7*
1399th Engineer Construction Battalion   *9*

Chapter 2

December 7, 1941: A Morning That Changed Our Lives Forever

I Saw His Face! *by Conrad Tsukayama*   *13*
Dead Silence *by Tokuji Ono*   *29*
Eyewitness at Wheeler *by Tom Mizuno*   *32*
America Is at War! *by George Akita*   *34*
Days of Infamy: The Journal of George Akita   *36*
Honor Thy Country *by Seiso Kamishita*   *45*

Chapter 3

Boys to Men

Now I Am a Man! Departure Diary *by Robert N. Katayama*   *51*
The Life and Times of a Kolohe GI *by Jesse M. Hirata*   *54*
Soft Green Soldiers *by Hideto Kono*   *69*

Chapter 4

Our Place in the Sun

The Trailblazers: The 100th Infantry Battalion (Separate)
by Lyn Crost   73

New Visions: Fires to Be Kindled by Ben H. Tamashiro   77

Two Years, Eight Months, and Nineteen Days That Changed My Life Forever
by Samuel Sasai   81

Kuni no on—Gratitude to My Country by Yoshiaki Fujitani   94

Two Songs by Warren T. Iwai   103

Chapter 5

Oya no ai—The Love of a Parent

Kuni no Tame ni . . . For the Sake of Our Country
by Kikuyo Fujimoto   107

Mother's Love and Kagezen by Robert T. Sato   110

Okaasan . . . Best Friend by Robert T. Sato   112

Two Sons . . . Four Shiny Stones by Minoru Kishaba   113

Chapter 6

An Ocean Away . . .

From Relocation Camp to Military Service by Robert K. Sakai   121

The Journey of a Mainland AJA by Ernest Uno   135

Chapter 7

From the Front Lines

Dad's "Boys" by Albert Farrant Turner   151

Japanese Dog Bait by Raymond R. Nosaka   155

Sargeant Shigeo Joe Takata: He Set the Standard by Tsutomu Tom Nagata   158

First Christmas Overseas by Ben H. Tamashiro   160

Secret Mission by Richard M. Sakakida   163

Comrades in Arms by Michael M. Miyatake   170

The Adventures of an MIS Marine *by Ben I. Yamamoto*   177
We Loved Our Country *by Sakae Takahashi*   186
Monte Cassino: Purple Heart Valley *by Robert T. Sato*   189
Hell in the Vosges *by John Tsukano*   191
Stalag VIIA *by Stanley M. Akita*   203
Bringing Home the Proud Colors *by Henry S. Kuniyuki*   219
Singing the Mess Hall Blues *by Ronald M. Oba*   223
The "Pineapple Soldiers"—Hawaii's Forgotten Battalion
by A. A. Smyser   227
"Dear Mom" Letters *by Chaplain Hiro Higuchi*   232
"Dear A": Letters Home *by Chaplain Masao Yamada*   255
The Making of the 100th *by Chaplain Israel Yost*   265
Letters From the Front *by Katsumi "Doc" Kometani*   273
If I Am Filial . . . *by Hoichi Kubo*   278

Chapter 8

We Are Our Brothers' Keeper

Sunken Eyes at Dachau *by Edward Ichiyama*   285
Dachau, 1945: What Have We Learned? *by Tadashi Tojo*   289
The Spirit of a Three-Year-Old Child *by Takejiro Higa*   291
In the Spirit of *Okage Sama De* *by Governor George R. Ariyoshi*   303
Trees of Aloha *by Fujio Takaki*   311
A Conversation with the Emperor *by Kan Tagami*   315
Humanity in Action *by Kenneth K. Inada*   321

Chapter 9

Coming to Terms

Fellow Citizens of Japan . . .   327
On the Way to Sugamo Prison *by Sohei Yamate*   328
An American—Not a Japanese Living in America *by Ted T. Tsukiyama*   335
Shared Ethnicity *by George Akita*   340
Sanji and Me *by Joe H. Shimamura*   343
Lucky We Came Back *by Walter "Biffa" Moriguchi*   346

Chapter 10

Taking Ownership

The Dream for Tomorrow—Letters between Joseph R. Itagaki
and Charles R. Hemenway   *351*
Journey to Washington Place *by Governor George R. Ariyoshi*   *359*
Building Behind the Scenes *by Mike N. Tokunaga*   *370*
Issei and Citizenship: Proud Americans *by Robert T. Sato*   *380*

Chapter 11

Building Bridges

Serving for Two *by Kaoru Yonezawa*   *385*
Mission Accomplished *by Don Seki*   *388*
Tomosu Hirahara Rests at Epinal *by Ben H. Tamashiro*   *392*
Rededication *by U.S. Senator Spark M. Matsunaga*   *395*
Patriots Still *by Edward Ichiyama*   *401*
Thicker Than Blood *by Edward Ichiyama*   *403*

Chapter 12

Let There Be Peace On Earth

We Must Teach Our Children to Want Peace
by U.S. Senator Spark M. Matsunaga   *407*

EPILOGUE

The Light from One Corner . . . *by Bishop Ryokan Ara*   *409*

SO PROUDLY WE HAIL: HONOR ROLL OF WORLD WAR II
AMERICANS OF JAPANESE ANCESTRY   *413*
THE CONTRIBUTORS   *423*
INDEX   *435*

U.S. Senator Daniel K. Inouye

Foreword

I was seventeen years old when aircraft of the Japanese empire attacked Pearl Harbor. After the initial shock, I felt anger at the Japanese for their hostile intrusion on our island. At the same time, I felt apprehension over what might happen to those of us who shared common ancestral roots and resembled the people of the nation that had attacked us.

The U.S. government promptly assumed total control of the governance of Hawaii through the declaration of martial law. We were powerless to challenge the control over our affairs inasmuch as Hawaii was a territory of the United States. As such, we could not elect our own governor or our own senators and representatives to represent our interests before federal authorities. Martial law was administered, for the most part, by newly assigned military officers who were unfamiliar with Hawaii's multiethnic population and even less able or willing to differentiate between the issei Japanese, who were ineligible for U.S. citizenship, and their nisei offspring, who were American citizens by virtue of their birthplace.

In the early stages of the war, all residents of Japanese ancestry were declared "enemy aliens" by the governing authorities, who believed that people with Japanese roots would side with Japan. This led to unreasonable and humiliating treatment of all Japanese, including U.S. citizens of Japanese ancestry. In time, however, the question of the loyalty of Japanese Americans was reassessed, due largely to the exemplary behavior of Japanese Americans who volunteered for the Hawaii Territorial Guard and the Varsity Victory Volunteers, and the outstanding performance of those who were already serving in the U.S. Army before the Pearl Harbor attack who were subsequently brought together to form the 100th Infantry Battalion.

In January 1943, the U.S. Army announced plans to form an all-Japanese American regimental team for combat assignment in Europe. Japanese American youths were invited to volunteer for the regiment, which was designated the 442nd Regimental Combat Team.

The response was overwhelming. Among the volunteers were young men in Hawaii and on the mainland whose parents had been rounded up earlier by military authorities and held under armed security in remote internment camps. I was among those who volunteered for the combat team. When I was getting ready to ship out of the Islands for army training on the mainland, my father came to bid me farewell. "America has been good to us," he said. "We owe a lot to this country, and if you must give your life, so be it. Whatever you do, do not dishonor your family or your nation."

The wartime exploits of the Japanese American 100th Infantry Battalion/442nd Regimental Combat Team in the bloody European battlefields and the Japanese American intelligence units that provided language support to U.S. Army, Navy, and Marine forces in the fiercely fought battlegrounds of the Pacific have been widely acclaimed. Numerous citations and grateful acknowledgments were presented by the president of the United States, military field commanders in Europe and the Pacific, and from fellow combatants of the Allied forces who fought alongside the Japanese Americans.

The Japanese Americans who returned to Hawaii after completing their military service had another battle to fight on behalf of themselves and thousands of their comrades who had sacrificed their lives for freedom and equality—a battle for equal opportunity for all residents of Hawaii and equal status for Hawaii as a political subdivision of the nation.

Over the past fifty years, the home-front battle has been successfully waged for the most part. The people of Hawaii have made considerable progress toward achieving a level playing field for all ethnic groups. Hawaii's political status was upgraded from a territory when, in 1959, it became the fiftieth star on the American flag. Since then, the governorship of Hawaii has been held by Americans of Caucasian, Japanese, Hawaiian, and Filipino ancestry. Hawaii's people have also elected persons of diverse ethnic roots to represent them in the U.S. Congress. I had the honor of serving Hawaii as a member of the U.S. House of Representatives in 1959, and, since 1963, have served as a U.S. senator.

I believe Bishop Ryokan Ara and the Tendai Educational Foundation are rendering a valuable service in documenting and publishing the life experiences and innermost thoughts of America's World War II veterans of Japanese ancestry, who went to war against the country of their parents' birth and endured prejudicial treatment from some of their fellow Americans. Even as the soldiers fought against Japan, the Japanese cultural values instilled in them, often unobtrusively by their parents, influenced their thoughts and actions in the battlefield and in their pursuit of equality and a place of responsibility and respect among their fellow Americans.

I highly recommend this fascinating book. By virtue of their American citizenship and their Japanese ancestry, Japanese Americans have a high personal stake in continued good relations between America and Japan. There should be no paths laid today that might lead to another dreadfully devastating war, similar to the one that came to a close just over a half century ago. This is my fervent wish.

Hideto Kono

Introduction

In 1995, during observances marking the fiftieth anniversary of the end of the war in the Pacific, the Tendai Educational Foundation, led by Reverend Ryokan Ara, bishop of the Tendai Mission of Hawaii, commissioned a Japanese-language book entitled, *Hawaii no nikkei beihei: Watakushi tachi wa nanto tatakatta no ka?* (Hawaii's Japanese American soldiers: For what did we fight?). The book was published by Heibonsha, a noted publisher in Japan, with editorial contributions by several prominent Japanese American World War II veterans.

Hawaii no nikkei beihei sought to help the people of Japan better understand America and its people, particularly those of Japanese ancestry, through events that transpired during World War II. Japanese Americans, through no fault of their own, were thrown into a war that pitted the country of their birth against the country from which their parents had emigrated. It was not until 1952 that these first-generation Japanese were allowed to become naturalized American citizens.

Following the successful publication of the Japanese book, Bishop Ara expressed the desire to produce a similar book in the English language to reach a broad readership. Again, the goal was to share the deep-felt sentiments of the Japanese American soldiers.

Although many excellent books on the World War II experience of the nisei soldiers have already been written, we hope this volume will provide some insight into the veterans' feelings about their wartime experiences—their fears, their disappointments, their hopes, their dreams—not only for themselves, but for their families and their communities.

Japanese Eyes . . . American Heart consists largely of the personal reflections of some of Hawaii's Japanese Americans who participated in World War II and their struggle for equality upon their return to Hawaii. To these testimonies have been added observations of a few others who worked closely with the Japanese American community and who played significant roles in these efforts during the war years. Gathering personal reflections by the veterans was the biggest obstacle we faced while compiling this book, for there was a characteristic reluctance on their part to share their thoughts, feelings, and deeds. That reluctance stems largely from their parents' culture, which encourages modesty and frowns on calling attention to one's own accomplishments.

Cognizant of that reluctance, Bishop Ara sought assistance from several veterans who had helped him publish *Hawaii no nikkei beihei*. An ad hoc group, the Hawaii Nikkei History Editorial Board, was formed and appealed to many World War II nisei veterans living in Hawaii to write about their experiences, with emphasis on what they thought and how they felt before, during, and after the war. The board faced an added urgency because most veterans were already in their late seventies and early eighties.

The editorial board, which met regularly at the Tendai Mission office, included myself, a veteran of the 442nd Regimental Combat Team and the Military Intelligence Service (MIS); and Rev. Yoshiaki Fujitani, former bishop of the Honpa Hongwanji Mission of Hawaii, also an MIS veteran, who served as cochair of the board. Others on the board included attorneys Edward Ichiyama and Robert Katayama, both veterans of the 442nd; attorney Ted Tsukiyama, a 442nd and MIS veteran; and Dr. Robert Sakai, emeritus professor of history at the University of Hawaii and a veteran of the MIS. Rounding out the editorial board were retired educator Jane Komeiji, a member of the board of directors of the Japanese Cultural Center of Hawaii and coauthor of the book *Okage sama de* (I am what I am because of you): *The Japanese in Hawaii, 1885–1985*. She was joined by the daughters and son of men who served in the 100th Infantry Battalion: Mimi Nakano (daughter of Shizuya Hayashi), Drusilla Tanaka (daughter of Bernard Akamine), and Cary Miyashiro (son of George "Oscar" Miyashiro).

The editorial board enlisted the services of Karleen Chinen, former editor of *The Hawaii Herald*, whose father, Wallace Seiko Chinen, served with the 100th Infantry Battalion. Ms. Chinen had the monumental task of editing and organizing the various testimonies, which were received in a variety of forms and styles.

I wish to thank the members of the Hawaii Nikkei History Editorial Board and those who submitted their personal testimonies for inclusion in this book. A heartfelt thank you also to many others who contributed to the publication of this book, among them, members of the Club 100, the 442nd Veterans Club, the Military Intelligence Service Veterans Club, and the 1399th Engineer Construction Battalion veterans group.

Finally, may I offer special thanks to Bishop Ryokan Ara, whose unwavering support and encouragement sustained us throughout this project. I believe *Japanese Eyes . . . American Heart* will help to promote better understanding of the contributions of Hawaii's Japanese Americans to international peace and goodwill.

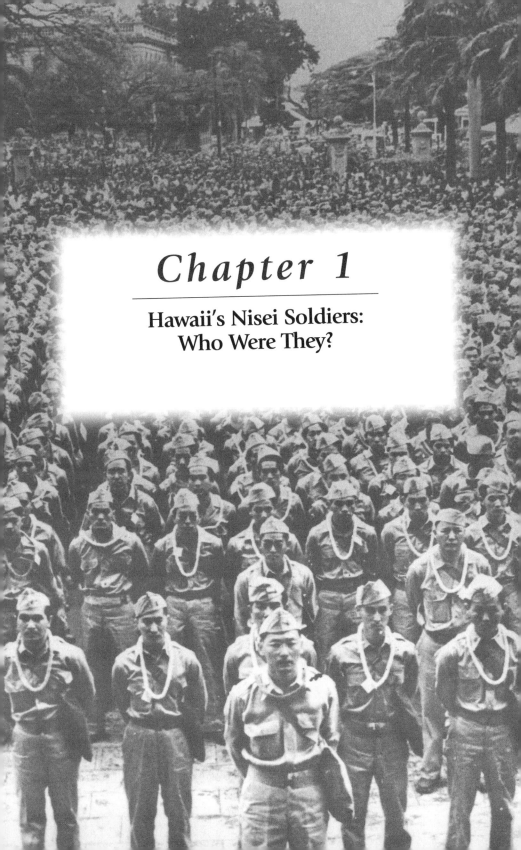

Chapter 1

Hawaii's Nisei Soldiers:
Who Were They?

100th Infantry Battalion (Separate)

The Purple Heart Battalion

With the exception of a few of its officers, the 100th Infantry Battalion (Separate) was the first combat unit in U.S. Army history to be comprised exclusively of Japanese Americans from Hawaii. The unit was made up of 1,432 men serving in the 298th and 299th Regiments of the Hawaii National Guard who had been drafted prior to Japan's attack on Pearl Harbor. In the weeks following the attack, the soldiers guarded Hawaii's beaches and coastlines from a possible land invasion by Japanese military forces.

On May 28, 1942, Japan's naval forces were approaching Midway. In anticipation of a Japanese attack on Hawaii, all Japanese American soldiers in the 298th and 299th Regiments were placed in a separate unit called the Hawaiian Provisional Infantry Battalion. They were shipped out of the Islands in the darkness of night on June 5, 1942—their destination a secret.

Several days later, San Francisco's Golden Gate Bridge appeared on the horizon. After disembarking in Oakland, the unit—renamed the 100th Infantry Battalion (Separate)—was transported by train to Camp

McCoy, Wisconsin, and subsequently to Camp Shelby, Mississippi, for combat training.

Throughout their sixteen months of training, the army remained silent about whether the 100th would be sent into combat, and if so, to where and with whom. Finally, in September 1943, the 100th was dispatched to Oran, Africa, and attached to the 34th "Red Bull" Division. On September 22, 1943, the "One Puka Puka" hit the beaches of Salerno, Italy.

For the next nine months, the 100th fought from Salerno to Rome, battling a tenacious enemy throughout a bitter winter. The unit faced its toughest test at Monte Cassino, a mountaintop monastery occupied by the Germans, and suffered tremendous casualties. That battle earned the 100th its nickname, "The Purple Heart Battalion."

On June 11, 1944, the casualty-depleted 100th was bolstered by replacements from the 442nd. The 100th was subsequently attached to the newly arrived 442nd Regimental Combat Team (RCT), a unit of nisei volunteers from Hawaii and the mainland United States. The 100th was designated the First Battalion of the 442nd, although it was allowed to retain its original name, the 100th Infantry Battalion.

Thereafter, as part of the 442nd RCT, the 100th contributed significantly to driving the German army north to the Arno River by September 1944. From October through November 1944 the 100th/442nd joined the 36th Infantry Division in northeastern France for the Vosges Mountains campaign. The 100th participated in the liberation of Bruyeres and Biffontaine and the rescue of the Texas "Lost Battalion"—an effort that earned it a Presidential Unit Citation.

In April 1945, the 100th/442nd was attached to the Fifth Army in Italy, where it pierced the long-held Gothic line and drove the German enemy back into the Po Valley, forcing Germany's surrender on May 2, 1945.

During its eighteen months in combat, the men of the 100th buried 337 of their comrades. For its service to America, the 100th Infantry Battalion and its soldiers were honored with 3 Presidential Unit Citations, 1,703 Purple Hearts, 1 Congressional Medal of Honor, 24 Distinguished Service Crosses, 147 Silver Stars, 2,173 Bronze Stars, and 30 Division Commendations.

From unwarranted distrust in the wake of the Pearl Harbor attack, this "guinea pig" battalion earned the distinction of being the most decorated battalion for its size and length of time in combat. Without a doubt, the 100th Infantry Battalion paved the way for other Japanese American soldiers to prove their loyalty to America in battle in World War II.

Japanese Eyes . . . American Heart

442nd Regimental Combat Team
Go for Broke!

The 442nd Regimental Combat Team was organized on March 23, 1943, in response to the War Department's call for volunteers to form an all-Japanese American army combat unit. Over twelve thousand Japanese American volunteers answered the call.

Ultimately, 2,686 volunteers from Hawaii and 1,500 from American concentration camps assembled at Camp Shelby, Mississippi, in April 1943 to undergo military training.

The 442nd RCT was comprised of the 442nd Infantry Regiment, 522nd Field Artillery Battalion, 232nd Combat Engineers Company, Anti-Tank Company, Cannon Company, the Medical Detachment, and the 206th Army Ground Forces Band. After about a year of training at Camp Shelby, the 442nd was sent overseas to Italy on May 1, 1944. There, it was joined by the 100th Infantry Battalion (Separate), which had been designated the First Battalion of the 442nd RCT.

The 442nd was assigned to Gen. Mark Clark's U.S. Fifth Army and underwent its baptism of fire at Suvereto on June 26, 1944. For the next ten weeks, the unit engaged the German army in the mountainous Italian terrain, driving the enemy forces north to the Arno River.

On August 15, 1944, the Anti-Tank Company was detached from the 442nd and ordered to make an assault glider landing in the U.S. Army's invasion of Southern France.

From October through November 1944 the 442nd served in northeastern France, where it fought with the 36th Infantry Division in the dark and bitter-cold forests of the Vosges Mountains. The French towns of Bruyeres, Belmont, and Biffontaine were liberated in the Vosges campaign, which was also highlighted by the rescue of the Texas "Lost Battalion." The 442nd suffered more than eight hundred casualties in the process of rescuing approximately two hundred Texans.

In late March 1945 the 522nd Field Artillery Battalion was assigned to the U.S. Seventh Army, which needed the 522nd's fire support in the Allied assault against Germany. While on that mission, it encountered and liberated Jewish survivors of the Dachau death march and other concentration camps.

The 442nd was returned to Italy in April 1945 at the specific request of General Clark, who wanted the unit to help the Fifth Army breach the German Gothic line, which had blocked the Allied advance for six months. The 442nd broke through the German defenses at Mount Folgorito in less than a day—and in the next three weeks forced the German army to retreat north to the Po Valley, where it finally surrendered on May 2, 1945.

In just ten months of combat against Germany, the 442nd RCT compiled a remarkable fighting record. It was achieved at a high price, however: over seven hundred killed and missing-in-action. The 442nd was honored with 9,486 Purple Heart Medals; 7 Presidential Unit Citations; and 18,143 individual decorations for bravery, including 1 Congressional Medal of Honor, 52 Distinguished Service Crosses, 588 Silver Stars, and more than four thousand Bronze Stars.

With its battle cry, "Go for Broke!" the 442nd Regimental Combat Team earned the honor and distinction of being the most decorated unit of its size and length of time in battle in United States military history.

Military Intelligence Service
America's Secret Weapon in World War II

During World War II, over six thousand nisei (second-generation Japanese Americans) served the Allied forces, performing secret military intelligence work against the Japanese military. Their work dispelled any doubt that as Americans the nisei were willing to fight an enemy with whom they shared a similar ancestral background.

On November 1, 1941, the U.S. Army secretly opened a Military Intelligence Service language school at the Presidio in San Francisco to teach and give training in military intelligence in the event of war with Japan. Following the outbreak of World War II, Japanese Americans with the required language background were recruited from the 100th Infantry Battalion and 442nd Regimental Combat Team, as well as from Hawaii and America's concentration camps. In all, over six thousand nisei graduated from military language schools at the Presidio and also at Camp Savage and Fort Snelling in Minnesota.

The MIS graduates were dispatched to every combat theater and participated in every major battle and invasion against the Japanese military. They were assigned to the U.S. Army, Navy, Marines, and Air Force and "loaned" to British, Australian, Canadian, New Zealand, Chinese, and Indian combat units in every phase of the Asia-Pacific war until Japan was defeated.

Beginning in May 1942, MIS nisei participated in the Aleutian and Solomon Islands invasions, in Gen. Douglas MacArthur's drive through New Guinea and the Philippines, and in the Central Pacific invasions of Tarawa, Kwajalein, Majuro, Eniwetok, Saipan, and Guam. Nisei led the final assault on Iwo Jima and Okinawa. Operating out of New Delhi, India, they helped drive the Japanese army from Burma, reopening the Burma Road to China.

The nisei linguists translated enemy documents, including orders, battle plans, maps, diaries, and letters; interrogated Japanese prisoners of war; served as order-of-battle specialists; intercepted and deciphered enemy communications; composed and broadcast surrender appeals and other psychological warfare tactics; and flushed caves of enemy soldiers and civilians. Volumes of intelligence material were gathered in the process and converted into successful Allied strategy and operations against the Japanese.

Until recently, very little was known about the invaluable service provided by the MIS nisei, primarily because their work was strictly classified.

The Military Intelligence Service was America's secret weapon in the war against Japan—a secret weapon that Gen. Charles Willoughby, G-2 chief in the Pacific, credited with saving a million lives and shortening the war against Japan by two years.

1399th Engineer Construction Battalion

The Chowhounds

The 1399th Engineer Construction Battalion was an all-Japanese American military unit stationed in Hawaii during World War II. It was the only unit of its kind to serve in the Pacific war against Japan.

The 1399th was activated at Schofield Barracks on Oahu on April 26, 1944. It consisted of Japanese American soldiers from a number of companies: the prewar 395th Quartermaster Battalion, 370th Engineer Battalion, 1536th Dump Truck Company, and 1525th Base Equipment Company, as well as draftees from the April through August 1944 drafts. The 1399th rose to its peak strength of 993 men in November 1944.

Throughout the war, the 1399th and its predecessor units constructed vital military defense installations on the island of Oahu. The 1399th completed more than fifty-four major defense projects, including construction of a million-gallon water tank in Wahiawa that is still in use, jungle-training villages, artillery emplacements, ammunition storage pits, water systems, warehouses, the Flying Fortress airfield at Kahuku, auxiliary roads in the mountains, rest and recreation camps, bridge repairs, rock quarry operations, and other military defense facilities.

Gen. Douglas MacArthur twice requested that the 1399th be assigned to the Philippines. However, the War Department considered them essential to the defense of Hawaii and refused to put them in direct conflict with the Japanese enemy.

In recognition of its contributions and sterling service, the 1399th Engineer Construction Battalion was presented the Meritorious Service Award in October 1945. Always standing in the shadows of the other Japanese American combat units, the 1399th Engineer Construction Battalion, known as the "Chowhounds," truly earned its reputation as the unsung heroes of the Hawaii front during World War II.

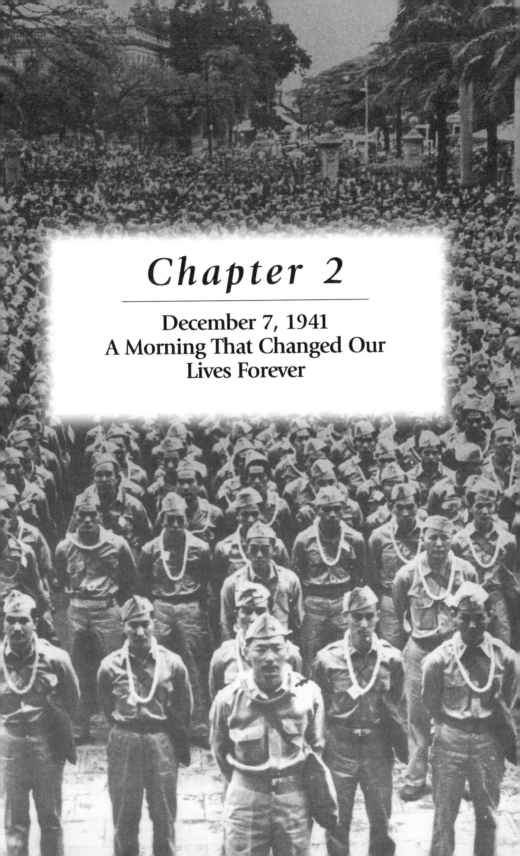

Chapter 2

December 7, 1941
A Morning That Changed Our
Lives Forever

Conrad Tsukayama

100th Infantry Battalion

I SAW HIS FACE!

I saw his face! I saw the face of the Japanese pilot in his fur-lined helmet, looking down at us through his goggles.

That is the very first image that flashes into my mind whenever I think back on all the events that took place over a half century ago. Now, in the golden years of my life, I see December 7, 1941, as one piece, but an important one, nevertheless, in a large mosaic. The mosaic's pieces represent my life and the lives of many nisei like me who served our country in World War II. When the pieces are all put together, we see a complete picture of our lives over the past eighty years.

I was born in Ewa on the island of Oahu, although I have no recollection of my life in the sugar plantation community other than the childhood stories related to me by my mother. After completing their contract with the plantation, my parents opted to become independent farmers and moved to Kailua on the Windward side of Oahu. Farmers in Kailua lived in scattered farm clusters, where they grew specialty crops. We, in the Oneawa group, grew watermelons closer to the Mokapu Peninsula.

There were a few Native Hawaiian fishing villages scattered along the seacoast. Still, we rarely had any contact with people of other ethnic backgrounds.

Although the community was made up primarily of Japanese immigrants, it lacked the facilities and support that we might have enjoyed in a plantation setting. The Kailua Japanese Language School was the only real facility available to us. Thus, it became the center of our community and the institution that bonded us together.

While the Buddhist temples served the youngsters in the plantation camps, the Community Christian Church became the center of activities for youngsters in Kailua. We became "Americanized" through Boy Scout troops, YMCA (Young Men's Christian Association) clubs, organized athletics, and other such recreational activities.

Education and knowledge of culture were very important to the Japanese parents of the early 1920s. They sent their children not only to English-language school as the law required, but also to Japanese-language school. After all, they planned to return to Japan eventually and wanted to prepare their children for that time.

Our growing-up days, therefore, resembled a country lifestyle in a prefectural village in Japan. It was a natural setting for cultivating the Japanese culture.

The little clusters of farmers were organized as support groups, which made up the larger Kailua Japanese Community Association. Japanese immigrants were noted for being an organized, caring, law-abiding, and tight-knit group. Perhaps too much so—other ethnic groups may not have felt very comfortable with them. For instance, the ceremonies and rituals for weddings and funerals were performed strictly according to set practices, and Japanese holidays were celebrated on the same day as in their homeland. New Year's Day was a great holiday that was enjoyed by everyone, with the traditional *mochi* pounding and feasting that seemed to go on forever.

When the Japanese naval training ships docked at our ports, it was a big treat to visit the ships. It was always exciting to watch the wrestling and kendo competitions between the Japanese cadets and the locals. Occasionally, officers from the ships were invited to speak to the assembled farmers. To an audience homesick for Japan, it must have been the treat of a lifetime. They came home impressed with Japan's superior and advanced naval weaponry and, no doubt, felt honored to be visited by a ranking naval officer here in distant Hawaii.

As the years passed, generation gaps began to emerge. Americanization had started to take hold with the children, who were beginning to ask uneasy questions: Why are we trying so hard to be Japanese? Why aren't we visiting our own battleships at Pearl Harbor? The answers to those and many other questions became obvious as I progressed in age and expanded my exposure to other aspects of Hawaii's multicultural society.

Our parents lived as though they were in Japan, and in their quest to return home, they were missing the Americanization opportunity that was open to them. It was partly because of this miscalculation that the Japanese ethnic group was generally not warmly and comfortably accepted.

Over time, I had gotten the impression from local Japanese people that Pearl Harbor was off-limits to anyone of Japanese ancestry. Thus, visiting American warships was out of the question.

By the late 1920s, changes were evident not only in the living conditions in Kailua but also in the makeup of the community. There was an influx of new farmers, the economy had begun to improve, and there were new highways and water pipes and electricity.

Most of the issei, by then, had established family roots in Hawaii and had come to realize that they probably would not be able to return to Japan. But they realized, also, that living in Hawaii wasn't really all that bad; perhaps Hawaii would be the land of promise for them and their children.

Little did my parents realize that by joining the local Christian church and constantly tolerating the modern behavioral changes taking place in their children—behavior that would be considered rude or offensive in Japan—that they, too, had gotten caught up in the process of change.

By 1936, due to family misfortune, I had left school after completing the tenth grade and started to work to help support my younger brothers and sisters through school.

The compulsory military training program was in effect. Thus, on November 14, 1941, with my pockets stuffed full with monetary gifts and with best wishes from my neighbors and friends, I was escorted to a neighboring town to board a bus for Schofield Barracks. During the physical examination I was found unfit for military duty due to flat feet, an arch condition detrimental to becoming an infantry soldier.

I was totally devastated. I protested vehemently because it was a disgrace to my family to be rejected. I pleaded and explained that it was not possible for me to return to civilian status like this. I had received numerous bon voyage envelopes and it would be embarrassing beyond words to return them to all my well-wishers. Thankfully, the officer finally relented and I was sworn in as a private in the United States Army. Life in the army was a big change, but I enjoyed the early phase of my training.

On Saturday night, December 6th, I was at home on a weekend pass, telling my family what a soldier's life was like. Early Sunday morning during breakfast, we heard unusual activities at the Kaneohe Naval Air Station. It was normally very quiet and peaceful on weekends, but that day we heard explosion after explosion.

As soon as someone commented on the commotion, we turned on the radio, just in time to hear the radio announcer interrupt the morning program and repeat excitedly: "This is the real McCoy! The Japanese are attacking Pearl Harbor!"

The family rushed out the door, and there, on December 7, 1941, I saw the face of that Japanese pilot. He looked calm and confident. Maybe this was his way of displaying his arrogant superiority, or perhaps he was communicating to us not to worry, that all would be okay.

The Japanese Zeros (the model of plane used by the Japanese in the Pearl Harbor attack) were on their strafing run and they peeled into their dive. Mushrooming clouds rose above the hill that obstructed our view of the naval air station, only two air miles from where we stood. Judging by the black clouds of smoke now visible high above the hill, I concluded that extensive damage had been inflicted.

The life of a simple country boy, a raw army recruit from a small village in Kailua, turned a new course that day. But I was not alone, for December 7, 1941, affected every living soul in Hawaii.

My very first impulse that morning was to pick up a stone and hurl it against the low-flying Zeros or communicate my anger with other gestures. But fright and the fact that I could not defend myself if the pilots trained their machine guns on us made me give in to my better judgment and drop the urge to strike back.

Many harsh words were directed at the pilots as, one by one, they passed from view. My anger was based on betrayal, the deepest hurt that can be inflicted. The deep-rooted respect and admiration for the Japanese instilled in us from childhood was shattered. They were mercilessly killing their own emigrant citizens.

By this time the radio was blaring that all military personnel were to return to their units immediately. Our anger and confusion subsided temporarily. We said our farewells, giving each other big emotional hugs, telling everyone to take good care of themselves.

I assembled my military gear and, in uniform, was prepared to walk to my buddy's home when he drove up, eager and excited. I still remember Father's parting words: "Be a good soldier." Mother's were those of a mother: "Come home safe."

Along the unimproved farm road, dust trailed the 1937 model Ford as we sped on, dodging potholes. Neighbors standing along the roadside waved farewell to us. Here I was, twenty-four days in the army and, in a few hours, a participant in the Pacific campaign. The only war training or experience I had came from playing soldier in the corn field as a child.

My sisters and brothers, whom I had been impressing just the night before with the nomenclature, description, and demonstration of the U.S. Army gas mask, would have been mightily shocked if they knew that I didn't know how to load my Springfield '03 rifle with ammunition.

We waved to the last of our well-wishers. Speeding along the paved highway, heading toward the mountains of Nuuanu Pali, my chest swelled with pride. I felt like a great hero. My buddy's car did not have a radio, so after a brief discussion of the morning's excitement, he advised me to expect massive confusion and to anticipate some prejudicial treatment from the regulars. He had completed basic training more than eight months earlier and was assigned to a Schofield engineers unit, so I took his advice to heart.

Traffic heading toward Honolulu seemed normal for a weekend, but my mind began to race, trying to understand why Japan had attacked us. Common talk among the issei all through the years was that Japan's aggression in conquering other nations was to satisfy its need for more land for its growing population. The Sino-Japan War, for example, was an expansion for Japan, which was intended to also position Japan strategically for eventual war with Russia.

This simple picture was painted in our minds time and time again from as far back as I could remember. What I couldn't understand was why Japan had done this to the United States. To put it mildly, I felt Japan had made its last mistake by irritating the world's mightiest power.

As we headed north to Schofield Barracks, the traffic approaching Pearl Harbor indicated huge turmoil. As we began the climb up Red Hill, through Moanalua, we could actually see Pearl Harbor. My heart began to beat out of control.

Pearl Harbor was a scene of devastation. Black smoke belched forth from explosions. I could see the twisted metal frames of the harbor infrastructure and the bottoms of capsized battleships. Pearl Harbor was literally on fire.

The rest of the drive to Schofield was solemn and distressing, marked by an inescapable feeling of doom. At Schofield, soldiers moved about like zombies in determined haste. A few trucks loaded with armed soldiers were moving out, presumably to occupy prearranged zones or sectors of defense.

My buddy dropped me off at the base entrance.

Our training area, where rows of tents were situated, was a scene of mass confusion. We were a bunch of frightened draftees without a leader. The assigned cadres had reported to their units and only supply clerks and mess personnel were on hand to take charge and supervise.

First, ammunition was issued. Then the big question: "Sergeant, how do you load this?" *Bang!* Order of the day: No loading of rifles.

We were issued tents, blankets, mess kits, canteens, knapsacks—all the necessary equipment to make up a combat pack. As excited yet nervous recruits reported for duty, one soldier was taught how to assemble all this gear into a combat pack. It was his job to then pass along the instructions to the next man. Packs, naturally, were not uniform.

By late morning, soldiers were loaded onto trucks. After many changes of orders, we dug trenches in the parade grounds and elsewhere to defend against possible landings by paratroopers. Lines of trenches zigzagged around Schofield.

The evening meal of field rations, consumed in pitch-darkness among unfamiliar soldiers, was an experience I will never forget. It was scary moving out to position that night, holding hands with an unknown buddy and led by a newly assigned young junior officer, who sounded confused yet impressively composed. Our instructions: Watch for enemy paratroopers landing.

Many changes of positions occurred before the night was over. Late that night I was pulled out of the trench and assigned to man a .30-caliber heavy machine gun. The officer in charge took my left hand and placed it on the trigger. He then placed my right hand on the bolt to load and then on the grip to traverse the pedestal-mounted gun, with instructions to aim at and shoot down enemy aircraft. The machine gun was loaded with tracer bullets to give the shooter an idea of how far ahead of an enemy aircraft he should be when firing.

During the early morning hours, a "friendly" aircraft attempted to land at the nearby airfield. Thank goodness I had already been relieved of the machine-gun assignment. Tracer bullets lit up the sky. There was no word about the friendly craft after that.

Rumors of paratroopers landing were rampant. Along with orders, rumors were whispered in our ears all night long.

With daylight the next morning, there was some semblance of order, relief, and composure—although a sergeant did forget a group of soldiers out in the boondocks without any food or water until almost nightfall. In the meantime, we were allowed to fire off a couple of rounds of ammo and learned safety and operating procedures for handling the rifle. Recruits from the fourth draft also trained and were assigned security and defense duties.

Our defense positions were assigned during daylight hours. We moved out at dusk, following our assigned leaders. This time we were organized and knew the other members of our newly formed squad. On the third day, draftees like me with Junior ROTC (Reserve Officers' Training Corps) training, which was limited to marching only, were organized into advance groups and given a higher level of training for two weeks.

Our group was assigned to the 298th, a federalized National Guard unit, and then moved out to the Windward side of Oahu. I was in the group that reported to D Company. It was a break for us to be with all local soldiers and especially comfortable to be serving with men with whom I could communicate in our island pidgin.

The National Guard was racially mixed and made up of ordinary working men. Except for the Native Hawaiians, we were all children of immigrants who had shared similar experiences. Basically, we all struggled for recognition as full-fledged American citizens.

My squad leader was a soft-spoken young Portuguese man. My platoon sergeant was a warm yet stern Native Hawaiian gentleman, the type of individual you trusted enough to follow on any dangerous mission. Our company commander was also Portuguese, a mature lawyer-type. What a great outfit. The Hawaiian unit was unique.

Regimentation was more like that found on a community football team, far different from the normal army organization. Officers and NCOs (noncommissioned officers) *led* us instead of ordering us around, and orders were more of a request than a command.

Being assigned to a local unit was definitely a break and a blessing, and every ethnic group contributed to the unit's cohesiveness. The underlying attitude that developed among the locals was that of "all for one and one for all"—loyalty to each other. Your fellow soldiers will take care of you and fight for you, whatever the risk.

This attitude was a local trait. Soldiers from the mainland could not get over it. Many times, the way we were willing to support a friend against the odds must have seemed crazy. What it meant, though, was that the mottoes "Remember Pearl Harbor!" and "Go for Broke!" really echoed natural feelings held and expressed by the soldiers from Hawaii.

From the lonely beginning, there was a common struggle: the experience of nonwhites in Hawaii, trying to pull themselves up the ladder, socially and economically. A support group of minorities developed, all pulling together to improve their conditions. This spirit of *ohana* (family), an extended-family concept that prevailed in school, stayed with us throughout our lives and was a way of getting ahead in the larger world.

We were all Hawaiian at heart. The basic *ohana* spirit came from the Native Hawaiian people, an ethnic group filled with genuine aloha, the magic ingredient that brought together the hearts of all the oppressed immigrants' sons. We carried this spirit of aloha wherever we went, and it became the spirit of the 100th even more intensely after Pearl Harbor because we had been singled out as "Japs." In a society in which all minorities struggled to gain acceptance, we were determined to prove to the world that we were indeed loyal Americans.

Among these ethnic groups, the nisei took great pride in the accomplishments of their fellow nisei. We idolized role models and worked hard to become role models for others.

For five months the 298th Infantry worked along the Windward Oahu coastline, preparing defense positions, constructing obstacles for invaders, and participating in air-raid drills and exercises to stop invaders. Among ourselves we created our own strategies to destroy our enemies.

While all these activities were going on, we nurtured our camaraderie and bonded in our determination to do our best as fighting soldiers from Hawaii. As the days and weeks passed, we had more time to compare notes about our experiences, our younger days, and our schooling. A few even shared their dreams for the future.

Being in this unit with all local leadership was a very special island situation—like belonging to a high-school football team. There was a desire to excel as a school, as a team, as a community of ethnic minorities, as a community of individuals with a shared background from Hawaii. For the nisei, "one for all and all for one" became our spirit *(tamashi)* and it paralleled the Japanese warrior spirit, bushido. We became the "American samurai."

We were out to show our loyalty and spirit to the doubters, particularly those who feared the ethnic Japanese and felt they couldn't be trusted. The Japanese immigrants were not an easy group to warm up to. They were close-knit, extremely ambitious, and, oftentimes, aggressively colonial in their attitudes and institutions.

Other ethnic groups in Hawaii were friendly, but they were outnumbered by the Japanese and did not feel very comfortable with their oftentimes overbearing cultural ways. Additionally, the white elite kept their distance and would not allow nonwhites into their circle.

To the nisei generation fell the task of turning this situation around and bringing all those of Japanese ancestry fully onto the

American scene. When the war came, our unique background and the support and friendship of other ethnic minorities helped realize this goal.

In time, improving defense positions, training, and watching the horizon for enemy landings became routine. I respected my Hawaiian sergeant and, particularly, a *kibei senpai* (American-born mentor who had been schooled in Japan), "number one gunner," Sakae Ishizuka. He was my mentor and took particular interest in teaching me all there was to know about the 81mm mortar. His heavily accented English was not only a soothing voice, but he had a particular sternness that kept me on my best behavior.

Then one day our routine was broken. All of the nisei soldiers were ordered to report back to Schofield Barracks. Rumors had been quietly circulating that we could be a potential problem in combat, that recognition problems could be harmful to the troops, especially to the nisei soldier himself. A chill fell upon us as we were loaded, without fanfare, onto trucks. Our gear was assembled in the same area where this frightful journey began.

The next day we assembled in a theater and were told of the army's secret plans to move us to the interior of the United States. We were told to turn in our weapons, which would be issued to the fresh troops arriving from the mainland to replace us.

I was one of many who cheered about going to the mainland. When my initial excitement died down, though, I realized that there were quite a few old-timers, such as early draftees and guys in the Reserves, and serious thinkers who received this news with hesitation. One of them was my buddy, who was married. Others, I'm sure, also had reservations about leaving their families and going on an uncertain voyage. Emotions were mixed as small groups formed—some bubbling with excitement, others soberly engaged in serious discussions.

And so it was that we were all loaded onto a train a few days later with curtains drawn, a secret move of the Hawaiian Provisional Battalion. There was only one elderly Japanese mother waving good-bye to us as we switched tracks outside of Schofield. A handful of nisei girls waved from the pier as the SS *Maui* pulled away from the dock. Only a few people knew that the nisei troops had sailed away. Realizing that it might be our last Hawaiian sunset, even the adventurous souls among us prayed quietly as we watched the sun sink below the horizon.

The navy immediately took charge. Chow lines were formed and continuous instructions blasted over our ship's communications system. We began to settle down, memorizing crew assignments and station numbers in the event of an enemy torpedo attack. The danger seemed to lurk more during the hours of darkness when a sense of helplessness gripped us, as we were packed like sardines in a can deep below the waterline.

This was one of the most disturbing and depressing experiences of my entire military career—surrounded by moaning, seasick soldiers; feeling miserably sick yet forcing myself to eat against the protests of a topsy-turvy stomach and pounding headaches; scared that I would not survive until morning; and dreading the prospect of another day of this agony.

Finally, after days of this misery, I took my blanket and struggled up to the deck, sure that I would not make it to morning. I woke up in heaven: We had arrived. Wild cheers broke out aboard and airships quietly floated overhead. My misery was over, and I was cheering, too, to see now, in the distance, the Golden Gate Bridge and the Bay Bridge.

We finally docked, only to be ushered from the ship to a waiting train. Again, the curtains were drawn. When, for the first time word came to lift the curtains, we saw the expanse of the land, vast to those of us from the small, geographically isolated islands of Hawaii. This was the United States of America that we had dreamed of seeing all those years.

We traveled for days, losing track of the states whose borders we crossed. The curtains were drawn whenever we passed through cities, but we were able to sneak peeks through the cracks and got a pretty good idea of the size of the cities and saw the bustling people along the station platforms.

The faces were very different from what we were used to in Honolulu. It was a new experience indeed to see farmlands stretching for miles in every direction, outhouses, and white "haole" farmers behind teams of horses. In Hawaii, we never saw white farmers—they were all executives working in offices; they were plantation supervisors, doctors, teachers, lawyers—but never laborers.

When we finally arrived at Camp McCoy, Wisconsin, the train stopped in front of a POW (prisoner-of-war) camp to switch tracks. One of our nisei officers threw down his cartridge belt in disgust, saying we had been betrayed by the army. No sooner had he gotten out his anger than the train began to move again. This time it stopped in the area of a tent city. We unloaded and moved into our assigned tents, our home for the next few months until construction of a modern barracks was completed.

Then came a few days of settling down and introduction to our new unit designation: the 100th Infantry Battalion (Separate). Our unit also included Hawaii boys from another heavy weapons company, the 299th Infantry, from the neighbor islands.

Our NCOs now were all nisei and the squads and platoons were organized with the most senior and best qualified leaders. Some received temporary promotions to corporals and sergeants, replacing the Hawaiian NCOs of the unit we had just left. We learned also that our commander,

Lt. Col. Farrant "Old Man" Turner, and the executive officer, Maj. James Lovell, had volunteered for this special assignment. On the battalion staff was a well-known nisei athlete and dentist, Dr. Katsumi Kometani. There were other nisei officers, all commissioned through the University of Hawaii Reserve Officers' Training Program.

All had reported for duty on December 7 from their respective civilian jobs. Many on staff were schoolteachers. All of the company commanders were white officers from the Hawaii units, the 298th and the 299th. They had either volunteered or were selected by the battalion commander.

The segregated unit, as surely we were, was a blessing in molding our unit as a fighting team. The battalion commander, our "Old Man," was a fatherly figure who had lived among us and knew the situation firsthand in Hawaii: the conditions, the lifestyle, the nisei's dreams and ambitions. And now he had a tremendous responsibility involving the human lives, families, and the future of this group of citizens who had been victimized because the white leaders in government and the military—in their shock and panic after Japan's surprise attack—could not differentiate between these American people of Japanese ancestry and the Japanese Zero pilots who had started this agonizing confusion.

The colonel was determined to do his utmost to straighten things out, at least for these otherwise lost souls. His executive officer was a respected schoolteacher and a successful high school athletic coach. With dedicated volunteers such as these and the cream of the nisei commissioned officers, the colonel had the perfect chemistry to move forward in proving the loyalty and performance of his troops.

We know that the "Old Man" swallowed many derogatory comments, but we know also that he challenged generals of larger units with his "dynamite in a small package" routine.

Again, the Japanese upbringing, the many special threads that made up the Hawaiian extended family, and the common denominator—the need to prove to the world that Americanism is not a matter of color or ethnicity—drove us to perform.

The esprit de corps and the development of a superior nisei infantry unit took place on the training grounds of Camp McCoy under the leadership of the "Old Man" and his support staff.

Now that we were segregated as a nisei unit, audible encouragement of "*Yamato damashii* (spirit of Japan)," "*Gambare! (Go for it)*" and those cheerfully shouted reminders of favorite foods from home, "poi," "*laulau (meat and/or fish wrapped in ti leaves and steamed)*," and "kimchee" were often heard, sometimes dangled like an imaginary carrot to get the troops through that extra record-breaking mile, or to excel in gun-drill competitions.

Behind the effort was loyalty and a desire to serve our nation, the United States. The slogans "No Give Up," "Give 'em Hell," "Go for Broke" (which was commonly used even before World War II), and "Remember Pearl Harbor" were accompanied by our own unique ethnic shouts, like, "*miso shiru!*" and "*manapua* (Chinese pork cake)!"

Shouting encouragement with *miso shiru*—the Japanese word for many a nisei's favorite soup made from bean curd paste—didn't mean support for Japan any more than our "Banzai!" which we kept muted in case it was misunderstood. We weren't shouting the praises of the emperor of Japan. We were sharing expressions of unity and solidarity as a group from a particular ethnic background, fighting to be free and recognized, and to keep our country, America, free.

After the money changed hands in the wild crap games each payday, and during the quieter evenings, our conversations drifted to dreams of home and loved ones. Sometimes the mood generated reminiscences of Japanese *shushin* (ethics), stories that touched on *on* (obligation, duty), and beautiful words of appreciation, like *okage sama de* (because of all you have done), which would remain forever in our vocabulary.

The few times our commander addressed all of the troops together, his well-chosen words of advice for us included, "Don't try to drink Wisconsin dry," "Treat the girls like you want others to treat your sisters back home," and "Don't start any trouble, but finish it."

He started a payroll deduction plan to set up a battalion fund to be used when peace came and we all returned home. (When peace finally did come, we were able to use these funds as seed money to buy the property for what is today Club 100. The 100th is still organized as a battalion under the Club 100 name and has as its motto "For Continuing Service.")

Individual savings plans were initiated to purchase Victory war bonds and at the same time support America's war effort. To keep the boys busy and occupied, arrangements were made to organize sports, athletic programs, community leagues, and interservice tournaments.

Judo classes were started and instruction teams established to teach postmilitary police personnel. The classes were opened to other stations, compliments of Camp McCoy. Through it all, the emphasis was primarily on qualifying the 100th for combat and proving to Washington the combat usefulness of this unique battalion. Our commander was adamant that he would not accept any assignment for us other than a combat role.

Programs were also instituted through such activities as arms demonstrations and war-bond drives to promote relationships in the outlying communities and to educate others that these citizens from Hawaii were 100 percent American.

Churches and civic organizations showed interest in supporting servicemen. Many soldiers were "adopted" into families away from home, relationships that were nurtured and continue to this day. The aloha spirit was also spread through entertainment provided by the troops at various community functions. These are the pleasant memories and experiences of our wartime years.

Our move to Camp Shelby in Hattiesburg, Mississippi, was a great letdown for the troops, however. First, there was the fact that we had to leave a beautiful modern barracks and our circle of civilian friends and experiences, such as the novelty of winter and a snowy white Christmas, which until then we had only seen in Christmas cards. Second, training was more severe at Camp Shelby. Third, the camp itself was a step down—dilapidated hutments with smoky charcoal heaters in a chigger-ridden pine grove. There was no incentive to mix with the local community. Hattiesburg was a soldiers' town with lots of bars and pool halls—like Wahiawa next to Schofield.

It did, however, remind us of our mission and the fact that comfort wasn't a part of it. Evidently, physical misery is good training. When the going got tough, we all knew that we could expect more discomfort as we moved up to an increased amount of physical training and advanced to the next level of small-unit tactics and maneuvers.

Conditions got so tough that, at times, the kitchen could not keep up with us. On one occasion, we got separated from the kitchen crew. By the time it caught up with us, the macaroni and cheese that had been prepared for us had spoiled and we had to wait another day to eat. We were on a tactical maneuver, and silence was mandatory. But from somewhere in the night, a lonely voice was heard in a mixture of Japanese and pidgin: "Okaasan, I no like play soldier already."

The Louisiana maneuver is one that many of us remember—the Blue forces versus the Red forces. The performance of the commanders and staff—down to the last soldier in the squad—was rated. Our performance was critiqued, graded, and rated. These were mock battles, with the umpires' colored flags telling us to withdraw, or that we had the offensive advantage to initiate aggressive maneuvers. "Enemy" troops were captured, and umpires made sure they remained captured and were no longer in the play.

The 100th Battalion never withdrew because the withdraw-flag always disappeared. Several intermissions were called because of this infraction. In fact, in one instance, a high-ranking officer of the battalion was rumored to be the culprit. This was the kind of spirit and actions that were part of the Hawaii-bred 100th Infantry.

The daily after-action reports noted that our troops did not play the game according to the rules, that soldiers flagged as casualties and prisoners were escaping and returning to their units, and that the troop-strength count did not correspond with that of the umpires. This kind of behavior from the top leaders down to the last soldier reflected a cohesive mentality and definitely played a major role in the combat performance of the nisei.

Finally, the day arrived for our departure for overseas. We left the shores of the United States on a Victory ship in a huge convoy surrounded by navy escort ships. Ironically, though we were headed for combat, we felt more at ease than we had on our first ocean voyage from Hawaii, and we shared the quiet confidence of belonging to a mighty and victorious force. One thing has stayed with me from those days aboard the ship—lines from a hymn we sang in daily worship service: "He died to make men holy. Let us die to make men free."

After disembarking at Oran, North Africa, we were dismayed to learn that the combat-trained 100th was to be assigned as railroad quartermaster troops. That assignment changed rapidly when the 34th Division, which was scheduled for a landing at Salerno, Italy, was short a battalion and Maj. Gen. Charles W. Ryder accepted the 100th to become a part of the 133rd Regiment.

So there we were in a staging area in Africa, preparing ourselves for a beach landing as part of a combat division that had just concluded a victorious assignment in North Africa. Last-minute bits of advice were passed down by veteran combat officers of the 34th Division, but instead of giving us an uplift, they actually made us more nervous.

Now all the big talk and the spirit of the "American samurai" needed to be carefully and calmly stored deep within, so it could be expended later in a rational, timely, and even sacrificial way. As we cleared our minds for orders and instructions, our hearts were filled with thoughts of home, of the path our journey had taken to bring us to this point, and of the unknown journey ahead.

Before we knew it, we were on ships nearing the landing area. Ships and more ships—a few transports and many navy gunnery ships. Assault vessels circled and zigzagged. Then came the order to disembark. In a few minutes we were crouching behind the landing platform heading for the Salerno shore.

Our craft never made it all the way to shore. The ramp was released in chest-deep water. We waded to shore with our gear and were ordered to keep moving and to clear the shoreline for others, which was like nothing we had experienced in any of our training. It was impossible to walk in boots filled with water and sand. Off came the boots. Knapsacks and blankets were discarded—mortar ammunition wasn't. Some opted to take only the raincoat. Others even discarded their cumbersome gas mask and replaced it with food rations.

Our greatest fear was to be left behind. It was crucial to keep up with the man in front of you. So the nisei, at an early stage of our combat experience, were already making quick adjustments, just to keep in step with the squad and be able to fight.

The episode at Hill 600 is a classic example. Night movement through an enemy minefield and damaging and fierce fighting finally resulted in our taking the hill. Many of our boys were either killed or wounded. Evacuation of the wounded and the movement of supplies up to the forward troops had to wait until a path could be cleared through the minefield.

There was a temporary stalemate with no food or water. Attempts to take and secure the hills to the right and left had been unsuccessful, and the flanks of the 100th were exposed. Then came the order to withdraw. To this, the 100th replied: "We are not withdrawing. We will stay and hold this hill." It was, in retrospect, a repeat of our Louisiana maneuvers.

Many of us had heard of the Japanese San Yuushi and their heroic three-man human bombers in Manchuria and of the fanatic Japanese kamikaze pilots. The heroics of the 100th were not senseless acts of sacrifice but instinctive actions aimed at preventing casualties and protecting and assisting our comrades. We did not want to let them down. We lost many lives at Hill 600, but we had made up our minds that we would not leave our dead buddies there in a lost cause.

The battle for Cassino in Italy and our efforts to rescue the "Lost Battalion" in the dense Vosges Mountains of France tested our courage and brought forth the extra cohesiveness of the nisei soldier. In these two battles, the nisei units did, indeed, display that extra determination, the will to push and to show that they had more reason to fight than merely to win a battle. It meant killing the enemy, or getting killed—a situation faced by any soldier in the thick of battle.

At Cassino, our mission for the Fifth Army was to take the abbey, located above the town, from the enemy. The 100th was ordered to make a frontal attack in broad daylight. But first we had to cross the flooded valley and the Rapido River in order to occupy a position north of Cassino. All of this was to be done in plain view of the trigger-happy enemy. Clearly, the odds were against us.

The officer assigned the suicide task was faced with a situation in which he might have to disobey the order to save his men and be court-martialed for it. He feared they would be massacred in a frontal attack in daylight. But the men encouraged him to give it a try. The outcome, as expected, was a display of guts and performance and a needless loss of lives. The few surviving soldiers commented that it was a miracle we had reached our initial objective. The troops were pulled back under the cover of darkness after committing battalion after battalion of young lives—the higher command was finally convinced that crossing the flooded valley was an impossible task.

There were many examples of suffering and ugliness, but many as well of individual heroism and valor. The scenarios may have been different, but the experiences were not peculiar to the 100th. Each American fighting unit had its own share of heroes. This war was won because of a concerted effort by U.S. military forces—and we salute them all, particularly those that fought side by side with the 100th—as well as by American citizens at home.

Word that the Germans had surrendered was greeted with quiet celebration in and around our company. Naturally gratitude and thanksgiving filled our hearts. But we also felt reverence and a special aloha for the buddies we would be leaving behind, their resting place on foreign soil marked with white crosses.

When the war ended, I really believed that it would be the end of all wars—that people and nations had had enough of killing and destruction, that our nation's leaders would never allow that kind of destruction and loss of life to take place ever again, that all efforts would be toward a permanent world peace.

I still believe in that dream. . . .

Tokuji Ono

100th Infantry Battalion

DEAD SILENCE

Most of us local guys were out on weekend pass. I had a bad tooth, so I had a dental appointment—Sunday morning, mind you. It must have been a 7:30 appointment. The dentist's office—I think it was one of the Hayashi brothers'—was right around Smith and Hotel streets.

I got out of the office about eight o'clock. As I walked to the bus stop to go back to Kalihi, I heard all the emergency vehicles blasting their sirens and rushing off toward west Oahu. Between the low buildings, I could see some dark smoke. I thought it might be Kalihi or the airport area. Because of the nature of the smoke—everything was heavy and black—I thought it was an industrial fire, so I thought nothing of it.

I got on the bus. The bus driver did not know what was going on. By that time, most of the emergency vehicles must have gone out to Pearl Harbor, because I didn't see any more. So I just went home.

As soon as I got there, my older brother told me that I'd better listen to the radio. The announcer was repeating over and over again something to the effect that the United States was at war with Japan. I remember he said, "All military personnel, report to your base."

That meant guys like me, even though I was in civilian clothes. In those days it was still peacetime so, as soon as you got home, you took off your uniform and wore your "civvies," civilian clothes. Now I took off my civvies and put on my uniform. I had to go back into town because the buses going to the different military installations all started at the old Armed Forces YMCA.

In a sense I accepted the fact that the radio announcement was correct, that war was declared. But I hadn't heard or seen anything in and around Pearl Harbor, so the idea of war seemed far-fetched. I just went casually—like so many others, I'm sure—to the Y to wait for the bus.

Most of the guys there, the GIs, the sailors, weren't really aware of what had happened. There were two major thoughts: One was that it was a mock battle being put on, a training exercise meant to look realistic. The other was that somebody was filming a Pearl Harbor movie, trying to inject all the realism they could into it. Both scenarios made sense.

By that time, it was well after eight o'clock and all the bombing had stopped. But we saw one Japanese plane flying over the city, coming up pretty low. You could see the *hinomaru*, the red circle, the "rising sun," on the plane. I swear we could see the pilot. He didn't do any strafing or drop a bomb, so I thought, this can't be war. I think of war as bombs exploding here and there, and none of that happened to those of us who were around at that time.

We got on our buses. I remember the next sequence of events vividly. While going out to Schofield—I think most of us were draftees, but there were a few other regular army people—we just talked to each other because it was a long ride. The conversation, I recall, was very light— you know, guys saying they had a big party last night and something about drinking a lot, and some guy had a nice date with his girlfriend. Everything was upbeat, light, and merry.

As we approached Pearl Harbor, we saw all the smoke rising. When we came right up to Pearl Harbor, we could see the half-sunken ships—and what was left of some sunken ships—and all the damage, the planes in the water, smoke coming up. Everyone just looked, stunned. I guess each one knew without having it confirmed by others that this couldn't be a mock battle or a movie, no matter how realistic. This was the real thing. For several seconds, there was just dead silence in the bus.

Then, as we drove away from Pearl Harbor, the conversation started coming back again. But the tone was entirely different. Guys asking each other, "Eh, you married?" "You got children?" "You get family?" or things of that sort. It was more subdued, serious. I can't recall what I talked about; maybe I didn't say anything. There was a complete turn around in the atmosphere and subject matter. I remember that to this day.

Tom Mizuno

442nd Regimental Combat Team

EYEWITNESS AT WHEELER

On December 7, 1941, I was on my way to Haleiwa to visit my parents with my big brother and his wife and our friend, Kosaku Isobe. It was a chilly December morning, but nice and quiet.

We drove past Pearl Harbor. It was a typical Sunday morning; nothing unusual was happening. But the scene suddenly changed as we approached the airstrip at Wheeler Field. There were lots of planes overhead, and we thought the military was training at this early morning hour of 7:55 A.M.

Suddenly, we realized that Wheeler Field was being attacked by Japanese planes. We were right there, watching as the hangars and the airplanes on the ground were bombed. I saw kamikaze pilots dive right into the hangars.

Wheeler Field was across the highway, which was next to some train tracks. We parked our car alongside the tracks, near a tall water tower, and watched the attack. We were stunned.

When one of the planes flew over us, I saw the red ball insignia of Japan. I told my brother that this was definitely an enemy attack. The planes dived into the base camp residents' area and fired at parked cars. The security guard at the gate was in shock.

There was nobody else around, so we drove to Wahiawa where my sister lived. I told her to turn on the radio, and, sure enough, we heard that Pearl Harbor was attacked at the same time: 7:55 A.M.

We left her place and got on Kamehameha Highway, headed toward our parents' home in Haleiwa. We passed the old iron bridge and drove up the hill, where the pineapple fields came into view. As soon as we started up the hill, enemy planes fired at us from behind, strafing right alongside our car. I thought, "God, we're gonners now." One shell fell right on the hood of our car! I thought it was a bomb.

When we reached the fork in the highway, we headed right, toward the CPC (California Packing Company) camp around the bend. We saw another enemy plane. He was flying so low that I could see the pilot clearly. I stuck my head out of the car window. I guess he didn't fire at us because he could see that we were Asian.

As we drove along the highway, past another pineapple camp, two cars passed us, driving at high speed toward Haleiwa. The drivers looked like they had just seen a ghost!

There was a small airstrip—hidden under a row of *kiawe* trees—alongside the Kawailoa turn. Usually there were about six fighter planes hidden under the trees. The army was able to launch those planes and from outside the Haleiwa Japanese School, we watched the "dogfight" between the U.S. fighters and the Japanese Zeros about a mile offshore. We were scared to death. It was like watching the movies—except this was real!

After war was officially declared, the draft board began signing up boys eighteen years and older for military service. Kosaku Isobe, who was with us that terrifying morning, volunteered for the 442nd. He was later declared missing in action in France. I, too, volunteered, but they didn't take me because I worked for the pineapple company in Honolulu, and agricultural workers were needed to continue producing food. I was finally drafted in August 1944—they were short of men. That's how I became a member of L Company.

But the event I still remember most about World War II was that December 7, 1941, morning at Wheeler Field. As the years passed, I wondered why I hardly ever heard people mention the Wheeler Field attack. But I was there and saw with my own eyes the hangars at Wheeler Field go down like toothpicks.

George Akita

Military Intelligence Service

AMERICA IS AT WAR!

America is at war! We are now engaged in a life-and-death struggle to secure for ourselves and for those who come after us the right to live our lives as we see fit. We are fighting for the perpetuation of the democratic way of life—the American way of life—against the encroachment of totalitarian dictatorship. It is immaterial whether there is an actual declaration of war or not. We are partisans in a real war—a war between two diametrically opposed views of life. The outcome of this titanic struggle will determine, for centuries to come, the map of the world and the very way of life for millions of human beings.

Because of the seriousness of the position we are in, President Roosevelt has proclaimed an unlimited national emergency. What is the citizen's role during this crisis? I think the time has come when we must conceive of our citizenship more in terms of duties and responsibilities rather than of rights and privileges if we so wish to preserve these ideals and institutions that have been secured for us by the blood and tears of American patriots.

In normal times citizens are expected to be usefully employed, law-abiding, and loyal. This and more is expected today. Those called to the colors must willingly and gladly contribute to the defense of our sacred American tradition. Others can cooperate with the constituted authorities and engage in a wide range of civilian preparedness activities. Here in Honolulu the Major Disaster Council has outlined defense measures, which if carried out, will greatly aid in repelling any enemy invader. Every citizen in whose heart burns the love of democracy is morally bound to assist in its defense by storing food, cooperating in blackouts, training for some emergency unit, and engaging in other activities as directed.

Most important of all, we must hold to a mental and emotional attitude in keeping with the seriousness of the time. We must be constantly on the alert to detect propaganda designed to undermine national unity. One lesson, the history of war thus far reveals, is that before the unscrupulous dictator orders his engines of destruction to march, he invariably sows the seeds of discord, suspicion, and disunity among unsuspecting peoples.

Because of the racial makeup of our citizenry, the ground is especially suitable for propagandists to stir up racial hatred and intolerance. More than ever before, we must exercise tolerance.

There must be a sincere willingness now to submerge personal and class interest for our national welfare. Labor and capital must lay aside differences to speed up defense production. Constant strife and the bitterness engendered between the partners in production are the objectives of our enemy. Only by making America an arsenal of democracy can we hope to emerge triumphant when that fateful day comes.

Finally, in our hearts and minds there must be a deep and abiding faith in democracy. We must feel that democracy, our way of life, is worth sacrificing for, fighting for, and dying for.

From tropical Hawaii to the rock-bound shores of Maine, from the snow-clad plains of the Dakotas to sunny Texas, let us, Americans all, rally around the Stars and Stripes in the defense of our way of life. With the love of democracy burning in our hearts and minds, we cannot fail—we must not fail.

George Akita
December 6, 1941, essay
W. R. Farrington High School

George Akita

Military Intelligence Service

DAYS OF INFAMY: THE JOURNAL OF GEORGE AKITA

Sunday, December 7, 1941

According to the Army Intelligence, the bombings began at 7:55 A.M. on December 7, 1941.

It's a grim reality now. Yes, it actually happened. Those hard-headed isolationists who have been shouting that it can't happen here must shut up now.

It was a quiet Sabbath morn. What irony! Most people were going to church with the prayer of thanks that we have so far escaped the horrors and death of warfare. And to think that just on Thursday I led a discussion based on the *American Observer* on the topic, "Can Hawaii be attacked?" The answers were mostly no's. They say that our navy is too strong, the distance too much, Japan can't even conquer China, Japan's power has depleted, etc., etc. I still can see Mrs. Caricof smiling a queer smile. She must have been thinking, "What do these young perches know about it. They talk as if they knew all, huh."

From the conversations that I have listened to, most people thought that the heavy antiaircraft fire they heard that morning was just part of a gigantic war maneuver. The feeling that war with a major power was imminent was very high for a few days prior. As for me, I paid little attention to the guns and went on finishing my HBTS lesson sheet. (I hope that Mr. Carbaugh doesn't get to read this, for he's always after us for doing last-minute work.)

But as I had just finished combing my hair, I heard the *rat-tat-tat* of a machine gun from a swooping plane; then and there did I begin to realize that this was the real McCoy. I hurried to HBTS. Almost met death. Had I left the house earlier, I might have been in the place of a Patrick Chong, who was killed by a bomb that exploded by Schumann Carriage Co. I had planned to get to HBTS by passing Schumann Carriage Co. Whew!

At HBTS the students were tense. Mr. Carbaugh wisely taught the students a new, inspiring song, "Are We Down-hearted?" It goes:

Are we down-hearted?
No! No! No!
Are we down-hearted?
No! No! No!
Troubles may come and troubles may go,
We'll trust in Jesus,
Come weal or woe.
Are we down-hearted? (whistle)
No! No! No!

Never heard the students of HBTS sing so lustily as they did sing that song.

When I got to church the last amen was just being said. An unexploded antiaircraft shell burst right across the street from the church. It killed two young boxers, injuring two more, while an aged grandmother escaped without injury. Whew!

Went to choir practice this afternoon. No practice because only a few reported. Just sang hymns to brace ourselves up, for we were very nervous as anyone could have seen. Boy did we strain our tonsils.

I doubt now that we can hold our Christmas concert. All the rehearsals for nothing. What a Christmas this will be, too. But I guess the closeness of death will make all appreciate Christmas more. "Peace on Earth Good Will to Men" seems hollow now. But I guess God has willed it so—.

It's funny how the course of our lives can be changed in such a short space of time.

I guess we Japanese are in for it now. Especially Mom and Pop; they're aliens. But the U.S. government has promised not to molest the nationals unless they by their actions and deeds make themselves detrimental. I have faith in the U.S. government.

We have to be brave. This crisis will test out our guts and gumption.

Planning to stay at Central Intermediate School—as messenger boy and kitchen helper. Mom didn't want me to go. She was afraid. Pop told her that no matter how young I am, since I was a citizen of America I have to help America whenever I am able to. Even to die for America. I like his attitude.

Just read 3rd [newspaper] extra, saying, "Martial Law Declared." Army's taking over now.

Had peaceful, eventful night. Only heard spasmodic antiaircraft and machine-gun fire.

Planning to stay again tomorrow night.

But this worry was superseded by a still greater worry. I am endowed with the great blessing of American citizenship, but what about my parents and the other aliens in Hawaii?

They are the ones that need the most sympathy, and understanding.

They are torn between two nations, haunted with the fear that they might have to be separated from their children in the event that this government feels it expedient to deport all nationals, although this is quite unlikely. They (my parents) are doing everything to compile [comply] with the commands of the authorities in charge and fearing at every moment that they might commit an error, bringing shame and disgrace to their name. They do not understand English very well. They will be looked upon with suspicion. Indeed their position is not enviable. Yet they have to be brave and endure all. Yes, it is they who have to be bravest and show a front of happiness.

But I'm sure that my parents have absolute faith in God and they believe that what He has willed for them is just, and they will take it like good Christian soldiers.

God bless them.

Note: According to the diary's author, George Akita, the Honolulu Bible Training School (HBTS) was located on the old Mission School grounds near Honolulu City Hall in December 1941.

Nuuanu Congregational Church was situated at the corner of Nuuanu Avenue and Kukui Street.

Monday, December 8, 1941

Experienced the first serious, total blackout last night from sundown. We were standing by at Central Intermediate School, my alma mater, in case there was another bombing and the hospitals became overcrowded.

Came home in morning to have breakfast. Can't expect any good food now. We'll be lucky if we have enough to eat.

Heard President Roosevelt's biting message before a joint session of Congress, asking them to declare war against Japan.

Took Mom to our barber shop. Doubt if we, or rather she, will have much business today.

Went to market to buy some crackers at Mom's advice. People storming to every available store to buy and store up food.

Met Pop on way home told him about the people storming to stores to stock food and told him to do the same. He told me that the people are now excited and panicky, but about a week later they will return to normal and that will be the best time to buy food.

I think that Pop's attitude and way of thinking is superior.

It was [because of] his farsightedness and good judgement that I'm not a dual citizen. He is a firm believer that we cannot serve Jesus and mammon, so he decided that we cannot serve Japan and United States at one time and he cut off our Japanese citizenship.

Congress voted to declare war. The vote: 476 to 1. The same woman who voted against war in 1917 voted against it [again].

Stayed at Central. Had peaceful night.

All in all, the second day of war was very peaceful.

Tuesday, December 9, 1941

Stayed at Central Intermediate School. Had an eventful night. Was on the 2:30 to 6 o'clock shift P.M.

Helped to prepare breakfast for emergency hospital workers. The eggs, cocoa, mush were overdone and didn't taste so good, but had to eat it. Can't crab any more now.

Rested till noon.

When I read the [news] papers it had General Orders from Army Headquarters and issued by Lt. General Walter Short. In brief, they are:

- General Orders No. 1
  Governor Johnathan B. Poindexter, Mr. Charles M. Hite, Mayor Lester Petrie, Mr. Charles Hemenway, Acting Attorney General Ernest Kai as advisory committee to the military governor.
- General Orders No. 2
  All liquor establishments and sale of liquor prohibited.
- General Orders No. 3
  Military commission was named to try any person as may be properly brought before it.
- General Orders No. 4
  This concerns the trial of civilians.
- General Orders No. 5
  Policy on alien Japanese. Tells how aliens should act and conduct themselves. They must also give up—firearms, weapons, ammunition, bombs, shortwave radio receiving sets, transmitting sets' signal devices, codes or ciphers, cameras, any map of Hawaii, etc.
- General Orders No. 6
  Schools, both public and private, on Oahu are ordered closed until further notice.

Also today all stores were closed as they had to take an inventory of all their supplies. Service stations had to close up. Heard many times on police calls that a certain store or certain station was selling things illegally.

Had an official air-raid alarm at 4:30 P.M.

President Roosevelt then spoke. He said that we will win this war no matter how long it took. Had another alarm about 5 P.M.

Lights out at sundown (about 6 P.M.).

Stayed home tonight.

Wednesday, December 10, 1941

Stayed at home last night. Couldn't sleep at first, as the blackout begins at nightfall.

One thing this blackout does is to keep children home and out of trouble. (Guess most of the kids will grow tall sleeping from dusk till dawn.)

It has been reported that since the blackout Sunday the crime rate in town has been reduced to an all-time low.

Woke up feeling fresh. Stayed home all morning, putting finishing touches to my scrapbook and diary.

Food stores and gasoline stations reopened today, at least all who received licences. Gas rationed to half a tank. Everything is under strict military control. Vegetable seeds, drugs, foodstuffs, etc., all controlled.

Went to Central cafeteria to assist in preparing food for emergency hospital workers in the afternoon.

Had an official air-raid alarm from 3:00 P.M. to 3:15 P.M. One long blast of the siren indicates the beginning of the raid. And short blasts of the siren indicates the end. Those sirens reminded me of death screeching her icy warning.

Was on the way to Central when William Suzuki told me that I was under sixteen and had no pass, so I had to go home and report at 6:00 A.M. the next morning for cafeteria duty. I went home feeling that even if I am too young to do active defense duties, I can at least help by feeding the people performing those duties.

I went home and had lots of time to do some thinking.

This war's getting dreary. No attacks since the sporadic attack on Sunday and a small raid on Pearl Harbor on Monday night. But we better not be caught napping as we were that day. Never can tell when those Japanese may come again. (Maybe after the next big raid I might not be able to finish my diary. Cheery thought, eh?) They'll receive a hot reception this time. The fingers of our defenders are just itchy.

By the way, I better not go too early tomorrow. I might be shot at. Those guards are known to be overzealous. They readily shoot.

In other words, they shoot first and ask questions later. They're serious and mean business so . . .

Seriously, however, I began to ponder over our position as American citizens of Japanese ancestry.

Thursday, December 11, 1941
Say, this war's getting really monotonous. No action at all. Although I'm not begging the Japanese to come.

Went through the same routine: cafeteria duty, home and scrapbook, a shower at the Y, the newspaper, and report to Central again at night.

Only one thing happened that broke the monotony and is worth my time recording.

Well, tonight Mr. [Kim Fan] Chong (my teacher at Central Intermediate School) got tired of the monotony so he decided to go to Room 39 in an adjoining building to get some ukes and guitars to "make merry."

He got hold of Mr. Gomes the janitor and I to go with him. Mr. Gomes was afraid to go because he heard and read of people being shot for staying out on the streets. And I don't blame him, too, because I didn't feel too enthusiastic about going out of our safe refuge and [taking] the chance of getting shot. Mr. Chong, however, insisted and on we went. Mr. Gomes [was] grumbling and scared out of his pants, always saying, "Come on, come on, make it snappy. We should have done this in the daytime. The quicker the better."

We came through with flying colors, Mr. Gomes and I sighing great relief.

I'll bet I'll laff or rather laugh at the way I am writing this mediocre diary of the day-to-day happenings of this war. The English, mistakes, the way I put things will certainly put shame upon me when I grow big and old enough to appreciate this diary.

Friday, December 12, 1941
Nothing much to write about now. Practically everything is getting back to normal now. That is, anything that the army has not taken over or has deemed important to national defense.

Yesterday Germany and Italy declared war on the United States. What irony! The United States has been arguing for months whether or not she should enter into war against Germany and Germany declares war on us first. (Although this move was not unexpected after the Japanese attack on us.) The United States retaliated and declared war against the Axis.

This war's going to be a long war. Even worse and more terrible than the first World War. New engines of destruction, and all the major powers of this world fighting against each other. We all will suffer whether we win or not. Men are fools. Slaughtering themselves when they should be helping each other. What they need is Christ in their lives . . .

Saturday, December 13, 1941

It was reported by the police department that this was the quietest and most peaceful weekend in the history of Honolulu. The blackout sends every unauthorized person scurrying home at dusk, decreasing crime and accidents tremendously.

Went through the same routine throughout the day, cafeteria duty, home and scrapbook, and back to Central. Things are more or less settling down and you can hardly see cars around as before the war because of gasoline rations.

Sunday, December 14, 1941

Exactly one week after the attack on Oahu by Japanese planes.

Honolulu is a changed city now. I can hardly imagine that just a fortnight ago, Honolulu was a busy metropolis buzzing with activities. Cars honking loudly as they went rushing by, masses of shoppers crowding to Kress, Sears and Roebuck, Liberty House, and the shopping districts, Xmas lights and Xmas spirit everywhere, and in general the holiday spirit prevailed.

Theaters and stadium crowded to capacity, parties and banquets galore, drunks, bums, cliques of boys, servicemen everywhere.

Such is but a glimpse of Honolulu life before the attack.

Then it happened. Everything was thrown topsy-turvy. Funny how things like wars, famines, pestilences, and disasters happen so suddenly and change the course of life and of history itself.

Honolulu's citizenry has faced and has gone through that transition admirably. Everyone performed their individual duties, whether small or large, commendably.

What are some of the most eminent changes Honolulu has gone through as a result of this war?

Firstly, everyone is tense. Waiting and watching. Preparing. People are taking the horrors of war seriously now that they have gotten over the shock of the first raid.

Secondly, I'll want to record my individual—or shall I say personal—views of what I have witnessed so far.

Here they are. The streets and downtown areas are conspicuously void of both servicemen and civilians. I guess the servicemen must remain on the alert after being caught napping last Sunday so they can hardly expect leaves.

The civilian population stay at home because they are afraid to be caught away from home during an air-raid and because the authorities have requested that all should stay at home if possible. I can hardly find a shoe shine boy around but newsboys are all around, for selling papers is a thriving business now, with everyone desiring to learn of the latest developments of this war and of instructions from general headquarters. I know of a newsboy who made 30 dollars the first 2 days of the war.

I see many establishments blacked out as to use [of] lights during the blackout.

Soldiers, HTG [Hawaii Territorial Guard] can be seen guarding important places and public utilities such as the Armory, Iolani Palace, Honolulu Rapid Transit Co., Hawaiian Electric Co., Mutual Telephone Co., etc. (I forgot to include the ROTC boys over 18 years of age doing guard duty.)

Monday, December 15, 1941

Honolulu's really settling down now. Fewer violations of blackout rules, orderly crowds, no rushing of cars as [during] the first few days of the attack, more people flocking and planning to go to town and do their Xmas shopping. I guess we're catching onto the technech [technique] of war-torn England.

Well the happenings of this day are few. Sale of drugs is controlled to prevent hoarding. We're not allowed to have any fireworks around just as we are restricted from having firearms. What a quiet New Year's this will be. The animal lovers will be happy now. They have been squawking about the use of fireworks because animals can't stand noise.

Gasoline has been rationed to 10 gallons a month. As I went to HBTS yesterday I saw crowds that extended from Punchbowl to Alapai Streets waiting to get their turns to obtain ration cards from city hall.

Japanese Hospital was taken over by the army. I wonder if Anchan (Akita's older brother, Hajime) will have to work for the army. I doubt it because he's an alien.

Mail service will continue but it will be censored. We must compile (sic) to these rules if we plan to write: Avoid rumors; we must not describe specifically or in detail any action we have witnessed; we must not describe any *location of military or commercial vessel and defense and military equipment. *Not location but movement.

President Roosevelt spoke today in commemoration of Bill of Rights Day. He said that we must not lay down our arms till we secure the liberties we so much cherish.

Bomb-proof shelter plans were published in the newspapers today. Every male citizen is required to build one for the security of his family. The shelters are holes dug in the ground, 6 feet by 2 feet or as long as is convenient for the use of the family. Additional comforts may be planned in that "grave" as according to the wishes of the head of the family.

I forgot to add more restrictions as I was in a hurry to get through. We must write in English as much as possible. Photographs must be of personal nature. In general we must not reveal anything that will be of interest to the enemy in case the mail fell into the hands of the enemy.

This was like any other day. No excitement at all.

I see everywhere windows taped to prevent them from shattering. Police officers can be seen wearing helmets.

Trenches are being dug at schools and at places where people congregate a lot, as the public library. These trenches are to serve as air-raid shelters. The measurements are, that is, according to my calculations, 4 feet by 2 feet.

I see fewer cars, due to rationing of gasoline. I see many headlights covered with blue paint or covered with blue cloth to travel during the night. Some are apt to forget to cover the taillights though.

Everything is quiet after dark. (6 P.M.)

No cars, except for autos authorized to move after dark. No civilians. No lights to be seen. No merrymaking. All saloons and beer joints are closed. It is pitch-black. Honolulu has settled down at last. It gives you an impression of a ghost town.

The reason why my English and my mistakes are terrible is because I have but little time to finish my scrapbook and diary.* I'm saying this because when I get to read it years later I might not laugh and say to myself what a stupid boy I was.

*Little time because I spend so much time in the Central Intermediate School cafeteria preparing food for emergency hospital workers.

Seiso Kamishita
100th Infantry Battalion

HONOR THY COUNTRY

After graduating from Waimea High School in 1938, I immediately took a job at a service station to help support my family. There were six of us kids; I was the third of five boys and we had one sister. My father was out of work, so my mother took on the heavy burden of supporting us. She got a business license to sell vitamins and other items.

Then she heard on the radio that a Honolulu drugstore was looking for an agent on the outer islands. She immediately contacted the owner of Seiseido Shoten, the drugstore, and was given the franchise to sell their products on Kauai. Everything was going well until sometime in 1940 when the United States government instituted the draft.

Any able-bodied male who had reached the draft age and who passed the health and physical requirements was inducted into military service. My older brother received his notice to report for a physical examination in the first round. I knew he would pass his examination and be inducted, so I wrote to his draft board requesting that his induction be postponed until a later date because the family needed his more substantial income. At the time, I was only earning $1.75 per day.

In my brother's place, I received my notice to report for the first draft. I passed the exam and was inducted into the U.S. Army on December 10, 1940. Our basic training was conducted at Schofield Barracks' tent city under the tutelage of regular army officers and non-commissioned officers. After completing basic training I was transferred into the Hawaii Army National Guard's 299th Infantry Regiment, I Company. We were eventually shipped over to Kauai and stationed at Barking Sands.

There we were kept busy building a theater, a cafeteria, and additional barracks. Sometime in 1941, I was detached from I Company and assigned to C Company, which was stationed at Wailua, Kauai. I was chosen for this duty because I could type. Besides, C Company was based closer to headquarters, which was located at the Lihue Armory.

On December 5, 1941, I went to see the first sergeant for a weekend pass. Although he did not deny me a pass, I was questioned at length about where I could be contacted in case of an emergency. I clearly remember my reply because I had planned to go goat hunting at Waimea Canyon in Kokee and there was no way I could give the sergeant an exact location of where he could contact me.

Realizing the futility of questioning me any further, he granted my weekend pass. On my way home to Waimea, I had a feeling that something was amiss. Because of that, I didn't feel comfortable about going goat hunting the next day, December 6, 1941.

Why all the questions, I wondered. Since we were on either Third or Fourth Alert, I decided to cancel my hunting trip and instead returned to C Company. When I arrived at our base, I was reprimanded by the mess sergeant. He reminded me that I was supposed to be on pass and that he had not ordered enough rations for me. I offered to pay for my dinner rations, but he relented and let me stay.

I was still in bed early Sunday morning when I heard the radio from the adjoining tent. The announcer's voice was cool and deliberate. He said that Pearl Harbor was being attacked. This is war—not maneuvers, he emphasized.

It took a minute or two for the terrible news to sink in. Someone yelled that Pearl Harbor was under attack. The bugler sounded the alert and we assembled for a briefing on the situation. That marked the beginning of my war experience. I was stationed at headquarters at Lihue Armory.

One night, not long after the Pearl Harbor attack, I was standing guard outside the armory building when a Japanese submarine surfaced outside Nawiliwili Harbor and fired a series of flares and artillery shells. Many of the shells were duds, however. The following day, a sergeant from the engineer group asked for volunteers to dig up the unexploded shells. I volunteered along with three others. We dug up two shells so the intelligence people could study their size and where they were manufactured.

Conditions of war at the time prevented anyone from being granted a pass. Eventually, I was transferred back to I Company, which was ordered to guard the shoreline from Hanalei to Haena. Subsequent events in the Pacific region made the Hawaiian Islands much more secure, and eventually the ban on passes was lifted.

I want to share with you a true story about something that happened to me in my own home. Many would find it hard to believe.

One day, while on my first pass since the securing of the Islands, I went home to visit my family in Waimea. I was met at the kitchen steps by my mom and dad, who were waiting for me. Their heads were bowed and they were holding hands. I was taken aback because in all my years growing up, I had never seen my parents holding hands. I didn't know what to make of it.

My mother spoke first. "Seiso, Father and I have something to ask you." "What is it?" I asked. My mother continued without hesitation, "You are an American soldier. Your country is America—a wonderful country. Our country, Japan, attacked your country. That makes us your enemy. If you feel that it is your duty as an American soldier to shoot us, we will be proud of you."

I was totally flabbergasted. "*Bakatare* (Fools)!" I shouted. "If both of you intend to kill me, only then will I shoot you." They thanked me and asked what they could do. My request to them was simple: "Just obey and do whatever my government asks you to do."

My dad finally spoke. "Seiso, as an American soldier, you must not bring shame to your country, yourself, or your family. Do your best, even if you must give your life." He said in conclusion that a true Japanese will give his life to the country of his birth.

With those formalities over, we sat down for the dinner my mother had prepared. I was just about to tell them about the Japanese submarine at Nawiliwili when my mom interrupted me. She cautioned me not to tell them anything. She said that in case they were interned and questioned, they would have nothing to say. The less they knew, the better. They would have nothing to hide or to tell if they were interrogated. In retrospect, I believe that my parents were smart, obedient, and very cooperative.

The Japanese way of thinking is hard for many to understand. I was surprised to learn of a similar situation when I visited my former platoon sergeant, Hisa Shimatsu, in Kekaha after the war. Hisa was promoted to second lieutenant—a battlefield commission—while attached to C Company. He told me that he was captured by the Germans and sent to a prison near Berlin, where he was visited by a representative of the Japanese Consul and questioned at length. He said he was surprised by the representative's comment that he must do all he could for America.

"America is your country. *Shikkari yare* (Do your best)!" he was told. Hisa was as surprised as I was. After that, I felt comfortable telling him about my experience.

I am still reluctant to tell people of other ethnic backgrounds about the incident with my parents because it seems so hard to believe. Who in their right mind would ask their son to shoot them just because they are aliens? Believe—or don't believe. I know the truth.

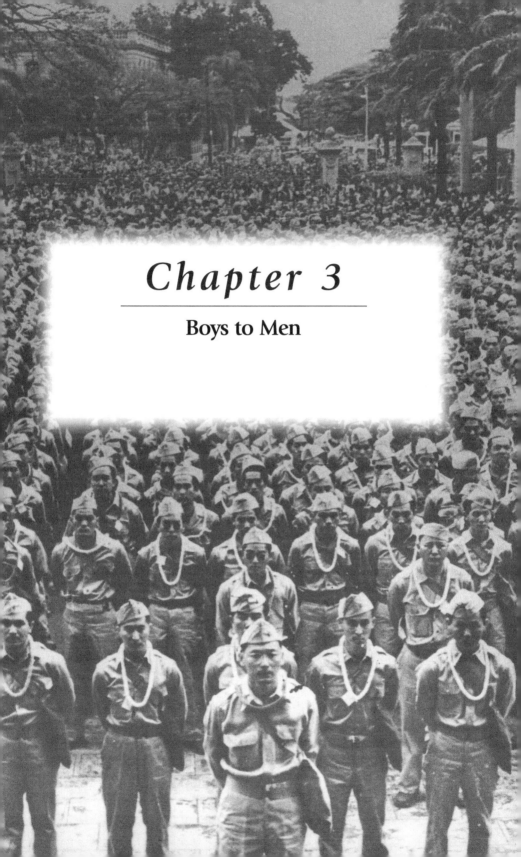

Chapter 3

Boys to Men

Robert N. Katayama

442nd Regimental Combat Team

NOW I AM A MAN! DEPARTURE DIARY

March 22, 1943

Physical exam today! Went through exam like a tank on an assembly line. Think I'll pass (hopefully).

March 23, 1943

Suspense as to whether I will be able to pass physical exam. People are already bidding me farewell! Farrington won high-school basketball championship.

March 24, 1943

Passed physical exam! I quit my job at CPC and bid all my coworkers good-bye. Walked around town jubilantly, but somehow sad.

March 25, 1943

Inducted today! Now I am a man! All my neighbors gave me a send-off. The army issued us clothing. Mine were not a bad fit. Army life is sure confusing.

March 26, 1943

My first drill in marching. Wasn't as difficult as I had expected. We have to do our own laundering and make our beds. Visited our PX (post exchange). At night we saw a show at the USO (United Service Organizations) recreation hall. Bad presentation.

March 27, 1943

We had our general classification and mechanical aptitude test. The test was easy compared to the UH [University of Hawaii] test. We had drill again. We are all excited at the prospect of going into town tomorrow.

March 28, 1943

We had to eat early. We marched down to the railroad depot [at Schofield Barracks], a long distance. The train ride was very uncomfortable. From the [Iwilei] depot we marched to the palace grounds to be given a farewell ovation. About 17,000–20,000 people were there. Our farewells were very heartbreaking. After the ceremony, we got home [Schofield Barracks] at a late hour, and were we tired. We had to eat in the dark so could hardly see what we were eating.

March 29, 1943

I had my first KP (kitchen police) duty this morning beginning at 5:45 A.M. Life [isn't] too hard. I took out a $10,000 insurance policy. I also had my interview. In the afternoon we had our inoculations. The tetanus shot was terrific. Thereafter we suffered.

March 30, 1943

My typhoid shot became painful. We went on policing [ground clean-up] duty. After lunch we had our blood typed. We also received our tags ("dog" tags).

March 31, 1943

My first leave. I went home and saw Dad, Mama, and Grandma. My bank account was changed to a joint account. I went to school and talked about my experiences in an army camp. _____ and I fixed things together again and I took her to eat. I went to her home and we listened to some music. I had my first kiss with _____ [*hon-ma* (Japanese slang: for real)]. Went home and said good-bye to everybody.

April 1, 1943

I went on latrine duty. The job was very dirty. Afterwards we had our marching drill. During the afternoon I only slept and moped (lovesick) over _____. I wonder how she feels? That night _____ [another soldier from Farrington High] and I had a long talk about our former school-mates. _____ talked to me about his girlfriend.

April 2, 1943
We went to school [Farrington High] to have our special graduation cere-monies. The exercises were very touching. _____ gave me her picture, "With all My Love, _____," and a small locket as a good luck charm. Friends gave me a lot of gifts. I parted with my friends again for the last time. Tears sprung from our eyes for the first time.

April 3, 1943
We had to eat breakfast at 6:15 A.M. We exchanged our "Hawaii" stamped currency for the regular ones. A general and a colonel gave us a pep talk in the open-air theater. We were ordered to pack all our belongings into one bag and to stay in the camp area. Looks like we'll be leaving soon.

April 4, 1943
Woke up at 3:30 A.M. and prepared to leave for the mainland. Boxcars took us down to the (Iwilei) depot, after which we had to walk quite a ways with our barracks bags. I almost dropped from exhaustion. We were loaded into a transport (ship) like sardines in a can. At about 12:00 P.M. I saw a tugboat turn over in the harbor. We left Honolulu harbor at about 2:15 P.M.

April 5, 1943
Seasick! Life is miserable.

April 6, 1943
Getting over my seasickness. Had my first meal in two days. Someone had a phonograph on board and the music sounded very good. Had my sec-ond inoculation. Our AJA (Americans of Japanese Ancestry) unit is to be called the 442nd Infantry.

> Postscript: On April 7, 1943, we were all ordered to surrender our diaries to our superiors. I subsequently learned that we had been encouraged to keep diaries so that they could later be reviewed by the federal agencies to ascertain the depth of our loyalty. As may be noted in my naive but "American as apple pie" thoughts, there was nothing to fear. My diary was returned to me in 1990.

Jesse M. Hirata

100th Infantry Battalion

THE LIFE AND TIMES OF A *KOLOHE* GI

In 1937 I came to Honolulu from Kona and worked as a live-in at a grocery store in Waikiki for about three years. I figured I needed too much capital to open my own store, so I changed my occupation to dry cleaning. I worked in Kaimuki, where the owner did not speak English, only pidgin. I learned fast. Later I went to work for McInerny in the pressing department and pressed all kinds of expensive garments. By then I was ready to open my own cleaners.

When I was ordering equipment for a cleaners of my own, I received notice for the fourth draft. I was twenty-three years old.

I was a soldier for five weeks, then Pearl Harbor was bombed. I rushed to report to post from a weekend pass. We went in [Kenneth] Harano's car, Hamano and myself. Traffic was jammed, so we stopped directly in front of all the bombing. Japanese Zeros were diving directly into the ships, exploding, and smoke was everywhere.

We got out of the car in all that hell. Then a shore patrol officer poked a pistol in my ribs and asked his superior, "This is a Jap. What I do with him?" I dared not swear at him. His superior said, "Let him go."

We looked below at all the smoke. Ships were tilting, burning; and above were bombers and Zeros, some circling, some dropping bombs. I swear I saw a Zero dive into the smokestack of the ship where the USS *Arizona* is now, and heard an explosion. It was total chaos.

It was close to noon when we reached Schofield. My tent had bullet holes in it and there were two spent bullets on my bed. I put them in my pocket. I don't know what happened to them.

At Schofield, everybody was running around. The cadre gave two of us a water-cooled machine gun, which we did not know how to operate, and set us up in the center of the open field. I remember I felt unsafe.

That evening, we were taken up a hill with trees. They expected paratroopers to come down to occupy the Islands. All of us rookies were jittery and scared, so it was very dangerous. Someone yelled, "Halt!" and no one answered. They shot. Some cows got it. Another guy yelled, "Halt!" No answer. *Bang!* In the morning, I saw it was a cement elevation marker, flat on its back.

Later, the guys saw all kinds of different colored blinking lights, saying it must be some kind of enemy signal. Where they were pointing, I could not see a thing except darkness. They started shooting. I would not shoot at something I could not see until the cadre kicked me, ordered me to fire. So I fired in the dark. Next morning, a family friend we called "Cockarm" from the 298th, who was in the position where we fired, said, "How come you guys shoot at us?"

Still on the hill, a rookie looked up between the leaves and must have seen clouds, but to him it looked like a parachute. He yelled "Parachute!" and fired. A large branch with a cracking sound came crashing down. Did we scramble!

More confusion: There was shooting at a friendly plane flying overhead, going in to land at Hickam. A GI was shooting his automatic Thompson, his finger frozen on the trigger out of fear. He was shooting on the ground all around. Two others jumped on him to wrestle the gun away. Soon after, they took away our bullets.

They passed out sandwiches in the dark. I don't know what kind of sandwich I ate, but I was still hungry. Needed riceball.

A few days later, we rookies were transferred into the 298th. Guarding the shores from Waiahole to Kahaluu was like a picnic—Samoan crabbing all the time we were on guard duty, and fishing during the day.

The first two months, I was on duty on top of the hill above the banana patch, which was our observation post. We reported passing ships and planes above. I did not know anything about how high an elevation the plane was flying, nor the azimuth reading of the ship passing. Many times, I reported ships passing. Headquarters told me that, according to my reading, a ship was way inside Waiahole Valley.

Up on the hill, we erected a three-man shack with a corrugated iron roof. Human bones came out when we were digging the foundation. Although we carefully put the bones in a carton and placed a helmet on top of it at night, next morning the helmet was on, but the bones were gone. Real spooky.

Not knowing any better, we built the shack on top of where we had dug. When the shack was finished, we started sleeping in it. At night, the strangling started. Not an actual strangling of the throat. It was strange: could not breathe; legs, arms could not move. I tried to reach for a flashlight under the pillow, but my arms could not move for a few seconds, although it seemed like much longer.

I was there for two months. All the while, replacement after replacement was coming up reluctantly as news about the ghost spread throughout the company. Then I caught a bad cold, which forced them to replace me. Replacements were hard to come by. I took care of my cold at company headquarters at the Waiahole Buddhist church and Japanese school—a wartime takeover.

While there, a haole sarge we called "Red" said, "You local guys all believe in ghosts. There is no such thing." So he went as a replacement, I guess to prove a point. He got choked that very night. Instead of waiting for a replacement, the proper thing to do, he ran all the way back to headquarters. I guess he became a believer.

When I got well, I was put on guard duty around the company. After guarding, around midnight, I got choked. Old man Komoda saw me and, after it released me, asked, "You 'wen get choked?" I believe it got me because I urinated outside that night after I finished guard duty.

Earlier I had moved my bed and was just about to doze off when, in the dark, I saw this black smokelike thing, twirling with energy, coming down on me, so I gave a scary yell. It missed me. From the other end of the dorm, a Puerto Rican GI said, "Hey, somebody getting nightmare?"

Another ghost was one we called "Cowboy," because he walked the boardwalk every midnight, from the house to the ocean. [James] Iwasa, "Happy" Sasaki, and I were stationed there. Every evening we waited, quiet and tense, for his walk. Happy suggested we shoot him. I wasn't for it, so I decided that I would hold the flashlight while they shot. That night he came, and walked a few steps. They fired the whole clip, which holds eight bullets each.

It was Iwasa's watch; we went to bed. Then Cowboy came back. In the house this time. Happy and I jumped up from a loud crashing noise. The phone was also ringing. The table was on its side, Iwasa was sprawled on the floor, phone still ringing. According to Iwasa, the ghost grabbed his leg and lifted him upside down to the ceiling. His voice wouldn't come out to yell for help. He tried to pound the table, but his arm wouldn't move. Then the phone rang, so the ghost let him go, and he crashed down on the table. The phone was an inquiry asking if we were the ones firing.

On another gun position I was ordered to clean the machine gun, so asked the sarge if I could fire a few bursts before cleaning. "Okay, not too much." I aimed at Chinaman's Hat and fired about five bursts. To my surprise, five net fishermen came out from the back of the island with their hands held high. I did not capture any subs, but these were my first captives.

Our picnic ended when we were gathered to form the all-AJA outfit. We shipped out for Oakland, though we did not know it then, on June 5, 1942. From Oakland, we boarded a charcoal-burning train, with soot all over. At our first stop, since we were not allowed out, most of the boys wired home through our colored porter, who was all smiles, as each one was giving him ten- and twenty-dollar bills.

Camp McCoy was hot, one hundred-something in the shade. We felt listless in the daytime. We were well-received in Wisconsin. Speaking with the locals, our good English came out automatically and many made girl-friends.

I wondered if I had made a mistake, because I cut all ties with my girlfriend before I left so she could go on with her life instead of waiting for me. I might not come back, or maybe come back crippled. So, I did not go steady stateside. Instead, three of us looked at maps and hitchhiked to other cities. It was faster than waiting for a train or bus.

I found out girls stateside are very aggressive—girls fourteen or fifteen are very mature. In some of the towns, as soon as we got off the bus, girls came up, said hello, and slid their arm into ours.

On one hitchhike, a farmer picked us up. He talked about the sneak attack on Pearl Harbor and said, "Good thing they rounded up those Japs and put them in the compound. You can't trust them. . . ." And if he caught one of them, he would kill them with his bare hands. He dropped us off where he was going to turn off. We thanked him—and then told him we were those Japanese Americans. I think he pressed on the gas too hard, for the car went hop-hop-hopping.

Milwaukee was the best. The beer was good. Eighty percent of the population were Germans. They understood our situation, as they, too, were questioned by the FBI. In the nightclubs, they wouldn't let us spend a cent. They joined our table, then others came and said, "When you are through with them, could you pass them over to our table?" First time I was there, I got carried away, and woke up at a couple's home.

At Camp McCoy and in the nearby town of La Crosse there were plenty of fights with other outfits, especially if they called us names like "Japs," "Oriental Creeps," or said how proud they had been of their uniform, but now "even Japs are wearing it."

A big fight started outside a club in the street because we did not stand up for their Texas anthem, "Deep in the Heart of Texas." Sometimes in town, the soldiers prodded the Mexicans in their outfit to start a fight with us.

Once, three of our boys came tumbling down the stairs from a bowling alley. Others passing by asked what happened. "Those Texans threw us out," the boys said. Unlike today's youth, the nisei was strong, as many took boxing, judo, karate, and kendo. In those days, martial arts were not known stateside.

So, they told the three, "Let's go back in." When they pushed the door open, a Texan said, "I thought I told you—" Before he could finish the sentence, he was punched out. Others were tossing six-footers in the air. In no time the alley was cleared of Texans. The owners thanked our boys profusely, as the Texans were not paying—they had just taken over. The owners loved these "gentleman soldiers," as the town used to call the 100th, and they later moved to Hawaii and opened a bowling alley.

Because of so many fights, Dr. Kometani gathered the judo guys and made us practice. We wore our green fatigue uniform, without the buttons, and used GI mattresses for tatami mats.

A few days later, we were trucked to the gym, which was filled with GIs. Jimmy Shintaku was the emcee, explaining what the GIs would see and said something like, "The bigger they are, the harder they fall." He beckoned to me and we were the first to demonstrate. I threw him over my shoulder with a loud yell. Of course, Jimmy helped with the fall; he is a third-grade black belt. He fell so nicely, flat on his back. He got up, holding his back like it hurt. The whole gym stood up. Then the rest of us partnered off and bodies were flying all over the stage. The GIs were so amazed, they did not sit down until the demonstration was finished.

Jimmy explained that we held back from hurting or crippling anyone because we were in the same army, fighting the same cause.

I was on the floor when a big GI approached me softly and asked if I could teach him. I told him it took me fifteen years to be where I was. This was not something someone could learn in a few weeks. He bowed his head and started to walk away. I called, "Hey, Joe, where are you going in this war?" He said, "Rumor is the Pacific." I told him, "Hey, I feel for you, because the Japs there are better than we are; plus, they carry the long sword." I shouldn't have said that. I hope he did not go AWOL (absent without leave).

At Camp Savage, Minnesota, the Military Intelligence Service was having a hard time because they were all scholars. When we first went in a bar there, the bartender would not come when we called him. After more noise on our part, he finally came over and said, "We do not serve Japs." There were lots of Seabees there, snickering. So whatever was on the counter, we threw against the mirror. Busted it all and took off before the MP (military police) or SP (shore patrol) showed up.

Halfway through maneuvers, lucky me, I sprained my ankle and went to the clinic. While waiting for the 100th to return, we were taking a stroll when a second lieutenant, just graduated from officers' school, ran across the street to us and said, "Don't you recognize an officer when you see one?" I told him we do not go around looking for officers to salute. He said something about a court-martial. We smashed him cold and continued our stroll. Ninety days of school and arrogant already.

Nothing much to say about the South. There were not too many fights at Camp Shelby. We saw abusive treatment of blacks. The blacks ran scared of the whites. We were with a dark-skinned Hawaiian, Eddie Kaholokula, in a theater line and this white soldier gave Eddie a punch, which made him fall. We yelled, "He's not black!" while chasing the soldier.

At Shelby, we had an eighteen-day furlough coming up. Train fare almost eats up a private's pay, so I partnered with Keichi Tanaka and played craps, hoping that one of us would make good. Keichi did not do well, but I made a little over a thousand dollars, so we were off to New York.

New York was great. We had to cross the street to see the top of a building. We found out they call those buildings "skyscrapers." With our Pacific Campaign ribbon on, which others did not have that early, at most bars two drinks were on the house. Cab drivers said, "This is on me, boys," and we could line up for free tickets for good shows. We went to see Frank Sinatra, a rising star. The women went crazy for his singing—yelling, crying, shaking in a frenzy. Real crazy.

We saw and toured for eighteen days, and my wallet was still fat. In fact, I gave some money to a buddhahead (Japanese American from Hawaii) who got rolled. You see, chorus girls who wanted to break into show biz could not make ends meet with a few hours work as chorus girls, so the extracurricular work, easy picking.

We figured that as long as new soldiers were coming in on furlough at the YMCA Sloan House where we stayed, the outfit was not shipping out yet, so we stayed almost a month.

Camp life again. We went through basics many times while waiting for Washington to make up their minds about what to do with us buddhaheads. Basic training was like hand-to-hand combat. The army manual instructions were baby-play for those who had knowledge of martial arts—like putting on the bayonet with a long and short thrust. Looks silly to a kendo man, like blocking a knife. Throwing the opponent—to a judo guy, that was baby-play. So it got tiresome.

Many times, bigwigs from Washington visited to observe us, the "pineapple army," and to see what an all-Japanese American outfit looked like. They had been looking at reports of the overall performance of the nisei outfit, so every time one of them visited, we had to dress up, shoes shined, and so forth, then parade before them.

Once, our platoon agreed that when the sergeant yelled, "Count cadence count," instead of shouting, "One, two, three, four . . ." we would shout, "*Ichi, ni, san, shi* (Japanese for one, two, three, four) . . ." over and over. The sergeant, who did not know of our agreement, was taken by surprise. He was telling us in a subtle voice, "Shut up, shut up . . ."

Then it was time to sail to Oran, North Africa, and then Salerno and the baptism by fire. It was raining so hard, the ground was running with water. The march was uphill. Exhausted, I cut some olive branches and slept on them.

As we were waiting to advance the next day or so, my buddy, whom I had always traveled with, told me he had a feeling that he was going to die. I scolded him for talking like that. But he knew, because he gave me his plastic cigarette case and gave a lighter to our other buddy.

As we were advancing, the enemy started firing 88s—our first fire. My ill-fated buddy was right in back of me as we were rushing forward into a ditch when a shell exploded behind me. I turned to look and his head was gone. Two 88s were firing at us, so there was no time to stop or think, just to dive into some kind of shelter. I could not go back to my best buddy as we were attacking two half-tracts that were firing the 88 shells.

We usually moved at night, except for the scouts who crawled forward in ditches, culverts, ravines, and any route unseen by the enemy. All through Italy, the enemy always occupied the higher ground where they could see us, so the outfit moved at night. It was blackout, so blown-out bridges were a problem. You could hear the men ahead falling in, a helmet-rolling noise, and the thud of bodies. I guess because we were young and nimble I did not hear of any that got hurt or died from it. But when you are exhausted and straining your eyes in the dark, you catch yourself sleepwalking.

At a river crossing, of which we had many, Douglas Tanaka, the boxer, could not swim, so he was holding on to me. He kept saying, "Deep, deep . . ." He was more afraid of the water than the shells exploding around us. I asked him, "How come you born in Hawaii and yet cannot swim?"

He said something like, "Boxers' muscles pull a certain way, so swimming does not match; spoil the muscle." I kind of thought he was pulling my leg, but, still, with all the dancing they do, who knows.

During training, the infantry followed the tanks under protection of their armor. But in combat that never happened; they followed us way in the back—like the time we pushed off from Anzio, which is flat landscape. You could feel the Germans watching us from the hills. As a scout, I went out first. In my heart, I told the boys, "Good-bye, this is it."

We advanced right up to the outskirts of Rome. Only then did we see tanks advancing to an objective. They had cameramen and newsmen to show the world the liberation of Rome. By then, we were stopped and ordered aside so they could roar into Rome as the conquerors. What a farce. As they were passing us, an artillery shell exploded ahead of them. They all stopped and the general ordered our company to go ahead of the tanks. Then the shelling stopped, and they put us aside. A shell came in again. The third time the general ordered us, no one moved for him. He mentioned "court-martial." That's when we started spitting at him, the deep kind. He was still shaking his swaddling stick and saying, "court-martial." That's when one of our guys stood up and fired a couple bursts in front of his feet with his tommy gun, which made the general dance, and he got off our backs.

Hachiro Ito was first scout and I was second during the attack of Hill 600 or 601. The enemy started rolling down plastic grenades, which we were slapping aside. They were also firing at us, so we were in a prone position, firing uphill. Then I saw Ito struggling to take out the grenade that lodged under his left shoulder. I yelled, "Roll over!"

Just then it exploded, and his left arm from the shoulder was hanging on by the skin. I put the arm on his stomach. First thing he asked was how was his face. "Your face okay." Then he grabbed his arm with the good one and asked whose arm it was. "Mine. Let go so I can work on you."

I had to say that, or else he would have died from shock right there. All that time, I was sticking my fingers in the gushing blood, with every heartbeat trying to grab the artery and tie it. But it had shrunk in like a stretched elastic being cut. Soaked in blood, I could not grab it. I got so frustrated, I cried out loud while he died in my arms.

Writing and reliving this kind of memory is still painful.

One day, I forget if it was spring or summer, but there was no snow, we were sitting by the bank of the road. The Germans started firing airbursts about a football field away—too far to be dangerous. We were smoking, talking story with Ralph Asai. Suddenly, Ralph stopped talking in midsentence. I looked at him; nothing seemed wrong. I talked to him, shook him. No answer. No movement. What was wrong? Checking him closely, I found that a paper-thin shrapnel, a freak one, must have come in like a disk that sliced the back of his neck. It had cut all his nerves and there was nothing I could do. So I took the cigarette from his fingers, laid him down, and closed his eyes. I sat there looking at him for a while until it was time to move forward.

By this time of the war, we had become so emotionally strong that tears didn't come out.

Where I was born we did not have cheese. Coming to Honolulu, working in a grocery store in Waikiki, they sold all kinds of stink cheese. I used to cut pieces from the big round cheese to fill my telephone orders. I tried the pieces that chipped off. Ugh! Yuk! Phew!

When our first meal, if you call it a meal, came, they carried it on their backs, as mules were all gone. Guess the lighter ration to carry was the cheese and crackers. It was not the time to be particular. Today I buy cheese.

Charlie Tanaka was passing out the rations hole-to-hole. When he came to mine, there was a dead German about two yards away, facedown, one arm out in front like he was crawling. Charlie, with rations, did not have his gun and wanted to quietly tell me with lots of hand motions about the enemy sneaking up on me.

"Oh, this guy . . ." I reached over and shook him. I told Charlie I always tell him good morning during the holding of the hill.

The Germans must have pulled back. At early dawn, I looked at the hill ahead where the Germans were and saw the whole hill moving! I ran to sleeping and tired Lieutenant [Young Oak] Kim to tell him about it. He pulled out his field glasses and told excited me, "Go back sleep!" I peered through the glasses; it was a shepherd moving his whole white flock.

Now that the enemy had pulled back, I remembered a well down the hill a ways, so I asked Kim if I could go for some water. He said go alone. I guess he did not want the enemy to see too much movement. So I gathered some canteens from the boys. [Kenneth] Kaneko saw this and volunteered to go with me. "You better ask Kim." He got the okay. We went into the olive grove, which was terraced. The well was in the upper corner of the terrace.

We were filling the canteens with the bucket we pulled up when an artillery shell exploded in the lower corner of the terrace. The Germans had the well zeroed in. We flew a foot or so, grabbed the cans in the dust and smoke, and took off.

Then I realized that I forgot my rifle, so, stupid me, I timed the shelling. As soon as it exploded, I rushed in in the smoke and grabbed my rifle and ran. Stupid, because many rifles were available from the dead and wounded. What if Kaneko had gotten killed. Of course, I would have felt bad.

Another time, when an 88 shell did not explode but was smoking, we waited a few seconds. Nosey Kaneko stood up to look and it exploded. A shrapnel hit his stomach area and he was out of breath. An examination showed it hit his bullet belt and one clip was bent in half.

Another time he was hit, a thumb-sized shrapnel was sticking out from his jacket by his heart. All pale, he carefully took off the jacket and pulled at the shrapnel. It was still hot. What a relief, though, it was shallow. Band-Aid would do it.

When we were by the Po Valley, where they grew rice—every family had rice—one of our professional chicken thieves stuck his hand in the chicken coop and grabbed one by the neck. He spun it to keep it quiet. We took it to the next door, and the lady cleaned the chicken. She boiled water in a big pot and put the whole chicken in. After enough oil came out, she took the chicken out, put in rice and a little salt and spices. She stirred once in a while, cut the chicken in pieces, salted it and fried it in olive oil, because that is all they had. The rice soup was done. I could hardly wait to dive into the rice. The rice soup with plenty of rice was so *ono* (Hawaiian for "delicious").

Another time, we were in the olive grove moving forward. I heard roaring tanks coming at us from the front at full speed. Good thing we were spread out while advancing. I dived by the wall, above which was another terrace. The tank just leaped over me to the lower terrace without slowing down. Other men on the right and left were doing the same—they were running for their lives.

It made me feel stupid the way we put our lives on the line in battle. When a bomb explodes near you, the pressure inside your body goes outward. When two Messerschmidts raided us, spraying us with machine-gun fire, we ran like in the movies and the bullets followed. Luckily there was a stone wall. I dived over and hugged the wall. The bomb exploded on the other side of it.

I must have been out for a while because when I came to, rocks were on top of me. I had to push them off. When I heard the boom, it sucked the air out of me. I checked myself. Legs, hands moved. No bleeding, a little groggy.

I went over the broken wall and saw one of our boys with a rip, more of a slit, sideways in his stomach. His intestines pushed out a bit, but were not damaged. He was alive and kept saying, "I finish, I finish." I assured him he was okay while cleaning the intestine where it touched the ground. I laid him down in a better position, all the while assuring him he would be okay, so try to relax. I used two first-aid kits on him.

Talking about intestines . . . After a long walk, our feet hot and sweaty, we came to a stream. I splashed water on my head and face; it was so cool. I cupped my hand and gulped water, then I noticed something from the corner of my eye. I took a good look. It was a dead German, about ten feet up, intestines all out, flapping all the way down to where I was.

Never mind the water; it was too late. I just did not know human intestines are that long.

At night we took turns on guard duty so we had to find out where our relief was sleeping. I forgot who it was that came to wake me. He was calling, "Jesse . . . Jesse . . ." and shaking another guy. When I answered, he looked my way and asked, "Who this guy?" He must have thought I was really sound asleep with all the shaking.

I answered, "Oh, that's a 'good' German." He sort of pulled away. We had a saying, "A 'good' German is a dead German."

Sometimes walking to the front under cover of darkness got monotonous, just following the one in front. Once I stopped, and when the guy in back bumped me, I jumped over an imaginary ditch and went on the side to watch. Two guys jumped. The third one searched for the edge of the ditch with his foot and said, "Shit, no mo' nothing?"

Once, to make conversation, I asked out loud, "What's the date today?" Who keeps dates up there. But one guy knew. He yelled, "September 15." I said, "Hey, that's my birthday." Everybody sang "Happy Birthday" to me.

At Christmas time, many received gifts. Once, stateside, someone received a mayonnaise gallon jar of poi, but the glass jar was all broken— really messed up, the glass mixed up with the poi. I saw them fold up a mosquito net several times and strain it.

On the front, a few received boxes of assorted chocolate bars. We passed them out among the boys, local style. Then a new *kotonk* (Japanese American from the mainland) approached and wanted to buy one. The local boy had a surprised look when the *kotonk* said he wanted to buy. "We don't sell; we share," he said, and gave him a bar. It was little things like that at the beginning till he learned our local style. Then we got along fine. Some wanted to learn and blended right in.

I once had animosity toward the 442nd when they joined us in Italy. We went over to meet friends, relatives, to talk story, and explain what we had learned in combat—like the sound of artillery shells coming in. If the whistling continues, it's going to pass overhead. But if the whistling stops, it's going to fall by you, so always, while moving forward under shelling, you had to look for a place to dive.

This group of eighteen-year-olds I met told me in a cocky manner, "Naw, we don't need you guys' help; watch us go." Well, the first few hours they went into battle at Belvedere they got so busted up by artillery, the 100th was ordered to go and help right away. I remember running into the shelling and actually tackling down the ones standing up. The 100th destroyed the German SS battalion, killing more than they captured. The 100th received a Presidential Unit Citation for that battle, and the 442nd was made humble like the rest of us.

Once, the machine gunners set their guns by a second-floor window at night and fired sporadically. American bullets, unlike German, make a big flash that the enemy can see, so the gunners hung blankets on the window and fired through them. I hope I am not giving away an American secret.

On guard duty up in the hills, there was a hurricane. The snow fell sideways, so cold, we were almost frozen. The replacement didn't show, so I walked against the wind to find shelter. I saw an ambulance with no one around, so I took off my wet shoes and slept in there. Many more hills past Civitavecchia, many were getting frozen feet. A doctor came to examine them. He separated the men after checking their feet—those who could continue and those who must be hospitalized.

I saw Captain [Sakae] Takahashi outside with a forlorn look, for he was losing many of his good men. Frozen feet try to swell in the shoe. There is no room, so it hurts. After the doctor checked my swollen feet, I had a hard time putting on my shoes.

I was sent to Africa because the hospitals in Italy were filled with the seriously wounded. The quack said my feet may have to be amputated. I told him, "No way." There were a lot of our men there, walking softly and nimbly.

It's like when you fold your feet, Japanese style, under you and your feet go to sleep; it was hard to walk. Only your pain goes away after the blood circulates again. Ours, we walked like that for months. My treatment was two jiggers of whiskey a day and some kind of vitamins. I played poker daily and when I ran low on cash, there were lots of buyers for my whiskey.

Back in Italy, I was classified Class B. I was at the replacement depot in Bagnoli, near Naples. I was sent to work at the 300th General Hospital, pushing the Italian labor in the kitchen, but I started off on the wrong foot when the interrogating captain said, "So you're a Jap." I told him, "I'm not a 'Jap,'" but a better American than he was. At this, all the frontline haoles who went there for the same thing, to work, said in unison, "Yeah!" The captain's face got all red.

When promotion time came, a haole who could not read good got stripes, and I received a cluster on my Good Conduct Ribbon. To receive it, I had to go into the office to accept it like it was a big deal. At the front, they used to toss them in the foxhole, even the Purple Heart. I should not have done it, but after the captain read me the citation and handed me the papers, I ripped them up, and after throwing them in the waste basket, saluted him smartly and walked out.

Walking in Naples, a man and woman called out to me. They introduced themselves as professors and said, "You are wearing an American uniform, but you are not like the black and white soldiers. What are you?"

I told them I am of Japanese ancestry, like there are Americans of Italian ancestry. "No!" they said in disbelief. "Japanese are not good-looking. They have small-rim glasses with teeth sticking out." I told them, "You have been reading too much of Mussolini's propaganda." Then they shut up and I walked away.

One morning my MP captain asked me if I could speak Japanese. Next day, I was shipped out stateside. When we were near France, our ship received a radiogram to load up ammunition from France and head for the Pacific. We were dumped at LeHavre, France. So with our directive papers in hand, we were free. No boss. We could go to any camp and eat. The papers let us into the PX, so we had the black market for spending money. We, eight of us, traveled slowly through France. When we saw enough, we boarded a ship named the *Sea Tiger* and traveled from the other end of France to the port of Marseilles. The Mediterranean was foggy, so we heard fog horns day and night.

After landing stateside, we had a twenty-one-day delay before reporting to Camp Ritchie, Maryland. The *kotonk*—I forget his name—who was with us invited Harold Kanemura, Fred's cousin, and me to Cleveland, where his wife was. His wife's maiden name was Hirata—that I remember.

There were lots of AJAs there. Some newspaper personnel saw us, and the editor went all over the city looking for us. When he found us, we went to his office to talk story. We came out on the front page in the morning edition. Many AJAs came to see us and show appreciation. A guy gave us the use of his Chrysler. A couple from Kauai told us our apartment was too small and invited us to come to their house.

With the Chrysler at our disposal, six of us headed for Canada through Niagara Falls. In Buffalo, New York, we hit a railroad track on our Class B tires. We went to the service station, but since everyone was on wartime rations, he could not sell tires or gas without a coupon. He suggested the only way was to go to city hall, which controls the coupons. So off I went half a block down: no cap, wrinkled shirt. I explained to the clerk, who said only the mayor could okay it and he was busy that day. What a quandary.

Talking with others in the car, there was no solution: The clerk would not pass minor problems to the mayor. Then a bright idea hit. I combed my hair, put on cap at a smart angle, put on my Eisenhower jacket with all the ribbons—borrowed more from the others—and marched smartly to city hall. Everyone's head turned to look. I went closer: The clerk went for the mayor. Citizens were around me. I explained our predicament to the mayor, who, looking at the citizens, said—or was it a political speech—"I'm sure the citizens of this fair city would be glad to help someone who did so much for our country . . ." In his office, he gave me coupons for sixty gallons and three tires. I thanked him several times and left with a smart salute. I thanked the citizens, too—gave them a salute and a big smile.

The mayor said more, but you wouldn't be interested. All political. He even used that opportunity to shake the hands of the voters there.

Don't get me wrong. I have appreciation and fondness for Buffalo. It was my first time at Niagara Falls; awesome.

We reported to Camp Ritchie, a military intelligence camp. Haole women in service there could speak perfect Japanese, so we kept quiet. I thought, "Shame, Japanese and no can talk." There was nothing to do except go to the movies and rent rowboats in the camp lake. They put us on KP, but we refused to work. I guess we felt we did our part in the war. MPs came, and we were ready to fight them, so they did not touch us. The reason we were sent there was for the occupation of Japan.

While at camp, I was picked to go to the White House, representing the 100th at President Truman's memorial fund for President Roosevelt. Terumi Kato from Hawaii and two *kotonks* went, too. Kato had lost a leg, so I helped him during the visit. We stayed at the Mayflower Hotel in Washington, D.C., where lots of politicians stay. Earl Finch told me to put on my Eisenhower jacket with all my medals and walk around in the lobby to show the haole politicians what we did. Not one senator or politician came up to me, but I could hear them talking that they were worried that the Japanese were going to sue them for putting them in internment camps.

Hideto Kono

442nd Regimental Combat Team/
Military Intelligence Service

SOFT GREEN SOLDIERS

My niece, Elizabeth Nakaeda, was thirteen years old when I was shipped to Camp Shelby, Mississippi, for basic infantry training as a member of the 442nd Regimental Combat Team. I was Elizabeth's only uncle and the only soldier she could write to in intimate terms. I, too, felt a need to convey to her how I felt as we at camp were engaged daily in marching in unison and undergoing basic infantry training.

The forest surrounding Camp Shelby was abundant with pine and maple trees. The leaves of the maple trees in early May were yet tender and light green. I couldn't help but compare ourselves—all in our late teens and early twenties—to the tender leaves which, in time, must become hardened to surmount their impending adversities and challenges. I put my feelings in a short poem and sent it to my niece.

I had forgotten all about the poem until Elizabeth, now Elizabeth Kunimoto and a professor at the University of Hawaii, surprised me by reciting it at the celebration of my sixtieth *(Kanreki)* birthday. Many of my fellow Shelby trainees in E Company who fought in Europe did not have the luxury of living through the autumn of their lives. I am grateful for the circumstance that led me to be transferred to the Military Intelligence Service, and for being healthy enough at age seventy-five to be able to continue to be of some service to my family and my community.

Soft green leaves
The May breeze gently stirs
As
Soft green soldiers
March

Soft green leaves
Before the autumn breeze to thee
A lovely hue bestows,
And to peaceful slumber slowly sends

Let not thee
The summer storms,
The autumn gales
To tattered shambles
Rend and crush

March
Soft green soldiers
As the May breeze blows
Soft green leaves

Pvt. Hideto Kono
Camp Shelby, Mississippi, 1943

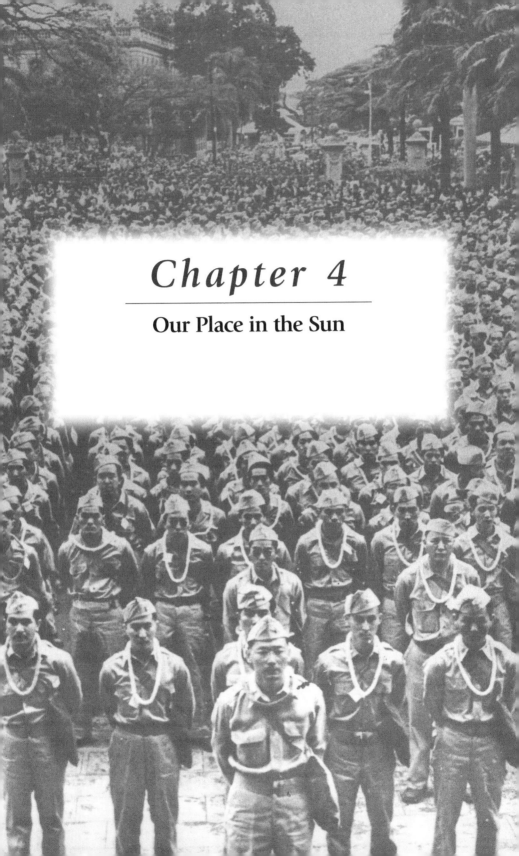

Chapter 4

Our Place in the Sun

Lyn Crost

THE TRAILBLAZERS: THE 100TH INFANTRY BATTALION (SEPARATE)

There was always a special note of pride in a man's voice when he told me, "I was in the original 100th Infantry Battalion." The words themselves conveyed not only the pride of this special band of men from Hawaii, but also the suffering they had endured fighting for the United States.

Unlike most American troops that fought on foreign soil, the men from Hawaii had seen bombs fall on their homeland, threatening their families—and this awakened in them the desperate need to fight against prejudice to protect the liberties that they had been taught belonged to all Americans. That original 100th Infantry Battalion was to become a legendary battalion of legendary men, like those who fought for freedom and justice in America's earlier wars.

On the night of June 5, 1942, these Japanese American soldiers and their haole officers sailed out of Honolulu Harbor for an unknown destination. Perhaps it would be the mainland United States. Perhaps they would be drowned at sea by marauding enemy submarines. Japan was already fighting to take Midway Island, and if it succeeded, might launch an invasion of Hawaii, whose Japanese population, as well as its American-born sons, were suspect because their ancestral origins were the same as the enemy. Yet, as members of Hawaii's National Guard, they had stood watch on that terrible night of Pearl Harbor, ready to kill or be killed, to protect Hawaii's mountains and valleys, its military installations, and its miles of shoreline against an unexpected invasion.

They were a microcosm of Hawaii: schoolteachers, factory workers, manufacturing officials, mechanics, agriculturists, salesmen, civil engineers, workers from sugar and pineapple plantations and from dozens of other island occupations. And 95 percent of them were children of immigrants.

For the Japanese American soldiers on board the SS *Maui* that night, it was the beginning of a journey into American history that has no equal. The original 100th Infantry Battalion, that band of men rushed out of Hawaii so ignominiously, was the first military unit that ever faced the challenge of proving, on a battlefield, loyalty to the United States. They had taken as their motto, "Remember Pearl Harbor." No one had a more valid claim to it. And, echoing their love for Hawaii, their battalion flag displayed the feathered helmet of ancient chieftains and the taro leaf that Hawaiians believed was a protection from evil. No matter where they were to go, they would never forget their beloved Islands.

Nisei linguists of the Military Intelligence Service were already spreading throughout Pacific battle-torn islands, but their very existence was so secret that America would not begin to learn about them for another two decades. The 100th Battalion would be the first public proof of Japanese Americans' loyalty to the United States and what they would do to protect it. After a training period, prolonged because they were constantly scrutinized for signs of disloyalty, the 100th finally landed on the Salerno beachhead of Italy on September 22, 1943. One week later, it suffered its first death when Sgt. Joe Takata was killed in an encounter that won the battalion its first Distinguished Service Cross. The men of the 100th would never forget Joe Takata. Each year, on the Sunday nearest the date of his death, they would hold a memorial service for their men who had died in battle or who had succumbed later to the aftermath of wounds or the ravages of age.

Army units that fought beside the 100th, military leaders who commanded it, and war correspondents who watched it would never forget this unique battalion as it wrote its history in blood, tears, and unsurpassed courage until it reached the rock-encrusted slopes of Monte Cassino, where it rose from the ignominy of suspicion to the acclaim of an admiring nation as it faced one of the greatest defense bulwarks of World War II: the German Gustav line. It was on those slopes, pounded by rain, frozen by the cold of winter, that the 100th Battalion's undaunted courage created the legend of the nisei soldiers, the "little iron men" who just never retreated. And it was there, by their heart-wrenching deaths and wounds, that they earned the sobriquet by which they would be remembered: the Purple Heart Battalion. Their bravery at Cassino, widely featured in newspapers and magazines, was the first glimpse the American public had of its nisei soldiers and what they would do to help preserve historic liberties of the United States.

When the 100th had landed at Salerno it numbered 1,300 men. When it finished fighting on Monte Cassino five months later, its effectives totaled 521. This was the end of the original 100th Infantry Battalion, as those men who had sailed from Hawaii in 1942 now called it.

They had fought not only a foreign enemy, but also prejudice and suspicion. And they had set the standard for Japanese American soldiers who followed. That band of men who had left Hawaii under a cloud of suspicion had won the admiration and trust of the United States Army from privates to generals, who now quarreled among themselves for assignment of Japanese American troops to their commands.

Replacements for the original 100th's decimated ranks came from the 442nd Regimental Combat Team, which was still training at Camp Shelby, Mississippi. Now reinforced, the battalion carried on the magnificent record it had established during those first months of fighting. It was next sent to Anzio, and after the breakout there, it once more did the seemingly impossible. When two battalions (twice its number) failed to conquer the last enemy roadblock on the road to Rome, the 100th finally broke through, thus allowing Allied troops to maintain their schedule and enter the Eternal City on June 5, 1944—one day before the great Allied landing on the Normandy coast of France. Poignantly, it was also the second anniversary of the original 100th Battalion's departure from Hawaii, shrouded in secrecy, hurried because America doubted their loyalty if the enemy invaded the Islands.

When the 100th Battalion was combined later that month with the 422nd Regimental Combat Team, which had just arrived from the United States, it was allowed to retain its own name in this new combination because of its impressive record during nearly nine months of fighting. The two units were now known as the 100th/442nd Regimental Combat Team as they fought northward in Italy to cross the Arno River, then in France to rescue the "Lost Battalion" of the Texas 36th Division, and finally, in Italy to launch the Allied assault through the Apennine Mountains, which ended the war on the Italian front.

The original 100th Infantry Battalion was the first Japanese American combat unit in the history of the United States. In fulfilling the trust given it, this unique battalion helped erase much of the nation's suspicion of Japanese Americans and cleared the way for thousands of them to join the 100th/442nd Regimental Combat Team, which became the most decorated military unit in American history for its size and length of service.

Lt. Gen. Mark Clark would never forget the 100th Infantry Battalion, which he had watched closely since it joined the United States Fifth Army at Salerno. In 1982, when he was no longer able to travel to Hawaii to celebrate the battalion's fortieth anniversary, he sent this message: "I witnessed your magnificent performance and the respect with which you were held, not only by the American troops, but by troops of many nationalities who fought together in the difficult Italian campaign."

With such a long history of outstanding battlefield action, it is not surprising that the highest ranking Japanese American field officer in the United States Army during World War II came from the ranks of that original 100th Infantry Battalion. Maj. Mitsuyoshi Fukuda had advanced from a lieutenant in command of a platoon to commanding officer of the 100th Battalion, the first Japanese American to command an infantry battalion in United States history. Breaking precedent again, he was promoted to executive officer of the 100th/442nd Regimental Combat Team.

Major Fukuda was the last member of the original 100th to leave Europe. In recognition of the battalion's remarkable record, he was sent to Washington to be received by War Department officials. At that time he requested that something be done to perpetuate the memory of the 100th Battalion. He need not have worried; Hawaii would never forget those men who had left it to fight and die on foreign soil, far from the Islands they so deeply loved.

As years pass, statistics of decorations and the numbers of men killed and wounded may be forgotten. But the record of that original 100th Infantry Battalion and what it meant in the acceptance of Japanese Americans as loyal citizens of the United States must be remembered. If it had failed in its first months of fighting in Italy, there might never have been a chance for other Americans of Japanese ancestry to show their loyalty to the United States as convincingly as the 100th did on the battlefields of Europe. The 100th had proved that loyalty to the United States is not a matter of race or ancestry. And it had set an example for people of all nations who seek sanctuary here to fight for those values and concepts of government that have made the United States a refuge from the hunger and despair that haunts so much of the world.

Yes, I will remember well that courageous band of men from Hawaii—that original 100th Infantry Battalion. Those of us who knew them and what they stood for and what they did could never forget them.

Ben H. Tamashiro

100th Infantry Battalion

NEW VISIONS: FIRES TO BE KINDLED

The following is a speech delivered by Ben Tamashiro at a conference of the Association for Asian American Studies in May 1991.

In my readings recently, I happened to come across this line by Plutarch: "The soul is not a vessel to be filled, but a fire to be kindled."

Then just the other day, I felt a bit of that fire when I visited the traveling Bill of Rights exhibit at Aloha Stadium and saw the original two hundred-year-old parchment on display. As to why it should affect me so, I think that, much as photographs provide us with graphic accounts of the past, often it takes a piece of paper, like the Bill of Rights, to help move us into the future.

I recall something like that happening to me fifty years ago when President Roosevelt signed into law the first peacetime draft. A country boy, I had been wanting to get away from Kauai to experience the outside world. My father had preceded me with similar dreams when he left

Okinawa in 1907, riding the crest of the emigration wave from Japan to Hawaii. He had visions of returning to his homeland with money in his pocket. But as it turned out, life on the sugar plantation was too harsh for him, so he learned to be a tailor, struggling to make a living at it.

Once he said to me that if I would take after him, he'd teach me everything he knew about the trade. I turned him down—turned him down, I think, not so much for the drudgery of tailoring as I saw it daily, but more because I wanted to be my own self. And that is how it was for me, trying to grow up to be an American here in Hawaii at a time when this place was a territory and its major industries just sugar and pineapple.

And what of the world beyond Kauai? It was a longing and a vision that the draft suddenly opened up for me. My circumstance, however, was much in contrast to my father's. He had been literally pushed out of Okinawa by his mother, who wanted to get him away from the possibility of being drafted into the Japanese army. The beginning of the twentieth century was a great time for young men in Japan inasmuch as the country had just won the Sino-Japanese War and had followed that up with a victory in the Russo-Japanese War. Afraid that my father would never survive the rigors of army life, his mother pushed him off to Hawaii.

Ironic, then, that his son could not wait to be drafted. I volunteered but did not tell my father until after the deed had been done. My induction date was December 10, 1940.

At Schofield Barracks, where draftees underwent their basic training, I had written home that I was well-fed and enjoying the training—so much so that after the termination of the one-year duty, perhaps I would like to join the navy. This threw the family into a dither.

Anyway, as the end of the one-year term approached, I found myself sitting in the company office, typing up discharge forms for those of us who were in that first draft. Then, just three days short of discharge, along came December 7. I recall taking the whole bunch of papers and dumping them into the wastebasket.

The real problems, however, brought on by the Japanese attack on Pearl Harbor could not be so easily pushed aside. For example, my father used to lead me into the garage every so often and there we would don our kendo masks and armor and bang away at each other with the bamboo swords. Perhaps that is how Saigo Takamori, the grand hero of the Meiji Restoration, came to be one of my heroes. Undoubtedly, it was this kind of learning, even as we studied American history in school, that contributed to the havoc raised in the minds of authorities as to what to do with the nisei boys at the outbreak of war.

For those of us already in the army, they had no choice but to tolerate us for the moment. Plans, however, were afoot to spirit us out of harm's way because of questions about our Americanism. After all, we were just one generation removed from the land of the perpetrators of the debacle at Pearl Harbor. Fortunately, there were others who knew us for what we were and had faith in us that we were Americans at heart.

In actual practice, too, there were other fires burning within our souls. For instance, though we lived next to a Buddhist temple, on Sundays I somehow chose to attend Sunday school at a Japanese Christian church a couple of miles away. And our big heroes of the day were Babe Ruth and Lou Gehrig and the whole batting order of the New York Yankees—along with George Washington and Abraham Lincoln. And Saigo.

As for that vision of fifty years ago, when I threw that batch of discharge papers into the wastebasket, I was in for the duration—four years, eight months, and twelve days, as it turned out to be—much of that time spent with the 100th Infantry Battalion, the first all-nisei combat unit in the history of the U.S. Army. I was swept, along with fourteen hundred other boys who left Honolulu in June 1942, through the Golden Gate, up over the Rockies, down through the midwestern plains, and into Camp McCoy and the winter snows of Wisconsin, the first snow for most of us.

We were then shifted down south at the beginning of the new year, to Camp Shelby, Mississippi, and thrust into the hot and steamy swamps of Louisiana in an endurance test of walking miles and miles with full field packs and one canteen of water a day. For a diversion, we cut open the bellies of tree snakes and tried to catch the fast and slippery armadillos.

I saw all there was to see of training. But I began to wonder whether it would end this way—just training and more training, without a full testing of Americanism to convince the doubting Thomases. I had written home, voicing a wish that we would be sent into combat. It was not long in coming.

Soon we were on our way across the Atlantic, and into Oran, North Africa, where we were integrated into the 34th Infantry Division. The 34th, an Iowa National Guard unit, was the first division to be sent overseas following our entry into the war. The division landed in England, led the charge at North Africa against Rommel and the Afrika Corps, and was now headed for the beachhead at Salerno, Italy.

I remember well that morning in September 1943 in the surf at Salerno. The whole battalion climbed down the side of the ships by way of landing nets into waiting landing crafts. We circled for a long time in the water until the whole battalion had gone over the side into the landing crafts, then all together headed for the beach. Most of the crafts sailed right up onto the sand and the boys hardly got their feet wet. But our landing craft got stuck on a reef and the coxswain, instead of going around the obstacle, decided to buck it. He reversed his craft, then slammed it into the reef, intending to go over it. Again he backed up and, with engines roaring, slammed into the reef a third time. Seeing that he couldn't make it, he just lowered the ramp and directed us to jump off. By now, the whole battalion had gathered on shore and was watching us.

First off was the executive officer, Maj. James Lovell, one of the handful of white officers with us. He was a big six-footer. I was next. He stepped off into the unknown depths of the reef, and when I saw him go under, I was sure that little me would drown. But there was no way out. Stepping off, I immediately sank in waters way over my head. Touching bottom, I gave a big kick to propel me upward. That, and the buoyancy of my full field pack shot me back to the surface. I dog-paddled in until my feet touched sand. Such was my introduction to sunny Italy.

Caught in a mortar barrage early on, I was hit on the leg and laid up in a field hospital for several weeks. I returned in time to enter into the battle for Cassino beginning January, a battle which turned out to be one of the greatest in World War II. Hit again, this time in my arm, and laid up for several months in a hospital in Naples, the wound turned out to be what I call a "million-dollar wound" in that it got me out of the fighting front for good.

While recuperating at the hospital, I ran into my brother-in-law's brother, Hideo Akiyama, who had come over from the 442nd Regimental Combat Team at Camp Shelby as one of the early replacements for the 100th. He was headed for Anzio to join the 100th there. Opening his wallet, he gave me his only twenty-dollar bill, saying he wouldn't be needing it where he was going. I tried to dissuade him, arguing that he'd need it later. But he proved to be right: He was killed at Anzio.

There are countless such stories of visions and dreams waiting to be told. Their value is that they serve as links to the past and provide inspiration for the future. And as with seeing the Bill of Rights and feeling a flame start up within me, I believe that gatherings such as this help to keep those dreams alive even as they generate new visions.

Samuel Sasai

442nd Regimental Combat Team

TWO YEARS, EIGHT MONTHS, AND NINETEEN DAYS THAT CHANGED MY LIFE FOREVER

I was born on September 3, 1924, in Haleiwa on the island of Oahu, the third child and only son of Tamaki and Kazu Sasai.

My father, who was the third son of a farmer in Okayama, was born in 1889 (Meiji twenty-two) and immigrated to Hawaii in 1909. At the time of my birth, he managed Bishop Bank's (now First Hawaiian Bank) Haleiwa branch. In 1929 we moved to Honolulu, where he worked as an insurance agent for the remainder of his career. He died in 1984 at the age of ninety-four.

My mother, Kazu Uno Sasai, was the third daughter of school-teachers. She was born in Hakodate, Hokkaido, in 1895 (Meiji twenty-eight). On her mother's side, she was descended from a warrior family of the Aizu Clan, which remained loyal to the Tokugawa shogunate at the time of the Imperial Restoration (1867). However, they lost a war with the troops of the new Meiji government and were banished from their home-land (now Fukushima Prefecture) to a barren portion of what is now Aomori Prefecture in northern Honshu. Eventually, some clan members settled on Hokkaido Island across the Tsugaru Straits.

My maternal grandmother became a schoolteacher. She taught at the Iai Girls School, an American Methodist Church mission school which still exists today in Hakodate. She met and married my grandfather, Kanemitsu Uno, who was originally from Matsuyama, Ehime Prefecture. He was the school's principal.

My grandfather Uno, the second son in the family, was actually born a Naito. He, too, came from a warrior family who served the Lord of Matsuyama. Being a second son, he was adopted by my grandmother's family—the Uno family—which did not have a male heir. After twenty-five years as principal of the Iai Girls School, grandfather retired and moved his family to Tokyo. The family then immigrated to Hawaii, arriving on October 15, 1913.

Shortly after arriving, my grandfather married off his two elder daughters. In fact, my mother was married to Tamaki Sasai on October 18, 1913, three days after arriving in Hawaii. Her marriage lasted seventy-one years, and on April 18, 1995, she celebrated her one hundredth birthday.

My mother was a well-educated woman for her era, having graduated from the equivalent of a high school in Tokyo before coming to Hawaii. She was determined that her two daughters (my older sisters) receive a good education. She must have successfully badgered my father because we moved to Honolulu, the big city, when I was five. My sisters were able to attend city high schools and graduated from the University of Hawaii.

As her only son, my even-more-determined mother enrolled me at Castle Kindergarten (located where the Noguchi Arch is situated on the grounds of the Honolulu Municipal Center), then at Lincoln Grammar School on Victoria Street, across from Thomas Square, which I attended from 1930 to 1936. During this period in Hawaii, there was a dual public-school system. Some schools were "English Standard" schools: Lincoln was one of them.

In 1936 I advanced to Roosevelt High School in Honolulu. At the time, Roosevelt was a six-year junior and senior high school. It was also the only "English Standard" high school on Oahu. On December 7, 1941, I was a seventeen-year-old senior, only six months away from graduation.

I mention the "English Standard" schools because they were strange animals. They were public schools, funded by the taxpayers of Hawaii; and yet, there was discrimination against anyone not white who wished to enroll. A prospective student was required to pass an oral language examination. Children of immigrant parents, obviously, had a difficult time speaking "standard" English. Thus, a de facto private-school system existed within the public-school system, with the children of white parents who spoke English as a cradle language being accepted at the "standard" schools and all others (immigrant children) being directed to "regular" schools. It took determined immigrant parents to invade the "standard-school system" with their children.

To give credit where credit is due, the teachers in Hawaii's public-school system (regular and standard) molded an entire generation of children of immigrants in accepting the United States of America as their own country, the constitution of the United States as their own governing principle, and the ideology of democracy as their own way of life—this in addition to teaching reading, writing, and arithmetic. They certainly deserve a "well done" for their efforts.

My own experience in the standard-school system parallels those of my generation throughout Hawaii, whether they were in regular or standard schools. I can point to many of my teachers as outstanding professionals and caring human beings.

And yet, in all of these early years there were instances of overt racial discrimination. I mention two instances only as they affected my development as a young adult soon to be involved in the maelstrom of World War II.

Once, in junior high, I asked for some help in locating an item in the school library. The librarian, a white woman, snapped at me and said, "Why don't you go to a school where you belong?!" The memory of that rebuke has remained vivid in my memory.

Another experience happened during my senior year in high school. Remember, school started in September and, unbeknownst to us, the surprise bombing of Pearl Harbor was only three months away. I was a member of the Roosevelt High School Reserve Officers Training Corps. Those in the senior class became officers of the cadet regiment. We had been informed that our test scores would determine our rank, that is, highest test score, highest rank.

Thus, my test score being the highest, I expected, in my innocence, the highest rank. When the appointments were announced, I was shocked to find myself about tenth from the top. I immediately asked for and received an appointment with the young U.S. Army lieutenant, our instructor, who was on detached service. When I reminded him of his earlier statements to us about test scores determining rank, he was very embarrassed. After a long pause, he finally said, "It's just one of those things . . ."

The ugly truth slowly sank into my brain. Obviously, no son of a Japanese immigrant could possibly hold the highest rank in the cadet regiment when there were sons of white parents available, no matter what his test scores. So I learned a major and bitter lesson on what it was to be yellow in a country dominated by whites.

In discussing the education of the children of Japanese immigrants, it is very important to consider the influence of the Japanese-language schools on the nisei generation. I am certainly no expert in this field and can speak only in generalities.

First of all, our parents came from a culture that revered education and educated people. They knew instinctively that for their children, the only way out from continued labor on the sugar plantations was higher education. Thus, their constant sermon was to study hard, and somehow, some way, they would sacrifice and put their children through the University of Hawaii.

However, at the same time they were amazed, appalled, and afraid of the rapid Americanization of their children. The nisei could barely converse with their parents in Japanese and only basic human needs were addressed. Even this was in the dialect of their parents' home province. So, the parents banded together and out of their meager incomes contributed enough to establish a private Japanese-language school system. Such schools were established in many towns and on all the major islands with Japanese communities.

Regular public schools ended their day at about two-thirty P.M. We then had to race across town to get to our language school by three-thirty P.M. There was one hour of instruction each afternoon and two hours on Saturday morning. The teachers were very strict and sometimes physically abusive. I hated every minute because the forced attendance every afternoon and Saturday morning made it impossible to participate in athletic activities and club activities at the public school.

The curriculum at the Japanese-language school was primarily reading and writing. There was one subject, however, which was unique to Japanese education. It was called *shushin*, which probably can be loosely translated as "moral training." A great deal of what I know about *on* (debt of gratitude), *giri* (duty and obligation), *chugi* (loyalty), *shinbo* (endurance), *ganbari* (perseverance), and other moral precepts probably came from these *shushin* classes over the twelve years I was forced to attend language school.

Despite my less-than-kind thoughts about the Japanese-language schools, I must acknowledge that my present-day ability to read, write, and speak Japanese, however limited, I owe mostly to the twelve years of hated language-school training. It enriched my life tremendously.

It should also be remembered that these language schools produced in the nisei population the only pool of partially trained Japanese linguists in the entire United States. Were it not for this pool, America would not have been able to field as many translators and interpreters as it did during World War II. It has been said that the military intelligence work of this unique group shortened the war by many months.

In 1940 or 1941 I remember being involved in a family and community tug-of-war when the subject of renouncing Japanese citizenship came up. Japan claimed me as a citizen because my parents were Japanese citizens. This legal concept was known as jus sanguinis—law of blood. On the other hand, the United States of America conferred citizenship on me because I was born on American soil. This legal concept was known as jus soli—law of land.

There was a great deal of debate, but the upshot of it was that a dual citizen could renounce his Japanese citizenship *(kokuseki ridatsu)* by signing and swearing to a written request submitted through the local Japanese Consulate General. For most nisei, this was a moment of decision closely watched by the white community as an indication of how the nisei thought and felt.

Although my parents were unhappy about the necessity of making such a decision, they told me that the decision was mine. My father spoke with considerable sarcasm about current immigration laws prohibiting them from becoming naturalized Americans even if they wanted to, while at the same time Americans agitated about nisei retaining dual citizenship.

There was no hesitation on my part, and, in due course, my name was stricken from the Sasai family register in Okayama Prefecture. That must have been cause for a good deal of conversation in the Sasai family household in Okayama. Now I was solely an American.

Life for a high-school student was both placid and predictable in one sense and very volatile in another. Daily routines of school and study continued as always. Social life tended to be hectic, not only because of our age group, but also because throughout that period of grades seven through twelve—1936 through 1941—the world was poised on the brink of conflict. Even in Hawaii, a mere dot in the vast Pacific Ocean, we could feel the gathering tensions. In Europe, Adolph Hitler was already moving to consolidate his hold on Austria, Poland, and other countries adjacent to Germany. Soon he would engulf Russia, England, France, Belgium, and the Netherlands. In Asia, the Japanese military was already in China and Manchuria. These events created great underlying tension and urgency in our lives. And so life went on, routinely, yes, but somehow, disturbingly unstable.

Then came that unforgettable Sunday—December 7, 1941. My father had gotten me up early that morning because he wanted my help in repairing a leaky garage roof. Our home was located in the Sheridan district of Honolulu. While working on the garage roof, both of us noticed black clouds of smoke rising over the western side of Honolulu. Then we began to see exploding antiaircraft shells high over the city. The civilian population on Oahu had become accustomed to constant military drills and maneuvers and both of us commented on how realistic the maneuvers were that morning.

My sister was in the kitchen, preparing our Sunday breakfast. Turning on the radio, she heard a male voice, full of emotion and urgency, say that Pearl Harbor had been attacked. He kept repeating, "This is the real McCoy! Take cover! This is no drill! Take cover!" My father and I hastily came down from the roof. As the radio announcer gave additional details of attacking aircraft with the "meatball" insignia of Japan, both my parents looked at each other and used the same despairing word—"*Masaka* (Can it really be)?!"

The ensuing days and months became a kaleidoscope of blackouts, rationing, directives from the military government, rumor upon rumor, fear, uncertainty, confusion, and shock. Stories abounded regarding leaders of the Japanese community who had been picked up by the FBI for reasons nobody knew for sure.

Six weeks into the war, the nisei University of Hawaii Reserve Officers' Training Corps cadets who had been taken into the Hawaii Territorial Guard were suddenly mustered out, obviously because they were not trusted. The nisei already in the active military through the selective-service process were out with their units defending the beaches of Hawaii from possible invasion forces. Six months later, in June 1942, they were suddenly relieved of their duties, their weapons taken from them. Within a short time they were shipped to the continental United States. Again, a case of not being trusted.

How I hated the Japs for bringing this upon us! The suspicious looks, the whispered rumors, the outright hate-filled remarks all caused by the sneak attack on Pearl Harbor. My maternal grandparents had taught me that *bushi* (Japanese warriors) always announced themselves before attacking. Here they were, however, hiding behind delayed diplomatic relations and attacking like cowards without a declaration of war.

How I hated the Japs for bringing this upon us. We were having a hard enough time establishing ourselves in America, and now this. Would we ever be accepted in the land of our birth?

In June 1942 I graduated from high school and that September, matriculated as an incoming freshman at the University of Hawaii. It was truly a helpless, impotent feeling, trying to be a college student when the entire world was engulfed in a conflict the scope of which had never happened before in the entire history of the world. On top of everything, my draft status changed from the most eligible, 1-A, to 4-C, "enemy alien." How insulting!

Just after New Year's in 1943, the war news, which until then had been only one way—bad—for the United States, began to have bits and pieces of good news. Although highly censored, there was an uplifting feeling of renewed hope after a string of defeats in places like the Philippines and New Guinea. It was at this time, perhaps in late January or early February of 1943, that we heard an announcement that the United States was organizing an all-Japanese American combat unit made up entirely of volunteers. This was electrifying news that opened substantially new vistas for us.

Then, as now, I am not a lover of war, killing, and violence. Yet, in my heart of hearts, I knew that unless we nisei showed our true colors then, by volunteering en masse and subsequently performing in outstanding fashion, we would have no hope, no future in the United States for our parents, ourselves, and our posterity. I knew that prejudiced feelings like "Why don't you go to a school where you belong?" and "It's just one of those things . . ." would continue forever. As young as I was, I knew we had to seize this opportunity or lose all.

Without my parents' knowledge, I volunteered and was accepted into the unit that was subsequently designated the 442nd Regimental Combat Team, Army of the United States of America. On March 24, 1943, I was sworn into the military service and became Pvt. Samuel Y. Sasai, army serial number 30104879.

I remember my final day at home. As I said good-bye to my parents, my mother fixed me with an unsmiling glare, formally bowed to me, and said, "*Kiyotsukete itte irrashai* (Go with care)." I knew she was furious at me, her only son, for volunteering and placing myself in harm's way when I did not have to. She accepted the inevitable, but in her anger, could only bid me a formal good-bye. It was only later in training camp when I received a letter from her that I knew the depth of her feeling. She ended the letter by saying, "*Hoshi no hata wo yoku mamorinasai. Sasai no ie ni haji wo kakeru koto wo shitara kikimasen* (Protect the country. I won't forgive you for bringing shame to the Sasai family)." She never wrote to me again, and I kept up with my family only through letters written by my older sister. It would be three long years before I saw my mother again.

Twenty-six hundred of us left Hawaii on board the SS *Lurline* in early April 1943. We landed in Oakland, California, five days later, transferred to a troop train, and began a cross-country journey that ended in the state of Mississippi at a place called Camp Shelby.

While we were on the troop train and still within the city limits of Oakland, I saw a sight that amazed me and has remained indelible in my mind. A crew of men on a city refuse truck were picking up trash containers and tossing the refuse into the bed of the truck. By itself, there was nothing special about what I was seeing. It was *who* the trash collectors were that mesmerized me. They were all white men! In Hawaii prior to World War II, it was always Native Hawaiians and Asians who did the manual labor. The white man was always boss.

For the first time in my short life of eighteen years, I began to see what it was like outside of Hawaii's segregated society. In the years to come, remembering that one sight gave me immeasurable amounts of confidence as I competed in a white man's country. It removed forever the poverty of spirit that had been ingrained in us.

Mississippi in the 1940s was vastly different from what it is today. My first impressions amazed me. Why is a black man's urine so different from a white man's urine that it required separate toilets? Why must a black man have to stand packed behind a white line on a bus when there was lots of room in front of the line? Why do the black men have the "best" seats in a movie theater up on the balcony? An innocent boy raised on an island in the middle of the Pacific Ocean learned that there really was a place called "n----- heaven" in a theater.

My political leanings toward the left probably began somewhere about then—anything, any political party except that which retained the status quo. Whatever it took to change the way things were done, whether in Mississippi or in Hawaii.

I was assigned to the Anti-Tank Platoon of the Third Battalion, 442nd Infantry Regiment. My specific job was being the gunner of a 57mm antitank gun. Our military training progressed rapidly. From civilians to raw recruits, from raw recruits to an untested but combat-ready regimental combat team in just twelve months. It is just amazing what can happen when motivated teachers and intelligent students merge under pressured conditions. By March or April of 1944 we were desperately packing our equipment, preparing for movement overseas for combat duty.

On May 2, 1944, we left Hampton Roads, Virginia, and spent twenty-eight long days and nights packed five-high in the cargo hold of a Liberty ship. The freighter zigzagged as part of a large convoy across the Atlantic Ocean and Mediterranean Sea before we finally reached Naples, Italy.

On June 6, 1944, while the fateful Normandy invasion was taking place, we, too, were on landing craft, making the run onto the Anzio beachhead. We finally caught up with the 100th Infantry Battalion north of Rome, near the ancient town of Civitavecchia. The 100th, which had preceded us into battle, was the same group of men who had been summarily yanked off of Hawaiian beach defenses and shipped to the continental United States in 1942.

On June 26, 1944, our regiment went into our first battle and fought continuously thereafter until July 21st. The initial shock of realizing that "they," the enemy, were trying to kill me quickly turned a greenhorn into a veteran.

Seeing my first friend killed in action was an emotionally traumatic event. It took many hours before I was able to stomach food again. If I close my eyes, I can still see his pale, bloodless face, his body crumpled and lying in a drainage ditch alongside a dirt road.

When shock after shock, near miss after near miss occurs, when a comrade who spoke to you a few minutes ago is killed or wounded, a human being gradually becomes hardened. Our emotional rubber band may stretch and stretch and eventually snap, but for most of us it was a matter of enduring—*gaman* (perseverance) and *ganbari.* Soon, all frontline soldiers become no better than animals. They become savages with no resemblance to the civilized humans they were only a few short months ago. In retrospect, I wonder how I could have been the way I was during those months in combat. Unbelievable.

By the time we entered the fight, Germany was already facing defeat. They were being pushed backward in France and Italy, and on the eastern front, the Soviet army was compressing them. On both fronts, massive tank and infantry battles were taking place. The feared panzer (tank) units of the German army were being chewed up. The mountainous terrain of Italy precluded the use of mass armored battles in our area.

For us in the battalion antitank platoons, and for me as a gunner whose assignment was to aim and fire the 57mm antitank gun, this meant no work. No work meant life because our 57mm gun was no match for the tanks of the German panzer divisions. Our projectiles would never have penetrated their armor. Thank you, Lord! We hauled that 57mm gun all the way up the Italian peninsula and all over eastern France and never once fired it in anger.

Our battalion commander knew that we had no work. Since we were just sitting idly, he soon found work for us. He assigned us to our medical detachment and we became litter bearers, carrying wounded men from the battlefield to where they could receive medical attention.

Being a litter bearer is a strange assignment for someone who has been trained for combat. We had to store our weapons and go out on the battlefield with nothing but a Red Cross armband to protect us. Being without a weapon added a new dimension to combat experience.

On occasion we would "liberate" a chicken from a deserted farmhouse. Because there was no refrigeration, we tied up the chicken and carried it alive until we had a chance to cook it. Sometimes we would "liberate" a head of cabbage, break it up, put the pieces into our steel helmet, sprinkle on some salt and bouillon powder, massage the cabbage, and lo and behold, we would have Japanese pickled cabbage, *oshinko*.

I mention food because the combat ration issued to us, called K rations, was so unpalatable we ate it only to keep from starving. Twenty to thirty consecutive days of this fare required extreme hunger before we could stomach another meal of K rations. It can be said that something is better than nothing, which is true, but under these circumstances, having fresh chicken or fresh vegetables was a heavenly treat.

After our first two battle engagements in Italy, the 442nd was transferred to France in September 1944. I observed my twentieth birthday lying in a drainage ditch near Florence, Italy. We traveled by transport ship from Naples, Italy, to Marseilles, France. From there we went by train, that is, on freight cars of the French National Railway.

The freight cars were already famous from World War I and had acquired the name, "40 & 8s," which came from the prominent sign painted on the boxcar: "*40 homme et 8 chevaux*," "forty men or eight horses." To put it mildly, it was an experience that is hard to forget. Packed into the boxcars without water or food, except what we carried, no toilets, no nothing, we existed for three days until we reached our destination in the Vosges Mountains region of northeastern France.

Here in the Vosges Mountains we engaged in the battle for Bruyeres and the battle to rescue the "Lost Battalion." There is no need to recount the two battles because they have been well described many times. I think it more important to talk about the human side of the terrible thirty or so days that ensued.

It rained and rained and rained. Then the rain turned to sleet, which then turned into snow. We fought a skilled and determined enemy, and, as always, on the ground of his own choosing. Covered with mud and wet to the skin, we shivered and fought. We lost so many in dead and wounded that in these two battles our combat team ceased to be an effective fighting unit.

What makes men continue to fight under such adverse conditions?

I think there are many reasons that are special to each individual. Some of the reasons were common to all. For example, we all fight to survive. When living or dying becomes an issue, any animal, including the human animal, will desperately fight to survive. In the Vosges Mountains we were fighting an enemy who had been pushed back to the very border of their own country. This last-ditch, backs-to-the-wall fight led to extraordinary efforts on both sides. Both sides fought and clawed to survive.

Another reason was probably the comradeship that had developed during our year of training in Mississippi and during our first combat experience in Italy. The cohesiveness that develops between men who endure and suffer together, who face death together, is more than being brothers. We fought well because we could not let our buddies down. This feeling of unity and responsibility toward your comrades is a strong reason for a unit to perform well.

Perhaps there are many other reasons: our parents telling us not to bring shame upon the family name; our moral training at language school, with its emphasis on loyalty. Most likely, it was a combination of many things: family, school, church. Underlying all of these reasons was the belief that we had to prove what really needed no proving: We were, in fact, Americans in our hearts, and that the color of our skin and the slant of our eyes had nothing to do with it. There may be many more reasons, but these are the ones I can think of as providing the glue that kept us together. They made us *gaman* (persevere) and *gambaru* (push forward) under tremendous physical and mental stress.

At the end of the battles in France, our regiment was so depleted that we were sent to southern France and spent the final winter of World War II defending the Franco-Italian border. Subsequently, fresh reinforcements arrived to bring us back to full strength and we were ordered back to Italy to participate in the final assault on German defenses in Italy. By now, the 442nd was a seasoned assault regiment, and when the attack began on April 5, 1945, we proved ourselves well. A month later the German army surrendered.

For those of us who survived, it was a feeling of relief rather than elation. It was finally over. We had lost so many comrades along the way. Why had God so blessed me that I was able to survive when others had perished?

In the dark forests of the Vosges Mountains, I never thought I would live through the fighting. And yet, here I was, a survivor. I vowed then that I would consider each day from that day on as a bonus day and would try to live life to the fullest, not only for me, but for my comrades who fell and gave their all.

It took us approximately six months after hostilities ended in Europe to return home and be discharged from the military. Midway through that process, the United States dropped the atomic bombs on Hiroshima and Nagasaki, which hastened the war's end in Asia.

On December 13, 1945, I became a civilian once again. I was able to return and say, "*Tadaima kaerimashita* (I have come home)" to my mother. Two years, eight months, and nineteen days! From age eighteen-and-a-half until twenty-one years and three months. The experience of those turbulent months, although short in relationship to my seventy-three years of life so far, were probably the single most influential period of my life. I was young and impressionable and those impressions, both good and bad, have remained with me to this day.

As a civilian I married, finished college, fathered two sons, and worked at a local bank for thirty-two years until retirement. During the last fifty years, not a day has gone by that my way of thinking, of speaking, of doing things in general has not been influenced in some way by my few years in the military.

Camaraderie between those whose friendship was forged in the white-hot crucible of combat is a "forever" relationship. We may not see each other for years, but when we do meet, it is as though we saw each other yesterday. We pick up where we left off.

The strong bond between those who have looked at death together—and at close range—is not easily broken. The strong dependence on each other to execute specific assignments so we could all survive is not easily forgotten. Those who conquered fear—who know breathtaking, spine-tingling fear and yet stand up to face the enemy and do their job— these people know each other. These comrades are welded together forever, whether they like it or not.

Nisei soldiers happened to come at a critical point in the history of the Japanese in the United States. Their performance fully justified their supporters' position that it is heart and mind that are important, not appearance.

The position of the Japanese American in American society is a reasonably comfortable one now. However, I believe that the fight for equality of opportunity and for enduring civil liberties is a never-ending one, requiring constant vigilance and active participation. As our own example proved, constitutional safeguards are easily voided if circumstances are right and mob hysteria prevails.

Why were we strong in battle? I think we nisei did only what was expected of us as citizens of the United States. I can only say that my comrades and I did our best and were willing to give all. Whatever the many influences on us, whether home, family, school, or church, they must have somehow come together at the right time and place for us to have succeeded as we did.

I believe there is nothing wrong and everything right about nurturing the concepts of *on, giri,* and *chugi.* They may be Japanese concepts, or probably more correctly, Confucian precepts. Wherever they came from, they are worthy of continuing application.

It also appears to me that the parting words to so many of us from our parents included the warning to not bring shame *(haji)* upon the family. This concept, broadened, could make us not want to bring shame upon not only our family but also our friends, our community, our country. What a better world we could live in if we all behaved in a way that would not bring shame upon ourselves as well as those who support us.

I hope our children and future generations remember that liberty and freedom from tyranny were purchased at a price—a price paid for in blood. Hopefully, they will value these precious gifts enough to work diligently for their preservation.

Yoshiaki Fujitani

Military Intelligence Service

KUNI NO ON—GRATITUDE TO MY COUNTRY

For me, the war years were exciting and interesting, but never dangerous. I was not among the many nisei who not only volunteered to serve in the armed forces but also jumped into the fray with great dedication and valor.

I have always wondered what made the nisei what he was. Certainly, it was his upbringing, not only within his family but also his Japanese culture; his education, both English and Japanese; and his religion.

In my own background, I clearly see the influence of the Hongwanji ministers who spoke frequently about the four *on*, or gratitudes, of which we must always be conscious. There is the gratitude toward parents, whose kindnesses we can never repay. Then there is gratitude to our country, which provides us with safety and protection. There is gratitude to all beings who sustain us in many ways, and lastly, gratitude to the Buddha, who is always with us, no matter what our shortcomings may be.

The second *on*—gratitude to our country—is what the Japanese soldier had in mind when he fought for the emperor. While we say, *"kuni no on,"* or "gratitude to my country," the Japanese said, *"kimi no on,"* or "gratitude to the sovereign," or emperor. Buddhism wasn't the only teacher of this lesson. Our language-school teachers, who, in my case were Hongwanji ministers, also taught this at the Hawaii Japanese High School.

As a young man, I remember the visit of the Japanese plenipotentiary, Mr. Yosuke Matsuoka, Japan's delegate to the League of Nations prior to World War II. In his speech in Hawaii, he emphasized that the nisei were Americans, and that in order to be exemplary Americans, they should be loyal to America. This sentiment was echoed repeatedly by our religious leaders, Japanese school teachers, and our parents. A good nisei, therefore, was first a good, loyal American.

Confucianist ethics, which pervaded Japanese culture, must also be acknowledged. Virtues such as filial piety, courage, propriety, duty, shame, family over self, and honor and loyalty all bear the stamp of Confucianism. This ethic was deeply ingrained in our parents; the Buddhist ministers and language-school teachers taught it and lived it; and nisei like me accepted its veracity without question.

I was the second child—and the first son—of Rev. Kodo and Aiko (Furukawa) Fujitani. My early years were spent on the island of Maui, where I was born in August 1923 in the small east Maui community of Pauwela. There, I attended Haiku School.

When I was twelve, our family moved to Honolulu, where Father had been assigned as resident minister of the Moiliili Hongwanji Mission. I continued my schooling at Washington Intermediate, McKinley High School, and the University of Hawaii.

I was a sophomore at the university when Pearl Harbor was bombed by the Japanese, throwing the entire country into chaos and creating a mountain of problems for people of Japanese ancestry in Hawaii as well as on the mainland.

At the time, enrollment in the Reserve Officers' Training Corps for two years was mandatory for all male students, except those with exceptional reasons. On December 7, 1941, the University ROTC boys were ordered to report to the campus. We were handed the old Springfield '03 rifles we used in our drills and parades and told to install the firing pins that had been taken out to prevent accidents. Armed with this five-round, bolt-action rifle with chrome-plated bayonets for parade use, we were mustered into the Hawaii Territorial Guard (HTG), which gained distinction as the only ROTC unit in the country to see any military action.

For a month and a half we guarded water tanks in the hills, gas tanks at Iwilei, and the piers of Honolulu Harbor. The vast majority of the boys, who were eighteen or nineteen years old, were of Japanese ancestry.

Thus, it was understandable that military authorities in Washington, D.C., who knew nothing about the nisei, would have some hesitation about arming young boys who looked like the enemy to serve in a military unit to guard against a Japanese invasion.

But when the unit was assembled one night in January 1942 and informed by our weeping commanding officer, Capt. Nolle Smith, that the HTG was being disbanded, we were all stunned and angered. We joined the captain in shedding tears. The disbanding of the HTG was taken as a rebuff and rejection. It angered everyone, but with the wise counsel of older community leaders, such as Hung Wai Ching, then executive secretary of the University Young Men's Christian Association; Shigeo Yoshida, a respected school principal; Mitsuyuki Kido, a schoolteacher and later, political leader; and others, a handful of students began recruiting volunteers to form a labor battalion. One hundred sixty-nine boys responded, from which was formed the 34th Construction Engineer Regiment, more commonly referred to as the "Varsity Victory Volunteers," "the Triple V," or the "VVV."

I joined the Triple V, not so much out of a patriotic fervor—although I did feel good about serving my country—but more out of my desire for adventure and to be with my friends. The Triple V remained in existence for about nine months. The boys worked hard, building barracks and roads, fixing fences, and breaking rocks in the quarry.

A few months after the Triple V was organized, however, I learned that my father, a Buddhist minister, had been imprisoned because he was considered a "potentially dangerous" enemy alien. Suddenly, whatever patriotic feeling I possessed disappeared.

Deep down, I had known that someday this would happen, and it finally did. Most of the Buddhist clergy and language-school principals were arrested within days of the December 7th bombing. Father had been spared, however. He enjoyed four extra months of freedom. I am not sure why that happened, but I was told that a nisei officer who served with G-2 in the provisional government had vouched for Father's behavior during that period.

After the war, I asked Father how he was questioned when he was arrested. He said, "I was asked what I would do if a Japanese soldier came to me to ask for help. The answer I gave was, 'I will not report him, nor will I let him stay. I would send him away.' " I thought that was the only truthful answer he could have given as a Japanese with Japanese ties, living in an enemy country with his American children. Life must have been very complex for the issei during the war.

The inevitable finally happened. Father was incarcerated at Sand Island. In my frustration and anger, I could not understand why the father of a young American man who was willing to serve the war effort as a volunteer laborer should be treated so callously.

And then there was the other, more practical consideration that Mother would be left alone to take care of six young children. Of the eight siblings, my older sister and I were the only ones old enough to work. So I decided to leave the Triple V. After telling our supervisor, Ralph Yempuku, of my plans, I was immediately visited by Hung Wai Ching, who tried to dissuade me from leaving. But I wouldn't change my mind and returned home.

I took a job with the American Optical Company, located in the Alexander Young Hotel building in downtown Honolulu, cutting and shaping lenses for eyeglasses. I worked there from May 1942 until the end of 1943.

In order to contribute to the war effort—and primarily for reasons of camaraderie—I joined the Civil Defense Fire Engine Unit, stationed on the grounds of the Moiliili Japanese School. Being a brash nineteen-year-old, I volunteered for and was assigned to be the driver of the army vehicle that had the water pump in tow, which was our fire engine.

The fire hose was neatly folded on the truck, and the volunteer firemen sat on the side benches built into the vehicle. The driver's most difficult task was to drive the truck in reverse, since the two-wheeled pump attachment would wobble right or left if the driver wasn't careful. I thought I had gotten proficient in driving it, but many years later, after the war, the fire crew got together to reminisce about the early days, and the truth finally came out.

"Maybe you *thought* you were a good driver, but every time we went out for a spin or for training, we hung on tightly to the truck. You were such a rough driver!" I was told. In retrospect, maybe I was.

In November of 1943, just when I began missing my old playmates and classmates, I was approached by Sgt. Edwin Kawahara, a teacher at the Military Intelligence Service Language School (MISLS) at Camp Savage. He had come home to recruit men for the Military Intelligence Service.

The anger I had felt when Father was interned had subsided. I had been feeling somewhat empty about sitting out the war, so I was ready to go with Sergeant Kawahara. I was inducted January 3, 1944, at the induction center in Wahiawa.

After a brief orientation and adjustment period, the new recruits were loaded onto a troop ship at Honolulu Harbor for the trip to San Francisco, which seemed like an eternity. From San Francisco, we continued on by train over the Rockies to distant Minnesota. I remember marveling at the beauty of the snowcapped mountain ranges. It was the first time most of us had seen snow-covered mountains and countryside.

Upon reaching Camp Savage, at that time the site of the Military Intelligence Service Language School, I wrote home to Mother, telling her of the breathtaking view of a military camp blanketed with fresh, pure, white winter snow. The snow was always powdery, perhaps because of the lack of humidity and the extreme cold in that part of the country. It was hard to make snowballs to play with. I still remember the magnificent view of the camp in the bright morning sun.

With the coming of spring, the snow began to melt and turn into chocolaty mush. On that occasion, someone wrote home saying, "That stuff is still with us." I'm sure most of us felt the same: philosophically, we accepted military life and life itself as being a combination of good and bad, beautiful and ugly.

Soon we were following a routine of marching to class every morning and then marching back in the afternoon, laden with home-work; visiting the post exchange to get trays of 3.2 alcohol-content beer; taking a shower; going to bed; and getting up in the morning to begin again, ad infinitum. The monotony was broken only by an occasional forced hike in the countryside.

On one occasion, when we were far away from camp, we were surprised by a summer squall that drenched us to the bones. Undaunted, the boys began to sing as they strode down the road, impressing the com-pany commander. When the march was over, he made a point of praising the boys for their esprit de corps and grit.

In May 1944 Camp Savage was closed and the school was trans-ferred to Fort Snelling, located on the outskirts of St. Paul, Minnesota, where our military-language studies continued. It was about this time that I was permitted a furlough, so I went to visit Father in Santa Fe, New Mexico. It was an emotional meeting.

I presented myself at the internment camp office, asking to see my father. After what seemed a long wait, Father was permitted to leave the barbed-wired and heavily guarded compound. He was dressed in a tan suit, sporting a goatee. He was in good health and spirits. It touched me to think that he felt he had to be dressed in a formal way to greet his son who was serving in the U.S. Army. I forget what we talked about, but it must have been small talk about what he did every day and what I did every day, and the like. It was an incongruous scene: A son in the U.S. Army meets his father who is suspected by the government of being a "potentially dangerous enemy."

On that occasion I met "Pistol" Yasutake, formerly of Kauai, who seems to have been a liaison for community relations. During my visit with him at his home in Santa Fe, he prepared a lunch of rainbow trout, which he had caught himself. I also remember visiting an art museum in Santa Fe and viewing beautiful paintings by a woman artist whose surname was Best.

Our class graduated that October and was sent on to Alabama for basic training. I was separated from my class and sent to Camp Ritchie, Maryland, to join the Pacific Military Intelligence Research Section (PACMIRS). I was separated because I had injured myself while playing football the previous August. For a month and a half, I was confined to the post hospital while my fractured kneecap mended. I was in no condition to undergo the extreme physical punishment rumored to be the norm in basic training.

At Camp Ritchie, our daily work consisted of translating military documents. Some of our top translators, especially those who had been educated in Japan prior to the war, played an important role in translating extremely important documents that actually hastened the end of the war.

Although we were never told for what particular activity, all of the PACMIRS personnel were presented a Commendation Ribbon with Pendant for our meritorious service.

My memories of Camp Ritchie are rather spotty. PACMIRS was comprised of officers and enlisted men and women from the Allied nations: the United States, Canada, Britain, and Australia. There were small groups of American WACs (Women Army Corps) and Canadian WACs, with whom we fraternized, but there was a clear demarcation between the officers and their noncomissioned officers (noncoms). However, there were excursions and other activities to entertain the soldiers.

One day, soon after arriving in camp, we were surprised to see about two dozen Japanese soldiers in full combat gear—complete with grass attached to their helmets as camouflage—darting through the trees near the camp parade grounds. Their rifles, affixed with bayonets, were Nambu pieces. We were puzzled by what we saw until a sergeant came along and told us that the men were nisei, many from Hawaii, who had been selected for their small stature, to simulate the enemy in the jungles of Asia and the Pacific Islands.

I have always remembered that scene, wondering how the young men felt about acting out the role of the enemy. I also wondered what else those men were ordered to do as American soldiers. We later learned that the group was known as the Military Intelligence Training Unit, which sounded as legitimate as the Military Intelligence Research Section, of which we were members—but I don't think I would have wanted to trade places with them.

The war with Japan finally ended in August 1945. After a few months of preparation, a segment of our unit was sent on temporary duty. We arrived in Tokyo in November. We were to select and translate any documents relating to the Japanese war effort. We were billeted with the Allied Translator and Interpreter Section in the Nippon Yusen Building. Our "office" was the Tokyo First Arsenal (Tokyo Daiichi Zoheisho) in Otsu ward.

Books, journals, and pamphlets collected from military and non-military libraries were dumped on the floor. Our job was to select those with any possible military value. The others were discarded. I don't remember the fate of the discarded materials, but I do remember feeling that it was a great waste—like the reactionary book-burning we have witnessed in our country, but in reverse. Books with no military value were simply thrown away.

Our temporary duty lasted four months. For me, that was long enough. During that period, I was able to meet my Grandmother Shite Furukawa, whom I had not seen for fifteen years, since she and Grandfather returned to Japan in 1930. Grandma Furukawa had escaped the holocaust of Toyama City, which was literally leveled by incendiary bombs, and was living in the hills of Yatsuo Village.

I remember vividly this scene from my visit with her. It was snowing heavily in Toyama. Yatsuo Village was covered with a thick blanket of snow. I remember walking through deep pathways cut in the snowbanks. I had mixed feelings as I walked up the narrow path, my arrogance as a conquering warrior showing in the uniform of an American soldier. But I wanted also to be welcomed as someone who belonged; after all, I was the grandson of Grandma Furukawa. I have long forgotten the details of my meeting with Obaachan, but I know it was a warm one that ended too soon.

My father's brother's family lived in Tokyo. My uncle, the former police chief of Niigata City, had died earlier. His wife, three sons, and two daughters lived in a part of Tokyo that had escaped the firebombing.

I visited them on occasion, bringing food items to share with them. Whenever I visited, Mrs. Yokoyama, my aunt, would serve dishes that I knew they could ill-afford. Once, she served a kind of large mussel called *taira-gai*. It wasn't very tasty, but I knew they were depriving themselves for my benefit, and I appreciated that. On another occasion, she served deep-fried bee larvae, which looked and tasted like shrimp. Gourmet food—I had it in Tokyo.

My three male cousins were in the Japanese army. The youngest was an enlisted man who had been assigned clean-up duty in Hiroshima after the bombing. My middle cousin was a second lieutenant in the accounting department; the eldest, Masayuki, was a first lieutenant in the infantry, stationed in Hachijojima, an island located just south of Tokyo. He was in charge of constructing fortifications. When I mentioned that we had translated a handbook on fortifications that had been picked up in the South Pacific, he smiled and said, "That's the book we used to build our bunkers on Hachijojima." When we left Japan, Masayuki gave me the sword he had carried in the Japanese army. We joked about the vanquished giving up his arms as a sign of surrender. Unfortunately, I gave that sword away about fifteen years later.

What was most painful to see in Tokyo were the hungry—young people as well as old. On several occasions I was approached by people who normally would have felt ashamed to ask a total stranger like me to share whatever I could with them. Once I had just left the post exchange with a round can of Almond Roca candy. I forget for whom it was intended, but when a man who appeared to be a father with children waiting at home asked me to share something, I gave him the tin of candy. I was left with such a feeling of despair, for I knew that can would soon be empty, and the hunger would still be there. It didn't help that the people's faces looked so much like mine. That feeling of helplessness remained with me until I left. Of course, I am well aware that "escaping" from Japan was a selfish solution for me alone.

I served in Washington, D.C., for six months after our temporary duty in Japan, doing more of the same work: translating military documents at the Washington Document Center. The top-ranking noncoms in our unit had remained in Japan to serve on the war crimes tribunal, leaving the organizational table of PACMIRS open at the top. As the next ranking noncommissioned officer, I soon found myself a master sergeant, a rank I held until my discharge in December 1946. I didn't have any special duties, but as the ranking noncom in our barracks, I was in charge.

Many of the young men with whom I bunked were from Arkansas and Oklahoma. Thus, every morning, we were awakened not with the bugle reveille, but with a large—and loud—dose of hillbilly music.

In October 1946, I received a letter from home, informing me that Father had suffered a heart attack. I immediately applied for an emergency leave, walking my papers through the proper agencies in the Pentagon. Seats on the MATS (Military Air Transport Service) plane were on an availability basis and I was held up at Fairfield Suisun Air Base in California for a day. Fortunately, I managed to return home without too much delay. Much to my relief, Father had recovered substantially and there was no longer an emergency.

Once back in Hawaii, I reported to my designated post in Wahiawa. I was told that since I had the prescribed number of months of service, I was entitled to a terminal leave of a few months. Thus, I was discharged in December 1946, ending my military career.

As I reflect on the shaping of our lives as nisei, I cannot help but remember another important aspect of our upbringing. Our public schools, and especially the enlightenment shared by teachers like Dr. Miles E. Cary, who emphasized the values of democracy, working together, asserting ourselves, and contributing for the benefit of the whole, helped us grow immeasurably. I was fortunate to have had teachers at McKinley High School, such as Mrs. Ruth Gantt, Mrs. Helen Griggs, Mrs. Ethel Spaulding, Mr. Archie Jackson, and Mrs. Erma Logan-Smith. They helped to mold my life just as much as my spiritual mentors: Rev. Jikai Yamasato, Rev. Eimu Miake, Rev. Chiro Yosemori, Mr. Ernest Wakukawa, and others at the Hawaii Japanese High School.

But there definitely was another element that played a role in the tenacious dedication of the nisei—and that was the very human feeling of wanting peer respect. I have personally admitted to myself that I didn't want to be seen by my peers as a coward or a quitter, and that fear has influenced my decisions on many occasions. Personal pride, I believe, played an important role in the dedication of the nisei.

The nisei was a superb fighter, both in Europe and in the Pacific, because of characteristics he shared with the Japanese soldier. Some people call it *Yamato damashii* (spirit of the Japanese)—except the nisei had another reason to fight. It wasn't simply his loyalty to his country, but a desperate need to prove to others in his beloved country that although the enemy looked very much like him, his loyalty was to America—and he was willing to give his life to prove that loyalty so that not only his family, but others, could have a better life. I believe this was the nisei's way of expressing his gratitude to his country. The respect gained by the nisei was earned at a very dear price, and we should be forever grateful for their sacrifice.

Warren T. Iwai

100th Infantry Battalion

TWO SONGS

Before we left Camp Shelby, they gave us the battalion colors, signifying we were ready for combat. We were standing in formation that afternoon with our combat packs. We had our rifles in front of us.

The order, "Present arms . . ." was given. The 442nd band began playing "Hawaii Ponoi." Standing at attention, I had this tingling sensation from the top of my head to the tips of my toes. I had read about things like that in books, but I didn't think they really happened. It did happen to me, though, and I'll never forget it. That's the last thing I remember about Shelby. I said to myself, "Hawaii . . . my home."

Later in Oran, North Africa, Allied military headquarters, we had American troops, British troops, and French troops. Every evening, we had what they called a "retreat parade," when the flag of each country is lowered. Troops from each country are represented at the parade.

For one of these formations, our platoon from C Company went. We were all ordered to present arms again, standing at attention. First they played the British national anthem and then lowered the British flag. Then they played the French anthem, "Lilting Marseille." Then they played "The Star-Spangled Banner."

Again, I felt the same sensation that came over me at Camp Shelby when we received our battalion colors. Standing at attention, I felt so proud. I said to myself, "I'm an American soldier." But I was bashful about telling people how I felt, so I never discussed it with anyone.

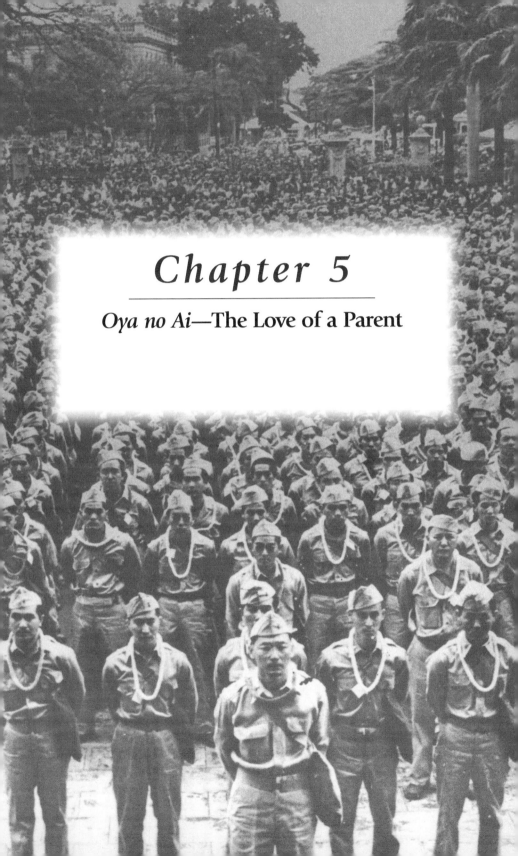

Chapter 5

Oya no Ai—The Love of a Parent

Kikuyo Fujimoto

KUNI NO TAME NI—FOR THE SAKE OF OUR COUNTRY

Many people have asked me how I felt to send my two sons off to war. My response is always the same: *"Kuni no tame ni . . .* for the sake of our country."

My husband, Hikosuke Fujimoto, worked as a steward for Queen Liliuokalani, so for a time we lived at Washington Place, and later at Paoakalani, the queen's summer residence in Waikiki. There were about eleven or twelve boys from the Waikiki area who went to war. I remember some of their family names: Nakamura, Takashige, Hikida, Kawasaki, Komori, and Nadamoto. Even though quite a few of our sons had gone to war, my husband and I never talked about it with the other parents. You have to remember, this was just after the bombing of Pearl Harbor, so people still looked at us as if we were spies. So we never got together to talk in groups.

I wasn't angry about that. *Shikata ga nai* (It cannot be helped). . . .
Japan bombed Pearl Harbor.

Kunio is my second child and the eldest of my two sons. I had to accept his having to go to war with the 100th Infantry Battalion. My younger son, Hikoso, who is two years younger than Kunio, later volunteered for the 442nd.

I had to let them go for the sake of our country. Yes, I worried about them. Every day, I sat in front of our *butsudan* (Buddhist altar) and prayed that they would remain healthy and safe. After Kunio left Hawaii for the mainland, I was able to get a message to him. I told him to take care of himself and to do his best.

Kunio was injured at Hill 600 in Italy and was finally sent home in June 1944 after the 100th Battalion pulled back from Cassino. When he arrived in Hawaii, the war was still on. I'm glad he returned home safe, but I know also that we had an obligation to the United States of America.

I had a Japanese spirit; after all, I was born in Japan in 1898. But America has been good to my family. Things happen in life, and we just have to accept them.

I never, ever thought that my children should fight for Japan just because my husband and I had come from Japan, or because my boys were of Japanese ancestry. I gave my children to America, so I had no claim to them. *Okage sama de* (By the grace of God), they came home.

In 1982, the fortieth anniversary of the formation of the 100th Battalion, I was asked to speak on behalf of the issei generation at Club 100's anniversary banquet. This is what I told the people attending the July 3, 1982, banquet.

I was asked to represent the issei, to share with you at this fortieth anniversary celebration banquet our joy and honor in being a part of such a special group. I am one of the mothers whose sons served in the army and fought on the battlefields.

As I recall those days, my thoughts turn especially to the families of those men who died while fighting so valiantly for this country. I would like to extend my heartfelt condolences to their families.

Like the epitaph on the monument at the National Memorial Cemetery of the Pacific, we also salute the Americans who gave their lives to preserve the beauty and freedom for all mankind.

Because of your faithful service to our country and your great accomplishments in all activities after the war, we, the issei, are able to live with pride as Japanese Americans. To the 100th Infantry Battalion, the issei would like to thank you from the bottom of our hearts. Presently, many of you are parents and grandparents. I sincerely hope you will not have to endure the same experiences we encountered during the war. Let us all hope, pray, and strive for world peace on Earth.

As an issei, I thank you for inviting me tonight to take part in this celebration. Congratulations, and may God bless you all!

Robert T. Sato

100th Infantry Battalion

MOTHER'S LOVE AND *KAGEZEN*

Totally exhausted, nisei soldiers (seven samurai) were sitting on their dirty helmets, trying to develop some kind of conversation. But no one cared to start. These hopeless and futureless seven GIs were giving up on just about everything. Our company started with the full strength of approximately two hundred, but only thirty-two were left. Yet we felt we must keep fighting until it was over. The main trouble was that we could not ask for any more replacements from the 442nd Regimental Combat Team.

Suddenly, usually quiet Pfc. K. muttered to no one in particular, "If I am lucky enough to go back to the Islands, the first thing I do is to go for that steaming hot rice, sashimi, my mother's favorite miso soup with tofu in it, and *oshinko* (pickled vegetables). M. asked what *oshinko* is, but no one bothered to answer.

These seven samurai, including myself, were still clinging to a ray of hope.

Our friendly but man-of-few-words Pfc. F. wanted to know who in the United States has the power to declare war. "President, of course." Answering immediately was none other than Pfc. T. "That's not right," I said. "Our Constitution precisely states that the Congress has the power to do so. Those 535 lawmakers (100 senators and 435 members of the House of Representatives) make the decision, and that's final."

I didn't understand why F. asked that question. F. is the only son in the family, and his loving mother always wrote to him, "I am offering *kagezen* (a meal set for an absent person) in front of your picture every morning. Offering steaming hot rice with *umeboshi* (pickled plum) and a cup of hot tea with the hope that you will enjoy this meal with Mother every day. My dear son, I do this because I don't want you to feel hungry wherever you are at the battlefield."

Kagezen is usually offered before the sun rises. He showed me the letter twice, and each time he told me not to mention the *kagezen* to anyone. I said, "Why? Your mother is doing a wonderful thing and you should be proud of her." He said he doesn't want anyone to criticize his mother's doing.

"My mother always think about me. For instance, she doesn't know anything about the foxhole, but she constantly reminds me to dig little more deeper so that I may survive."

"You really have a wonderful mother. Your mother is trying her best to save her only son's life in the battlefield," I offered.

F. said, "My mother doesn't want to say it openly, but I know she wants me to come back alive some day." His mother's familiar words: "Don't worry anything about the home front. We are doing just fine every day. Please take good care of yourself and do your best to fight for the country."

Robert T. Sato

100th Infantry Battalion

OKAASAN . . . BEST FRIEND

Suddenly, the sergeant informed us that the enemy was counterattacking and there were many casualties, including some litter bearers, which was very unusual. The sergeant said, "Bob and M., report immediately to the aid station to pick up some casualties from the hill."

I was digging my foxhole like mad, and I must admit that I wasn't too happy to go. On the way, we saw many wounded, but our mission was to take care of the most seriously wounded soldier first.

When we arrived at the scene, he was lying facedown, so we couldn't recognize him. But judging from his heavy breathing, we knew he was in trouble—probably hit by shrapnel. A trickle of blood ran down his face. We were instructed to handle him very carefully, so we tried to lift his body as slowly as possible.

All of a sudden, I heard something like "Okaasan . . ." from his somewhat twisted, bloody mouth. My partner said he heard it, too. But the soldier's voice was so soft that I couldn't make out what he was saying. I felt very uneasy. I had some experiences in the past in which "Okaasan . . ." was usually the last word spoken by the seriously wounded nisei soldiers in battle.

"Please don't die," I thought. We must take him to the station as fast as we could to save his life. We were moving double-time almost all the way.

When the time comes, no matter how strong the soldier is, his okaasan, his mother, is his most powerful and best friend in this whole wide world.

After all that commotion, I went back to my position, only to find that the foxhole I had been digging had been hit directly by enemy mortar shells. My pick and shovel had completely disappeared. I was at a loss for what to do. I would have been killed instantly if I had still been digging that hole. It was the litter-bearer duty that saved my life.

I experienced several narrow escapes in both the Italian and French battlefields, and this, definitely, was one of them.

Minoru Kishaba

442nd Regimental Combat Team

TWO SONS . . . FOUR SHINY STONES

In October 1994 I fulfilled a dream I had held for decades of returning to Europe where I had fought with the 442nd Regimental Combat Team in World War II. The occasion was the fiftieth anniversary of the 442nd's liberation of the French towns of Bruyeres and Biffontaine.

I was surprised that some of the boys in my company, Anti-Tank Company, still called me by my nickname, "Chappie." They had given me that name because I sometimes read passages from the Bible to them.

Being back in Europe after all those years made me very reflective. It brought back memories of how lonely and homesick I had felt during the war . . . especially in the evening after I had dug my foxhole and sat down to rest.

Although Anti-Tank Company was not involved in the actual liberation of Biffontaine and Bruyeres, the memorial ceremonies in the forests outside the two towns rekindled so many memories. The liberation had taken place just as my company was leaving southern France to rejoin the 442nd in the Vosges Mountains. We had been detached from the 442nd and attached to the 517th Parachute Infantry Regiment for three months. We arrived in the Vosges just in time for mop-up duties. We also chased the last of the Germans out of Bruyeres, which they had occupied for four years.

During the memorial service, it hit me that here I was in a place where I had experienced something fifty years earlier. I was so scared back then, and yet, I had a "gotta do it" kind of attitude. Tears filled my eyes as a lone bugler played taps. I couldn't help but remember the boys who had died on those battlefields.

I remembered the loneliness, the cold, the snow and mud. The trees looked pretty much like they did fifty years ago. Of course, in certain places, it looked like they had been chopped down and replanted.

Back then, the forests were so thick and dark it was hard to tell where the enemy was hiding. But I could hear them sometimes. My hearing became so sharp. As we approached the Germans, I could hear them cock their weapons.

Fifty years later, the weather was so different from what it had been in 1944. Back then it was bitter cold. In 1994, the weather was so nice and beautiful. The leaves were showing off their autumn colors.

In 1944, it was so cold that I got trench feet, a frostbite condition that many of the boys got because our feet were always in wet, cold, icy conditions. Our blood circulation was bad because we didn't have a chance to take off our wet shoes and socks, dry them off, and massage our feet. My condition was so bad that I was sent to the field hospital near Epinal, which was a few miles away. I was told that the best treatment for trench feet is to keep the feet elevated and in cold surroundings.

I stayed at the hospital for about four days. Unfortunately, the hospital ward was heated, which only made my feet hurt more. So I persuaded another soldier—he had trench feet, too—to go back to our outfit. They released us from the hospital and we walked back and rejoined the 442nd.

Many times during our travels in 1994, there were places I couldn't recognize. Some of the others in our group were disappointed but I wasn't. I was satisfied because I knew that I had been there at one time. I knew there would be many places that I wouldn't recognize because we hadn't been there long enough to get to know the place. Still, knowing that I had been in the area during the war was satisfaction enough for me.

I grew up in Mahinahina, which was a sugar-plantation community in Lahaina on the island of Maui. My parents, Choyei and Uto Kishaba, had immigrated to Hawaii from Okinawa.

During my senior year at Lahainaluna High School, a recruiter came to the school to recruit young men for the National Guard. After listening to his talk, I decided to volunteer.

But the next thing he said broke my heart: Anyone who met the age requirement could volunteer—except for those with Japanese surnames. I was crushed. I went back to my classroom. I was so depressed and disappointed.

Several months after I graduated, the call went out for volunteers for an all-Japanese American unit, the 442nd Regimental Combat Team. I was eighteen at the time, the youngest of five boys in our family, and number seven of nine children. I was the first nisei from Lahaina to volunteer. My brother just above me in age, Susumu, volunteered, also.

The first thing that came to my mind when I volunteered was that I was going to see the mainland. After all, going to America was just a dream for a plantation boy like me. I was on cloud nine for weeks after I volunteered. I was so proud that I was going to be an American GI and that I was going to see America. The reality of my decision to volunteer finally sunk in the night before I left Lahaina.

My father, my oldest brother, Susumu, and I were in our living room. My dad, he's not the talkative type. But my brother, the older one, told Susumu and me that we had to train extra hard, because the Germans were good soldiers.

What he said hit me. I looked at my dad, who sat silently. Knowing we might never see each other again, the four of us cried together.

The 442nd volunteers from Lahaina were scheduled to report for induction the next day. That morning, my mother made *miso shiru* (soup) for us. She sat at the table with Susumu and me while we ate. Neither of us said very much.

As I gulped down my soup, she asked me, "You want some more?" I told her that I had had enough. That's when I really broke down and cried. My mom cried, too.

There were seventy-seven volunteers from Lahaina. We were supposed to meet the army trucks in town. My dad wasn't feeling well that morning, so he had stayed home. But my mother came into town with us. Things were fine until we climbed onto the truck. Then my mom grabbed my arm. She wouldn't let go. I started to cry. Susumu told me not to cry because I was making Mother cry.

Oh, my mom. Even now, I can still see her crying. When you get emotional, it's hard to say anything. As the truck pulled away, I could see my mother running after the truck, crying, as she watched the truck take us off to war. That sight stayed with me for a long, long time.

While in basic training at Camp Shelby, quite often I dreamed of being back home in Lahaina. The dream was so clear. I was at home, in our back yard, cutting the lawn or lying around. Both Susumu and I wrote home to our parents regularly because we wanted to ease their fears.

When we returned home after the war, my mom and dad greeted us at the airport. When we got home, my mom showed us four shiny stones she had picked out after we had left Lahaina. She told us that she had taken them with her wherever she went. She said the four stones represented our four feet—Susumu's and mine. Every night, when she went to the *furo* (bathhouse) to bathe, she carried the stones with her and washed them, as if she were washing our feet. And then, when she went to bed, she lay the stones close to her body in her bed to keep our feet warm and safe.

She said that when the family came together at the table for dinner, she always placed pictures of me and Susumu—and Susumu's friend, an I Company boy from Hilo named Sadaichi Kubota—at the table so we would never go hungry.

My father was a camp groundskeeper for Pioneer Mill. He worried about our safety, too. He told us that whenever he saw a Jeep coming up the road—a cloud of dust following it all the way up—his heart began beating faster. He always wondered why the Jeep was coming his way and whether there was bad news about me or Susumu. Dad said he was always relieved when the Jeep drove past him. But he'd always wait a few minutes, wondering whether the driver had made a mistake and was turning back, before putting his mind at ease.

It's funny how things repeat themselves. Many decades later, years after my wife, Molly, and I had moved to southern California, our eldest son, John, came to me one day. It was during the Vietnam era. "Dad, I have to go register for the draft," he said.

It never dawned on me that one day my own son might be going off to war. Fortunately, John was never called up. But my fear for my own son's life was very real, and it made me realize and understand the fear my own parents had felt when Susumu and I went off to war.

During my trip to France in 1994, several bright-eyed young French girls came up to me in Biffontaine. They wanted me to autograph their book because I had been part of the team that had liberated their town a half century earlier. It didn't matter to them that I was not one of the liberators, per se, nor that they were not even born at the time. These children knew that they were free because of the sacrifices the AJA soldiers had made fifty years earlier.

Seeing the children running about, enjoying the festivities, gave me a good feeling about what we had done in October of 1944.

But I benefitted from the experience as well. I grew up on the plantation. For people like me, the haole was always the boss. The haole was the teacher; the haole was everything. So haole, to us, was upper class, and we were lower class. Training at Camp Shelby opened my eyes to a class of haoles who were not necessarily the bosses or the teachers, or the upper class in society. For the first time in my life, I saw poor haoles, uneducated haoles, and the class structure of society, and it changed my views.

World War II was a cruel war. But it opened up a whole new world for nisei soldiers, like me, from Hawaii. Before, we thought only about Hawaii . . . Maui . . . Lahaina. The war broadened our thinking.

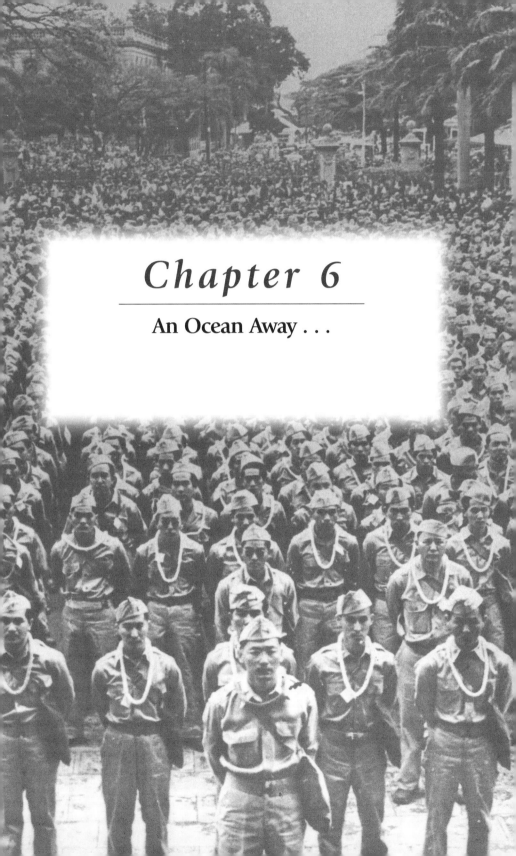

Chapter 6

An Ocean Away . . .

Robert K. Sakai

Military Intelligence Service

FROM RELOCATION CAMP TO MILITARY SERVICE

When I was born in 1919 in Riverside, California, my father gave me my Japanese middle name, Kenjiro—after a Japanese diplomat who had participated in the Versailles Peace Conference. My father was a farmer whose view of the world stretched far beyond his farmlands. He was interested in history and in international relations, and he hoped that I would one day carve out a career in these areas. I think I fulfilled his dreams in at least two phases of my life: my service as a translator and interpreter with the Military Intelligence Service during World War II and, subsequently, as a professor of East Asian history.

My parents faced many social, economic, and legal challenges bringing up five children. Even as a child, I was aware of the difficulties they faced trying to farm without even so much as a bank loan. Although Father had acquired a piece of undeveloped desert land, antialien land laws prohibited him from owning it. Thus, he entrusted title to the land to a Caucasian church friend, to whom he paid a sum of money annually. Fortunately, Mr. P. A. Robinson was an honorable man who turned over the deed to my older brother when he came of age just before World War II broke out.

As for educational and social problems, my gentle but determined mother succeeded in having my elder sister transferred from a segregated class for non-English speaking Mexican children to the regular first grade. As children, we accepted the fact that the town swimming pool was closed to us. Most of these legal and social barriers were beyond our capacity to remove. Besides, we were too busy trying to survive economically.

In elementary school I got along with my classmates, and in high school I participated in sports and student government. My warmest memories are of my high-school teachers, who encouraged me and gave me confidence. Teachers like Miss Bernice McCollum, Mr. E. B. Dykes, and Miss Elsie Smith believed in developing the full potential of their students, regardless of race, and I truly appreciated their interest in me.

Another phase of my life that influenced my decisions and behavior occurred in 1934, at the end of my freshman year, when my younger brother and I accompanied my mother on her first trip back to Japan since leaving in 1912. My mother wanted us to learn, firsthand, about Japan.

We stayed with her four siblings, who lived in different parts of Japan, thereby giving us a broad view of the country. I enjoyed many interesting discussions with my relatives.

By 1934 Japan's relations with Western nations, particularly the United States, had become strained. Severely criticized for its invasion of Manchuria, Japan had withdrawn from the League of Nations.

The country's mood was reflected on the walls of the Nihonbashi Mitsukoshi Department Store in broad murals that depicted the city of Tokyo in flames with enemy planes overhead. A mock air attack on Osaka caused a blackout even in Kobe, where we were staying with an uncle. I also witnessed an air-raid drill for elementary schoolchildren who scrambled into underground shelters while a plane dropped sandbags onto the school grounds. At a middle school I watched with astonishment as two units of students charged each other with realistic-looking wooden weapons.

Fortunately, I also saw the cultural expression of the people in their temples, museums, and theaters, as well as the many beautiful national parks and forests. It was a memorable and educational trip. I liked the Japanese people, but I disliked the authoritarian regime that fostered militarism. More than ever, I gained an appreciation for the privilege of living in America, despite lapses in American democracy.

In January 1938 I enrolled at the University of California at Berkeley, where my major, Far Eastern history, enabled me to put in perspective what I had observed in Japan. This gave me the confidence to refute the arguments of an eminent University of California political science professor in a public forum in the fall of 1941. The topic was the likelihood of war between Japan and the United States.

The professor flatly discounted the possibility. If war did break out, he said, the Japanese navy would be sunk in two weeks. I said that we should be aware of the tense situation in Japan, with radical militarists in control of the government and the people feeling desperate and victimized by the Western nations.

And yet, when war did indeed break out, I was no more prepared psychologically than anyone else. I had been studying for my last exams before graduation when I heard the news. All of the academic information that I had been stowing in my head suddenly became inconsequential. My worries now focused on the present.

I somehow managed to finish my exams and rushed home to the desert community of Indio in Coachella Valley. Berkeley had been blacked out every night since the Pearl Harbor attack, and guards patrolled the streets. By comparison, Coachella Valley seemed calm. After all, the agricultural valley was isolated by mountains and deserts; the population was sparse and scattered. Readers of the local weekly newspaper were not informed of the Japanese "problem." These readers were preoccupied with their own worries.

The FBI arrested a very popular and community-minded Japanese-language teacher and an elderly gentleman who happened to occupy the position of president of the Coachella Valley Japanese Agricultural Producers Association. Both were issei. My father, the acknowledged leader of the Japanese community, had preferred to ask others to serve in official capacities. Still, with his bag packed, he was ready to join his two friends. To his embarrassment, the FBI never bothered him.

Most of the valley population never knew that Japanese farmers had quietly turned in to the police station any tools and implements that might be misconstrued as weapons or signaling devices to aid the enemy. These farmers were further handicapped in their work when their financial assets were declared frozen. Only money for subsistence and to pay the wages of laborers was permitted to be withdrawn from bank accounts. Travel was restricted to a three-mile radius. Most of the stores, banks, and churches patronized by the Japanese were located beyond the three-mile restriction.

Other people probably did not realize how deeply wounded and angered Japanese Americans were by the daily hate columns published by the large regional newspapers. Even the prestigious *Los Angeles Times* engaged in scurrilous attacks on "treacherous Japs." In the general climate of panic and hysteria, little could be done to challenge these false reports. If the media sought to fuel hatred toward the Japanese and drive them out of their farms, businesses, and homes, they succeeded.

Anyone with even one-fourth Japanese blood was driven from the West Coast within months of the Pearl Harbor attack. First to be ejected were Japanese living in Zone A, areas considered militarily sensitive. Many were given only forty-eight hours to dispose of their property. Most were temporarily relocated in "assembly centers," which were horse-racing stables that had been converted into living quarters.

Those of us in Zone B were given a little more time to carry on as farmers. But just when the crops were ready to be harvested, we were ordered to evacuate. The crops left on the vines were harvested by opportunists who raked in profits while the growers lost all of their investments.

My family was one of sixteen Japanese families residing in northern Coachella Valley. Our notice to evacuate came in early May 1942. We were instructed to bring only what we could carry to the town of Indio. When we boarded the bus, the town was still asleep. Only a few faithful Mexican employees came to see us off. We were not told of our destination. Not knowing what our future held, we were anxious, bitter, and resigned.

At about noon our bus crossed the Colorado River and turned north. We soon came upon a large camp filled with rows of ugly, black tar-papered barracks. This was Poston I, our relocation center.

Life in Poston was uncomfortable, depressing, and dehumanizing. There were three separate camps, each surrounded by barbed wire and guarded by soldiers. Poston I was built to accommodate ten thousand people, Poston II and III for five thousand people each.

The need for living space, however, had been calculated not on the basis of family needs but on the military assumption that each twenty- by twenty-five-foot room should be filled by up to six people. Thus, large families were split up, some members sharing a room with a different family. Next to our barrack three newlywed couples occupied one room. Except for army cots, the rooms were bare, so new arrivals hung sheets for privacy and began making furniture with lumber from the scrap heaps. Not even the hospital barrack had air conditioning; two newly born infants reportedly died of dehydration as a result.

The resilience of the internees was remarkable. Everyone cooperated, knowing it was up to them to make the most of primitive surroundings. For example, each block had a communal kitchen and dining room that fed up to three hundred persons. Volunteer cooks worked in steaming kitchens, preparing and serving meals at a cost of thirty-seven cents per day per person. The daily fare during the first few months was bread and cheese, or rice, sauerkraut, and ersatz weiners with a half-pint of milk for infants and the sick. Many Japanese were unaccustomed to and disliked cheese and sauerkraut.

Each block selected a manager and elected a representative to serve in the community council. Police and fire units were organized; experienced farmers began cultivating the desert, rich with silt from the Colorado River. Athletic, social, cultural, educational, and religious activities were organized by capable leaders.

During my first year in Poston, I served on the community council, chaired the education committee, and taught the "core course" for a high-school senior class. This class had opened in October 1942. By the end of the month, seven outside teachers had abandoned the class, several of whom had been recruited from mental institutions and were taken out in strait jackets. I began teaching in November.

Though isolated from the outside world in a prisonlike camp, it was possible to subscribe to the *Los Angeles Times* and other periodicals. Unfortunately, news reports about the early phases of the Pacific War were discouraging. To make matters worse, the "Jap"-hating rabble-rousers were still given prominent print.

There were a few Caucasian administrators at Poston who were decent and fair-minded, however. Some were "dollar-a-year" volunteers who sacrificed comfort and income to help in the camps. They were truly dedicated to the democratic principles of fair play and did their best to offset the injustices inflicted on the internees.

One person on the outside whose generosity and concern I will always remember was Miss Anita Shepardson. In March 1942, during the curfew period, Miss Shepardson had arranged a shower in Fullerton for my future bride, Sady Kitaoka, to announce our engagement. Prior to our marriage in October, Miss Shepardson saved up her precious gas ration coupons in order to travel roughly four hours from Fullerton, California, to Poston, Arizona, with a carload of dresses, suits, and shoes from which Sady could choose her wedding attire. On our wedding day, she brought us beautiful fresh-cut flowers (nonexistent in Poston), wedding cake, and nuts and candy. Neither of these trips and favors had been requested of her. Her dedication and sacrifice and that of other individuals like her helped me maintain my faith in American society and the American people.

I believed that the democratic process would ultimately vindicate us. That was what I tried to convey to my high-school seniors, who were understandably disillusioned and bitter. Ironically, the theme handed down for the school system was "democracy," so the students had opportunity to vent their feelings as we explored the realities of democracy.

In early spring 1943, army recruiters arrived at Poston seeking volunteers for the 442nd Regimental Combat Team and the Military

Intelligence Service. I volunteered for the MIS. Americans of Japanese ancestry had been prohibited from military service after Pearl Harbor. Those already in the army prior to December 7, 1941, had been disarmed and transferred to noncombat duties.

This turn of events created turmoil in camp. "After the treatment we have received, why should we volunteer?" was one view expressed. In class I emphasized that this was the opportunity to prove that we were worthy American citizens. There was no question in my mind what I would do, but teenagers were influenced by their parents and others. Some in camp saw the call for volunteers as a cynical move and resorted to fistic violence against volunteers.

A telegram from Col. Kai Rasmussen, commandant of the Military Intelligence Service Language School, arrived in June, instructing me to report to Camp Savage, Minnesota. I was elated, but in my self-centered joy I had not stopped to think of my parents' feelings. They had brought us up to be good citizens and to be appreciative of America. They trusted me to act accordingly and did not question my decision. When my wife and I were about to leave our family and friends, Mother and Father smiled with pride, although, undoubtedly, they were worried about my safety and the possibility of my confronting relatives in Japan as combatants.

My wife was as eager as I to leave Poston, for she did not want our child to be born in a place where we had been incarcerated and where our civil rights as citizens had been denied.

Leaving camp made us feel like we were being released from prison. But it wasn't until we reached Kansas City, enroute to Minneapolis, that we felt we were in a nonhostile environment. We were met in Minneapolis by Sady's college friend, Annette Edwards, a graduate student at the University of Minnesota who helped us get settled.

We had left camp with two hundred dollars that friends had contributed from their meager earnings (people employed in camp earned between twelve and nineteen dollars a month). We could not afford to use pay phones to check on housing, so Annette arranged for Sady to use the church phone. Meanwhile, Annette and I knocked on doors to find an inexpensive rental. After a few days we found a tiny, one-room kitchenette with a foldout sofa, stove, and kitchen table for sixteen dollars a month. Sady somehow managed to stretch the two hundred dollars four months by not riding streetcars and saving a few cents bargain-shopping. I began Japanese-language study, commuting to Camp Savage six days a week.

I had expected to be inducted into the army soon after reporting to Camp Savage, but my local draft board at Berkeley, California, had not sent my clearance for enlistment. I was nevertheless admitted to the language program as a volunteer civilian student and received free lunches for my participation.

Class was already in session when I entered my assigned classroom. As I scanned the back of the room for an empty seat, the *sensei* (instructor) called me to the front and ordered me to address the students for five minutes in Japanese! This type of intense instruction continued for over three months, for we were expected to be competent for combat service as interpreters, translators, and interrogators.

My classmates were nisei volunteers from Hawaii. Though West Coast and Hawaii nisei had experienced racial prejudice in different ways, we were alike in our determination to do our best because thousands of American lives depended on our ability to extract information from the enemy. We were aware that our role was uniquely important, for in a sense, we were the eyes and ears for the American war effort.

My clearance finally arrived in September, just in time, as the two hundred dollars brought from Poston was nearly exhausted.

I went for my physical examinations for induction, happy that I would finally be in the army. After five days of exams, however, disaster struck; I was rejected because of poor eyesight. Dismayed, I reported the situation to Colonel Rasmussen, who instructed me to return for retesting. I passed on the second try with the commandant's assurance that with proper glasses my eyesight would not impede my language work. The uniform I now wore was symbolic of my restoration to full citizenship, and I could hardly contain my happiness.

In Minneapolis I had been able to study as long as I wanted, but now at Camp Savage lights were out at eleven P.M. Having missed nearly two weeks of class, however, I needed extra study time to catch up. I bought an extension cord, placed the light bulb in my helmet, and studied every night past midnight with a blanket over my head to conceal the light. The consequence was disastrous. After a week, my eyes would no longer focus; I thought I was turning blind. I lost another week of class while I rested my eyes. Formal class work ended soon after, and fortunately, I was able to graduate with my classmates.

The newly trained linguists were sent to Camp Blanding near Jacksonville, Florida, for basic training. Despite limited military training at Camp Savage, the discipline and motivation of the Japanese American troops impressed the instructors.

One evening after a strenuous day, a tall, handsome first lieutenant approached our cottage, calling out my name. He was Lt. Ralph Fisher, aide to the commanding general of Camp Blanding. Lieutenant Fisher had been the student body president at UC-Berkeley. I wondered how he knew me. He said he had spotted my name while going over the list of new arrivals and had come over to chat. He was troubled by the government's relocation of Japanese Americans from the West Coast. Lieutenant Fisher represented America at her best, a gentleman with a sincere concern for others.

A weekend pass to Jacksonville reminded me of the serious gap between democratic ideals and reality, however. The discrimination I had experienced as a Japanese American was largely a product of wartime hysteria, while the degrading treatment of blacks in the South had persisted for generations.

After basic training, we returned to Fort Snelling. A two-week furlough for the Christmas holidays gave Sady and me an opportunity to visit our parents and show off our two-month-old son. The reunion with family and friends in Poston was joyous, but it was soon time for a final farewell and to return to Minneapolis. Our Military Intelligence Language School class was ready to be shipped overseas.

Military intelligence language personnel were in great demand from Washington, D.C., to Alaska, the Pacific area, and the China-Burma theater. I was in a team of ten, carefully chosen for our different capabilities. All of us were Japanese Americans from the West Coast and Hawaii: three were *kibei* (born in America but educated in Japan). Over half of us had attended American colleges. We became a close-knit team.

In June 1944 we received our long-awaited order to prepare for departure from friendly Minnesota. However, again a barrier was raised. I could not go overseas because of my twenty/four hundred eyesight. I again appealed for help and the barrier came down. My wife assured me that all would be well at home, although I wondered when I would see my son again, now eight months old and in the prime of his charm.

Our train took us to Fort Lewis, Washington. Since we had a few days to wait before boarding ship, we asked for permission to see Seattle. The request was denied. I thought it was because Seattle remained off-limits to Japanese Americans, even though we wore U.S. Army uniforms, but it may also have been due to the secret nature of our mission.

The sea journey to Honolulu was uneventful, thanks to the U.S. victory at Midway in June of 1942. From the ship we were taken directly to the camp of the 81st Infantry Division, commanded by Major General Paul Mueller. Known as the "Wildcat Division," it was formerly the Tennessee National Guard unit. Intensive jungle training followed, and we participated fully with the Wildcat soldiers so we would not be mistaken for the enemy in the heat of future combat.

Ready to fight, the 81st boarded several transport ships. With a convoy of destroyers, we zigzagged across the Pacific for forty days, until one morning the towering mountains of Guadalcanal loomed before us. Japanese soldiers were reportedly still ensconced in its dense forest.

After a ferocious battle in August 1942, the Americans had gained control of the coastland, enabling us to stretch our weary sea legs on land and to have our first experience interrogating Japanese prisoners. By this time they had reverted into relaxed human beings and were no longer the battle-hardened fanatics of their reputation.

Our fleet resumed its seemingly lazy zigzag course in the South Pacific. Seven days later, on September 15th, we were offshore from the Palau Islands. A battleship, cruisers, destroyers, and airplanes from a carrier began an unbelievably heavy bombardment that completely enveloped the islands of Pelelieu and Angaur in dense black smoke—so dense that it appeared the islands had been sunk by the tons of steel that had rained upon them. Yet, when the 1st Marine Division stormed ashore on Pelelieu island, they were met with a deadly hail of fire from the enemy. A foothold on the beach was finally secured after two days of bitter fighting.

On September 17th the 81st Division went ashore on Angaur Island, where they met with the same fierce resistance. Trees had been chopped down in the naval bombardment and tropical vines made camouflaged machine-gun bunkers even more invisible and dangerous to the American soldiers. After several hours of intense struggle, the 321st and 322nd Regiments had penetrated only a few hundred yards from shore.

The ten men in our language team were paired off and attached to the marines on Pelelieu, with the 323rd Regiment on a feinting mission toward Ulithi Island, the 322nd and 321st Regiments, and Division Headquarters on Angaur. Sergeant Hiroki "Chico" Takahashi and I were assigned to headquarters.

When we got ashore and began digging in for the night, our shovels clanged on so much coral rock that when we lay down for the night in shallow trenches our bodies were half exposed. Bullets seemed to whiz by just over our faces. The discomfort of jagged rocks against my back was further compounded by a huge coconut crab that dropped on me from a tree above. Its claws were so big and powerful that they could snap off a man's wrist.

Members of the language team were not allowed to be on guard duty that night. There was the ever-present danger of enemy snipers slipping through our lines and causing havoc. Many of our soldiers, who were engaged in battle for the first time, were trigger-happy, firing their semiautomatic guns at the slightest rustling sound. Japanese Americans faced double jeopardy because they looked like the enemy.

The battle for Angaur and Pelelieu lasted several weeks, with heavy casualties inflicted on both the marines and the infantry units. The enemy was not massed in conventional warfare formation. They were scattered in hundreds of caves and bunkers. Many were camouflaged with fresh-cut leafy branches and strapped up in the trees, enabling them to pick off advancing American soldiers with deadly accuracy. GIs respectfully referred to these snipers as "dead-eye Charley."

Members of our language team were considered nonexpendable—too important to be exposed to danger. But in this close-encounter warfare, the policy meant nothing. No one was out of range of enemy gunfire.

Sergeant Shinso Chojin, a *kibei* about five feet tall, received a Bronze Star for heroism when he rushed under fire to the side of an American soldier shot by "dead-eye Charley," administered first aid, and helped drag the soldier back to safety. Sergeant Masao Abe received a Purple Heart when he was shot in the thigh by a soldier hiding in a cave from which Abe was bringing out prisoners.

The effort to persuade enemy soldiers to surrender was very important because they were a valuable source of military information. This dangerous task could be accomplished only by our linguists.

At Division Headquarters, mailbags full of captured documents piled up for sorting and translation. Some required on-the-spot translation; others were for later translation, and still others were sent to Joint Intelligence, Pacific Ocean Area in Honolulu for careful analysis. Our translation work at Division Headquarters varied in difficulty, sometimes testing my skills. I was often amazed at how intense pressure could dredge up information from the recesses of my brain.

Prisoners were sent from the frontlines to headquarters for detailed interrogation. When handled properly, they provided vital information about their unit, its strength, location, morale, their officers, supply situation, and so on. That kind of information came easily from lower-ranking soldiers who had been trained never to surrender, but never trained on what *not* to say should they be captured.

Ironically, if a Japanese prisoner was accosted by a Caucasian officer, even if the latter spoke fluent Japanese, the prisoner tended to freeze up, anticipating cruelty. If the captor had a Japanese face like himself, he visibly relaxed. Because of their brutally harsh training and the propaganda they had received about the cruelty of the Americans, Japanese prisoners were unprepared for considerate, humane treatment, which proved effective in interrogation.

For example, a tough, burly sergeant who was a twelve-year veteran of the campaigns in Manchuria, China, and the Pacific Islands, responded to my interrogation. One day he said he wanted to become an American soldier. He said the Japanese considered him dead because they did not recognize Japanese prisoners. Thus he wanted to be "reborn" and to join our division. He said he knew Japanese military tactics and could anticipate Japanese moves in any situation. The sergeant agreed to accompany us to the edge of a broad ravine. Across from us were Japanese military positions. Lying prone next to me, he lined up my carbine to point out the location of the Japanese headquarters, supply dump, and other facilities. The howitzer behind us then fired off shells according to his directions.

Instead of pressing a prisoner who was reticent, I would quietly offer to let his family know, via the Red Cross, that he was well, albeit a captive. This suggestion made him cooperate instantly, for such information would bring shame to his family.

But I also met an infantry captain from Utsunomiya who knew his rights as a prisoner of war (POW). I asked him whether he intended to commit suicide if the opportunity arose. "Of course," he responded. He said there was no way Japan would win the war. He said he had been assured that Japanese warplanes would protect his forces if the Americans attacked. When the attack came, however, the sky was filled with American warplanes; there was no Japanese support.

The captain believed Japan would surrender. When questioned whether all of Japan's citizens should commit suicide, he finally realized the futility of his own suicide. Instead, he became determined to live to help his country recover after the war. To my surprise, he now asked that his family be informed of his situation and well being.

Combat casualties and tropical illness in the Palau Islands had severely weakened the Wildcats. The Division was eventually transferred to New Caledonia for rest, recuperation, and reorganization. I was told to speak to battalion units about the psychology of the Japanese soldier.

My lectures attracted the attention of higher authorities and I was called to Noumeia, the capital of New Caledonia, where I spoke to field-grade officers. I was intrigued that officers of the U.S. Army would request information about Japan from a sergeant.

During our stay in New Caledonia, U.S. military policy was relaxed to allow qualified Japanese Americans to become officers. Sergeant James Kai, Sergeant Kei Kitahara, and I were invited to take the examination for admission to Officer Candidate School (OCS). After passing the written tests we were interviewed individually by a board of officers.

I was asked whether I had relatives in Japan. Yes, I said. Although I knew very little about him, I had an uncle on my father's side who was a businessman in Manchuria. On my mother's side, I was very fond of my aunt and three uncles with whom I had lived while visiting in Japan in 1934. "Then why are you willing to fight against the Japanese?" they asked. I told them that as an American, I was outraged by the attack on Pearl Harbor. But I told them also that I was fighting not against the

Japanese people, but rather against their military leaders who had led the country into war against the United States.

I wrote home that I might soon be back in the States to enter OCS. In the meantime, our rejuvenated 81st Division was again in dangerous waters, heading to another battle zone.

We arrived at Leyte in the Philippines on May 17, 1945. Heavy fighting there was almost over. The mission of the Wildcat Division was thus to locate and eliminate or capture remaining Japanese soldiers. This involved many small-sized reconnaissance and probing actions that sometimes took us through waist-deep swamps where buffaloes wallowed and from which we filled our canteens for drinking water. Two little decontaminating pellets put into the canteen for two hours made the water safe to drink. Members of our language team were essential for these reconnaissance missions.

One day, Sergeants Kai, Kitahara, and I were flown in to Division Headquarters. After a brief ceremony, Commanding General Mueller pinned single gold bars onto our collars, instantly transforming us into commissioned officers, a status and lifestyle to which we were unaccustomed. Perhaps because we were needed in the field, we did not get the opportunity to return to the United States for OCS.

On August 14, 1945, we welcomed the news of a cease-fire between Japan and the Allies with cheers and yells. We had been training strenuously for another beach assault. The plan was to use the 81st as a diversionary force on the coast of Kagoshima, where the Japanese were waiting for us. Now that the fighting was over, my mission also was over, I thought. Soon I would be able to rejoin my family, whom I missed very much.

A few days later, I was shown into a top secret building of Division Headquarters, where the general and his staff planned strategy. A curtain along a wall was drawn open, revealing a huge map of Japan. They wanted me to explain the differences between the terms *ken*, *gun*, and *machi* (prefecture, district, town) and where military government headquarters should be located. I knew then that we were going to Japan.

From the torrid Philippines we were sent to Aomori, northern Honshu's snow country, in early September. We stormed ashore with fixed bayonets only to be greeted by a handful of Japanese civilian officials. General Mueller explained that the U.S. military was in charge of security for the area and that the Japanese were expected to cooperate. Later, while observing action on the beach, a few local males walked around me, wondering aloud among themselves, "Who is this Asian-looking person dressed in American military uniform? He must be Chinese or Korean." I kept them guessing with my amused silence.

I was now in charge of a small group of language personnel who were required to translate or interpret a variety of materials. The military police needed to talk to local police officers, investigate criminal activities, issue orders to brothels, and so on. Visits had to be made to all the schools to inspect how they carried out SCAP (Supreme Commander, Allied Powers) directives for elimination of militaristic material from textbooks. Disarmament and demobilization of Japanese forces, destruction of airfields, confiscation of weapons, elimination of coastal defense facilities, conversion of military industries—all required the help of language personnel.

The team also observed and reported on political rallies, translated local newspapers that affected security in the area, and interpreted for the general when he gave instructions to the governor and other local officials. In short, we were classified as "essential."

The 81st Division returned to the United States after a few months and was replaced by another unit. Members of our original language team also either returned home or chose to stay in Japan as civilian employees for the Allied Occupation. I was still in uniform, classified as "essential."

In the summer of 1946 I was transferred from Aomori to IXth Corps Headquarters at Sendai as commanding officer of ten new language personnel. Our responsibilities were even broader at the corps level, but with disarmament accomplished, attention now was directed to democratization. Besides supervising the daily translation of newspapers and assigning interpreters to help other officers, my principal task was to ensure maximum cooperation from Japanese suppliers in securing building materials, house furnishings, and even measuring cups and spoons that would be needed with the anticipated arrival of thousands of U.S. military dependents.

My predecessor, a Caucasian language officer, had been frustrated working with the Japanese. His knowledge of the language was limited, and he assumed that the Japanese suppliers were stubbornly uncooperative. It became clear to me, however, that there simply was no supply of seasoned lumber to construct the required hundreds of homes. There were no good nails, nor glass for windows, nor cotton sheeting. They had all been destroyed in the firebombing by Allied planes. The tinsmith had no idea of how to replicate American measuring cups and spoons because of the difference in measuring systems. The carpenter ordered to make beds for American officers could not believe that such big beds were needed for tall Americans. Once we understood what they could do and what they were incapable of doing, we received full cooperation from the Japanese.

With good working relations finally established, I requested release from service. But the personnel officer still considered me "essential." Units had come and gone, and I was still in the army. I felt like a victim of bureaucratic red tape, so I requested aid from Senator Joseph Ball of Minnesota. His office responded by sending me his talk on agricultural policy.

Finally, I decided to apply to have my family join me as dependents. "If this request is approved, how long would I be committed to stay in the service?" I asked the major in charge of personnel affairs. "Indefinitely," he said. I tore up the application in front of him. His unsympathetic response reminded me of the hard-line attitude military officials had taken in the interning of Japanese Americans following the Pearl Harbor attack.

My superiors in IXth Corps, Military Intelligence, were unaware of my predicament. When I explained my situation to Colonel McCone, chief of military intelligence, he urged me to be patient. My travel orders arrived a few weeks later and I was back in the United States by the end of December 1946.

The captain at the military discharge center tried to get me to reenlist, promising me an immediate promotion to the rank of captain. But I knew I had fulfilled my obligation to my country, and my dedication was not to a career in the army.

I wanted to begin my graduate work in East Asian history. Lieutenant Colonel Higgins, my immediate superior at Sendai, promptly responded to my request for a letter of reference for admission to Harvard University's graduate history program. What pleased me even more was an unsolicited note from Colonel McCone sent to Harvard, expressing a positive view of my role as an American citizen.

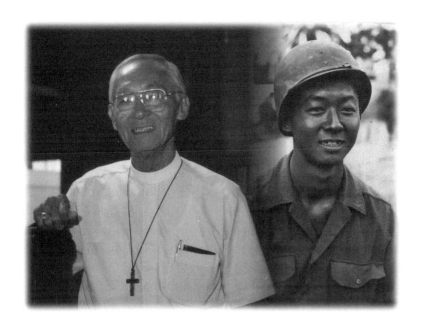

Ernest Uno

442nd Regimental Combat Team

THE JOURNEY OF A MAINLAND AJA

The Early Years

I was born in Salt Lake City, Utah, in February 1925, the seventh of Kumemaro and Riki (nee Kita) Uno's ten children. At the time of my birth, my father, a traveling salesman, was on the road. I'm told that when the hospital asked for a name for my birth certificate, my mother could not come up with a Japanese name, so she gave them the name of an American missionary, Ernest.

I was later given the name, Nobumaro, which I proudly used as my middle name until I graduated from college in 1950. When I was presented my diploma, the college president mispronounced my middle name so badly that it prompted a giggle from the audience. I was so embarrassed that to this day I refuse to use my Japanese name. I do not even use my middle initial when signing my name.

My parents came to the United States from Ishikawa *ken* soon after the turn of the century. They were married in Alameda, California, in 1912.

When I was still an infant, my father moved the family to Los Angeles, where I grew up attending public schools until the outbreak of World War II and the subsequent ouster of all people of Japanese ancestry from the West Coast.

My three brothers and I grew up carefree, although they were difficult years because of the Depression. Living in urban Los Angeles where job opportunities were scarce was rough for a large family like ours. It was even harder for people of Japanese ancestry, who at the time were denied government employment. Affordable housing for a large family like ours could not be found in the nicer residential sections of the city, so I grew up amidst small factories and light industries, away from the few communities that were predominantly Japanese.

As a result, I never attended Japanese-language school, although my older siblings did, paying their own way. I still cannot read or write Japanese and have only scant knowledge of the spoken language.

I grew up among predominantly Euro-Americans, with a small minority of Mexican Americans. None of my playmates or classmates at school was Japanese. In fact, I didn't know what it was to be Japanese, so I joined my friends in making fun of and mimicking the newly arrived youngsters from Japan who dressed and spoke funny.

Like any youngster looking for adventure and a chance to earn some money, I went door-to-door, selling magazine subscriptions. The magazines were rather big, so carrying my monthly quota was a struggle. A more profitable venture was selling newspapers at street corners every afternoon. It always felt good to head home with a pocket full of change and no leftover papers.

In my early teens I spent several summers peddling fruit and vegetables door-to-door. I don't remember encountering any overt acts of racial discrimination. However, I do recall my mother telling all of us to be careful how we conducted ourselves so as not to anger our neighbors. Furthermore, because we were Japanese, we should not be satisfied with being "just as good" as our peers; we had to strive to be better than the next person—because we were.

The real shock of being Japanese came with Japan's attack on Pearl Harbor on December 7, 1941. I remember a teacher telling me that I was not the same as the other students because I was Japanese—the same, sneaky, not-to-be-trusted people who bombed Pearl Harbor. I was ousted from school and separated from classmates with whom I'd grown up since elementary school. Even the red-haired girl whose hand I used to hold suddenly distanced herself from me.

In my adolescent years I was vaguely aware that my parents were different from my classmates' parents who spoke a foreign language. My father, who came to the United States at age twenty, spoke and wrote English fluently, without a hint of an accent. But there was no mistake that he was Japanese when he spoke to us at home of the greatness of the Japanese army as it overran the enemy in Manchukuo and China, in Indonesia and the Philippines.

We endured injustices and unfair treatment in restaurants and department stores. I remember being denied access to the YMCA to swim, except on a designated night not open to the general membership. As a result, my friends and I were in a segregated YMCA club that competed in sports only against other clubs made up of Japanese boys.

Pearl Harbor, December 7, 1941

On the morning of December 7th, I had gone to church and then home, where I had lunch before heading off to work in the fruit and vegetable section of a market just down the street from where we lived. I was setting out the fruit and vegetable stands while my boss prepared the produce for display. Suddenly, someone from the butcher section yelled out, "The Japs bombed Pearl Harbor! We're at war with Japan!"

I was stunned and bewildered by the announcement, for I had no idea where Pearl Harbor was and what the Japanese were trying to do. After recovering from the initial shock, my employer decided to close the fruit and vegetable section because of uncertainties about what kind of reaction the bombing might spark. At that point, he wanted to avoid any possible trouble.

After the Pearl Harbor attack, people spoke in hushed tones and we were told to be very careful of what we said and to whom we said anything. There were spies everywhere. There were rampant rumors about plans to round up all the Japanese and ship them back to Japan, or to move them all to a desert spot away from the Pacific coast.

In February 1942, my father was arrested and detained by the FBI as a suspected enemy agent. At the time, his incarceration seemed like a Charlie Chan movie—there was mystery and a hint of intrigue. There was tension in our family because it wasn't clear who should take charge in my father's absence. My mother set the tone for looking at the situation rationally by designating my eldest sister to speak for our family on issues relating to Executive Order 9066, the internment order issued by President Franklin Roosevelt.

Our family struggled. Even though my father had been gainfully employed until his incarceration, he did not earn enough to keep us comfortably fed and housed. Those of us who could, worked to help support the family. Therefore, we didn't lose much as a family when the order to evacuate came down. I remember having to sell my most treasured possession—my bicycle—which I had bought with my earnings from selling newspapers. My two younger brothers also had to sacrifice their bicycles.

Incarceration and Camp Life

The next sixteen months of our lives were spent behind barbed-wire fences patrolled by U.S. Army personnel bearing bayonet-mounted rifles—first at the Santa Anita Assembly Center and subsequently at the Amache Relocation Center. I was puzzled by the fact that the machine guns mounted on the guard towers were pointed inward, at us, instead of at the outside to fend off any possible attackers.

Santa Anita Assembly Center was a horse-racing track that had been hastily converted into a temporary internment center while the more permanent buildings were being constructed in the inner wastelands of the Midwest. Our family was assigned to a barrack that had been constructed on the vast parking lot. The government had also converted nearly all of the paddocks and horse stalls into quarters for the first groups of evacuees. Their callousness at making people live in stalls reeking of urine and horse dung was indicative of America's attitude toward the Japanese at the time.

Our next "home" was Amache Relocation Center, located in the southeastern corner of Colorado. For a teenager, life in the concentration camp, euphemistically called a "relocation center," was a waste. I had no interest in continuing my schooling, since the school program in the camp was a poor substitute for the real thing. Much to my mother's distress, I began hanging out with a gang of guys who had nothing better to do than smoke and play cards.

I resented being herded into a camp with my family and forced to live in a wooden barrack bare of any furniture other than an army cot with a thin mattress. The novelty of having to eat in a large dining hall with hundreds of others soon wore off. I disliked having to stand in long lines for every meal and jockeying for a seat at the long tables. After a while, the clanging of forks and spoons on the metal food trays became a deafening din.

At home, saying grace and singing out "*Itadakimasu* (Thank you for this meal)!" at mealtime came naturally. But in the camp dining hall with hundreds of others around, I used to wish that my mother would quit insisting that we join her in prayer. Much to her consternation, I broke the routine by finding a gang of guys who stuck together day and night, and with whom I would sit at mealtimes. I did not set a good example for my two younger brothers and sister, but at that point in my life, I was only interested in myself.

Instead of completing my senior year of school, I took a job with a silk-screen poster program in the camp, designing and producing freedom posters for the U.S. Navy. It was a creative and rewarding experience; I learned a craft and an art form while doing something productive. From a sullen drifter, I became a motivated and creative craftsman who was paid a respectable sixteen dollars a month.

When the war with Japan began, all eligible Japanese males were classified 4-C: "undesirable aliens." The War Department changed its policy in late 1943, restoring the nisei to 1-A status: "physically fit for active military duty."

At about the same time, the War Department required all nisei to fill out and sign a loyalty questionnaire. Anyone wanting to leave the camp had to complete the questionnaire before being allowed to leave.

Two questions generated much debate and concern for many nisei: "Are you willing to serve in the armed forces of the United States in combat duty wherever ordered?" and "Will you swear unqualified allegiance to the United States of America and faithfully defend the United States from any or all attack by foreign or domestic forces, and forswear any form of allegiance or obedience to the Japanese emperor, to any other foreign government, power, or organization?"

At about the same time, the War Department had decided to recruit, through voluntary enlistment, nisei from Hawaii and the continental United States to form a combat unit that became known as the 442nd Regimental Combat Team. This army unit was formed in response to the Japanese American community's plea to be given a chance to prove its loyalty to the United States.

A Call to Arms

The response from Hawaii was an overwhelming ten thousand volunteers. I was among the mere eighteen hundred who volunteered from the ten relocation camps on the mainland. The enlistment of nisei from the camps on the mainland fell far short of what had been anticipated.

The reason, I learned, was not so much the lack of enthusiasm and interest among the mainland nisei, but the rigid preinduction physical examination standards. With these strict standards, only one in four were eligible for enlistment. I remember how disappointed several of my buddies were when they were rejected by the induction board. When the War Department resumed drafting nisei, these men showed up in army uniforms overseas as replacement troops for the 100th Battalion and the 442nd.

In December of 1942, two of my older brothers had enlisted in the U.S. Army's Military Intelligence Service Language School and were sent to

Camp Savage, Minnesota. When I discussed the possibility of volunteering for the 442nd, I was rebuffed by my mother, who felt that two sons were enough for one family to give to the war effort. She said I could be of more help at home. After much pleading, she finally relented and allowed me to volunteer since I had recently celebrated my eighteenth birthday.

I failed my preinduction physical because of a double hernia. It was a crushing blow, for I had my heart set on answering the call and becoming a soldier to remove all doubts about my patriotism and loyalty to the United States. For a while my dreams of patriotism were dashed, until I learned that I could have my hernia treated by the medical staff at Amache.

Soon thereafter, I underwent surgery to repair the double hernia. Three months passed before I was allowed to be inducted into the army. Physically, I wasn't ready to undergo the rigors of basic training. The surgery and my lengthy recovery in the camp hospital had left me bent over at the waist. It took great effort and a lot of pain to stretch myself to stand erect. Even more painful were the lengthy marches and field exercises that caused me to strain at the waist and eventually suffer some adhesions. But the army would never know about that.

I had not been inculcated with the legendary virtues of the samurai. Terms such as *bushido* and *Yamato damashii* were foreign to me. I grew up learning more about "Honest Abe" Lincoln and Davy Crockett, apple pie and the American flag.

Upon joining the 442nd in training at Camp Shelby, I quickly learned what it took to become a real soldier the "Hawaiian way," and to be a member of a proud team. During one of my first long hikes, both my feet were in excruciating pain from fallen arches and ill-fitting army boots. Midway through the march, the pain was becoming intolerable. With every step, I contemplated dropping out. To make matters worse, scars from my hernia operation felt like they were pulling apart. I was miserable. I looked around for sympathy and support but found that no one else had dropped out.

Others were ailing, for sure. One soldier's rifle was being carried by another; others were marching with a fever and were so ill that they were vomiting. But no one wanted to be the first to drop out, to be a quitter. No one cried out for help. I quickly learned from the men from Hawaii that the motto "Go for Broke!" really meant that whatever is attempted, we go all the way; there's no quitting.

In training, I learned that in war, survival is the name of the game. To survive, each man had to hold up his end of the bargain. As a *kotonk*, I needed to change my attitude and behavior if I was to make it in this army outfit.

When I first reported to my assigned unit at Camp Shelby, I learned that my way of speaking would set me apart from the Hawaii boys and that I had to learn to listen and speak pidgin English. My early attempts at changing my speech pattern resulted in a lot of laughs. More important, I was adopting a different set of cultural values and mores, since the prevailing attitude among the Hawaii boys was that the *kotonks* were aloof and standoffish, acted superior, and talked too much like the haoles.

Perhaps it was naive of me, but during those early days of training, it never occurred to me that there was a problem between the mainland and Hawaii boys. The three or four of us in the same platoon slept and ate together with our Hawaii buddies and were well accepted. I don't recall being involved in any confrontation.

Our training at Camp Shelby molded us into a first-rate combat unit with high morale. The change in cultural values and mores had to do with how the boys from Hawaii were brought up, as opposed to the values and lifestyle of most mainlanders. In my case, I was born in Utah and raised in a neighborhood of Los Angeles where there were no other Japanese. The impact of this cultural isolation was that everything I did was patterned after a Western mode. For example, no one in my family would ever go out of the house without shoes and socks. My parents would never have tolerated our going out in public in slippers. The only barefoot people I saw in the streets were poor white children. By contrast, most of the soldiers from Hawaii came from either ethnically segregated plantation camps or from Honolulu, where the neighborhoods were somewhat segregated by race. In either case, they had a community that they could relate to; they had Buddhist temples and Japanese-language schools where they learned values and cultural virtues.

I quickly learned that there was a cohesiveness among the Hawaii soldiers that was alien to me. I was most conscious of this whenever we sat around in a bull session or were partying at the post exchange or USO club. Whenever the talk turned to such things as gang rivalries or a particular island camp, I felt totally left out. I even found it difficult to relate to other boys from the mainland, for we represented such a diversity of places up and down the coast, from Alaska to Mexico. As strange as it may seem, I often found myself yearning to be back at Amache Relocation Center where there were familiar faces, people I could talk with, especially girls whom I'd once known.

I know it was unfair of me, but often I felt like an outsider who was being discriminated against when it came to promotions within the ranks. I resented what I perceived to be favoritism among the Hawaii soldiers since I was in the minority in our platoon. I had to learn the hard reality that when it came to putting one's trust in a situation, a close friend would naturally get the call. This lesson taught me to overcome my resentment and to, instead, appreciate the bonds of friendship that brought our unit together. I depended on this bond of comradeship to sustain me throughout combat in Italy and France.

While in training at Camp Shelby I received word from my eldest sister that my mother, two younger brothers, and kid sister had left Amache to join my father at Crystal City, Texas. Crystal City was a camp for internees and their families who were deemed "undesirable aliens" and subject to deportation. I was told that my father had petitioned for deportation to Japan, and that my mother and the younger children were to accompany him. This news disturbed me greatly for it meant that I would no longer have a family at home, wherever that was, and that my being in the U.S. Army would pit me against my own family.

Soon after the family was reunited with my father at Crystal City, I received a lengthy letter from my father, which he had written in English. He explained that his loyalty was to the emperor of Japan, and that he truly believed that it was his destiny to return to the land of his birth. In this letter he admonished me to be the best soldier I could be, since it was my choice to take up arms as an American, and that he would be very proud of me if I died on the battlefield. I would be a hero then in his eyes, rather than a live coward if I should survive the battles and return home. He wrote something to the effect that my not dying for my country would bring shame to the family. I took this to be his way of saying good-bye to me.

The 442nd shipped out in early May 1944. For the next fourteen months we trudged up and down the mountainous terrain of Italy and slogged through the mud and mire of France. After Germany's surrender, I headed back to the United States to enroll in the army's Military Intelligence School and train to become a language specialist. As it turned out, Japan had surrendered and the war in the Pacific was over before I boarded a ship out of Leghorn, Italy.

By the time I reached the language school at Ft. Snelling, Minnesota, there was no need for additional language specialists, so I was discharged. I became a homeless civilian—homeless because we had been evacuated two-and-a-half years earlier from the only home I'd ever known. With my parents still interned at Crystal City, my two older sisters living in a cramped apartment in Minneapolis, Minnesota, and another sister and her husband and two children living in a flat in Chicago, I had no home to which I could return.

I was given a long furlough after returning from overseas. I used the opportunity to petition the government for permission to visit my parents at Crystal City. Permission was granted, so I set out for the Texas camp in full army uniform, my chest emblazoned with the appropriate decorations and awards.

Both of my parents, my brother Edison, and sister Kay were at the fence to greet me. This was my homecoming. I barely had time to touch my mother's hand through the chain-link fence and tell her *"Tadaima* (I'm home)!" when a guard admonished us that meeting at the fence was not permitted. We were to proceed to the visitors' cottage, where we could have an hour together—under the watchful eyes of an armed guard!

I can still picture my mother, stoically trying to hold back her tears of joy as she said to me in a firm voice, *"Okaeri* (Welcome home)!," that she knew I would return safely because she had faith, and that I had answered her prayers by coming home.

The Justice Department finally released my father in September 1947, and our family was reunited in Los Angeles, where I immediately began taking steps to pursue a college education. Having dropped out of high school, I wasn't sure what I needed to do to earn my high-school diploma. Much to my relief, a grateful school system awarded me a diploma based on the fact that I had spent the war years in the military and was honorably discharged. With my record showing that I had completed high school, I enrolled in college. After four years, I received a bachelor of arts degree in social group work. The degree qualified me to pursue a position with the Young Men's Christian Association (YMCA), which was my goal.

The Beginning of a Career

I encountered my first experience with racism and bigotry when I appeared before a personnel committee of a local YMCA. The interview with this group of businessmen went well; they were friendly and the interview focussed on my experience in working with people. Everything seemed upbeat until the conclusion of the interview, when I was asked if all things were equal and I was competing for a job with a white candidate, would I be willing to take the job at a lesser salary? I did not respond to the question, so I was not offered the job. I would have turned it down anyway. Undaunted, I continued to pursue a career with the YMCA.

I landed my first position in 1950, serving as director of youth programs for the YMCA of Honolulu. It was here that I first learned about the dual standard that prevailed among Christian ministers, social workers, and in private industry. Ethnic minorities were paid less than their white counterparts, most of whom were from the mainland. Back then, the rationale cited was that the "local" person had a lower standard of living and family and relatives on whom they could depend for help. They, therefore, did not require much to live on. Whites from the mainland, on the other hand, had no one to turn to for help. Furthermore, since they were so far from home, they were given extra money to make periodic trips back home every three years or so to get refreshed. Even with the advent of unionism in the Islands, these dual standards prevailed. It was not until the Democratic "revolution" of 1954 that change began to come about.

My wife, Grace, and I were newlyweds when we arrived in Hawaii in 1950 aboard the SS *Lurline*. My time in the military as a member of the 442nd made my transition much easier. I had gotten to know so much about island life and island ways from my 442nd comrades. That wasn't the case for Grace, who had a more difficult time adjusting to this new and strange environment so far from home. She had to learn to take off her shoes when entering someone's home and to train her ear to understand the pidgin spoken everywhere. The camaraderie among the Y staff and their families and the friendliness and acceptance we experienced at church, from our neighbors, and among Grace's coworkers at Pearl Harbor made us malihini (newcomer to Hawaii) feel at home.

We were in Hawaii less than three years, living in Leeward Oahu, when I was offered a similar position with the YMCA of Ventura County, California. As much as we enjoyed living in the Islands, taking the mainland job seemed in the best interest of my professional career, so we packed up and moved back to California.

For the most part, my experiences in Ventura's communities were positive and rewarding. Very few Japanese had returned to live in Ventura County after the war. As a result, Grace and I socialized almost exclusively with Caucasians. The teenagers with whom I worked were white, as were the children who attended the summer mountain camp I directed. There were no blacks.

In my three years there I can recall only one incident of racism, which occurred when I tried to purchase our home. We had gone to look at the model homes and were quite impressed, so we went to the sales office to fill out an application. I was told that my application would not be accepted by the developer. No reason was given, although it was obvious that they didn't want any Japanese there.

There was no such thing as fair-housing laws or Equal Employment Opportunity in those days, and since this was my first experience of having been rebuffed, I decided to ask a fellow Rotarian, who was a prominent and respected member of the community and a realtor himself, to intercede on my behalf. A phone call later, I was on my way to buying my home.

I spent approximately ten years on the mainland, doing YMCA work in three different places on the West Coast before receiving an offer to return to Hawaii for a position with the newly constructed Nuuanu Y. The offer came as I was about to make a career decision. Either I accepted the fact that there was a glass ceiling on job opportunities for me—despite my performance record which was considered superior—or move on, because no YMCA on the West Coast was ready to hire a Japanese American as its top executive. Had I not gotten the offer from Hawaii, I'm sure I would have left the YMCA organization.

Our return to Hawaii in 1963 was quite different. We now had a family: two boys and a girl, all born on the mainland. Urban subdivisions had begun to replace sugar fields. The Democratic "revolution" had taken place nearly a decade earlier, bringing forth men such as Dan Inouye, Sparky Matsunaga, and Nadao Yoshinaga. A number of other nisei rose to the fore as political leaders, heads of government departments, and leaders in the private sector. The power and influence nisei veterans wielded cannot be underrated. No more could we nisei regard ourselves as second to white power brokers.

Equal Opportunity

The YMCA was an example of the change that occurred. In the early 1970s, it was still a practice at the Central Y to fill its top executive position with a Caucasian—until the organization was challenged to discontinue this racist practice. I instigated that challenge when an attempt was made to hire a new executive from outside the Honolulu YMCA without first advertising the vacancy locally. I made my point and the Central Y had no choice but to open the search for a new executive to all of the local staff. A young sansei (third-generation Japanese American) was finally selected. This success was followed by the election of a nisei from a field of candidates from across the mainland to the position of general director of the YMCA of Honolulu.

My thirty-year career with the YMCA dated back to my days as a volunteer leader for a small group of boys in a Sunday school class. Their families had moved back to Los Angeles after the war. With these boys I had a chance to organize a club that would get them involved in a variety of YMCA activities, including a week in the mountains at a summer camp.

I began teaching Sunday school as a result of a seed planted in me by my 442nd chaplain, Hiro Higuchi. During the war, I had gone to Chaplain Higuchi for counseling after my buddy, a litter-bearer, was killed while carrying a wounded rifleman. The wise chaplain suggested that I might find some purpose and meaning in my buddy's death if I sought a mission for myself when the war was over.

Teaching a Bible class to a group of youngsters was the beginning of my search for purpose and meaning in my life. I also had to declare my major in college. I chose the field of social work, specializing in group work in preparation for a career with the YMCA. At that time, college classes in religion were required to qualify for employment as a professional in the YMCA, which was very much in keeping with my spiritual journey to find a mission to which I could devote my life.

Attending church was not required for doing YMCA work, but it was expected. This was not difficult for me, for I had attended church regularly as a youngster. As an adult, I had served as an usher at the morning worship services, and for a time, sang in the choir. I had even organized a young men's club at my Los Angeles church before coming to Hawaii in 1950.

My mother's Christian faith fueled my own spirituality and religious consciousness. Her faith was born out of her own need for spiritual nourishment as she struggled to provide for her ten children during the difficult Depression years. I remember her reading her Japanese translation of the Bible daily, and I often saw her in deep prayer. Etched in my memory was my visit with my family at Crystal City after returning from the war. My mother's first words to me were, "*Oinori shimashoo* (Let us pray)." Years later, she was reading a passage from the Bible to a friend dying of cancer when she, herself, slumped to the floor and died. She was fifty-nine at the time.

It was this undaunted faith, which I learned from her, that kept my marriage together and gave me the strength to go on with my work, even when the going got rough. Above all, I attribute my having survived a most serious illness, ulcerative colitis, to my abiding faith in God.

Throughout my adult life, I cannot recall a time when I wasn't involved with my church in one way or another. Even when I was skeptical of the theology of a particular minister or preacher, I held on to my belief in the redemptive power of God's love, and the basic doctrine of a Trinitarian God.

My faith is also a reflection of my roots as a third-generation Christian. My paternal grandmother became a Christian when my grandfather, an officer in the Japanese army, was stationed in Sendai, Miyagi Prefecture. She was a devout Christian who organized a Women's Christian Temperance Union group among the army wives. Following my grandfather's retirement from the army, they returned to their ancestral home in Kanazawa, where she taught Bible classes in her home. According to records of the Christian church in Kanazawa, my father's family played a major role in establishing Kanazawa's Christian congregation.

On a visit to my birthplace, Salt Lake City, several years ago, my cousin took me to visit the Japanese Protestant Church. My father's name was inscribed on a small plaque as one of the church's founders. It is no wonder then that my spiritual footsteps followed the path of my forebears.

They eventually led to my being ordained a deacon in the Episcopal Church.

Since being ordained, I have been involved in several ministries. As a 442nd veteran, I currently serve as chaplain for the 442nd Veterans Club. I also offer invocations and prayers on various occasions and am sometimes called upon to officiate at memorial services and burials of 442nd veterans who have passed away and to comfort families in their bereavement.

Another of my ministries involves serving as a volunteer for St. Francis Hospice, providing care and comfort to the terminally ill. I regularly visit with patients in the hospice facility, and, on occasion, visit patients in their homes, providing respite for their primary caregiver. I am sometimes called upon to offer a commendatory prayer for the departed. I have found that for the terminally ill in a hospice setting, the thought of death and dying is accepted with a sense of peaceful resignation. It is the bereaved who are not prepared to part with a loved one for whom care has to be taken to ease their loss.

I have already had to deal with the passing of several loved ones in my family: my parents and six of my siblings. The youngest in our family to die was my brother Edison, who, at the age of forty-seven, was in the prime of his career as an educator and social activist. He is best remembered as the nisei who gave birth to the idea that the United States government owed an apology and reparations to the thousands of Japanese Americans who were illegally interned during the war. Edison first spoke out publicly about the need for redress and reparations in 1972. At the time he was rebuffed by the national leadership of the Japanese American Citizens League (JACL) as well as many individuals, who opposed asking the federal government to apologize, calling it "radical" and going too far in faulting the government for something that happened in 1942. "*Shikata ga nai,*" they argued. What's done is done.

Accompanying the demand for an apology was a demand for a token cash payment for the losses incurred by those affected by Executive Order 9066. It was argued that an apology without some kind of payment or penalty was an empty gesture.

Opponents of redress and reparations were understandably disturbed that they would be perceived as greedy troublemakers and as unpatriotic for taking action against their government. After the war, many former evacuees had settled comfortably in small communities in the Midwest, having overcome some initial local resistance. Their school-age children were now accepted by their classmates and were doing well academically. It was unthinkable to take any action that would upset what they had struggled so hard to achieve. Let bygones be bygones, they argued. Furthermore, it was argued, Japanese Americans were such a small segment of the population: Who would ever listen to their plea for an apology?

Initial opposition to redress and reparations was formidable, and it took a great deal of courage, energy, perseverance, and money to fight a campaign to overcome this resistance. My brother Edison and a small, loyal group of followers who believed in the justness of this cause pursued the drive for four years, until his untimely death in 1976.

Several years after his death, however, the JACL had a change of heart and turned the issue of redress and reparations into a national campaign. Finally, in 1988, twelve years after Edison's death, the Civil Rights Act of 1988 was signed into law by President Ronald Reagan. Payments of twenty thousand dollars to each surviving evacuee began, which was a monumental achievement. Unfortunately, by 1989 when the first checks were sent out, 90 percent of the issei and a large number of older nisei internees had already died. I think it's fair to say that reparations were too little, too late. Twenty thousand dollars was a token amount that could never make up for the losses suffered, neither materially nor spiritually. But even this amount, along with the president's apology on behalf of the nation, would never have happened without the influence of U.S. Senators Daniel K. Inouye and the late Spark M. Matsunaga.

I am awed by the twists and turns of our fortunes as Japanese Americans, living in a country where we are such a small minority. Although my family's experiences differed from the immigrants who came to Hawaii, they faced their own formidable problems on the mainland, where they were confronted by organized campaigns to oust them from their homes and deprive them of their livelihood. My father recalled having to dodge bricks thrown at him by hoodlums on the streets of Seattle and of being pushed off the cable car in San Francisco while racial epitaphs were shouted at him.

In Hawaii there is a homogeneity among the Japanese, even among the third and fourth generations. There was a common ethnic identity as well as a shared lifestyle in the plantation camps. Language schools, religious customs, and colorful festivals reflecting the heritage of their Buddhist faith attributed to this bonding. On the other hand, mainland nisei who grew up in the Midwest had almost no other AJA with whom they could relate and share customs and family rituals. Until the attack on Pearl Harbor, these nisei never considered themselves Japanese. The war dramatically changed that for all Japanese Americans.

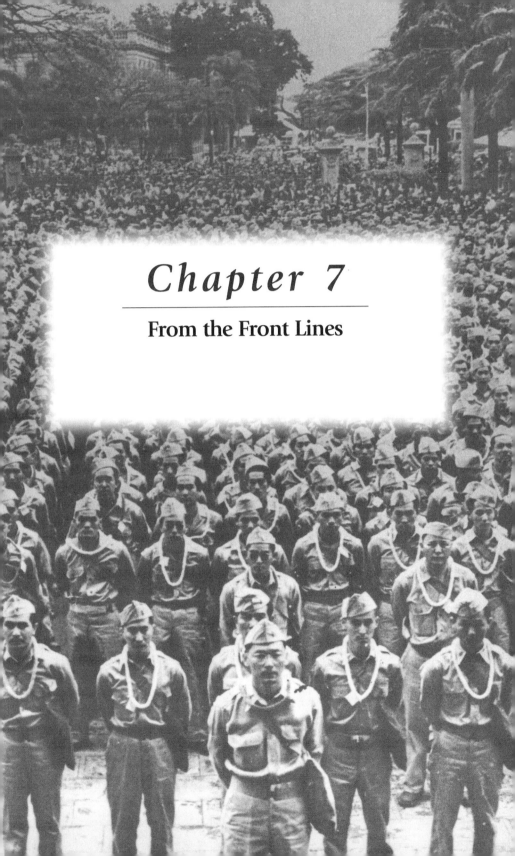

Chapter 7

From the Front Lines

Albert Farrant Turner

DAD'S "BOYS"

In this essay, Albert "Bert" Turner reflects on the fondness his father, Lt. Colonel Farrant L. Turner, held for the men in the 100th Infantry Battalion (Separate). The "Old Man," as the young soldiers referred to him, was a father figure to the "boys" from Hawaii.

As I look back on my father's life, I see a man who was honest, who cared for his fellow man, who never tried to attain personal gain by taking advantage of others, and who had a true love for Hawaii and all of its people.

As the treasurer of Lewers & Cooke, a building supply house in Honolulu, Farrant L. Turner worked closely with the construction trades and knew most of the contractors in town. To my knowledge, he treated them all fairly and did his best to enhance his company's business while assisting the small businessman contractor who purchased building materials.

In October 1940 the 298th Infantry Regiment, a National Guard regiment made up of men from the island of Oahu, was called to active duty. Key leaders in that regiment were Col. Wilhelm A. Andersen, the regimental commander; my father, a lieutenant colonel and the executive officer of the regiment; Lt. Col. Paul Porter, the S-3 of the regiment; and Maj. Jim Lovell, the assistant S-3 as well as the regiment's football and baseball coach.

When the regiment was called to active duty, wooden barracks were built toward the back of Schofield Barracks. Other units of the Hawaiian Division, also known as the "Old Taro Patch Division," were housed in quadrangles on the lower post.

My memory tells me that the ethnic composition of most of the officers was typical of our population. The senior leaders at the time were haole, but the company grade officers were of mixed ethnic background—probably there were more of Japanese extraction than of other ethnic backgrounds, but that is a guess on my part.

The officer corps of the regular army of the late '30s and '40s was made up almost entirely of Caucasian officers. I well remember that the Officers Club on the main post at Schofield invited the haole officers to become members. This invitation was not extended to the other officers. I am proud to say that none of the invited officers accepted the invitation. Instead, the regiment constructed its own Officers Club and all social functions for the officers and their families were held there. I know that my father was as much responsible for that decision as the other haole leaders.

In about April 1942, thanks to many leaders in the local community, it was decided that an over-strength battalion of men of Japanese extraction would be formed from men currently in the army. I know that Colonel Andersen wanted to command this unit, as did my father. Colonel Andersen offered to be demoted to Lieutenant Colonel so that he could command the unit. I suspect that my father was selected as the commanding leader of this group because he was of the appropriate rank and because of his many years spent dealing with local contractors.

Shortly after the war started, my father decided that I should finish my high-school education on the mainland. I was a sophomore in high school in 1941–1942. After much emoting, I convinced him that I should not leave Hawaii.

Suddenly one day in late May he came home for a couple of hours and advised my mother and me that we would be leaving for the mainland soon, as he was getting a new assignment. It was obvious this time that no amount of emoting was going to change his mind.

Mother and I were advised that we should be at Pier 10 on or about June 2, 1942. My father's instructions to those men who were going to be in that unit were that they would be leaving the Islands shortly, but that their families could not be told of their departure. Well, when the SS *Maui* sailed out of Honolulu Harbor on June 5, 1942, Pier 10 was sinking into the water with the weight of all of the families down to watch their husbands and sons sailing off. In retrospect, how could the families not be told, even though there was a security risk.

I remember the trip to Oakland. Forget the fact that Midway was attacked when we were several days at sea. No one knew where the ship was going (other than to the mainland), and no one, including my father, knew where the unit would be taken upon its arrival.

When we arrived in Oakland, my father said good-bye and said he would get in touch with us when he knew where he was going to be. My mother and I made our way to her mother's home in Illinois. Shortly after arriving there, we learned that the unit, now known as the 100th Infantry Battalion (Separate), was stationed at Camp McCoy, Wisconsin.

Several things stand out for me while the battalion was in the States. My father believed that competitive sports were a morale booster. Soon the unit had a baseball team, which played the local semipro and town teams, and a basketball team, which competed with other teams within one hundred miles of Camp McCoy. During the summer while I was in Wisconsin, it was exciting for me to watch the teams in action. The men were about six inches shorter than their competition in basketball, but because of their speed and fervor for the game, they competed well.

It was at Camp McCoy that my father proposed to the men of the 100th that a fund be started so that when they returned home after the war, there would be something permanent for them to latch on to. The fund grew as each man contributed to it on payday. When the unit returned home, there was sufficient money to purchase the current home of Club 100.

How do you build morale? I think the route to good morale is caring for your men and being a part of everything they did. My father was good at that, and it was apparent that devotion was a two-way street.

Dad was forty-six when the battalion landed in Italy—pretty old for a battalion commander—and I suspect the rigors of combat caught up with him. He lasted about a month in combat and then was evacuated because he had lost all feeling in one of his legs. Years later, doctor friends told him they thought he had polio.

I suspect that losing men who meant so much to Dad had an impact on him as well. Each man in the 100th was special to him and the losses the battalion experienced had to be very difficult for him.

In the years after the war, I well remember the tears streaming down my dad's cheeks when we would talk about the battalion and the many fine men who lost their lives.

The 100th Battalion was the most important thing in my father's life. He won many honors over the years, but nothing was more important to him than his achievements leading the 100th Battalion, from its formation until he was relieved of command in October 1943. He may have been relieved of command, but his leadership continued in many small ways once the war was over and the men returned home. Because of Dad, the men of the 100th Battalion will always be very special to me and my family.

Raymond R. Nosaka
100th Infantry Battalion

JAPANESE DOG BAIT

I kept this story of my experience during the war a secret for thirteen years after World War II had ended. I only began sharing it with others after the War Department declassified the information.

At Camp McCoy, Wisconsin, my platoon—3rd Platoon, Baker Company—was ordered to assemble in the mess hall. We were given an eight-page questionnaire to complete. The questions were rather general, about family history, and so on. There were no clues whatsoever of what lay ahead.

On November 1, 1942, twenty-five of us were selected from our platoon of forty. We were told to pack our barracks bags and be ready to move out at 7:30 A.M. the next morning. We were told not to talk to anyone about our orders.

It was cold when we left Camp McCoy the next morning in a covered army truck. There were no good-byes. We knew nothing about our destination or our mission. I felt uneasy about leaving my buddies behind without even being able to say, "See you later."

We boarded a transport plane. There were twenty-five of us: Robert Goshima, Masao Hatanaka, Noboru Hirasuna, Masao Koizumi, Herbert Ishii, Fred Kanemura, James Komatsu, Masami Iwashita, John Kihara, Katsumi Maeda, Koyei Matsumoto, Toshio Mizusawa, Taneyoshi Nakano, Tokuji Ono, Tadao Hodai, Seiji Tanigawa, Yasuo Takata, Robert Takashige, William Takaezu, Seiei Okuma, Patrick Tokushima, Takeshi Tanaka, Mack Yazawa, Yukio Yokota, and me. We were accompanied by Lt. Rocco Marzano, Lt. Ernest Tanaka, and Maj. James Lovell.

We were silent during the flight. I kept asking myself, "What is this all about? Why all the secrecy? Are we being returned to the Pacific to be kamikazes?"

Soon I began noticing greenery below us—an indication that we were entering warmer climates. Our plane landed several hours later, and I noticed a sign on the hangar roof: "Radd, Memphis, Tennessee."

We were not allowed to deplane while the transport was being refueled. Our lunch of sandwiches was brought to us. We felt like prisoners. I couldn't help but think of our buddies back at Camp McCoy who were probably wondering what happened to us.

Our next stop was Gulf Port, Mississippi, where we again boarded a covered army truck that had been backed up to our plane. We were taken to a pier where a Coast Guard boat was waiting for us. Several hours later, we arrived at Ship Island in the Gulf of Mexico. There were no stores, no cars—just a barracks building for us and old Fort Massachusetts situated on miles of barren sand.

We tidied up our barracks; after all, it would be our home during our time on Ship Island. The water was brackish and smelled like sulfur. So did we. When we showered, there were no suds from the soap. When the island was hit by a typhoon, we thought we were doomed. Somehow, we managed to survive.

Soon thereafter, Major Lovell explained our mission. We were there for "dog-bait training." I was so disappointed. After all, we had been trained as combat soldiers. What were we doing there?

I soon learned that we would not be training the dogs, as we had assumed. Rather, *we* would be used as the bait—Japanese bait—so that the dogs could be trained to sniff out and kill Japanese soldiers. It seems that someone in Washington, D.C., thought that we Americans of Japanese ancestry secrete the same odor as our ancestors, and that the dogs could be trained to sniff out the Japanese.

We commuted to Cat Island every day by Coast Guard boat. The island was mostly marshland and dense like a jungle. There were alligators, snakes, and millions of mosquitoes.

My first assignment was working with attack dogs. My right arm was wrapped in protective gear. The dogs were trained to leap and attack the soldier's throat. I was taught to quickly place my wrapped arm over my throat and then wrestle with the dog until the trainer commanded him to "stop," or "kill."

The most difficult time I had was when we were ordered to hit the dogs with sticks—this, after having become friends with them. As a dog lover since childhood, this seemed so cruel and was very difficult for me to do.

After about a month on Cat Island, I received a letter from home. There were rumors circulating that Hawaii's Japanese would be evacuated to concentration camps on the mainland. I was very angry. Why couldn't they trust us? What more did we have to do to prove our loyalty to America?

After five months of "dog-bait training"—and of having our mail censored—our group was disbanded and we were returned to the battalion. I never learned how or why our particular group of men was selected, or if the dog training was ever put to use in the Pacific war zone.

One of the most vivid memories I have of the war occurred in November 1943, a year after our dog-training episode. After being wounded in my thigh, I crawled to a nearby cave and took cover. When darkness fell, a stray dog came to me. I shared my C-ration dinner with the animal, who then lay down beside me. We kept each other warm that night. I felt warm inside, thinking I had the chance to befriend this stray dog, to, in a way, make up for the dogs I had to hit while in training.

I came home after I had been wounded. My dad was there to greet me. For the first time in my life, I saw him cry.

Tsutomu Tom Nagata

100th Infantry Battalion

SHIGEO JOE TAKATA: HE SET THE STANDARD

The 100th Infantry Battalion landed in Oran, North Africa, on September 2, 1943. We were housed in a campsite a short distance away. Soldiers who had stayed there earlier had nicknamed it "Goat Hill."

Several days later, it was my turn for night guard duty. At the guard tent that evening, I met the other NCO, Sgt. Shigeo Joe Takata, from B Company; I was from C Company. After the guards had been posted, we sat up all night, talking story and checking up on the sentries. Joe loved the game of baseball: He mentioned that he played for the Asahis AJA baseball team. We talked about many things that night and parted as friends the next morning.

The 100th Battalion landed at Salerno on the morning of September 22, 1943. The sky was clear and the sea was calm. The enemy was miles away as we started to get off the boat. When it was our turn to disembark, we climbed down the rope ladder into the landing barges. As I sat down, I saw our battalion commander, Lt. Col. Farrant Turner, and half of his staff already in the boat. We had a good landing; nobody got wet.

I remember seeing mullet swimming in the clear waters of the Sele River as we hiked up the hill. The vegetation turned from cactus plants at sea level to crab apple trees higher up.

It had rained heavily the night before, so those of us who had slept in the open field got up early on the morning of September 29, 1943, to clean our rifles. We had hiked and ridden trucks and then hiked again as we neared the battle zone. The farmers had harvested their chestnut trees and had piled the nuts in heaps in front of their farmhouses.

B Company took the lead as we crossed into "no-man's land." C Company was in reserve behind battalion headquarters. We passed some soldiers from another outfit who were sitting in their foxholes. Suddenly, we heard the sound of machine-gun fire and exploding mortar artillery shells up ahead. A spent shell fragment landed near me. I heard more rifle fire. And then there was silence.

I heard Colonel Turner, who was up ahead, reporting to the regiment by radio that Sgt. Joe Takata had been killed by artillery shells. Colonel Turner said that Joe's heroic action in leading his men to outflank the enemy had caused the Germans to withdraw. I also heard him say that he was going to recommend Sergeant Takata for a Distinguished Service Cross for Gallantry in Action.

The battalion had to move forward, but as we passed Sergeant Takata by the roadside, each of us offered a silent prayer to our brave comrade. I felt very sad that someone I had just gotten to know had been killed. Joe was the first of many AJA soldiers to be killed in action. I was proud that I knew him. He set the standard for the conduct of the men from that time on. He was leading his men and doing his job clearing the way. I felt that if he was willing to give his life for his country, then the rest of us should try to do the same.

Ben H. Tamashiro
100th Infantry Battalion

FIRST CHRISTMAS OVERSEAS

This essay was written in 1981 by Ben Tamashiro. In it, he recalls his first Christmas eve overseas—in Italy, 1943 with the 100th Infantry Battalion—after rereading a letter he had written to his sister Aiko in Hawaii.

Our conversation about family was sputtering along when my niece, Sandra Arashiro, said, "My mom has kept all your wartime letters."

Just like that, she said it, as though there was nothing to it. But in that instant, my mind banged wide open. "She has? She's never told me about it!"

"She's kept them in a little box, tied with ribbons. She turned them over to me some time ago." I could feel myself tightening up. "And I've read every one of 'em," Sandra added.

"No kidding!" Evidently the strain of my anticipation was reflected in the glow of my face, the light in my eyes.

She laughed. "You can have them if you want them."

That's how I recently came into possession of the letters I had written to my sister Aiko while I was a member of the 100th Infantry Battalion.

In the pile of yellowed envelopes was one postmarked December 28, 1943. I pulled out the letter from the slightly torn envelope: three yellowed onionskin sheets scrawled in black ink in my chicken-scratch handwriting. Censorship forbade citation of place-names so I had noted simply, "Italy—Xmas Eve, 1943" at the top of the first page. I read the letter, reread it. My first Christmas overseas!

The 100th had pulled back for a rest after having spent several weeks on the front lines and we were bivouacked some sixty or so miles northeast of Naples on a plateau of the Apennine Mountain range. The letter recalled for me a couple of things about the rest period.

For one, we had subsisted mainly on canned rations during that long stay on the front lines: canned hash, pork and beans, cheeses, and the like. Our digestive systems had accordingly gone "soft" on us, though we were not aware of this condition until that first chow line in the rest area when, to our shock, we discovered that our long underutilized digestive systems could not take the sudden ingestion of freshly cooked foods, not even fresh bread!

And, incongruous as it seemed, on another day we had to stand in formation to receive "Good Conduct" medals! Ours was not to question or reason why.

The big pyramidal tent we were in must have held six to eight of us. I had written, "Having used up our quota of candles the night before, and [with] no other means of light available, we had rigged up our own through simple ingenuity. A discarded ink bottle filled with bacon lard, a few inches of wrapping twine from Xmas packages, and, presto! 'round this makeshift light flowed the talk of the evening. Then someone broke in with a Xmas carol but that did not get far. But we all lustily joined in for one chorus of 'Pistol Packin' Mama!' and that about ended our attempt at a songfest for the evening."

Continuing the letter: "Even with the ebb and flow of our talk, we had constant reminders that this was Xmas eve of 1943—not exactly our idea of celebrating the coming of Christ, but as one lad remarked, we are certainly thankful that our unit wasn't on the line at this moment." The letter told of how each went off to bed until I was the only one up. "I could hear the footsteps of the relief guard going to post. Now the silence of the evening deepens and one begins to feel the cold creeping in. Outside, for one last look before going to bed. Visible overhead are just a handful of stars. One can readily note that it's mighty cold way up there. I hastily creep back to the comforting warmth of my bed, blow out the light, and prepare for sleep."

After the Christmas break, the 100th was to go back to the line, to plunge right into the bloody battle for Cassino. But for now, everything was peaceful and quiet, so much so it tempted me to quote that line from Thomas Gray's "Elegy Written in a Country Churchyard": "And all the air a solemn stillness holds." I suspect that we were far enough to the rear that roars of the cannons up front were audible only as faint rumblings.

"Then suddenly, the harmonious singing of several voices reached my ears. It's 'Silent Night! Holy Night!'" Reading the passages from my letter at this point in time, thirty-eight years later, I can still feel the excitement of that moment. "Coming clear and loud through the still night, it's too beautiful for words, so I know it can't be a group of fellows glowing with the spirit of Italian vino! I imagine several of the boys from the battalion had got together to form this caroling party. Two more carols, then the voices die away. And in the stillness that follows, I somehow can't go to sleep." I closed the letter to my sister with the hope that "by this time next year, there'll be peace on earth."

That was not to be, for the peace of World War II did not come for another eighteen months.

Shortly thereafter came the Christmases of the Korean War. Then still later the Christmases of the long and bitter Vietnam War.

At each of these Christmases overseas, undoubtedly many a letter similar to mine was written under the same kind of circumstance, expressing a like sentiment: how a solitary soul in the midst of a grim crusade can catch a glimpse of hope in just the notes of a Christmas carol.

But isn't that what Christmas is all about? All the improbable dreams of this whole big, wide world—dreams as unchanging today as those of yesteryear—riding on the light of a star guiding us to a manger and the birth of the child of tomorrow?

Richard M. Sakakida

Military Intelligence Service
Edited by Ted Tsukiyama

SECRET MISSION

World War II produced no greater American patriot and hero of the Military Intelligence Service than Richard Motoso Sakakida. In the war against Japan, he was a pioneer among nisei MIS personnel, having been recruited by the U.S. Army to perform undercover intelligence against the Japanese in Manila even before the December 7, 1941, attack on Pearl Harbor. Sakakida performed his mission efficiently, faithfully, and with loyalty, living up to the honor of his selection with distinction.

    After the Japanese army invaded the Philippines in December 1941, Sakakida served with the U.S. forces, which were relentlessly driven back to Bataan and Corregidor. General MacArthur utilized Sakakida's Japanese-language skills to perform invaluable military intelligence work against the advancing Japanese: translating, interpreting, intercepting, decoding, inter-

*rogating POWs, and conducting psychological warfare against
the enemy.*

 *From the last siege of Corregidor up until its capitula-
tion on May 7, 1942, Sakakida served as General Jonathan
Wainwright's intelligence man. In his autobiography,* A Spy in
Their Midst, *authored by Sakakida and Wayne Kiyosaki,
Sakakida recalls General Wainwright's sad surrender.*

Along with Gen. Wainwright and his staff, we lined up on both sides of
Malinta Tunnel awaiting the entry of the Japanese forces. I had the plea-
sure of standing right by the general. The day of the surrender was the sad-
dest day of my long military career. Neither the euphoria of the victorious
end to World War II nor the happiness that I have had the good fortune to
enjoy since retirement will ever erase the poignant sadness I experienced
that day on Corregidor. I shall never forget the sight of Gen. Wainwright,
dignified and unbowed, moving forward while we stood at attention, to
unbuckle his belt and holster with his pearl-handled pistol in symbolic
recognition of the surrender. I could feel tears welling in my eyes and I was
sure that I was not alone in paying silent tribute to our commander who
was there with us to the very end.

 *When the fall of Corregidor became imminent, General MacArthur
ordered Sakakida to leave and continue his work at MacArthur's
headquarters in Australia. Citing his moral obligation, however,
Sakakida asked Colonel Stuart Wood that his seat aboard his "flight
to freedom" be given to a fellow Hawaii nisei, Clarence Yamagata.*

The concept of *on*, or moral obligation, was too complex for me to explain
to him. It is something we owe to our Japanese forebears. I simply grew
up steeped in the efficacy of the concept. It involved a whole set of oblig-
ations that we learned to accept in relation to family, friends, community
and nation. It was also integral to our identity. Because of what we were,
we did accordingly. It was a kind of moral force that cemented interper-
sonal relationships, reinforced one's identity, and fostered community
cohesiveness. Looking after each other meant furthering the social better-
ment of all of us. Thus, to profit at the expense of others was to err, and to
give of oneself was necessary, no matter how painful. With my mother, all
of this was embodied in a fundamental rule by which many Japanese
Americans lived: never bring shame to oneself, one's family or to our col-
lective identity as Japanese Americans.

 Not everyone abided by those rules. All of this may sound improbable and overly idealistic, but that's the way our generation was raised in

Hawaii. Unlike others around me, Clarence treated me like a Hawaiian. As a fellow Hawaiian and friend, I owed him at least that much in return.

During World War II, Sakakida was the only nisei in the U.S. military to be imprisoned as an American POW by the Japanese army in the Philippines. He survived over three years of captivity—a continuous nightmare of fear, ridicule, and physical brutality—because of his Japanese ancestry. Just before Sakakida was captured, he was ordered to go undercover and gather intelligence from the Japanese military wherever possible. Sakakida was interrogated mercilessly as an American spy—which he was—by the dreaded Kempeitai and charged with treason. He faced his interrogators, determined to "out-samurai" his "samurai" captors.

Following the call-out of Wainwright and his staff, my name was called. I experienced a chilling sensation and tried as hard as I could to collect my wits as I was escorted to the office of the commander of the military "thought police," better known as the dreaded Kempeitai (*kempei* literally means military police; *tai* is a unit designation).

The Kempeitai had a reputation for terror and intimidation that virtually destroyed political liberalism and freedom in Japan in the 1930s and paved the way for the rise of Japanese militarism. Members could be identified by the white armbands they wore with red characters "Kempei" printed on them. When I realized where I was headed, I braced myself for the worst.

When we were growing up, many of the *issei* could not read English so they taught us by reading Japanese fables and fairy tales. They spent hours reading to us and explaining what those lessons were supposed to mean in our lives. Storybooks and fables were a significant part of our Japanese language school education. Many of the stories were grounded in mythology, but the stories seemed real to us because of the earnestness with which they were presented. My parents wanted those stories to serve as foundations for character and manhood.

Early on, I loved the world of the *samurai*. As I faced becoming a POW, I wanted to live up to the highest ideals of a *samurai*. I had to accept fate on those terms and refrain from blaming others for my fate lest I end up wallowing in remorse, self-pity and bitter hatred. It was the only way I could think of to avoid caving in to my captors.

Sakakida vehemently denied being an American soldier and spy, so the Kempeitai turned to savage beatings and brutal torture to wring a confession out of him. He never broke down and successfully concealed his true status as an American undercover agent,

even under unspeakable and unbearable torture inflicted upon
him by his captors. Sakakida described that agonizing ordeal.

I lied to my interrogators; I didn't like lying even while I was being tortured. Lying went against something of fundamental value that I was taught at home, in the classroom and by my religious teachers. The orthodoxy that defined my military responsibilities was my only hedge against self-doubt. I felt that, right or wrong, I had to do whatever it took to continue on with my mission. I saw it as a matter of duty as the interrogation took on a violent turn. From then on, I was put through a series of torture treatments and incessant beatings.

It began by having my hands tied behind my back and stringing me up to a rope that had been thrown over a rafter in the interrogation room. I was kept dangling with my toes just barely off the floor. The pain was excruciating and after a time it felt as if my arms were being torn out of my shoulder sockets. All the while, the interrogator kept asking me, "What is your true military rank?" I kept denying that I was part of the military. Soon the pain reached a point at which I thought I would have to scream, but the persistent questioning raised my blood to the boiling point. All of a sudden, the rage that welled up inside of me came on like some sort of divine intercession. Sweat poured out of my body and I was enraged as I had never, ever been before in my life. Suddenly the overriding pain was diminished to a level where my will to resist could be kept intact.

I don't know how my ravaged mind and body were able to muster the burst of spirituality that saved me from going over the edge, but for that I shall be eternally grateful. It gave me mental leverage and I vowed with a rage bordering on madness that I would not succumb to torture. By then, I knew that he would have to kill me or somehow separate me from my senses to get me to capitulate. Suddenly, I felt in control of myself.

The Japanese have always been known for their stoic acceptance of fate, even in the face of death. They refer to it as a capacity for *gaman*, or endurance, something that my parents and Buddhist teachers taught me as I was growing up in Hawaii. As early as I can remember, we were taught that it was shameful to cry when faced with physical pain, and I was determined to show him that on that score, I was just as Japanese as he was. I stared him right in his eyes. I also vowed that if I ever survived the war, I would someday hunt him down. At that moment, I felt that I could kill him.

Realizing that he was not getting his way with me, he decided to push the torture up a notch. He had some men strip me of my clothing until I was stark naked. He still kept me dangling from the rafters as he systematically took a lighted cigarette and inflicted burns on me. He started in the area of my thighs. As the days went on, he went up to the area of my abdomen before finally getting to my genitals, hoping all along that I would crack. The pain, added to the pain in my arms that already felt dislocated, was indescribable. I was subjected to the same torture day after day. There were times when I felt like screaming as loud as I could, but I refused to give them even that satisfaction. After a while, I began to lapse into a state of extreme nausea compounded by the smell of burning flesh—my own.

To this day, I don't know how I endured the ordeal. Perhaps it was my Buddhist upbringing that made me turn inward, looking for inner strength to counter the pain that had already reached an almost unbearable level. Fortunately, my rebelliousness and Buddhist faith held me in good stead. If I was enraged during the early stages of torture, I was by then delivered to a state of incandescent fury, particularly as he buried the cigarette into my penis. That was the last straw and I knew that in my state of indescribable rage, my torturer was not about to break the steel-like clamp on my nerves. I felt as if I had entered a dark tunnel and the light at the end was visible only to me. Today, I can count about thirty to forty scars from the ordeal.

Unable to "break" Sakakida by torturing him, the Japanese assigned him to the 14th Japanese Army Headquarters in Manila, where he was forced to perform English interpretation and translation work. It was the perfect foil for his undercover mission.

In August 1944, Sakakida planned and executed a prison break at Muntinglupa Prison, freeing hundreds of Filipino guerrillas who thereafter served as a pipeline for transmitting Japanese intelligence gathered by Sakakida to MacArthur's headquarters in Australia. After MacArthur's American forces invaded the Philippines in March 1945, driving the Japanese army into retreat, Sakakida escaped from his Japanese captors into the jungle, where he was wounded and incapacitated by fever and disease. He emerged in September 1945 and rejoined American armed forces and his former CIP (Corps of Intelligence Police) unit.

Working with the U.S. War Crimes Commission after the war, he was able to confront his former Kempeitai tormentors—and treat them with compassion and forgiveness. Sakakida shared that remarkable experience.

I spent nineteen years in Japan after the war. During this period, I took my first steps toward trying to live with the pain and anger that still filled me after my traumatic experiences as a POW. When I was being tortured in prison, all I could think of was surviving so I could seek revenge against every one of my tormentors. This rage was still bottled up inside me when the war ended. But once things began to return to normal, the rage began to subside, even though I was still tortured by the traumatic events of the past. I realized this when I encountered my assailants after the war.

During the occupation period, as chief of the Apprehension and Interrogation Division of the War Crimes Commission, I had access to all of the POW camps. I located the master sergeant, captain and major of the Kempeitai who were responsible for the torture I had undergone in Bilibid Prison. I had them brought to Manila and went to see them, wearing dark glasses to hide my identity. Through an interpreter I asked them, "We are looking for a *nisei* by the name of Sakakida. Did any of you know him?" They each replied in the negative.

I removed my sunglasses; their eyes widened in recognition. They were stupefied and showed no traces of the arrogance I had long associated with them. Looking frightened and guilty, my former torturers prostrated themselves on the ground as if ready to accept any punishment I chose to inflict upon them.

But by now I was far too removed from the rage I had felt while in their control; the war was over, and I had no desire to return to bitter hatred and killing. As soldiers in combat we had all done what was required of us. They had done their job, just as I had done mine by escorting the Japanese colonel to his hanging in Tokyo. I was ready to let bygones be bygones. I still don't know where that compassion and forgiveness came from. Wherever they are, I hope that those men have found peace, as I have.

What gave Richard Sakakida the inner strength to withstand and survive his terrible three-and-one-half-year ordeal as a prisoner of the Japanese enemy? Sakakida credited those Japanese ideals and values transmitted and taught to him by his issei parents.

The past year had been a time for self-examination and a reassessment of the roots of my heritage. There were myths and realities that I had to sort out for my own good. Myths were a significant part of my early upbringing, but I thought I knew the difference between myth and reality.

My musing led me to wonder whether our parents had pulled the wool over our eyes when they taught us about things like *Yamato damashii*, the mythical "Japanese spirit." I wondered about the tales of filial piety, honesty, loyalty, bravery and forbearance. "Was all that Japanese propaganda?" I asked myself. I remember many of my friends feeling that way as they grew older and became more Americanized. But when I was imprisoned, those ideas and concepts helped me survive.

As I composed my speech, I began to realize that all the things I had learned through Japanese materials were universal principles necessary for the healthy sustenance of any society, including American society. The *issei* probably thought so, too. That was their contribution to making us better American citizens. Because of that, by the time I became a POW, I knew exactly who I was and what I stood for as an American. Myths were translated into reality allowing us to experience a kind of "American spirit," not unlike the "Japanese spirit" that I had learned about as a child. Without that grounding, it would have been much harder to endure all the torture and humiliation in prison. I discovered that it is possible to have what I can only describe as a spiritual experience at a time of dire need. The price of faith is often steep and painful, just as it should be. That, too, was impressed on us by the *issei*, but I didn't believe it as a child. In spite of my earlier misgivings, those myths formed the basis of my identity and commitment to citizenship.

For his outstanding wartime service and incomparable demonstration of loyalty to country, Richard M. Sakakida was recognized with the following honors:

- *Admission into the Military Intelligence Hall of Fame at Fort Huachuca, Arizona;*
- *The Defense Medal, Liberation Medal, and National Defense Medal of the Republic of the Philippines;*
- *The Legion of Honor of the Republic of the Philippines;*
- *Naming of the operational facility of the 201st Military Intelligence Brigade at Fort Lewis, Washington, in honor of Lt. Col. Richard M. Sakakida; and*
- *Bronze Star Medal for the December 7, 1941, to May 10, 1942, campaigns in Manila, Bataan, and Corregidor.*

Michael M. Miyatake

442nd Regimental Combat Team/
Military Intelligence Service

COMRADES IN ARMS

On occasion, corps headquarters was asked to provide language assistance for its subordinate units, particularly those in constant contact with the enemy. Assistance was usually sought if a prisoner of war had been captured, or if there weren't enough men at the front to escort the POW to the unit headquarters for initial processing. The only alternative then was to ask a language specialist to volunteer to conduct the interrogation at the front.

GHQ (General Headquarters) had issued a directive to all commanding officers in the Pacific theater: They could not order language personnel beyond Division Headquarters. However, a linguist could volunteer to be sent to the front. This "loophole" was used in such emergencies.

One such request for assistance came from the 112th Regimental Combat Team, which was headquartered in New Guinea along the Driniumor River, near the village of Afua. The enemy, suffering from diseases and injuries and in need of medical treatment and ammunition, had been trying to penetrate our defense to escape toward the Pacific Ocean.

We knew we could be killed at the front, so I decided I would never volunteer. Nine other linguists had to make their own decision. If no one volunteered, the request would be sent to the higher echelon: ATIS (Allied Translator and Interpreter Section), located in Indooroopilly, Brisbane, Australia. That meant a delay of about a week and the possibility that vital intelligence information would be lost.

Later that day a volunteer stepped forward: Henry Morisako. It saddened me to think of him going. But my respect for him grew stronger because of his decision. I wished him the best of luck.

A Jeep came to pick up Hank that night. As he settled into the front seat, I noticed a sad, forlorn look on his face. His mission wasn't a difficult one, but it was a dangerous one.

Hank Morisako and I had volunteered for the 442nd Regimental Combat Team at the same time and, likewise, had also gone through basic training at Camp Shelby, Mississippi. Hank was selected for the Military Intelligence Service Language School because he had attended Japanese-language school in Hawaii. I had met him on the flight from Australia to New Guinea.

I was sad as I watched Hank leave. We had known each other for only a few months, but in that short time he had become my closest companion and confidant.

Hank must have been awfully busy at the front. For nearly two weeks, we heard neither from him nor about him. And then, out of the blue, our team leader called us together. Hank had developed dysentery, a common ailment in the jungles of New Guinea. A replacement was needed so he could leave the front. No one was willing to volunteer, however.

Someone had to replace Hank or he could not be evacuated. Intelligence information would also be lost. With each passing day, Hank's condition grew more serious. The boys knew what they faced at the front if they volunteered. So did I, but I was concerned about Hank. Time was of the essence: I couldn't imagine him suffering any longer. Finally, against my will, I volunteered. I'd never done anything so irrational before, and I knew I would regret my decision later.

The monsoon season had already begun. I was crazy to leave the comforts of camp life to live in the dark jungles of New Guinea. It was suicidal, especially because I had to go to the front, where I would be in constant contact with the enemy.

I was ready to leave in no time. All I carried with me were my duffel bag and a field pack filled with tools I would need at the front. My Jeep arrived after supper. It was pouring heavily when I left corps headquarters. Only the driver knew our destination.

Within minutes we were surrounded by darkness. We seemed to be going though unmapped terrain. It was harrowing weaving through the bushes in the torrential rain, which nearly blinded our view of what lay ahead. I was afraid our Jeep would fall into a ditch.

Fortunately, the enemy had been pushed inland and we were driving through an area secured by friendly forces. Two hours later we came to a clearing. I was welcomed by a group of nisei from the 32nd Division Headquarters Language Team headed by Sgt. Mas Yamamoto. It was too early to go to bed, so I went to the language team's tent to listen to their stories and advice.

I was told not to answer when my name was called by someone whose voice was not familiar—for the caller could be an enemy. They also warned me to be very careful, because I could be mistaken as the enemy disguised in an American uniform. Although I would be protected by scouts while enroute to the 112th Regimental Combat Team, the men would certainly consider me the enemy if they couldn't identify me by looks—for even among our own troops there were men who had never met a nisei.

I was also told that the enemy didn't know that nisei were gathering intelligence for Allied forces at the front. It was supposed to have been a secret, but I doubted that. The Japanese military was using nisei caught in Japan when the war began to assist in the field and at the front as linguists.

After breakfast, I was introduced to four scouts who were to escort me to the 112th, which was always in contact with the enemy. All intelligence matters, including information on POWs, were being forwarded by them.

When we left the 32nd Division Headquarters, we were advised to be on the lookout for enemy stragglers. We were ordered to report to any regimental headquarters of the 32nd Division and notify the commanding officer of our whereabouts and our plan to proceed to the 112th's headquarters. Even with the escorts, the thought that the men along the line had not seen me and may not be familiar with what a nisei looked like made me nervous.

What if one of them thought I was an enemy POW and shot at me? I wasn't taking any chances; I stuck close to the guards.

My instructions from the 32nd Division Headquarters seemed simple enough to follow, although I later wondered whether they really were. My movements would be slowed by the mud tracks left by the tanks and heavy equipment. I knew I was in trouble from the moment I began plodding into the knee-deep mud. With each step, my feet sank deeper. Progress was slow. I kept thinking I was crazy to have volunteered for this mission.

We finally came to a clearing—a sign that the Driniumor River was close. Suddenly I heard machine-gun, rifle, and mortar fire and grenades exploding. People were yelling. I scrambled for cover in a hole.

The enemy was staging a banzai attack. They were trying to cross over to our side of the river and penetrate our lines, hoping to escape to the coast and return safely to their country.

I found a hole half-filled with water and jumped in without worrying about getting wet. All around me I could see the guards taking cover. As soon as the all-clear sounded, the guards came over to help. I was alright, but my heart was pounding and my legs had locked stiff. I remained in the muddy water for a few minutes before getting out with the guards' help.

We hurriedly located one of the command headquarters and informed them of our whereabouts and the route we were taking to the 112th Regimental Headquarters. We then proceeded toward the riverbank and the 112th, which was situated a few hundred yards beyond the upper reaches of the river.

As we walked out of the area where the fighting had taken place, we had to step over hundreds of dead enemy bodies. Some were still grasping hand grenades, the pin already pulled. The slightest movement of a body could have set off an explosion at any moment.

The sight of blood-strewn bodies everywhere made me nauseated. I felt pity, then anger, and finally disgust to see so many young lives wasted. This was the first time I had witnessed the aftermath of combat. Walking through the area made me more determined than ever to get out of this mess alive and to let people know how pitiful and merciless the front could be. Relieved of the tension that gripped my entire body, I walked more freely toward the path that led deeper into the jungle.

We finally arrived at the command post of the 112th Regimental Combat Team, where we were met by the commanding officer, Brigadier General Cunningham, and his staff of three officers and an enlisted man. I knew I had to get to know as many men in the unit with whom I would be working—and make sure they knew me as well. I began with the general's staff, for I would be working closely with them.

Serving my country on the front lines as an American soldier whose job was to provide language assistance made me feel important. It made me forget the racial discrimination I had experienced. I vowed that I would serve my country bravely and dutifully. I was determined to protect my comrades and do whatever I could to save their lives, even if it meant sacrificing my own, for we were all fighting for a worthwhile cause.

What I had learned in school about democracy, country, duty, and honor did not seem as significant as being out there at the front, facing death. I realized that I had taken my citizenship for granted. I wanted to prove that I was as loyal an American as any other, but also that I was willing to go the extra mile by fighting an enemy who, like me, was of Japanese ancestry.

General Cunningham was a small-statured Texan, about fifty years old. His powerful handshake told me he was not to be taken lightly. He regretted Henry's having to leave but was happy to see me.

Though unheralded, the 112th should have been recognized as one of the most valorous combat units dispatched to the SWAPAC (Southwest Pacific Command). Originally a Texas calvary troop, it was organized by men with Texas roots. The unit had participated in much of the fighting in the southwest Pacific, clearing the enemy from the southern coast of New Guinea to Aitape. The 112th had lost a lot of Texans, who were replaced by men from the Midwest. By the time I joined them at the Driniumor front, most of the men in the unit were replacements from all over the United States.

I was taken to Henry's hammock, where he lay in a daze, suffering. He didn't move as I held his hand. I felt sad to see him so ill. He was too weak to get up or even raise his hand. In spite of his weak condition, Hank had completed all of the translation work that had come in to date.

After setting up my hammock, I was too tired to dig my foxhole in the muddy ground. I climbed into my hammock and fell asleep. It was dark when I awoke, so dark that I didn't realize I was in a forest with thick branches overhead. In basic training, we had learned that the first thing a soldier should do at the front is dig his foxhole. I had not—and would suffer the consequences that night.

After a supper of K rations, I walked to the stream, some twenty-five yards away. I washed up and returned to my hammock to sleep. Suddenly, I heard guns exploding from the direction of Afua in the mountains, followed by explosions as the shells struck the treetops above us. Shrapnel from the projectiles rained to the ground.

I rolled out of my hammock in a flash, looking for cover to escape the falling shrapnel. I hadn't dug my foxhole, so I wrapped my body around a large tree to shield myself.

Hank had rolled out of his hammock and slipped into his nearby foxhole. When he saw me holding on to the tree, he motioned for me to jump in with him. It was a tight fit, but I didn't hesitate, especially with the shells falling closer to our billeting area. Fortunately, we had our steel helmets on to protect our heads.

Enemy bombardments like these were routine, I later learned. The enemy always pulled their guns back into their mountainside caves after firing a few rounds, thereby escaping our guns.

I was grateful that Henry had been kind enough to share his foxhole with me, and it taught me a good lesson about the importance of digging my own. The next morning I dug my foxhole even before washing my face.

The enemy fired at us again that evening, and for several evenings thereafter. Each time I heard the booming sound of the mountain guns, I jumped into my foxhole, regardless of whether it was filled with water.

Our main objective at the front was to keep the enemy away from the coastal area by pushing them farther into the jungles—this I had to help do despite a bout of dysentery and a bad case of "jungle rot," which I contracted two weeks after I joined the 112th. Unfortunately, there was no medication at the front or in the jungle and I could only use what was in my first-aid kit.

The jungle rot started between my toes and quickly spread all over my foot. I had gotten this terrible ailment because I had to keep my boots on all the time, except when I slept—although I always kept my socks on. My feet were always damp from the humidity and perspiration. I hadn't worn a dry pair of boots since leaving the 32nd Division Headquarters.

Although I washed and hung out my socks to dry every day, they would never dry completely in the thick jungle. The branches of the huge trees formed a canopy of cover over us, blocking the sun from penetrating to the ground.

The small can of foot powder in my first-aid kit was gone in less than a week, and there was no more after that. The thick skin that covered the soles of my feet began to dry and crack, out of which a smelly, watery substance oozed. The skin was so dry that whenever I walked, it cracked and hurt terribly. The only thing I could do to keep the skin from cracking was to wrap my feet with dry undershirts, stripped like gauze and bandages. If I did not take care of the rot in this manner, my movement and activities would have been restricted. Each day, the smell grew stronger. Fortunately, no one else was around to complain about it. Each time the bandages were removed, dry scabs stuck to the gauze peeled off, exposing raw flesh. The pain was excruciating. Whenever I changed the bandage, cold sweat formed on my forehead, but the process had to be repeated, or gangrene might have set in—and possible amputation.

Infection resulting from gangrene was common in the jungle. I had seen many cases of it in the field hospital and I couldn't bear to see it attack me. I had to save every bit of bandage and take care of the rot myself, for there were no supplies of gauze or bandages at the front. Jungle rot was not considered a life-threatening condition. In fact, it was a common malady suffered by many men. Fortunately, I had the time to take care of it. There were others on the front line who couldn't unless they were relieved from duty or replaced by someone else.

The rot gradually improved. As it healed, it was replaced by blisters, particularly between my toes. By the time we were ready to leave the jungle, I was receiving supplies of sulphur powder, which dried the open wounds. Taking care of the rot and tending to my language duties kept me busy for the few months I was in the jungle until we received orders to return to Division Headquarters.

I helped Henry Morisako pack the morning he was to leave. The pained look on his face made me wonder whether he would make it to the coast, where a Jeep was waiting for him. To walk out of this jungle in his condition required stamina and fortitude. He walked away from me, unsteadily, toward the group of men who would escort him out of this jungle hell. I prayed that he would make it to the Division Headquarters.

I then returned to improving my area, which I occupied for several days before being ordered to a new position elsewhere. We moved every three to four days; otherwise, the enemy would zero in on our position and blast us with their mountain guns. Each time they fired, I jumped into my foxhole, cursing myself for volunteering for this duty. However, after the firing stopped, I consoled myself by thinking about the adventure I was experiencing and the things I could relate to others when the time came; if not to others, then at least to my children—that is, if I left the jungle alive.

Ben I. Yamamoto

100th Infantry Battalion/Military Intelligence Service

THE ADVENTURES OF AN MIS MARINE

I was born in January in the year 1920 in Pearl City, Oahu. By the time I was ready to attend school, my father owned an auto service and tire recap business near Pearl City. My parents wanted to give me the best education possible—English as well as Japanese—so I was sent to McKinley (public) and Mid Pacific (private) high schools. I also attended Japanese-language school.

My father wanted me to marry a Japanese, so when I began dating a non-Japanese girl, he sent me off to school in Japan. I attended a number of schools in Japan, including Waseda International College, which was attended by many foreign students. Most of us from Hawaii didn't do very well in Japan because it was easier to communicate in English among ourselves, and also because we were there largely at our parents' urging.

I returned to Hawaii and enrolled at the University of Hawaii. In my second year in the university ROTC program, I was drafted into the

U.S. Army. It was November 1941, one month before Japan's attack on Pearl Harbor. I was assigned to the ethnically mixed 298th Infantry National Guard unit. Draftees from the neighbor islands were assigned to the 299th National Guard.

In June 1942 the Hawaii National Guard units segregated those soldiers of Japanese ancestry and sent them to Schofield Barracks. There were about fifteen hundred of us. Soon after, we boarded a converted troopship, the SS *Maui*, and shipped off to Oakland. From there, we traveled by rail to Camp McCoy, Wisconsin, where we were formed into a Japanese American unit, the 100th Infantry Battalion (Separate).

My 100th Battalion buddies established a fantastic fighting record in Italy and France. But it was not my fate to remain with the outfit.

The commanders in the Pacific theater were desperate to learn the enemy's tactics and strategy. They needed Japanese-language specialists to interpret and translate voice messages and written documents and to interrogate captured prisoners. My service record indicated that I had a comparatively high exposure to Japanese-language training. In December 1942 I was directed to join the newly established Military Intelligence Service Language School at Camp Savage, Minnesota, along with about seventy others from the 100th Battalion. Our group was among the first to graduate from the school. Upon graduation in June 1943 we were transferred to Fort Snelling, where we awaited our assignment.

About a week after we moved to Fort Snelling, five of us—three Hawaiians and two *kotonks*—were shipped out. Again, we didn't know where we were headed. We were taken to the Presidio in San Francisco, where we were assigned to inspect boxes of Japanese documents from Attu and Kiska in the Aleutian Islands. We enjoyed the good chow there and took in the movies at the base theater, all the time wondering what was really in store for us.

The answer came about a week later when a truck arrived and drove us into the hills about five miles east of San Francisco to a place called Byron Hot Springs.

Assignment: Byron Hot Springs

I had heard Byron Hot Springs was a popular hideaway resort for Hollywood people and other celebrities before the war. There was a three-story building and, a short distance away, a warm mineral-water swimming pool and mud baths. Swimming in the mineral water was soothing, but I never mustered enough courage to submerge myself in the bubbling black mud. Those who tried it said they liked it.

The army had taken over this resort and converted it into a prisoner-of-war camp—more precisely, an interrogation center. There was tight security around the building. German, Japanese, and Italian POWs were held in the second- and third-floor rooms. Our offices were on the ground floor. There were interrogation sections for the different groups: The Italian section shut down shortly after our arrival. Several officers and enlisted men, all Caucasians, were already there as interrogators in the Japanese section. The section chief was a lieutenant colonel who had a good command of the language.

My baptism to interrogation came immediately when I was assigned an infantry lieutenant who had been captured at Guadalcanal. He told me repeatedly during our talks that he was captured only because he was unconscious. I remember this particular POW, not only because he was my first but also because of an interesting coincidence. He was a graduate of Doshisha University in Kyoto, where he had taken an English course taught by George Sakamaki of Honolulu. I told him that Sakamaki's younger brother, Ben, was a college chum of mine. We both agreed what a small world it was.

There weren't many POWs coming in yet, so I had this lieutenant for four or five days. He told me he would not divulge any military information but volunteered to talk about subjects my superiors might find interesting. And they did. They found his evaluation of our equipment, tactics, the fighting qualities of the army, marines, Aussies, and so forth very interesting.

Life was good there, working in an air-conditioned building and bunking in the same barracks with the service staff and German-speaking Jews who had escaped from their German captors and come to America. They had been hired by the U.S. Army as German-language specialists. We were like a family. The work was intriguing, too. I thought I had it made: All I had to do was stay put for the duration.

There was a steady flow of prisoners for two or three months, then the pace really picked up. I began interrogating two to three subjects a day, at times working into the evening. Occasionally, we were awakened at 4 A.M. and sent to Angel Island or to Letterman's Hospital in San Francisco to interview POWs who had just arrived there. Still, I found the work interesting.

After several months, however, my nerves were getting ragged. I was afraid that if I continued with this grind, I might end up a Section 8 candidate. I knew I would regret later giving up such a good position, but I decided to request a transfer. I think my superiors saw that we were approaching the breaking point, so after thirteen months at Byron, we, the first nisei assigned there, were transferred out. In the meantime, many reinforcements from Savage had arrived. Leaving Byron was a sad but necessary move for me because I was too burned out, physically and emotionally, to continue that type of work.

Assignment: JICPOA's Annex

After a brief return to Fort Snelling for a meeting with John Aiso, I received my new assignment: Honolulu, Hawaii. I couldn't believe my good fortune. Hawaii, after almost two-and-a-half years on the mainland!

I joined a group of fifty MISers, half of whom were army, navy, and marine officers. The remainder were enlisted men. This was JICPOA's (Joint Intelligence Center, Pacific Ocean Area) annex. This group had been loaned to the navy, and the men had gone on invasion campaigns with the marines to such places as Tinian and Saipan. Between campaigns, the men were kept busy translating captured documents in the office upstairs. Sleeping quarters were on the ground level. We received stipends from the navy, so we had our meals at restaurants. We generally went across the street to McKinley Grill.

The move to Hawaii was a good deal. It gave me a chance to visit my family in Pearl City and enjoy local food. I got carried away and even got married. What distressed me at this time was the anti-Japanese sentiments expressed by some in the local dailies—in spite of the great number of us in uniform putting our lives on the line!

The honeymoon didn't last long. We were told to enjoy our 1944 holidays because some of us would be shipping out with the marines right after the new year.

Assignment: Iwo Jima

After participating in a landing exercise off Maui, I kissed my young bride good-bye, and a team of us shoved off with Headquarters Company, 4th Marine Division, stationed on Maui. Again, destination unknown. We had no trouble blending in with the marines. For the few who were cool toward us, there were many others who went out of their way to put us at ease.

Two days before arriving at our destination, the company commander assembled the men for a briefing. Our destination, he revealed, was Iwo Jima. Our mission: Invade and secure the island, for it was needed as a refueling point for our Saipan- and Tinian-based B-25s after their bombing flights to Japan. The island was expected to be pretty "soft," for it had been heavily shelled and bombed for an entire month.

That assumption did not bear out. The marines learned only after landing that the enemy's weapons were carefully concealed in over a thousand caves with only the muzzles of the guns pointing out. Our month-long aerial bombing and pounding by naval guns had hardly made a dent in their destruction. Our reconnaissance photos did not show the clever network of their caves. The roughly twenty-two thousand enemy count was more accurate; they were not decimated as was believed. Thus, the backup marine divisions had to be committed, and what was supposed to be a campaign involving very little resistance developed into the fiercest slugfest in the Pacific.

I hit the beach on the fourth day and found a stack of dead marines and a group of live ones sitting with blank stares. These gyrenes had cracked. They were so gung ho on the transport, but two or three nights on the front lines had broken them. This was not an encouraging start for me.

We were assigned to an area near the airstrip and told to dig in and wait for orders. The first night's mortar barrage was a nightmare, with shrapnel landing too close for comfort. I regretted that I hadn't stuck it out at Byron. I noticed that the marines had large shelters fortified with sandbags, which they had gotten from the supply area about a hundred yards away. I started off to get some for my shelter construction.

As I neared the area, a shot rang out and a marine ten yards behind me fell to the ground: He had been shot in the forehead. Everybody dived for cover. As I started to get up, someone pushed me down. It was a Seabee officer, holding a .45 automatic a few inches from my face, demanding to know who I was. After grilling me and checking my identification, I told him that I was an interrogator with the 4th Marines. He let me go, but not without a stern lecture to stay in my own area. How were his men to know that I wasn't a Jap sniper wearing a marine uniform, he scolded. At the moment, I recalled something that either Colonel Rasmussen or Major Joseph K. Dickey had told us back at Savage: We could be shot at not only by the enemy when we went overseas, but by our own men as well. How true those words were, I realized.

The Seabees deserve a lot of credit for the work they did during the war. On Iwo, they worked nonstop under enemy fire to repair the airstrip. From the day I landed, our bombers were already landing for fueling.

After my brush with the Seabee officer, I didn't do much roving around on my own. Some of the other guys were used for cave-flushing and for searching for manufacturers' tags on enemy equipment. I was ordered to stay put and be available for interrogation. As it turned out, fighting on Iwo was so fast and furious—and in only eight square miles of terrain—that I rarely did any interrogation work. There were only two instances in which marine line officers came racing down in their Jeeps to take me to the front lines to interrogate captured enemy soldiers. In both instances, by the time we got to them they were barely alive and unable to talk.

When we got to our area to dig in, the stench of the dead was so overpowering that I couldn't eat or drink water for two days. Human parts of the dead could be seen in the volcanic cinder. After awhile, though, nothing bothered us and I subsisted on cheese and crackers. One day, one of the guys came back with a full case of *iwashi no kabayaki* he had found in a cave. We forgot about our rations for a few days and feasted on the broiled sardines.

We sailed back to Hawaii at a leisurely pace, relaxing topside day and night and enjoying the peace and quiet for a change. Some of our guys and several marines could be seen taking stock of the souvenirs they had collected on Iwo. Our faces clearly showed how happy we were to be the ones sailing away—still breathing—from that speck in the ocean.

Back home at the annex, there were a few parties for us. I still had the "shakes" from what we had experienced on Iwo.

Soon rumors began circulating that our next assignment would be with the 5th Amphibious Corps, assigned to take Kagoshima, Japan. Invading Japan was entirely different from the island invasions of the past, so the rumor weighed heavily on our minds.

Rejoicing replaced apprehension when Japan surrendered following the atomic bombing of Hiroshima and Nagasaki in August 1945. Two days after the surrender, we were flown to Guam, where the men were paired off and dispatched to the various islands that had been by-passed to inform them that Japan had surrendered and that they, too, should surrender. The guys later told me that getting the Japanese to surrender did not come easily. In many cases, the Japanese fired at them. Another guy and I were kept on Guam, but he was whisked away on a mission one night, leaving me alone.

Assignment: Guam

Early one morning, at about 2 A.M., I was awakened by a marine captain who wanted me to help him process about fifteen hundred POWs from Rota Island. At the time, I had no idea that I would be working until 2 o'clock the following morning, helping with the physical feeding, billeting, and so forth.

A funny thing happened when I lost my voice that afternoon: The captain who had gotten me out of bed noticed, grabbed me by my belt, and hoisted me into his Jeep. "You and I are going for some medicine," he said. He dashed over to the Officers Club, where we had a couple of beers. The medicine worked—a 100 percent cure.

Back to the POWs: Navy and marine officers were in desperate need of interpreters. It made me feel good to realize how indispensable I was.

The highlight of this episode was the arrival of the commander of the Marianas Islands, a vice admiral, to "greet" the POWs. I wasn't notified in advance that I would have to translate his speech. Perhaps no one knew that he was going to speak. The admiral was on the platform. I was about a hundred yards away when I heard the call for an interpreter. Answering the call on the double, I climbed the platform, panting. He looked at me from head to boots; it wasn't a look of approval. I realized then how shabby I must have looked, unshaven and in muddy uniform and boots. It had rained that afternoon and I'd had to slosh around in the mud.

After mildly admonishing me for keeping him waiting, the admiral commenced with his speech. I assumed that my role was to translate. His opening remarks were fairly easy, but when he began delving into such technical matters as the League of Nations, Geneva Convention, the treatment of POWs as mandated by international law, and so on, I knew this job was not for a mere Section 12 student like me. It called for the expertise of someone with a Section 1 or Section 2 ranking. Since there was no getting out of the situation, I bluffed my way through the ordeal in the presence of an all-Caucasian audience of marine and navy personnel, reporters, and photographers.

Without stammering, I pulled off a neat imitation speech translation that rivaled a performance of Chinese actors playing the role of Japanese in Hollywood war movies. The speech was no longer than five minutes long, but it seemed like an eternity to me.

After finishing his speech, the admiral decided to walk through the rows of POWs, asking many questions along the way. This kind of translating was right up my alley, and I showed the admiral how capable I was. He was especially curious about the wooden boxes, or *okotsu*, wrapped in white cloth, which many of the POWs carried. The admiral ended his inspection by thanking me.

As soon as I was able to, I sought out the Japanese commanding officer, a major, to explain the admiral's speech. He commented, "*Wakatta setsumei wa iran* (I understand; you need not explain). . . . *Daisho eigo wa shitte iru* (I understand some English). . . . *Kimi no nihongo wa mazui na* (Your Japanese is pretty lousy). . . . *Tsuyaku hei ka* (Are you a military interpreter)?" We both had a good laugh. He questioned me about conditions in Hawaii, adding that he had a sister living on the island of Hawaii.

My orders were to proceed to U.S. Navy headquarters in Sasebo, Japan, after thirty days on Guam, although the order didn't state how I was to get there. Nearly three weeks had passed, and, at the time, I was the only member of our outfit still on Guam. With the war's abrupt end, there was some confusion at the time.

After some inquiring, I got the name of our chief, a commander at Pearl Harbor. In desperation, I wrote to him, asking whether I should return to Hawaii for discharge, or go on to Sasebo. If I was to go to Sasebo, how would I get there, I asked. He replied promptly, saying he understood the confusion on Guam because it was much the same at Pearl. He suggested that I befriend the marines and hitch a ride to Okinawa on one of their planes and then continue on to Sasebo. He wished me good luck. In the meantime, the other interrogator had returned, so the two of us traveled to Sasebo in the manner prescribed by the commander.

Assignment: Japan

When we arrived at Sasebo, about half of our outfit was already there. I was assigned a tedious job: assist in inventorying the torpedoes in various storage locations. There were two Japanese navy officers and a crew of civilians. I was issued a .38 revolver, a holster, and twenty-one rounds of ammunition to protect myself. After all, we did not know how we would be received by the natives.

I packed my six-shooter with me the first two days and was careful not to let any Japanese get behind me. It was an awkward, uncomfortable relationship, with some of the Japanese men casting embarrassing glances at my gun. These people didn't look dangerous at all; in fact, they looked much like the issei back home. On the third day I left my firearms at home. They reacted beautifully. They warmed up to me and worked more enthusiastically. We shared our lunch with each other and played volleyball during our breaks, among other things. I started going to an officer's apartment for *sake* and learned to "suck 'em up," Japanese style. The other officer insisted that I accept his short sword as a memento, a navy issue, since they had lost the war. I still have it.

Some of the neighborhood kids came to our dormitory to visit with us. They looked malnourished and small for their age. We gave them what goodies we had. They tried to return the favors by giving us things.

One little boy gave me a natural pearl he had found on the beach. Another boy told me his mother wanted to do my laundry. Thinking that she offered to do this to earn some money, I let the kid take my soiled clothing home. The boy returned two days later with my laundry neatly folded. I tried to pay him, but he refused payment. This continued during my month-long stay in Sasebo. Later, when woolens were issued to us, I gave all of them to the boy to keep. He later showed me the mittens his mother had made from them.

When it became apparent that my departure was near, I gathered a carton of foodstuffs from my kitchen and made a farewell call on the boy's family. His mother, a young widow, served me *sake* and *sashimi*, which I knew she could ill-afford. I forced them to accept most of the cash I had with me.

I relate these stories to describe the friendly relations that flourished spontaneously with the Japanese. I'm glad I was able to come to Japan at this early period of the occupation, before ending my military service. As Americans, we were there not as arrogant conquerors but with hands extended in friendship and humanity.

One night a member of our outfit, who was a messenger and truck driver, told me he had arranged to take the next day off. He talked me into driving to Nagasaki for a view of the A-bombed city. We got a third guy to join us and left early the next morning for the three- to four-hour drive.

I was not prepared for what I saw of Nagasaki. I was shocked and horrified to see that there was nothing left of the historic city: It was completely obliterated. I shuddered at the thought that a miniature bomb of less than fifty pounds was capable of all that destruction. What I saw around me for miles defied all comprehension. All I could mutter was, "Oh, my God!" There was an eerie silence. The only life I saw were a few people poking around in the rubble. Some gave me a quick glance, their faces expressionless.

This was less than two months after the bombing. Interestingly, there was no knowledge of the health hazards of radiation at the time. Had there been, the entire contaminated area would surely have been tightly sealed off. We drove back to Sasebo mostly in silence, all of us visibly shaken.

It gives me a weird feeling to know that what we saw of Nagasaki in 1945 was a sneak preview of what to expect the next time around—only now we know that the next blast will make Hiroshima and Nagasaki look like mere firecracker poppings.

The day came to say *sayonara* to Sasebo when there was space available on a destroyer for a bunch of us. Had I known what a destroyer ride was going to be like, I would have declined. After twenty days of zigzagging across the Pacific, shedding twenty pounds along the way, I set foot on the deck at Pearl Harbor, reinstated to civilian status—November 15, 1945—four years and one day after induction into the army. Whew! What a ride the four long years had been! I thought about the guy who said, "Going to war is an experience you couldn't buy with a million bucks, but I wouldn't take a million bucks to go through it again."

This is the first time I put my World War II experiences in writing. It was like opening the flood gates.

There is no doubt in my mind that we MISers were the special tool needed to expedite the Pacific war, bringing it to an earlier end, thereby saving countless numbers of lives on both sides. I would also like to think that our service, along with the outstanding service of our nisei brothers in the European combat units, contributed much to help the cause of Americans of Japanese ancestry.

Sakae Takahashi

100th Infantry Battalion

WE LOVED OUR COUNTRY

The following narrative is based on an oral history interview with Sakae Takahashi that was conducted in 1995 by Karen Ishizuka and Robert Nakamura for the Japanese American National Museum.

I think the fact that the 100th Infantry Battalion was a segregated unit— and I want to make that distinction, *all* Japanese Americans—made for a real closeness among all of us. Most of the fellas in the 100th were from Hawaii; there were just a few from the mainland. The 442nd had quite a few from the mainland United States.

Many of the men in the 100th also knew each other—we played with each other, went to school together. So, we were close to each other and worked very well together as a unit. We all felt that not only should we do well in combat, but we should also do well in order to erase some of the discriminating stereotypes of the Japanese and to help the issei here in Hawaii.

We were Americans of Japanese ancestry and our country was at war with the country to which we traced our ancestry. In spite of that, I never felt torn about my parents being from Japan. My father told me, "You are an American citizen. This is your country. In fact, this is my country, too, because I've been a resident for almost all my life." Although he could not become a citizen at that time, he said, "Do the best you can for your country. But don't bring any shame, that's all." That's typical of the Japanese ethic.

In Italy, the Germans fought defensively—holding on to their strong points, trying to inflict casualties on us. Once we moved forward and could overwhelm them, they'd move back to another point. We seldom saw the enemy really in force. We ran into a lot of artillery fire, a lot of mines. Because they were on the defensive, the Germans laid a lot of mines. They threw a lot of artillery and used their tanks effectively. The tanks were all armed with deadly and dangerous "eighty-eight" guns, whose shells exploded before you could hear the boom of the gun. If they went over you, you could feel it graze by and hear the "whoosh" right over your head. It was very frightening.

I think once the guys got used to such enemy artillery fire, they knew when they were coming, so, as much as possible, they avoided getting hit by the exploding shells. But there were casualties caused by these weapons.

The Germans also had a knack for keeping the high ground. Those who went up ahead were usually pinned down with machine-gun fire. Very seldom did they fight close.

They also didn't like to fight at night. Our boys used to like to go out after them at night. Whenever we sent patrols out, if they ran into the enemy, invariably, they'd beat them. Once in a while, some of them might get hurt, but most of our night patrols were very successful.

It's hard to describe what it was like to be in combat. Everybody's scared, but you've got to move forward; you've got to overcome that fear. Once you start moving, you build up courage. The worst time is when you're sitting still and waiting, because that's when you start reflecting on what might happen and your fear of getting wounded or killed comes out. It's an awesome feeling, but you can overcome it. Once you start moving forward, especially if you're *successfully* moving forward, that fear gives way to the real fighting spirit. You want to go ahead and get it done with.

The 100th and 442nd suffered lots of casualties. Some people have said that we were expendable, that we were like "cannon fodder." I don't believe that. We just didn't have enough troops. We could have been much more successful, for instance, if the 100th had been the size of the 442nd—three thousand troops. But we were only thirteen hundred.

They used us because we were successful; we were good fighters. All the generals will attest to that. They could trust us. And the more fighting you get involved in, the more casualties you're going to suffer. By the time we reached Cassino, my company strength was down to only 46 men out of an initial authorized strength of 190. Most of them were casualties, killed or wounded; not too many were killed, but enough of them were. Most were wounded.

In my own personal experience, I've known discrimination, but I ignored it. There was an instance when I was on duty on the island of Kauai before I joined the 100th. The 27th Division, a New York National Guard unit, had been shipped out to Hawaii. One of its regiments was deployed on Kauai. There was a General Michael Anderson who issued a general order saying that the nisei in the service there could not visit their parents unless their parents were American citizens.

We completely ignored his order, because we felt that this guy was a stupid general. If we got caught, we got caught. But we weren't going to ignore our parents just because this guy from New York had this bias.

A side note: The strangest thing happened in connection with this General Anderson. When the first group of replacement officers came to me before Cassino, there was a young second lieutenant named Anderson. When he came to the unit, I asked him, "Are you by chance from New York?" "Yes," he answered. "Do you know a General Anderson?" "That's my father," he replied.

In Cassino, Lieutenant Daniel Anderson went out on a patrol with about five men. One of the guys got wounded and couldn't get over a wall, so Lieutenant Anderson went back, picked him up, and pushed him over the wall. While he himself tried to climb over the wall again, Lieutenant Anderson was shot in the head and killed. He was a great soldier.

There are people who discriminate, but the best thing to do is to ignore them, because there are more people who recognize the good things about you.

If I could leave anything for future generations in terms of the experiences of the 100th, I would want them to know that we fought for the United States because we loved our country. We were born and raised here and we were taught what democracy is, what it is to be an American. We participated like other soldiers. We'd grumble because of the discomforts and the things that we suffered. But we fought for our country because we were loyal to our country.

We also knew that there was a lot of discrimination, not only against the Japanese people here but against other racial groups as well. One of the ways we could mitigate or reduce discrimination was to show people that we were as good as any other American. If need be, we'd fight again. I hope future generations feel the same way.

Robert T. Sato

100th Infantry Battalion

MONTE CASSINO: PURPLE HEART VALLEY

The United States government made four draft calls prior to December 1941. Draftees were required to serve one year in the armed forces, indefinitely if war erupted.

In Hawaii, several thousand men were drafted and assigned to the 298th and 299th Infantry Regiment of the federalized Hawaii National Guard. It should be noted that slightly over half of the draftees were of Japanese ancestry.

The nisei draftees, however, learned sadly that enlistment in the navy, Coast Guard, marines, and air force was closed to them. However, issei parents were somewhat satisfied that their sons would be allowed to serve in the army. The nisei draftees were treated very well, not only by the issei, but the community also welcomed them.

During our basic training at Schofield, a weekend pass was issued to us quite regularly—that was the highlight of our army life. There was a very kind gentleman who lived in Kaimuki, who loved the nisei boys in uniform so much that he invited us to many restaurants and nightclubs. Some of us were not familiar with drinking but enjoyed the atmosphere, anyway. The nisei boys in uniforms were so popular that people invited them to many parties.

Richard Honda and I were invited to a farewell party together because his parents and my parents came from the same prefecture in Japan. The families, relatives, and friends, young and old, gathered to bid us "aloha" and gave us some envelopes containing money, and beautiful leis.

Richard and I were drafted at the same time in March 1941. Everyone shook our hands so happily, saying, "*Omedeto* (Congratulations)!" and "*Ganbatte* (Do your best)!" Those days, there was no such thing as karaoke singing, so people sang with samisen and sometimes with *shakuhachi* (bamboo flute). It was the most enjoyable and memorable party I ever attended.

I always wanted to know how Richard was killed in action in Italy. He was my very best friend. Many years ago, this heartwarming and amazing story was written by Raymond Nosaka of Club 100, based on the account of Richard Nakahara of A Company, who was digging a trench side by side with my friend, Richard Honda:

"Not too long ago, a letter written in Italian was received by the wife of KIA (killed in action) Richard Honda. Translated, it read:

> *Gentle Lady: Eight days ago, while walking up the mountain, looking for and digging up vegetables, I uncovered the body of your husband. Tag #30,100,958 T-43, Richard Honda. With all due course, I notified the American Command in Rome and they immediately took the body to the American Cemetery. I am sending you condolences from Italy. Signed, Potane Antoniccceo*

"We were in a small excavation at the base of a small cliff. It offered protection, but not completely, so Honda and I dug in a little more because we were on the firing line. He got tired quickly and I told him to lie down and be comfortable while I finished digging.

"Between three and four in the afternoon, an explosion caused the small cliff behind us to crumble. Honda and I were buried in the mass of rubble, stone, and dirt. However, I was buried up to my neck sitting up. Honda was completely buried for a few minutes. I felt his leg move, then it was quiet."

Richard was a good soldier and a kind-hearted gentleman, who never tired of smiling. Richard Honda, your tremendous accomplishments will long be remembered with deep affection and the highest admiration from all of us.

John Tsukano
100th Infantry Battalion/
442nd Regimental Combat Team

HELL IN THE VOSGES

The calendar says it's still October, but the freezing weather says it's winter. And it's still raining. When it's not raining, it's drizzling and foggy.

Our wet socks never dry out in our wet boots. Our attempts to keep our extra pair of socks dry by keeping them next to our bodies are unsuccessful. They remain damp. We are never completely dry. We are always cold and shivering; our teeth chatter. Our fingers are numb and are beginning to swell. Our eyes smart from the bitter cold. It surely must be the coldest and wettest October in living memory.

Why is it so? Are the steady and often violent bombardments upsetting the delicate balance of nature in the atmosphere, thereby starting a chain reaction of more rain, thunder, and more rain? Could this be true? Probably not. But it is an interesting theory.

The fog-shrouded forest and even the sky look gloomy and belligerent. Thunder roars and reverberates through the valleys and forests, again and again.

The towering pine trees reach ever upward. The dark clouds part and allow the sun's rays to filter through the thick forest, through the branches and leaves, to the ground. They create an illusion of many sunlit rays and paths to the heavens. The scene, though it doesn't last long, is inspiring and memorable.

Enemy artillery barrages, including the terrifying six-barrel *nebelwerfer* (screaming meemies) pound and torment us mercilessly. It seems that the enemy has an unlimited supply of shells. We wonder where they are all coming from.

In Italy we generally knew where the enemy was located. Here in the Vosges forests and mountains the enemy could be anywhere—in the front, back, side, or right under us. Machine-gun nests and foxholes are so cleverly camouflaged that we are not aware of them until we are practically on top of them. Another worry, which is constantly in the back of our minds with each step we take, are the diabolical personnel mines, lurking just a few inches underground.

The enemy has made one point perfectly clear: He is going to make us pay dearly for every yard we gain. We get a gut feeling that this campaign is going to be unlike any other we have ever been in.

Another night is approaching. Our imaginations begin to work overtime. The tall pine trees, silhouetted against the sky, begin to assume human characteristics. The shattered branches become shattered limbs, outstretched, ready to embrace us, or crush us. The leaves, swaying rhythmically in the wind, emit a whistling, haunting sound, beckoning, seducing us to Valhalla above us.

Still another night has come, and with it total, pitch-black darkness. We put our hands an inch away from our eyes to see how dark it really is. We cannot see our own hands. Darkness is absolute. We wonder if this is what hell is like. The sense of sound takes over. A crackling twig becomes approaching boots, the enemy's.

Even the artillery shells assume personalities, more evil and menacing in the night, ever prowling in the darkness, like hired assassins out to get us. The brilliant flashes of red, followed immediately by exploding shells, strike terror in our hearts.

The totality of the silence and darkness in the forest is inexplicable. But the enemy makes sure that shells are sent our way intermittently throughout the night. We suspect that the enemy is trying to prevent us from having a peaceful sleep, as much as trying to kill and maim us. If so, they are doing a good job. The combination of total darkness and silence in the foreboding forest is eerie.

Thoughts come floating to us, like in a dream sequence. Parents, sisters, brothers, and for the older soldiers—sweethearts, wives, children—

of carefree and sunny days. All beautiful and comforting thoughts. Then the sudden explosion of a single shell shatters the stillness of the night and along with it the beautiful thoughts, bringing us back to reality. The switch is startling and nerve-racking, especially when the shell lands right in our midst. Each close call begins to erode our nervous system. How much erosion can the human body take before it breaks down completely? Is there a limit to human endurance?

Our slit trenches give us a measure of protection. But since we are in the forest and had no time to cover the trenches with logs, they offer incomplete protection from the dreaded shrapnel falling from above. The shells land on the treetops, spitting out red-hot, jagged steel and splintered wood down on us in the slit trenches. It's no wonder our bodies become tense, waiting for the next shell. Not knowing when or where the next shell is going to land is disconcerting. It's Russian roulette. We often wonder if the enemy artillery men are aware of the terror they cause in us and how often they are in our minds.

There is much pettiness in war. Why would the enemy go through so much trouble harassing us in the night, keeping us on edge hour after hour, trying to keep us from sleeping? Of course, the question is rhetorical. This is war. We do the same to them. We are like children in many ways. We hit them. They hit us back. They punish us. We punish them back. We attack. They counterattack. They hold back a little. We hold back a little. Is there a subliminal message both sides are trying to flash to each other without being aware of it?

The universal desire for peace and goodwill must surely be in the heart and soul of every soldier, except for the demented who truly love wars. True or not, this noble thought of peace is quickly relegated to the deep recesses of our minds, as if we are ashamed of such thoughts. They disappear in the ever-present mist and we are back to the business as usual of killing the enemy at every opportunity, using every trick and tactic to demoralize him, crush his will and spirit to fight, as if noble thoughts of peace and goodwill had never crossed our minds. And the enemy does the same. Could this be because soldiers are afraid that these thoughts are unpatriotic and even treasonable?

This is not to say that the soldiers on both sides are entirely without humanity. Many acts of compassion by individual soldiers are seen and talked about on both sides. A young German prisoner, who must still be in his teens is dying. Quietly and trustingly, he entrusts his personal belongings to one of our men. His last words are, "Please tell my mother and father about my last moments and give them this pouch." Among the items in the pouch is a family portrait, apparently taken just before he left the family hearth for the army.

An observer for the German artillery is caught doing his job, spotting the movements of the 100th Battalion. He hears leaves rustling behind him. He looks back and sees the barrel of a tommy gun pointed at his head. A lightning thought races through his mind that this is the end for him. A close-up look at the soldier pointing the gun at him does not relieve the fear racing through his entire body. The soldier with the gun looks grim and fearless, unlike any soldier he's seen so far. Up to this instant, as an observer, he had only observed figures from a distance. Now he's staring into a face that does not measure up to what he thinks a soldier should look like. This soldier has . . . oriental features. His fear rises another notch. He soon finds out that his fears were groundless. He is passed on to other 100th Battalion soldiers and is given food and water. One of the 100th soldiers asks his name and the town in Germany where he came from. The information is stored in the memory bank of the 100th Battalion soldier. Many decades later, this bit of information is destined to involve the son of the famous German Gen. Erwin Rommel.

Our officers and men, for the most part, are devoid of hatred for the enemy. There is a maturity and understanding about the whole nasty business of war and the role of the enemy combat soldier that is truly remarkable. Once the enemy is a prisoner of war, he has entered into another dimension and is treated with respect and dignity.

Of course, there are exceptions, on both sides. One of them occurred on Hill D when the Germans shot and killed Sgt. Abraham Ohama as he lay on a stretcher, being evacuated by our medics. This incident occurred while the outcome of the battle for Hill D was still in question. It was a grave mistake on the part of the Germans, for every member in the unit who witnessed this incident was furious. Without orders, the entire unit charged and killed fifty of the enemy without taking any prisoners. Several Germans saved themselves by hiding and surrendering later, when things had cooled down.

The dreary nights wear on. It is still raining. Will it never stop? We are soaking wet. Our raincoats are no help. We are freezing and miserable. We want to strip off our soaking clothes for dry ones. But that's wishful thinking. Even if we could, we'd be soaking wet within an hour. We yearn to be dry again; we yearn for a warm bed in a quiet and safe place—more than food, more than anything. Our muscles are trembling and aching. Our lips are cracking. Our feet are throbbing and swelling. The shells are more frequent and insistent. They seem to want more blood. Thunder roars again. It portends all kinds of scary and evil happenings.

Rifle shots and the *ra-tat-tat-tat* and *brrrrrrrrrrp brrrrrrrp* of machine guns and the fast Schmeisser machine pistols puncture the night. They sound puny compared to the solid and heavier sounds of the artillery shells. We can understand the artillery shells firing away in the dark, but we can't understand the small-arms fire, as absolutely nothing can be seen in the total darkness. We wonder who is shooting whom and what are they shooting at. Who in his right mind would be prowling around on a night like this?

Surprise, surprise. We are. Like in a nightmare, we hear an urgent voice: "Get up, get up. We gotta move in fifteen minutes." It's no nightmare. It's the voice of the sergeant. We can't believe what we are hearing. Go where? It's so dark we can't see a thing, not even our hands right in front of our faces. We are still groggy. We must not have slept long. We obey immediately, automatically. To be the obedient soldier is ingrained in us. We pack our gear in the dark. We are ready to march at the specified time. We start marching. It's so dark we have to keep in touch by holding on to the shoulders of whomever is in front of us. We march for a couple of hours, groping in the dark. We slip and fall on the slippery ground. We don't know where we are headed. We wonder who is leading us. How does he know where he is going? The full field pack, weapons, and ammunition on our backs and shoulders get heavier and heavier. We are so weary. We are so tired. We are like walking zombies.

We are in and out of the forest. We must be backtracking. We must be walking in circles. We seem to be getting nowhere. After all the walking, we seem like we're where we began.

Dawn is breaking. The task of taking Bruyeres is already behind us. The four hills have been secured and the house-to-house fighting is over. Bruyeres is liberated at great cost. Hill D is taken, then reoccupied by the enemy, and retaken by the 3rd Battalion. We see a sign on the road. It says "Bruyeres." It means nothing to us, just like any of the dozens of towns the battalion and regiment liberated in Italy. They all look the same to us. We march on. Max Henri Moulin, leader of the FFI (Freedom Fighters of the Interior); Jean Drahon, scout for the 100th Infantry Battalion; Bello, scout for the 442nd; Serge Carlesso, the youth who lost his leg; Dr. Raymond Collin—we don't know them, yet.

We make a turn toward another group of mountains in the distance. We are now on flat ground, in the open. We notice a ditch running alongside the narrow road. It has stopped raining. It's only drizzling. The sun is trying to break through the dark clouds. We feel uneasy. Somehow, we feel exposed, naked. We know the enemy occupies the imposing hills in the distance. They are not the hills the 100th and the 442nd have already taken. They are new hills to be conquered. Just like Italy. There's always another hill to be taken.

Doesn't the enemy see us? We expect an artillery barrage at any moment. Our bodies are tense, ready for anything. What a target—a large part of the whole battalion exposed in the open. How could this be? Surely the officers must know what they are doing. They have the bigger picture. We enlisted men only know what's happening in our immediate small circle. We follow orders. But we also know that concealment, camouflage, surprise are all important in battle. These principles were hammered into us during training. But here we are, exposed in the open, telling the enemy where we are and where we are headed.

The expected artillery barrage so far has not materialized. What is the enemy doing? Here is a battalion that had inflicted so much damage, killed, wounded, and captured so many of their elite SS troops and materiel from Salerno to Cassino; Anzio all the way up the boot to Rome; Belvedere; Leghorn; Florence to Pisa; and practically to the Gothic line before we were transferred to the French front. Of course, the enemy doesn't know all this. Even so, this is too good a target for them to ignore.

The enemy is just not taking advantage of the opportunity to destroy their nemesis in Italy—the 100th Infantry Battalion. It's offered to them on a silver platter and the enemy is not feasting on the banquet. When we were in the thick forest, they always seemed to know exactly where we were and were never bashful about throwing barrages to groups even as small as squads. And here we are, almost an entire battalion in the open, perfect targets, and they are not lifting a finger to destroy us. We can't believe our luck, but we never let our guard down.

Our alert ears pick up the drone of airplanes. We look up. Two Messerschmidts with Nazi insignias under their wings appear out of the dark clouds and are diving down on us. We are caught completely flat-footed. They are so low that we can see the pilots' faces. Incredibly, unbelievably, the pilots hesitate momentarily to pull the triggers. Why? Perhaps they weren't sure of our identity. The target may have looked too overwhelmingly good to be true—a fighter pilot's dream.

That must have been the reason, for they immediately make loop turns and come screaming down at us again. In those precious fleeting seconds, many of us dive into the icy ditch. Others scatter flat on their bellies in the field. All hell breaks loose. Machine guns from the two planes are now spraying the area with bullets. Lying helpless on the ground, not daring to look up, we imagine and believe that a major disaster is taking place—hundreds of comrades being slaughtered, and we can't do anything about it. We hear the thud of bullets hitting the ground and making paths right down the field. No bombs are dropped, just bullets, hundreds of them.

It's over just as fast as the whole nightmare started. The planes do not come back at us. We wonder why. The sergeant calls out for the wounded. Nobody answers. A fast check is made. Miraculously, although the machine-gun bullets missed many by inches, nobody is seriously wounded or killed. Some are grazed. We pick up some of the spent bullets as souvenirs.

Suppose the planes were dive-bombers and unleashed bombs instead of bullets. Suppose the pilots pulled the triggers as soon as they came down at us, instead of hesitating. Such are the mathematics of war. It's a matter of seconds, of inches between life and death. The most obvious, the easiest targets, are missed. The most protected targets receive bull's eye.

We reorganize behind a nearby farmhouse. Now that we know we are discovered, we must get back into the protective covering of the forest. Several hundred yards of ground separate us from the forest. We are instructed to run for it, squad by squad, at several minute intervals. We run as fast as we can, slowed down by the heavy loads we are carrying. At the halfway mark we are caught by a mortar barrage.

A mortar barrage is different from an artillery barrage. We know when the shells are approaching in an artillery barrage. The mortar shells are silent and explode before we can hit the ground. There is no warning. For reasons we do not understand, the enemy lifts the mortar barrage just when they had us zeroed in. That is our cue to get up fast and sprint for the forest again. Suddenly the loads we are carrying are much lighter. It's amazing what a human body is capable of doing when it is in danger. Another miracle. Everyone makes it safely into the forest.

Our section is resting in the forest, catching our breath after that narrow escape. My sergeant and I are sitting back to back, leaning against each other, exhausted, when we are caught in an artillery barrage. The Germans are up to their old tricks again. They seem to have eyes that can see in the forest. It's uncanny. The screaming shells are landing right above us on the tall pine trees. Five are wounded, two seriously. My sergeant got it in his spine. He is unable to move. There is a gaping hole in his spine. He is paralyzed. Who is to say which is more merciful: death in battle, never to see loved ones again; or to return, only to be a burden. How long will love last in a family when a totally paralyzed veteran must be diapered and fed and washed for the rest of his life by family members?

A replacement recently arrived from one of the relocation camps on the mainland is seriously wounded in his forehead. The shrapnel went through his helmet and came out above his eyes after taking a chunk of his forehead off. Thick blood is oozing from the ugly wound. His face is covered with blood. Three of us are wounded in the back, not seriously enough to send to the hospital.

We are going deeper and deeper into the forest. We do not know what to expect. Is the enemy leading us into a trap? Surely, they must know where we are. Why aren't they trying to stop us? Not even a sniper is shooting at us. Our eyes are darting from one tree to the next. Our ears are listening to every little sound, even the rustling of the leaves. At the same time, we are keeping a wary eye for minefields. Some of those nasty mines are designed to pop up in the air when tripped and explode at the proper distance where they are most likely to destroy our reproductive organs. No artillery barrages impede our progress. We can't understand it. The going is too easy. That is why we suspect that we are being drawn into a trap. Nevertheless, we press on. . . .

Biffontaine is a tiny hamlet near Bruyeres. It is situated in a valley surrounded by hills. Apparently, the Germans did not expect a daring infiltration into their lines.

From the vantage point we occupy, we are able to see the Germans walking about in the valley. We can even hear them talking. We see a German soldier turn away from his comrades, open his fly, and urinate on some logs. After finishing, he kicks the logs a few times for no apparent reason. His performance makes us laugh, our first in a long time. There is absolutely nothing to laugh about here in this miserable forest.

We immediately start digging, for we know that we will be discovered, if we aren't already. Disturbing news comes to us from our sergeant that enemy movements have been observed to the rear of us. We keep asking ourselves if the enemy had sucked us in to trap us. Some of us suspect this because they have been known to use this tactic and it's been too easy getting here.

Our platoon is concentrated on a narrow ridge on the side and on the top of a hill overlooking Biffontaine. The Germans know the disposition of their troops. By deduction, it is easy for them to calculate the perimeter of our platoon. The Germans could muster every available gun, work out a systematic, degree-by-degree firing order, and lob shells on every square yard of our small perimeter.

We wait for the inevitable.

The Germans have us just where they want us. My gunner and I dig a deep hole under a big rock, afraid of what is in store for us. We exchange worried looks but say nothing. Night is fast approaching. Everybody is quiet, except our sergeant who reminds us to go easy on our rations and water. We receive an order to fire five rounds of heavy explosive mortar shells. We don't know what the target is—only the range, deflection, and instructions. As soon as we fire the first shell we know what is going to happen. By the time we finish firing the fifth shell, we are grateful that our slit trench is at least partially protected by the big rock. We wait for the inevitable in our slit trench. Sure enough, some minutes later—five, ten, fifteen minutes—enemy shells land to the right, left, forward, and back of our perimeter. They are merely shots fired for bearing— the teaser before a well-planned major barrage.

We await the onslaught of powder and steel that is sure to follow. Then the slaughter begins. It starts from the forward position. Like a slithery snake, it weaves to the right, then to the left, each time moving closer to where we are. We are in the rear of the perimeter. From the sounds we hear, we know that the Germans are using every gun they have—mortars, ack-acks, machine guns, the dreaded 88s. In our confused minds we even hear, true or not, the dreaded screaming meemies.

My brother is with the machine-gun platoon. I wonder what is happening to him. The barrage is so intense that many shells land simultaneously. The noise level is so high that many of us actually lose hope that we will survive. The barrage, increasing in intensity, creeps up to where we are. As it comes nearer and nearer our slit trench, my gunner and I are grateful that we dug our hole under a large rock. It seems like a long time before the full impact of the barrage falls around where we are. Two shells land directly on top of our slit trench. It seems that every square yard is plastered. We are saved by the rock. The earth itself is shaking from the barrage.

We are now shivering, not from the bitter cold but from fright and disbelief at what is happening around us. The barrage lasts twenty-five minutes, possibly longer. Old-timers in the 100th who fought at the Volturno and Rapido River crossings, "Purple Heart Valley," and at Cassino can't recall enduring artillery barrages more vicious than the ones the Germans are throwing so prodigiously here in the forests of the Vosges Mountains. The barrages have left an indelible mark on many of us, not because they are the worst barrages of the war, but because they have done something to our psyche that will probably stay with us for the rest of our lives.

After the barrage, there is silence, an eerie silence. The acrid smell of powder fills the air. As usual, the medics are the first to come out of their slit trenches to give first aid to the wounded. As expected, many are wounded seriously, a few are buried in their slit trenches. A grotesque sight catches my eyes. A shattered hand and arm is embedded on a shattered branch halfway up a tall pine tree and it's waving at me. It sends chills up my spine and makes me want to vomit. Our worst imaginations when we first entered the Vosges forests have come true. Trees with human parts. Humans with tree parts.

It's not easy to describe how it feels to be in the middle of an artillery barrage. It's not knowing what is going to happen from one second to another that is so terrifying. With chunks of jagged steel flying and falling all around us at high velocity, hearing them slamming the ground like buzzing bees beside our slit trenches, not knowing when or where we are going to be hit—the spine, head, neck, shoulders, buttocks, legs, or feet as we lay flat on our bellies, praying—not knowing whether the wound is going to be serious or not, whether it's going to paralyze or kill us.

What happens if we are paralyzed and don't die? Who is going to take care of us? How will we manage if we lose our arms and legs? What if we are blinded, or castrated? Horrible, awful, sickening possibilities flash through our minds because we have seen all of the above happen to our comrades in Italy.

It is the unknown that is truly frightening. It is also scary when we lose hope and do not care to live anymore, when we hear ourselves saying, "To hell with it, we may as well die." What are the chances, we ask, of a frontline infantryman coming out of the war unscathed? We already know the answer. Practically none. It's bad enough to go through one barrage—it has got to be one of the most gruesome tortures invented by the mind of man—but having to endure dozens only to die in the end . . . is sad. We are going to be here forever in this godforsaken forest. We have seen original 100th Battalion men who went through all the campaigns, from Salerno, only to die here in the miserable Vosges Mountains.

We feel isolated and vulnerable on the tortured ground. We are all caught up in a vortex over which we have no control. The thought occurs that the war is never going to end. Already the water in my canteen is almost gone. After a major barrage, our throats are dry and scream for water. We know we are in a spot. We are cut off, surrounded by the enemy, by his clever design or not. We can't seem to shake all these terrible, nasty, negative thoughts.

It is beginning to get dark. Nobody is talking. One of the recent replacements who is seriously wounded is placed in an open slit trench next to us. There is nothing more the medics can do for him. We are now surrounded by the enemy, so he cannot be evacuated. Both his eyes are swollen so much that he can no longer see. We don't know him. He is not from our company. Perhaps he is from one of the rifle companies.

We were told by one of the medics that he was in the batch of 674 replacements who joined the combat team in Naples before we left Italy for the French front. He and most of the others in that replacement group were *kotonks* from the mainland. Most of them had been drafted prior to or immediately after Pearl Harbor, before all Japanese Americans were declared ineligible for the draft. The War Department actually had sent a directive (not an order) asking for the dismissal of all Japanese American soldiers several weeks after Pearl Harbor. Many were discharged. Many more were not, but they were assigned to menial jobs from post to post. We wonder how many of these replacements are already dead. It is a pity that the first battle for this batch of replacements had to be so fierce.

It is not easy to describe how an old-timer who has been at the front for a long time looks at a new replacement, any replacement. With pity? With happiness? With indifference? With sorrow? With anger?

The old-timers may have looked condescendingly at this new replacement when he joined the battalion, but now as he lay in his slit trench, dying, they feel nothing but profound sorrow for him. We hear his tortured moans most of the night. We hear him calling out for his mother. We've seen and heard that many times before. Why is it that a dying man always calls out for his mother instead of his father?

It's very sad to see a comrade die. We try to make him as comfortable as possible. We don't think he is aware of what is happening to him, or what he is saying, or where he is. He is in shock. We have a feeling that he will be dead in a few hours, certainly by morning. We want to say something meaningful to him, whether he can hear or not. We want to embrace him. We do neither. We don't know what to say. We are clumsy at such tasks, knowing that soon—today, tomorrow, or the next minute or hour, we may be where he is now. By now we have seen too many of our buddies die to not know that. We wish the chaplain were here to say the last words to him. Certainly, he deserves at least that.

We look at the replacement now lying in the shallow slit trench and wish he had not volunteered. How many of us from Hawaii would have done what he did, had our own government betrayed us as it did him and his family? If he dies, as he surely will, how will his death affect his parents, brothers, and sisters, still locked up behind barbed wire? Will they understand his death? Will they believe that the death of their son and brother will contribute something positive?

The dawn confirms what we had feared all along. The young replacement died during the night. His hands are clasped together over his chest, as if he had been praying before he died. His eyes are swollen. Otherwise, he looks peaceful. We immediately think about his parents, about the telegram they will be receiving from the War Department, and tears come to our eyes.

For us from Hawaii, the tears are genuine and sincere. By now we have come to know our mainland *kotonks* very well. We have identified with them, and they with us. We are united in a common cause. True, at Camp Shelby we had some serious misunderstandings. But living together, working together, training together, sharing hardships together, and plain common sense unified us. The term *kotonk* was ostensibly how their heads sounded when the Hawaii boys knocked them together. The *kotonks* in turn dubbed the Hawaii boys *buddhaheads*, a corruption of the word *buta* (pig)heads.

Living and training together all through basic and advanced training, going to nearby and faraway towns and cities on passes and furloughs, engaging in countless philosophical as well as nonsensical conversations, standing up together against thoughtless civilians and soldiers who taunted us by calling us "Japs" during training, and finally fighting together as a team in searing combat—both groups had evolved to the point where we could look back to our Camp Shelby days with amusement, nostalgia, and affection. The names, *kotonks* and *buddhaheads*, gradually became badges of honor for both groups, names to be proud of, names to look up to, names we'd be proud to pass on to the next generation, and the next— as long as the 100th and the 442nd are remembered.

Stanley M. Akita

100th Infantry Battalion

STALAG VIIA

In the latter part of 1943, Stanley M. Akita, who was born in Honomu on the Big Island of Hawaii, was among 150 soldiers from the 442nd Regimental Combat Team sent to Italy as replacements for the injury-plagued 100th Infantry Battalion. Akita had volunteered for the 442nd in 1943. He was assigned to K Company and trained with the all-volunteer unit at Camp Shelby, Mississippi.

Upon his arrival in Italy, he was assigned to C Company of the 100th Infantry Battalion (Separate), which was engaged in battle at Anzio, Italy.

In the fall of 1944, the 100th, which in June had been attached to the 442nd Regimental Combat Team, was sent to northeastern France, near the Franco-German border. Their battleground was two small farming communities, Bruyeres and

Biffontaine, both of which were strategic strongholds for the Germans.

After liberating Bruyeres, the 100th sneaked about three miles into enemy territory through a gap in the enemy's front line. The unit then attacked the town of Biffontaine and captured twenty-seven German prisoners. Akita was one of six armed guards taking the prisoners and eleven wounded GIs back to headquarters when their leader, who had been wounded but was able to walk, lost his way in the dense Vosges Mountains. Shortly thereafter, the Americans were captured by the Germans.

The following is Stanley Akita's recollection of his capture by German soldiers on October 23, 1944, in the Vosges Mountains of France. It begins in the aftermath of the liberation of Bruyeres.

The weather was getting chilly, and we were miserable living in foxholes. The conditions were such that we had to cover our foxholes to protect ourselves from "tree bursts."

There were lots of rolling hills in this region of northeastern France. In the small valleys lived a few families who farmed the rich topsoil, which, for centuries, had washed down from the hills. Only the flat valley bottoms were cleared for grazing or farming. These open areas were surrounded with trees—and, in 1944, German soldiers.

On October 18, 1944, we entered the town of Bruyeres in preparation for an attack the next day on Hills "A," "B," and "C" by the 100th Infantry Battalion. The French were overjoyed at having been liberated by the Americans. We witnessed for the first time the actions of the French populace against collaborators. The men were beaten; women collaborators were shaved baldheaded and marched through the town.

The attack by C Company of the 100th went over exceptionally well. We had been assigned to attack Hill C, and our boys captured twenty Germans without firing a single shot. After the hills were cleared of German troops, we returned to Bruyeres and had hot chow, the first in a long time, and a restful sleep in a French home.

On October 21, the 100th Battalion sneaked three miles past enemy lines and prepared for an attack on Biffontaine, a hamlet consisting of about a dozen homes. Aside from our scouts capturing a few Germans on errands, things were very quiet. We spent that night on a ridge in the forest, looking down on the enemy. We ate our C rations cold. There wasn't much activity because the enemy didn't know we were right behind them.

The next morning, C Company, led by Lt. William Pye, attacked Biffontaine. Due to the element of surprise, the battle was fast and furious. By late morning we occupied Biffontaine; our casualties were not too serious: no dead, six litter cases, three "walking wounded," and twenty-seven prisoners.

During the day's battle, we had also captured a horse-drawn German ration wagon loaded with the famous German army bread, which consisted of 23 percent wood pulp, and a pot of soup. Since we were not accustomed to eating wood pulp, we gave all the German food to the prisoners, who were very pleased.

On the night of October 22, 1944, in Biffontaine, two of our men, Sgt. Mike Tokunaga and Minoru Norikane, were sent out to contact the ration patrol. We hadn't eaten all day and the men were eyeing the rabbits and chickens running around.

That night we took turns guarding the prisoners. During my watch, I gave them a few cigarettes. We also gathered hay for their beds. Overall, we treated them well and they appreciated it.

At 6 A.M. the next morning, October 23, the two men who had been sent out to contact the ration patrol, Tokunaga and Norikane, came back with baggy eyes. They unfolded their experiences of the night before. They had encountered so many Germans that they couldn't make any headway and ended up just barely sneaking away at the break of day.

I was assigned to be a guard and to take the prisoners to the rear. As I heard this story unfold, I had an uneasy premonition that something was going to happen to me that day. Up on the front line it was believed that the longer you went without a scratch, the harder you'd get hit—and I had already survived seven months without a scratch.

Feeling the premonition, I went to the C.O. (commanding officer) and told him that I would rather not take the prisoners back. He said very nicely that I should go back anyway and stay with the kitchen crew until we caught up with the outfit. Without pursuing the issue any further, we left that morning for what turned out to be, for me, one of the most interesting experiences of the war.

There were twenty-seven of us in this detail: eleven medics who carried no arms, six wounded litter cases, four walking wounded, and six guards who carried two M-1s, two carbines, and two pistols. I was one of the guards carrying a carbine.

With the premonition of danger still strong, I went up to Sgt. Saburo Ishitani and gave him my wristwatch and a beautiful rose gold German pocket watch, which was my souvenir. It was to be sent home to

Mother in case I didn't make it back. (When I got back home, I found out that the army had sent my family both watches: I still have the German souvenir.)

At about 9 A.M. we were going up a knoll. The sergeant leading the detail had an English-speaking Jerry prisoner with him who had already reached the top. There, before their eyes, within talking distance, was a company of 150 Jerries, relaxing and "chewing the fat."

Thinking fast, the sergeant told the English-speaking German to ask the Jerries if they wanted to give up and go to America. It seemed that they were tired of fighting, for about half of them threw down their arms, ready to surrender. The sergeant would probably have ended up a hero if all the Jerries had surrendered. But the lieutenant in charge, a true Hitler man, deployed some of his men to surround us.

In the meantime, one of our officers and a medic, who had been near the front of the group, had found out about the German soldiers before the rest of us. As they ran past me, I asked the officer, "What's cooking up there?" "Nothing . . . nothing . . . Just stick around," he replied. They both ran up to a high-ranking officer, who had been wounded and was being evacuated on a litter. They knelt down and whispered something in his ear. He then jumped up from the litter and the three of them ran quickly, disappearing into the forest. (We later learned that they had gotten back to the battalion safely.)

The rest of us, who didn't know the situation just yet but knew we were having difficulty finding the way, thought the three men were backtracking to find a trail. When I thought about it later, I wondered how a wounded person being evacuated on a litter could jump up and run away.

I was facing downhill, giving water to one of our wounded officers, Lieutenant "Chicken" Miyashiro, when I saw the Jerry below me going from tree to tree with his rifle at port. I couldn't believe my eyes. "How come I see one Jerry with a gun down there?" I asked Lieutenant Miyashiro. That's when he got suspicious and tried to get up. Just as I glanced toward the sergeant leading the group, I saw a Jerry take his gun away. I turned around quickly and saw three more Jerries. We were surrounded.

The only thought in my mind after entering the war was that I'd either get a "million-dollar wound" and go home a cripple, or get killed. The thought of being captured and held as a prisoner had never occurred to me. It seemed like a bad dream that I couldn't wake up from. After realizing we were actually prisoners, my morale was very low. My first thought was, "This is it." I thought it was the end for me and that I would never see my family again. A few of the others felt the same.

The twenty-seven German prisoners we had captured weren't happy, either, with what had transpired within the last half hour. They were thinking of the battles they would have to go through again for a lost cause. Only minutes earlier, they had been thinking of the States and of all the food they would have to eat. Most of all, they were assured of being alive and of being able to return to Germany after the war.

We had guarded German POWs in Alabama for a month, and we had told them as best we could with hand motions and with what little German we knew what the life of a German prisoner of war was like in America.

In my opinion, these frontline Jerries were "gentlemen." Even though we were their prisoners, they never took anything from us except our arms. They never stuck their hands in our pockets or took anything for souvenirs. I had a Parker pen with an arrow-shaped gold clip showing on my O.D. (olive drab) woolen shirt, and they just left it as it was. Even our American cigarettes, which were superior to the European cigarettes, were left alone. Only when we took out a pack of cigarettes to smoke would they come around longingly, but they would only take a cigarette when it was offered to them.

Prior to our capture, our Jerry prisoners carried the litters with our wounded. Now that we were their prisoners, we started to carry our own litters. And now, instead of going toward our lines, we were headed closer and closer toward Germany. It was so hard to find our way through the forest that even the Jerry officer stopped on several occasions to ask French farmers for directions. When the Germans saw us tiring under the weight of the litter, they would give their gun to their comrade and relieve us.

As gentlemanly as they were, the French people feared them. Once, when the Jerry officer stopped at a farmhouse for directions, we saw a vegetable patch with tomatoes, beans, and cabbage, all ready for harvesting. We made motions with our hands and pointed to our mouths to show that we were hungry. Without asking the Frenchman, who was watching, the officer just pointed toward the vegetables and told us to get some. We did. I never liked raw tomatoes, but they sure tasted good then. Even the cabbage tasted good, flavored with bouillon cubes melted in a little water. It reminded us of home where raw, sliced cabbage and shoyu were a common sight.

The artillery fire had faded to a soft boom by late afternoon when we came out of the forest near a small town. The wounded were separated from us and taken to a hospital. The rest of us were herded into a small barn with straw spread out on the ground.

It was almost dark when a guard came in and gave us a few loaves of that 23 percent wood-pulp bread. As hungry as we were, we couldn't stomach the bread. It was the same size and shape as our American loaf, but, instead of weighing one pound and being soft, it weighed one kilo (just over two pounds) and was very hard. You could kill a guy if you hit him in the head with it.

The German soldiers didn't gorge themselves with this bread, for it almost always made you constipated, as we learned. Instead, they carried a small pouch on their belt with a slice of bread about two inches thick and a piece of sausage, maybe three inches long. Whenever they felt hungry they would take out the bread and sausage and chew on a slice of each—like the way we ate dried abalone back home. They did this five or six times a day.

Although that night in the barn was uneventful, we were restless. We stayed up late, talking about foods we used to eat back home, like sushi, fish cooked with shoyu and sugar, and barbecue meat. We felt full just swallowing our saliva. We also wondered how our parents were going to take it when they received the telegram from the War Department stating that we were missing in action.

The next morning we were herded into a corner of a vacated shop in town and held there for a few days. The food was a little better there. Our dinner consisted of two slices of roasted meat, bread, a few pieces of lettuce, and a macaroni-like soup. While in the shop, we saw a mother and daughter, probably the shop's owners, playing up to the Germans. We knew that one day, they'd be shaved baldheaded and marched through the town as collaborators.

On the second night we were interrogated in pairs by a German officer who spoke English fluently. We entered a small, blacked-out room with a dim light. They wondered why we, as Japanese, were fighting so hard for the United States when Japan was their ally. An officer seated at a desk asked the questions:

German officer (G.O.): "Did you go to Japanese school?"

Stanley Akita (S.A.): "Yes."

G.O.: "What did you learn at the Japanese school?"

Frankly speaking, I was no scholar in either Japanese or English school. I went to Japanese school because I had to and because all my playmates went. Otherwise, I wouldn't have had anyone to play with. About the only thing that came to my mind as a reply was, "We learned to obey our parents and to respect the elders."

G.O.: "Do you like America?"

S.A.: "Yes."

G.O.: "Why?"

S.A.: "Because of the democratic way of life. Everybody is free."

G.O.: "Do you feel like an American?"

S.A.: "Yes."

G.O.: "Did you know that a cat born in the fish market isn't a fish?"

S.A.: "Yes, but he belongs to the fish market."

The next day we were transported to a small French town close to Germany. This time our quarters was a section of an abandoned textile mill. It looked more like an oversized dog kennel. We ate, slept, and relieved ourselves in that same room.

Our guard was a young Polish man. We told him about the life German prisoners of war lived in the States. He got so worked up that he planned to volunteer for frontline duties so he could surrender to the Americans.

The following day all seventeen of us were loaded into the back of a truck a little bigger than our pickup trucks. It seemed like a 1930 vintage with hard rubber tires and it burned alcohol. The back section was covered with fence wires, and the top was about four feet high. You either sat with your legs folded or stood up, stooping over. It looked like the dog catcher's wagon in comic books.

We learned that we were going to cross the German border through the Siegfried line. If there was a last-ditch line, we didn't see it. The years of work required to build that defensive line seemed well worth it, for the camouflage was perfect. At the border, there was a long line of gas, alcohol, and steam autos and wagons on both sides going in or out of Germany. They checked the goods and identification of everybody. As "military cargo," we passed through easily.

We passed through a small German village. When the children saw us, they came up yelling and waving their hands. We threw them whatever candies we had and they scrambled for them like chickens. They must have seen other American prisoners of war pass by and found that the Americans were a "soft touch" where children were concerned.

Late that afternoon we were herded into another abandoned textile mill, which was like a large hall with windows all around. The machinery had been stripped from the mill. We were housed on the second floor.

The guards were older the farther we went into Germany. One guard was an old man, about sixty years old, with graying hair and teeth missing from here and there in his mouth. He really meant to guard us with his life. The corporal had locked him in the room with us. He carried a full bandolier of arms and two potato-masher grenades.

Earlier, a cocky young corporal came in and tried to frisk us, probably looking for an American pen, money, or whatever he could get his hands on. We shied away from him and told him we'd report it to the officer. He finally gave up and left.

Food for the day was thin soup and—ugh!—the 23 percent pulp bread.

The night was one of the most miserable I have ever experienced. It was teeth-chattering cold. We had no blankets. All we could do was pile about six excelsior mattresses over our bodies, and still, we felt like we were sleeping in an icebox.

Early the next morning, we were assembled outside the building and began a twenty-kilometer march to Strasbourg. There were about six guards on bicycles. It wasn't anything like a death march or a forced march, but walking twenty kilometers on an empty, growling stomach was no fun.

Our "prison" was a big brick building six stories high, approximately one hundred fifty feet by fifty feet, with a barbed-wire fence around it. It seemed like an abandoned factory that had been stripped of all its machinery. We were led to the fifth floor, which was empty: They must have sent a batch of prisoners of war to the rear recently.

The only thing in the building was a long trough made out of sheet metal with a pipe running parallel to it about eighteen inches above the trough. The pipe had holes in it every two inches. When the water was turned on, about forty men could wash at once. The only other thing in the building, besides the toilet and "shower," was a mountain of burlap-bag excelsior mattresses.

In the confined area next to the brick building was another shed-type building, which was the prison mess.

This was the first time since becoming a prisoner of war that I felt we were really entering a prison. I guess the barbed-wire fence and the tall, brick building with bars on the windows did it.

Glancing down, we saw the cooks, who were prisoners themselves (Polish), showing us cigarettes. The only way we could get at the cigarettes was to tear up a burlap-bag mattress cover, which we weighted down with a nail tied to the end and then lowered down four stories. The two cigarettes the cooks tied to the end were American-made Pall Malls. We were really surprised to receive American cigarettes from Polish prisoners of war.

While in Strasbourg, we witnessed American planes called Thunderbirds for the first time. The planes were making a daylight attack on the industrial area of town and having a field day. They dived, bombed, and strafed without any opposition. Also, since entering Germany we saw a couple of P-38s circling overhead every day, reconnoitering previously bombed areas.

On our second day in Strasbourg, about fifteen more GIs (haoles) were added to our group. By this phase of our imprisonment, the cigarette situation was getting critical. To save cigarettes, five or six guys would share one. After the cigarette was smoked to a one-fourth to half-inch butt, we put out the fire and saved whatever tobacco we could salvage in a small container. After we got enough tobacco for one smoke, we'd make a cigarette out of newspaper and smoke it. We had to be careful when smoking "newspaper cigarettes," for we couldn't inhale too big a puff. That thing can choke you!

On or about the third day, we were taken to the train depot, where we rode the first decent means of transportation since our capture. It was a regular European passenger coach. The trip was an uneventful one.

We ended up in a red brick building, which was part of an old cavalry camp in Stuttgart. We were quartered in what had been a horse stable. The stable had no panes on the windows. The floor was sloped toward the center to a trough, which carried the waste to the end of the building.

The buildings formed a quadrangle. Although it was winter and there were a few mud puddles, it was a neat place to stay. Our bunks were triple-decked, made out of two-by-fours and one-by-sixes, with excelsior in burlap material for mattresses that rested on wire.

This is where we began receiving our American Red Cross food parcels. The parcel was about a twelve inches wide all around and six inches high. It consisted of five packs of cigarettes; one "D" bar (army candy bar); a package of M&Ms candy; a package of crackers; a box of dried fruit; and one can each of powdered milk, oleo margarine, meat or fish, and jelly. Each prisoner was supposed to get one parcel a week. However, due to the lack of other food, some prisoners ate all of their food in two or three days and starved for the rest of the week. The Germans punctured all of our canned goods because we could have kept the canned goods to eat during an escape, so we had to eat them fairly soon. Six prisoners shared one parcel every day. By the end of the sixth day, you would have received one whole parcel. We were supposed to save a little each day for Sunday "dinner."

By now, our meals from the Germans were pretty well set. For breakfast, we got a cupful of "coffee" that tasted like our local *habu-cha* tea. For lunch, we received a bowl of thin barley soup, and for dinner, four to six boiled potatoes, a sixth of a loaf of "sawdust" bread, and, occasionally, a one-inch slice of sausage.

A most revolting thing happened to us on our first day there. As we entered our quarters, we noticed two wooden barrels in a corner. Each barrel was shaped like a cone. The upper, open end was about twelve inches and the bottom about ten inches; they were to be used for our daily business. That day, the Germans brought our soup in two containers that looked exactly like the two in the corner. Needless to say, that first serving of soup didn't sell too well.

The nights were getting cold. With only our O.D. uniforms, we piled mattresses over us, and we still spent a very sleepless night. We caught up on our sleep during the day when it got a little warmer with the sunlight entering the stable.

Every day, prisoners were trickling in from here and there, so that there were quite a few in the stable—about fifty Americans and French. All the Hawaii boys were interrogated again. It was like the first time: What did we learn in Japanese school? What did they teach at the Buddhist church? Did we like America? and so on.

The next three days were spent in a boxcar enroute to our "home" for the next five months, a camp called Stalag VIIA, located about forty-five miles northeast of Munich. The boxcars were like any other boxcar, only a little smaller. There were four barred windows, two on each side, each about two feet by four feet. The famous phrase, "10 horses or 50 men," was painted on the boxcar.

Our train consisted of about six cars. Our car wasn't crowded, but we later wished it was at least three-fourths full. It was so cold at night we all slept side by side, facing first to the right and then to the left, turning whenever one got tired of sleeping on that side. One person would be flush against the back of the next guy. Whenever we had an opportunity to get out to stretch and relieve ourselves, we would pick up as much wood as we could and get temporarily warm by burning the wood in our steel helmets.

Whenever there was an air raid, each boxcar was locked from the outside and the engineer and all the guards would abandon the train in search of a safe hiding place. We prayed that the planes wouldn't bomb or strafe us.

Stalag VIIA was a huge camp that housed about twenty thousand prisoners of war from all of the Allied nations. It was surrounded by a double barbed-wire fence with machine-gun towers all around. Every fifty yards, there was a sentry on foot accompanied by a police dog on a leash. These dogs were trained to be fierce. The sentry came into the compound with his dog several times, and if a prisoner of war came too close to the sentry, the dog growled and showed its fangs.

Our first night at Stalag VIIA was spent in a barnlike building with no floors. The area was infested with fleas and bedbugs. Our bed was a bundle of straw spread out on the ground.

The next day we were taken to be deloused. As we lined up to enter the shower, we took our clothes off and hung them on a rack. By then, we had been relieved of all our valuables and didn't worry about losing anything. Also, because I was just five feet tall, I knew my clothes wouldn't fit anyone there. After the racks were filled, they pushed them into an airtight vault, which they filled with delousing gas. In the meantime, we showered and were led into a large room. We waited another two hours since the clothes took two and a half hours to delouse. It was a very uncomfortable feeling to just stand around naked with no pockets to stick your hands into. Just picture two hundred men not knowing what to do with their hands.

To our dismay, after retrieving our clothes, we were led right back into the flea-infested barn.

The following day we were taken to our permanent quarters. Our compound, like the others, was about a quarter of an acre in area and consisted of four units with approximately two thousand prisoners of war of many nationalities.

There were two sections to a building with over two hundred men in each. There were two wood heaters, although we had heat only when the work detail could find enough wood. We had no electricity. The only light came from two carbide lamps in the building. If your bunk was more than ten feet away from the lamp, you'd recognize the next fellow by his voice or his silhouette. Sometimes when the carbide ran out, we went without light that night.

Sanitary conditions were terrible. There was no such thing as a mess hall or dishes. Our only utensils were a used margarine can and our GI spoon, from which we drank our breakfast coffee and had our soup at lunch. The can was our lifeline; it went with us wherever we went. Everything from bathing to washing our cups and spoon was done at one tap outside the building. During winter, the ground didn't dry fast enough, so there was mud everywhere. The floor in our quarters was as dirty as could be.

The sewage situation was the worst of all. The latrine was a ten-hole outhouse in which we sat back-to-back. The waste dropped into a sloping trough and emptied into a large concrete tank alongside the outhouse. About once a month, the "honeywagon" would come and suck up the waste, which was used to fertilize the fields and lawns in the prison camp. During winter, the floor of the outhouse was muddy. Sometimes when the urinal plugged, the place was really a mess.

By then, we were getting our Red Cross parcels regularly. We still saved our cigarette butts so the fresh packs could be used for trading during work detail.

In a prisoner-of-war camp like the one we were in, the privates and Pfc.s were a little better off than the officers, noncoms, and medics. Under Geneva Convention rules, the privates and Pfc.s were the only ones the captors could use for work details. We were sent to Munich every day by train to clear the debris on the railroads and in town. Nowadays, whenever I sing the song, "I've Been Working on the Railroad," it brings back memories of Stalag VIIA.

The beauty of being able to work was that we could trade four cigarettes for one loaf of civilian bread—with no "sawdust." It was softer and there were caraway seeds in it. We could sell this bread in prison for one pack of cigarettes. Just imagine, a 400 percent profit. Privates like us who could get extra loaves were "rich." Cigarettes became our money. On work details in Munich, each German guard was responsible for ten prisoners. Before we started working, each prisoner tried to bribe the guard with two cigarettes. If the guard took all the bribes, he got a total of twenty cigarettes—and we had it made, for some German ladies were willing to trade their civilian bread for our cigarettes—two to four cigarettes for a loaf of bread.

Our overcoats had pockets sewn inside in which we could carry up to ten loaves. The best trading I ever did got me nine loaves of bread. I could just picture the packs of cigarettes I could get for that.

But one day I took a big loss. After work we had been marched back to the camp as usual, in groups of fifty. Every night the Germans picked a group at random for a shakedown. They were interested in finding prisoners smuggling in weapons or tools. Just my luck, that night our group was chosen for a shakedown. Those with bread were supposed to go to the back of the group and get rid of their bread by eating all they could, or by throwing their loaves outside the building. When I finally went up to be frisked, I had gotten rid of all my bread. There were about fifty loaves of bread on the floor and an assortment of tools.

When the German guard saw me, all he said to the other German was, "Look at the small soldier," and, without frisking me, tapped me on the head and passed me over. I could have kicked myself, for I could have gotten as many as four loaves past the guards.

Life in prison was routine. We got up at 4:30 A.M. and had our coffee. By 5:30 we were in the boxcars headed for Munich. The train ride took two to three hours, depending on how often we had air raids.

Once we reached Munich we were split up into groups, ten to each guard. The lucky ones got to go into town, where there were lots of civilian women and where trading was super if you had a good guard. We only got to trade when our work took us near the depot.

To get the guard in the right mood before starting work, each of us would bribe him by giving him two cigarettes. The luckier prisoners got to go to influential residences to clear the debris, which meant they would have a chance to sit at a regular dining table and use appropriate silverware and dishes and eat regular, good, hot food. I had an opportunity like that once when we helped a lawyer transfer his books from his bombed-out downtown office to his country estate. It was an enjoyable day.

The unlucky ones ended up working on the railroad, sometimes alongside political prisoners dressed in black-and-white-striped cotton clothing. They were all shaved bald for easy identification.

Work on the railroad wasn't too bad. Four to six men carried railroad ties about ten feet long. It took fifty men roughly three days to cover up a bomb crater about thirty feet in diameter and ten feet deep. It must have been a fairly good-sized bomb, for the crater was made on solidly packed ballast material. After a good day of bombing, the railroad yard looked like a field of giant pretzels. The rest of the area, including the buildings, was a shambles.

Wherever I went with the work detail, civilians would ask the guard if I was a Chinese soldier. When told that I was Japanese, the expressions on their faces showed they wondered how this came about.

One cold January day, I was on a work detail in Munich. It was so cold that we built a fire in a metal drum and gathered around it to keep ourselves warm. The guard ordered us to go back to work, but none of us paid any attention to him. After repeating his order three or four times, he came behind me and shoved the butt of his rifle into the small of my back. The blow knocked me down and I had to be helped up by my fellow prisoners. That hit was so bad that, for at least a month, I had a really hard time getting on and off the boxcar to go to work. My request to see a doctor fell on deaf ears.

In the city of Munich, most of the buildings were left with big gaping holes. Buildings with a wall completely blasted away or with large holes in the roof were demolished. All the town residents could do was clear enough debris so that an automobile could pass. In some instances, there was only enough room for a footpath for pedestrians and cyclists.

Regardless of the wartorn conditions, Germany was a very clean country. The people kept their homes spick-and-span. Whatever windows were not destroyed by the bombing were kept sparkling clean.

One of the best work details was the potato-digging detail. During my six months in prison, I got to go only twice. We dug up potatoes that had been stored underground after they had been harvested. They were stored in a trench four feet wide and eighteen inches deep that ran the whole length of the field near the camp. The potatoes were piled in the trenches, covered with a foot of straw, and then covered again with earth. This was done to protect the spuds from frost. After digging them up again, we would pile the spuds into the wheelbarrow—and at the same time fill our overcoats with them. You can just imagine the amount of spuds we took back to camp that night. My partner and I had fried potatoes, mashed potatoes, boiled potatoes, and potato soup. Potatoes were coming out of our ears.

Speaking of partners, almost all of the prisoners were paired off with another guy. We were then put in groups. One group with eight men was led by a paratrooper who was an ex-Golden Gloves champion. He had arranged with the leader of the department for each member to have a different work detail. One of them would always stay back so he could have supper ready by the time the other seven men got back. The advantage in having men in different details was that they could trade their cigarettes for bread and, sometimes, for other food items. Sometimes my partner and I didn't have a chance to trade. We usually had enough food stored away so we could go without trading for two or three days and still have substantial amounts to eat.

Life in prison wasn't all work. Every so often, maybe once or twice a month, when the air force ran out of targets, we got a Sunday off. If it was sunny, the blankets were aired out, the clothes were washed, and we cleared our quarters. We also tried to bathe then—about two hundred men to a tap—and get a haircut. I was one of the barbers. After cutting at least a hundred heads, I know dogs don't feel the fleas crawling all over them until they're bitten. Many times while cutting hair, I saw fleas leap off of a head. I'd tell the guy whose hair I was cutting and he'd reply, "That's funny, I didn't feel anything." Some of them thought I was joking.

Sometimes while on work detail, we'd have a "good Joe" for a guard. On those days, we took off our long-johns underwear and buried it in the snow for about an hour. Later, we shook the snow off and picked off the frozen lice and fleas. The fleas weren't too plentiful, maybe one or two, but depending on how often we bathed, we'd see at least a dozen lice frozen in our long johns.

Of the things we had to eat, the small quantities of cheese and sausage were the only foods that had any nutritional value. The rest was starchy food. This is where I learned to eat Limburger cheese. At the time I thought it was okay, except for the smell. Today I can't imagine how I ate that damn stuff.

In the spring the wild dandelions started to pop up. We picked the young leaves, chopped them up, and made a dandelion omelette.

During the early part of March 1945, about five hundred of us were sent to a small farm village about three miles from a railroad yard. I was separated from my partner and was the only one from Hawaii in this group. We were quartered in a huge barn. We slept directly on the ground covered with straw. Our toilet was the craziest damned thing I've ever seen. It was a log, about six inches in diameter and about fifteen feet long. It was built like a carpenter's horse, but only about eighteen inches off the ground. Directly behind the log horse was a slit trench. All we could do to use this toilet was hang our bare rear ends over the log. To make things worse, there was no screen to hide us. Every "Hans" and "Fritz" walking by could see us sitting on the log.

Our "bathroom" was just as bad—a wide-open space. The "bathtub" was a little stream that ran about fifty feet away, parallel to a road traveled daily by civilians. The only time we took a bath was when a whole bunch of us went. Most of the guys would bathe only once a week. Boy, you should see five hundred naked men in a stream at one time—there were all sizes and shapes. Just like the old swimming hole back home.

We walked three miles to and from work every day to clear up the mess at the railroad yard. One morning, right after reaching the work area, I felt so sick that I had to walk all the way back to our quarters, accompanied by a guard. I am really thankful to the guard for being so patient with me. I would walk a few hundred yards and feel so tired that I would have to lie down. I'd sleep for about fifteen minutes or a half hour and then get up and go another couple hundred yards and lie down again. I don't know how many times I did that, but the guard just stood by, not saying a word or hurrying me along. He just followed along like a faithful dog.

I don't know how long it took me to get back to the camp, but all they had for me was aspirin. Typical army—headache, backache, blisters, bruises—no matter what the ailment, aspirin was the medication. There were no medical facilities or doctors, just a guy carrying a bottle of aspirin, bandages, plasters, and salves.

The end of my imprisonment came sometime in the latter part of April. One night, at about 9 P.M., most of the men were fast asleep. After all, we had no electricity; only candles were used. Suddenly a few of us heard the staccato of an American machine gun—it was definitely not a German make. We jumped up and aroused the others. Nothing else happened, and those we had aroused said we were hearing things. We all went back to sleep.

Nothing happened the next day. It made those of us who had heard the machine gun the night before look bad. That night, at about 7 P.M., just after it had gotten dark, we heard a battle royal taking place in the woods nearby. We could hear the *rat-a-tat-tat* of American machine guns and the *burrp bur-r-r-p* reply of the German machine gun. This time, all of us heard it. We lit up all the candles we had and started packing our meager belongings. We were prepared to go at a moment's notice. The guards locked the barn from the outside. It was about 9 P.M. when everything finally quieted down. Some of us fell asleep. Others stayed up all night.

Bright and early the next morning, a guard unlocked the doors. When we went out, we found that only a handful of the fifty guards were left: The others had fled. All the buildings in the village had white flags of surrender hanging from their windows. The village of about fifty families was situated in a slight valley, surrounded by a meadow as wide as a thousand feet in some places. A wooded forest surrounded the meadow. It was from these woods that we saw our American tanks rolling out. We knew that we were liberated and would soon be wearing clean clothes, eating good food, sleeping comfortably, and, best of all, that we would be able to go home and see our loved ones.

The first thing the tankers offered us was a few loaves of white American bread. After six months of hard, brown, "sawdust" bread, the white bread looked, felt, and tasted more like cake than anything else.

Henry S. Kuniyuki

442nd Regimental Combat Team

BRINGING HOME THE PROUD COLORS

My World War II experience began with the disastrous bombing of Pearl Harbor by Japan. The strained relations between the United States and Japan had prompted the territorial government to establish first-aid stations and a block-warden system. For many months before the war broke out, I had volunteered for the Honolulu Civil Defense First Aid Corps.

When Pearl Harbor was bombed on December 7, 1941, I immediately reported to our designated first-aid station, located in the basement of a classroom building at Punahou School. Shortly thereafter the U.S. Army Corps of Engineers took over the entire Punahou campus. Much to my surprise, I was evicted from the first-aid station because I was Japanese. I immediately volunteered to be a block warden for the block surrounding our home.

My father, Aisuke Kuniyuki, was very active in Japanese community organizations such as the Shingon Mission and the McCully Japanese Language School. He was arrested by the FBI and held initially at the

Honolulu immigration station. Father was eventually transferred to the internment camp at Honouliuli and then sent to another facility in La Junta, New Mexico.

As the eldest son, I helped my mother manage my father's home-rental business. When the call for volunteers for an all-AJA combat team was issued, I was not among the Hawaii men who stepped forward.

However in August 1944 I was drafted into the United States Army and sent to Camp Fannin, Texas, for basic training. I immediately wrote to the U.S. Justice Department, requesting that my father be released from the internment camp and returned home. The Justice Department denied my request and transferred him to another camp, this one at Amache, Colorado.

At the time, Colorado Governor Ralph Carr was the sole voice of dissent among the Western governors:

> *When it is suggested that American citizens be thrown into concentration camps, where they lose all the privileges of citizenship under the Constitution, then the principles of that great document are violated and lost. If a man may be deprived of his liberty . . . without proof of misconduct, without the filing of charges, and without a hearing, simply because men now living in the country where his grandfather was born have become the active enemies of the United States, then we are disregarding the very principles for which this war is being waged against the Axis nations.*

At the time, few Americans could see the truth and wisdom in Governor Carr's position—not even the U.S. Supreme Court.

After completing basic training, my buddy and I received a ten-day furlough to visit relatives at Amache Relocation Center and other parts of the country before reporting to our embarkation point, Fort Meade, Maryland. We were surprised to see Japanese Americans living in barracks at Amache, surrounded by barbed-wire fences and guarded by American GIs with machine guns pointed into the compound.

Father was getting along reasonably well, although he was very worried about Mom, who was now living alone at home in Hawaii. My two other brothers had been drafted into the army after me. Another brother, who had been studying at Waseda University in Tokyo prior to the outbreak of the war, became a war refugee in Japan. For that reason, I had declined to serve as an interpreter in the Asia-Pacific theater when a recruiter came to Camp Fannin.

Several hundred nisei replacements like me were awaiting our orders at Fort Meade. In the meantime, an epidemic of German measles broke out among the AJA soldiers, requiring some to be hospitalized. The irony was that the stricken AJA soldiers were quarantined in the German prisoner-of-war section of the post hospital.

While at Fort Meade, I again wrote to the U.S. Justice Department, this time demanding that my father be released from Amache Relocation Center and sent home. I explained that I was scheduled to be sent overseas to the European battlefront, where I was willing to die for my country. The Justice Department finally released Father, permitting him to go—not home to Hawaii to live—but to Chicago!

Our battalion finally received its orders, so we set out for our port of embarkation in New Jersey. The company commander at Fort Meade had tried to retain me as a company clerk because of my specialist training at Camp Fannin, but the higher authorities denied his request because I was physically fit.

Going overseas to the European war front was quite an experience. We traveled on troopships guarded by Allied navy ships. The troopships' position in the huge convoy was changed daily to confuse the German submarine wolf packs.

Crossing the North Atlantic in midwinter was rough. Our protecting aircraft carrier collided with a destroyer, forcing the carrier to return to its home port on the East Coast. The alarm for us to abandon ship sounded several times after German subs were detected trailing the convoy.

After several days of crisscrossing the high seas, we finally arrived in Le Havre, France. A U.S. Army band greeted us with the "Hawaiian War Chant" as we walked off the ship. We were then placed in boxcars for the journey to Marseilles in southeastern France.

I knew how uncomfortable a boxcar was, so five of us volunteered to be in charge of the troop's duffel bags, which were placed in the boxcar immediately behind the steam engine. Thus five of us had very comfortable quarters on the train, sleeping on top of the duffel bags. The engineer allowed us to use the hot water from his steam engine to sterilize our mess kits during train stops.

Many young AJA soldiers suffered dysentery due to the unsanitary conditions. The boxcars didn't even have toilets in them. From our vantage point at the front of the long line of boxcars, we could see the poor GIs hanging out of the cars' sliding doors.

At Marseilles, we boarded another troopship, this one bound for Leghorn, Italy, where we finally joined the 442nd Regimental Combat Team. The unit was preparing for its final Italian campaign.

In late March 1945 the 442nd had returned to Italy from France at the specific request of Gen. Mark Clark, commander of the Fifth Army. The German Gothic line, which had held back the Allied advance for five months, needed a go-for-broke breaching by the 442nd. It took the 442nd less than a day to break through the German line at Mount Folgorito.

During the last battle, I remember traversing across carefully marked trails that had been cleared of land mines and going up the steep mountainside. From the top, we charged down the other side, causing me to severely sprain my right ankle. Italian partisans helped me mount their donkey, as I was unable to walk to the first-aid station located in the valley below.

I had assumed that the partisans would guide the donkey down the cleared crisscross trails. Much to my chagrin, however, the animal was given a whack on its backside, causing it to charge down the heavily mined hillside. I thought the donkey and I were destined for donkey heaven. By the grace of God, I made it to the aid station, where my injured ankle was taped.

Within three weeks, the German army was routed into retreating north to the Po Valley. The Germans surrendered on May 2, 1945. The 442nd was then assigned to occupy headquarters in Leghorn, Italy.

Because of my army administrative-specialist training at Camp Fannin, I was selected to be a company clerk for a medical detachment during the latter part of the Italian campaign. Most of the original 442nd volunteers had earned enough points to return home. I transferred out of Regimental Headquarters' Personnel Section and was reassigned to the Medical Detachment Headquarters. That gave me the opportunity for rapid promotion.

With the settling of hostilities in the Pacific theater, the 442nd Regimental Combat Team returned to the continental United States. After a long ocean crossing from Leghorn to New York City, we were quartered at Fort Belvoir, Virginia, where we prepared for a victory parade in Washington, D.C., which was reviewed by President Harry Truman.

It was a muggy, drizzling day and we were soaking wet to the bone. After the parade ceremony, we thought we would be hopping aboard a troop train to the West Coast. However, due to a race riot in California, we instead embarked on another ocean voyage—East Coast to Honolulu, via the Panama Canal.

We were honored with a grand reception upon arriving in Honolulu. As replacements for the 442nd Regimental Combat Team, it was an honor and a privilege to bring home the regimental colors.

During the army discharge process, I was among several men who were offered a direct commission to remain in the U.S. Army—which we all promptly declined. Two years later, however, I accepted a position with the Hawaii Army National Guard, which required my wearing a uniform once again. After serving thirty-two years on active and reserve status, I retired at the rank of lieutenant colonel in the Staff Specialist Corps.

Ronald M. Oba

442nd Regimental Combat Team

SINGING THE MESS HALL BLUES

During basic training at Camp Shelby, Sgt. Dick Masuda always called on me to do the close-order drills on the field because I had a loud voice. I counted cadence with the good *kiai* (spirit) I had learned from kendo exercises. I did all of the obstacle courses and hikes with a full field pack, and by the end of basic training had earned an expert rifleman badge. That prompted Sergeant Masuda to appoint me squad sergeant for the 1st Squad, 1st Platoon.

My officer status was short-lived, however.

One day, Capt. Tom Akins summoned me to his office. "Oooba, I want you all to report to the mess hall as a cook." Flabbergasted, I replied, "Sir, I was just appointed sergeant, 1st Squad." Captain Akins snapped, "Oooba, you want to be court-martialed?" Visions of being sent home, humiliated, filled my mind. "No sir," I snapped, and headed for the mess hall.

Incidentally, the soldier who took my place as squad sergeant was later shot in the head. His replacement, also, was wounded and sent home from the battlefield. I had better karma than my two replacements, escaping with only a perforated eardrum and three compression fractures in my spine suffered during a Jeep accident in Italy just three days before the end of the war.

Before leaving for battle in Europe, I was sent to the Cooks and Bakers School, where I learned to prepare a Southern menu that the boys didn't much like: hominy grits, rutabaga, liverwurst, mutton, yellow squash, black-eyed peas, corn bread, brussels sprouts, rhubarb, pig corn, and powdered eggs. I also went to the Butchers School to learn how to carve beef.

The following are just a few of my memories of being a cook with F Company.

One day First Cook Frank Dobashi baked a large pan of yellow layer cake, topped with icing. Along came the Hattiesburg Ladies Auxiliary to pay the boys a visit. Frank was proudly serving the ladies the fluffy cake when one of them declared that it was the "best cornbread" she had ever tasted!

As everyone knows, cornbread is gritty and firm—not as light as cake. After the ladies had left the mess hall, an exasperated Frank Dobashi tossed the entire pan of cake into the garbage can.

F Company's Capt. Joe Hill invited a captain from a haole outfit to lunch in an occupied hotel on Peirra Cava, high atop the Maritime Alps between France and Italy. I was asked to prepare lunch for the two captains. On the menu was steak and potatoes with vegetables. We had elegant china and silverware for this occasion, so I decided to prepare something special. Steak was special, but that alone wasn't enough. I decided to prepare fresh potatoes that the visiting captain would not forget.

Everything was ready except the potatoes. As the officers relaxed with their cocktails, I put the steaks in the frying pan and mashed the boiled potatoes. Melted cheese and milk were already on the double boiler. I blended fresh butter and salt and pepper into the potatoes, and then, at the last minute, folded the melted cheese and milk into the potatoes, which I served piping hot.

The visiting captain enjoyed a second serving, and then a third. The next day he sent his First Cook to get the "recipe" from me. Recipe? The disgruntled soldier left empty-handed, of course.

I was asked to take a detail of fresh food to a platoon of F Company men on the front lines in Italy. The detail was dropped off at the top of a hill, where a Sherman tank was battling a German panzer tank. I followed the trail down into the valley and through a vineyard then asked a captain where F Company was situated. He pointed to a hill beyond and ducked behind a rise as artillery shells exploded around us. The detail packed the three mermite thermal buckets used to store hot food and beverages, five-gallon water cans, and a sack of bread loafs on their backs and followed me.

We followed the trail down into the valley, through the vineyard, and onto the hill beyond. After delivering the hot food and feeding the boys, we followed the same route back up to the top of the hill. As we approached the rise, the crew of the Sherman tank and the other officers gave us a rousing round of applause. We had unknowingly walked through a minefield where a soldier had earlier been blown to bits.

On another food detail just beyond Bruyeres, toward Belmont, I was asked to take hamburgers, rice, corn, pineapple tidbits, and coffee to the men on the front lines. The detail was dropped off near a rise off the road. It was pitch-dark.

Captain Jack W. Rodarme suddenly appeared from nowhere. "What have you got there, Oba?" he whispered. "Sir, I have some hamburger, rice, corn, pineapple, and slices of bread." "Forget everything except the hamburger and rice," he said. "Why?" I asked. "The enemy is just over the rise and mess kits will make too much noise," he said.

Without making a sound, we served the rice in one of the soldiers' hands and hamburger patties in the other. The hungry young men disappeared into the darkness, gobbling down their rice and hamburger.

The boys had been battling the enemy for nearly a month without any respite. They were being fed C rations, with an occasional hot meal—when it could be scheduled. Thus the kitchen was stocked with only C rations, coffee, flour, salt, and sugar.

One day, the boys were given a four-hour rest period without notice. The captain asked the cooks to prepare hot food for the boys, who'd had their fill of canned rations. We heated up the beef stew from the C-ration cans, garnishing it with fresh onions and tomatoes. Still, the captain said that wouldn't do.

The mess sergeant was beside himself. "What can we do?" he asked. After thinking for a minute, I asked the kitchen crew to help me dig out the flour, sugar, lard, salt, and baking power from the kitchen truck. They virtually yanked the field kitchen out of the packed truck and set up the stoves.

I remembered that the recipe for biscuits called for two parts flour to one part lard. I proceeded to knead the dough until it was ready to roll. Then, using an empty C-ration can, I cut out the biscuits.

Hot biscuits came flying out of the oven as the boys marched up to the kitchen for their hot meal. They were disappointed with the canned beef stew, but the biscuits saved the day!

The troops guarded thousands of enemy soldiers at Italy's Ghedi Airport after the war in Europe had ended. All was quiet on the Italian front, and many a Hawaii soldier was dreaming of feasting on heaping bowls of hot rice and *hekka*.

Salted bacon, used coffee grounds sun-dried and repacked in their original containers, cigarettes, candies, soaps, towels, and more were traded for fresh eggs, tomatoes, round onions, bouillon cubes, green onions, cabbage, and eggplant. Although the army menu called for an occasional steak dinner, the boys passed on steak every time in favor of *hekka*. So, *hekka* it was.

Mas Yoshida cooked the rice and I took turns cooking the *hekka*. Chopped meat, round and green onions, and tomatoes were the main ingredients. We used bouillon cubes boiled in water for shoyu. It was even better than shoyu. Honest.

As soon as the rice was ready, Captain Jack Certain took his place at the table. Yoshida scooped a huge serving of rice onto the biggest platter he could find. He then cracked two eggs over the piping hot rice. The freshly cooked *hekka* was then served on top of the eggs and rice. The captain ate this concoction every day; he never tired of it. The boys loved *hekka* so much that they even took the leftovers to their tents for midnight snacks.

1399th Engineer Construction Battalion

THE "PINEAPPLE SOLDIERS"—HAWAII'S FORGOTTEN BATTALION

The following speech was delivered to veterans of the 1399th Engineer Construction Battalion by A.A. "Bud" Smyser, contributing editor for the Honolulu Star-Bulletin, *in August 1984. The event celebrated the fortieth anniversary of the battalion's formation.*

I have entitled my talk tonight, "Hawaii's Forgotten Battalion."

That's an overstatement, to be sure—"The Battalion That Stayed Home" is a more accurate title. But it doesn't catch the fact that stories of the World War II exploits of Hawaii's American soldiers of Japanese ancestry rarely focus on the 1399th Engineer Construction Battalion.

I was surprised—very surprised—in preparing this talk, to discover how few news references to the 1399th are in the library of the Hawaii Newspaper Agency, which files news clippings of the *Honolulu Advertiser* and the *Honolulu Star-Bulletin*.

(From Left) Col. C. H. Chorpening, Lt. Col. J. A. Malone and MSGT George M. Hoota, the battalion's sergeant major, admire the Meritorious Unit Plaque, which was awarded to the 1399th Engineer Construction Battalion for "superior performance and record of accomplishment and exceptional duty."

When we talk of the AJA effort in World War II, we very naturally focus on the tremendous battlefield effort in Africa, Italy, and France of the 100th Infantry Battalion and the 442nd Regimental Combat Team, the most decorated units of the war. Belated recognition also is being given to the Military Intelligence Service, AJA soldiers from Hawaii who served as interpreters for U.S. forces in combat in the Pacific and Southeast Asia— and who sometimes went on spy missions behind Japanese lines. They deserve every bit of attention and commendation they get. They paid a high price in lives and in wounded to prove the overwhelming loyalty of Hawaii's AJAs for America at a time when many were calling it into doubt. Many of them gave their lives with the clear object of helping Hawaii win statehood, despite its predominantly non-Caucasian population, and thus assure equal rights for its citizens of all races.

The fact that we are this week celebrating the twenty-fifth anniversary of statehood is in many ways a tribute to that effort. Statehood probably would not have been won without it, certainly not by 1959 and quite possibly not even by now, and perhaps never. Racial doubts would have held us off from statehood. The United States would be a poorer country because of it and Hawaii a far less happy place—more of a place with racial schisms, like Fiji, and less the relatively harmonious, prosperous state we enjoy today.

But no one praising the World War II military effort of our AJA soldiers from Hawaii should ignore the 1399th and the units that were

A jungle training village built by the 1399th Engineer Construction Battalion.

merged into it after the draft of AJA male civilians was resumed in 1944: the 370th Engineer Battalion, the 1536th Dump Truck Company, and the 1525th Base Equipment Company—all AJA construction units.

If you visit our Big Island, Mauna Loa and Mauna Kea volcanoes dominate the scene, each rising up more than thirteen thousand feet from sea level. It is very hard to perceive that at their flanks is another important volcano, Kilauea. It rises gradually to only four thousand feet and is thereby obscured by the giants. The 1399th is the Kilauea of the AJA military units, obscured by the giants, but possessing a proud record of its own.

I spoke a few days ago with Gardner Hyer. I think he is the only surviving officer who served with the 370th and the 1399th through the war, from January 1942 when he was activated from the army ROTC reserve until after V-J Day in 1945. He advanced in rank from second lieutenant to major and held just about every command in the battalion of nearly one thousand men, including a brief tenure as battalion commander. Now he is retired from the auto service business in Wahiawa.

"What kind of a unit was the 1399th?" I asked him. "How did it do?"

He had just been watching the Olympics. Using Olympic judging, he said, he would give the 1399th a score of "ten." Its men couldn't have been better. They did every job they were supposed to do. They completed construction projects ahead of schedule. They did them very well. On at least one big project, they were called in to finish a job another unit had goofed. And when urgent deadlines had to be met, they were the unit the army turned to.

He recalls only one serious disciplinary problem, and it was settled by a little off-the-record, man-to-man boxing match between him and the soldier involved.

He also recalls that your [the battalion's] accomplishments became known to higher-up officers passing through Hawaii. Gen. Douglas MacArthur's headquarters in the South Pacific twice requested that you [the 1399th] be assigned to campaign with him in combat. Both requests were refused for fear an AJA unit in the Pacific would be mistaken by our own mainland Caucasian soldiers as the enemy.

Even after World War II, you were remembered. In the Vietnam War, Hyer got a call from the Pentagon asking if two of your construction techniques on Oahu would be applicable in Vietnam. He said yes in both cases.

You will laugh that one was the building of latrines over running streams to obtain a flush toilet effect. But it was a serious benefit, and so was the use of bamboo instead of steel as reinforcing bars for concrete. Hyer said you found that in the short run, a year or so, the bamboo was just as strong as steel, or stronger.

You called yourselves the "Pineapple Soldiers" because you stayed home—and the "Chowhounds" because you were. One of your number, Shiro Matsuo, learned enough by being a mess sergeant for you that he went on to found Shiro's Saimin Haven, prosper, and bring back to Hawaii this year the GI who introduced him to cooking.

You got no Purple Hearts because this was not a combat zone. But you lost three dead in mishaps and suffered, I assume, injuries in the line of duty that no one counted as we count Purple Hearts.

You had weekends off in Honolulu—Saturday afternoon to Sunday afternoon—and you played hard at those times. Duke Kawasaki recalls the late Harold Sakata drinking so much beer that others sometimes had to lift him aboard the truck going back to Schofield Barracks from the Honolulu Central Library and other pickup points.

He also recalls that Harold suggested he and Duke wrestle together professionally after the war as the Togo Brothers. Duke refused, and that may have been just as well for Harold's later career as Oddjob of *Goldfinger* movie fame and Duke's as a state senator.

But when you worked, you worked hard and well.

Stanley Shioi, one of your members, was in construction work before World War II and has had his own construction company afterward. He knows the business as a pro.

He says the quality of your work was "tops" in comparison with other construction jobs. "Guys with no experience still did very good work," he said. "Japanese boys have very good hands."

Tatsuki Yoshida, another contractor from your ranks, agrees. "I'm amazed at the work we did without much background experience," he recalls. The raw material the unit had to work with was a cross section of young men from wartime civilian life: clerks, a fireman, agricultural workers, even a dentist.

A million-gallon water tank you built near Wahiawa is still in use by the Honolulu Board of Water Supply. Tatsuki also recently found one of your old campsites at Opaeula, in the hills above Haleiwa, at a spot where you opened a quarry.

You helped develop the airstrip at Kahuku for Flying Fortresses. You built jungle training villages in the hills, complete with main streets, side roads, and primitive equipment for combat simulation. You built warehouses, waterlines, and more. On Coconut Island in Kaneohe Bay, you built a rescue and recreation camp for the air force.

You did, in short, whatever the Army Corps of Engineers, headquartered on the Punahou School campus, needed done. You completed fifty-four major projects and you, too, are a decorated battalion.

As a battalion, you received the army's Meritorious Service Award on October 29, 1945, some ten weeks after V-J Day, when your demobilization was beginning.

You were draftees. Like most Americans, you didn't rush into service. But when you were called, you went where you were assigned and did your job as well as you could.

Because you were of Japanese ancestry, an ethnic group foreign to most Americans then, and because the war was with Japan, you and your families were discriminated against. You have relatives who were interned. The draft for you was suspended from 1942 to 1944. When you were mobilized, you were placed in ethnically separate units under mostly Caucasian officers. Early in the war, some units were denied ammunition.

In my inquiries, I even picked up a story I couldn't confirm with a second person of machine guns being trained on one unit of AJA inductees for a single night at Schofield, apparently because their mainland officers were afraid of them. The occasion must have been soon after Pearl Harbor.

Whatever discriminations you faced, you served well, with dedication and with good humor. You achieved the same kind of respect-building across racial lines here at home that the 100th, the 442nd, and the MIS did overseas.

In the nature of things, your record has gotten lost in the shuffle a bit. It doesn't deserve to be that way. On your fortieth anniversary, congratulations, and . . . well done.

Chaplain Hiro Higuchi
442nd Regimental Combat Team

"DEAR MOM": LETTERS HOME

Few things were as treasured during the war as letters from loved ones back home, or on the front lines. For a brief moment, they brought husbands and wives together, reunited young children with their soldier fathers, and allowed sons to tell their parents what they felt in their heart.

The following are selected letters written by 442nd Chaplain Hiro Higuchi to his wife, Hisako, whom he affectionately addresses as "Mom."

February 21, 1944
Dear Mom:

It's ten o'clock now but can't pass this lovely day without writing to you. The day started very nice and warm—got a little warmer, something like our summer weather, and although it was rather warm, it reminded me so much of home. To complete the day, we had a group of Hawaiian musicians (professionals) come and give us an hour and a half of home music. When the music ended with "Aloha Oe," "Across the Sea," and "To you, Sweetheart, Aloha," you could hear a pin drop. I watched the boys from the Islands—and was afraid most of them would break down and cry. It was wonderful—and so thrilling to know that in spite of wars and everything, they can't take that feeling for the Islands away from us.

I believe that's the big difference between the island boys and the mainland boys. Our boys from the Islands have a tradition back of them with Hawaiian music and songs. Since coming here, I haven't heard as yet one boy sing "I Love You, California," or any of the state songs. It is sad when you think of that—on the other hand, our boys sing and have a tradition of home holding them all the time. It made me so happy that perhaps Peter and Jane, too, will some day learn these songs and get weepy, too, when they hear them. It began a wonderful day and ended perfect.

No doubt the boys will go home to their hutments this evening, kind of sobered up and happy, too, in a way. There will be many a dream about Hawaii this evening.

The whole program was planned by Mr. Earl Finch—the benefactor of the boys here in Camp Shelby. He really does a lot for the boys here and spends a lot of time bringing happiness to them. He is only 27 years old, not a particuarly wealthy man, but spends thousands of dollars on the boys—bringing them music and giving parties for them. And the boys appreciate it, too.

I have sent a copy of the album to both Kamejiu and Ets and will send one to Sam tomorrow. I suppose Sam would be 1-A in the draft now. He had a leaking heart as a youngster, so I wonder just how it is now. I hate to see him in the army with all his responsibilities—taking care of his family and mine, too. I understand that Mr. Mikami was classified 1-A so guess there [aren't] many exemptions.

We are not in the fields this week but am afraid this break cannot last very long. If it is as warm as this, one would not mind, but this Mississippi weather is so funny—warm or hot one day and freezing the next. If it is as warm as this in February, I wonder what the summer heat is like. We have to take salt tablets in the summer time—otherwise the men get lightheaded, so they say. However, I can stand heat better than cold.

Guess I'll close this letter for the night. And end up with the music we sang tonight: To you, sweetheart, aloha—in dreams I'll be with you, dear, tonight—and I'll pray for that day we, we two will be again—until then, sweetheart, aloha.

February 23, 1944

Dear Mom:

Yesterday was Washington's birthday but in the army there's no such thing as a holiday. It was work just the same—and for the chaplain there is no such thing as a day off, [either]. However, since we have no regularly assigned duty at any time, we can arrange our hours to get a half a day or so off. I plan to take tomorrow afternoon off and spend it in town doing some personal business.

Last evening I had a memorial service for the brother of one of our sergeants in camp who died in the 100th. A very short service, but well attended. I dropped in to see Toshi Anzai after that to just chew the rag, so to speak. I have a few duties to perform but aside from that seems like a very easy day.

I have a few new roommates now. All haoles from all over the country. It's interesting to study the reaction of these fellers when they come here and find that their command is over AJAs. However they do fall into the spirit of it pretty well. We came out of maneuvers with top honors and [either] really looked good or we are really crack troops. At least we would like to think of ourselves as the latter. We have really gained the respect of the other groups.

The question that is strong in our minds is just where or when will the new draftees come in. It will make some difference to us, in that a lot of us may be transferred to train the new groups, but again only the War Department knows that.

Enclosing a little picture taken from the *Missionary Herald*—you probably have seen that by now but thought you might find it interesting. Daddy really doesn't look like that, I am sure—he certainly looks young. I have been gaining weight again after the maneuvers and weigh about 137 pounds now with leggings and boots. That's about eight pounds more than when I was commissioned into the army.

Chaplain [Thomas Eugene] West is having his leave next week and Chaplain Yamada the next. I am hoping to take my leave after they all come back—it will give me 8 months of service after that and some 20 days due to me. Eight months of service—doesn't sound very long but it has been ages for me. Let's pray and hope that it will be all over by the end of this year.

I still can't get over the fact that Peter is as tall as you said he was—perhaps you made a mistake. He must be almost as tall or taller than Karen by now.

Love to Obachan and Peter and write soon.

Love
Dad

July 20, 1944
Dear Mom:

In a village close by, church bells are ringing—probably morning mass. Even though it is near the front, bells of a church give one a certain sense of security and peace nothing else can give. All seems so quiet here—chickens running around and *paesans* (Italian for fellow countryman) walking here and yon. And yet in any minute this peaceful scene could be turned into bedlam.

Have been at my station the past few days just typing letters and daydreaming. Aside from the first week, haven't experienced very much in the way of shelling. Perhaps I am learning not to be places where they are likely to shell—or perhaps the heinies just don't have anything to shoot with. I hope the latter is true—but they seem to be still in there pitching.

It's over a year now since that bright morning I took my oath before the colonel and Peter and you. Since then I have seen much and have experienced things I had never hoped to experience. A year ago I had an impression that frontline duty was something like we experienced in Hawaii during and after the 7th. Now I know different—and yet I would not have gone without this experience for anything. It has been of great value to me personally and has given me greater values, which I would not have received as a civilian at home in a nice safe church.

Remember the letters I used to write from Shelby—I thought training was hard: the bitter cold and the marches too long. To us now, Shelby seemed like paradise and not one of us would ever refuse going back to it—we only regret that the training was not harder to prepare us for combat.

The other evening while dodging shells in a large building I came across a rather better classed Italian family who were also taking refuge in the building. They had four very cute children—four boys. These Italian children are blonds usually as youngsters and grow into brunettes as they grow older. It was so much fun to be with a youngster again—the children just followed me around. Of course we had to speak in sign language—they reminded me so much of Peter. One gets awfully lonesome for children after being away from his own so long.

We have all kinds of bets concerning the date of peace on this front. I still stick to the end of August—others claim it will be this month, while the majority thinks it will be over by Christmas anyway. The real cussed ones figure it to last another ten years or so. We all wish it would be over tomorrow. The way the Russians are pushing—and the lack of materiel the Germans face—it should be over sooner than we expect. Let's hope so anyway.

It must be grand in the Islands now with lights back. I daydream all day about home—the peaceful evenings, the soft breeze—and the smell of gardenias and ginger always in the air. Here in Italy all we smell wherever we go are manure piles and chicken coops. The houses all smell alike and one would have to be an Italian to appreciate it. The flies are awful—and animals seem to be accorded the same treatment as humans. Perhaps it is because wealth still is valued by the number of livestock a person owns. Why they house the animals in their home—I can't really understand. One can understand the bedlam of "home sweet home" with the cattle mooing, the pigs grunting, the chickens cackling, and the children yelling—the old man scolding the old lady and vice versa. Home was never like this—

One of the boys in our company had to go on patrol in one of the towns nearby. While hiding in a house he heard machine guns cracking nearby—after it was safe he crawled out and witnessed one of the most diabolical scenes. The Germans had lined up fifty-seven Italian men and boys and shot them down in cold blood. This is not a war-atrocity story, as it was not only witnessed by our man but also authenticated in our *Stars and Stripes*. And yet these German soldiers are just youngsters—how any man could do anything like that I don't know. Gradually from listening to the stories the men tell me I am beginning to think that the heinies are just blood-thirsty fiends—however when they are captured or in a tight spot, these youngsters all cry "Mama." Guess it is like feeding a child with gangster pictures day after day and then giving him a gun to shoot with—Hitler must have certainly filled these kids with blood lust.

Whenever we come into a new town—the villagers come running out, clapping their hands and cheering the liberators. They mob the Jeep to shake your hands and to hold you. Then in the next instant they come begging for "cigaretto (cigarette)" and "caramella (candy)." These *paesans* must think that we are fighting for them and have come to feed them. I still think that this country is a nation of beggers from the top down—I always think that they must have cheered old Mousso a lot when he was bellowing his way through the shoeless, naked Ethiopians—the conquering Romans, and so forth, and now they come crying, "*Guerra non buono* (war is bad)." If I knew any Italian I would certainly blast them with a sermon on "warmongering Italians."

I am planning to go out for a bath today if possible. I think I am keeping a federal housing plan for some of these Italian lice—even the lice around here want something for nothing it seems. I plan to get a haircut someplace—a shave and then a bath with a change of clothing. Find myself some nice house to sleep in tonight instead of a barn and have a grand rest. I need it.

Don't worry about Daddy—love and kisses for the kids. Keep an eye on Margaret's family—they need you.

Love
Dad

July 22, 1944

Dear Mom:

Hope my letters are reaching you OK—the last few days I have had chances to write to you but do not worry if at times my letters are spaced quite a bit. Everything is OK—and still healthy and kicking. Have managed to keep away from shell fire, although they do give me a scare once in a while. The fellers are out in the orchard picking plums and peaches, which surely adds to our diet.

One of the drivers told me this morning that the radio announced uprisings in Germany. Hope that is true—for it must be the beginning of the end. With Germany on its last tottering legs, so to speak, and Japan rooting out old Tojo—it sounds like peace should be just around the corner. Once the war is over, no one is ever going to get me away from my wife and family ever again. I am going fishing quite a bit and rest for some time before working again—we'll go on those picnics we were always planning on and have lunches for a king's feast. Lately I have learned a few twists about cooking which ought to come in handy then.

It has been easy and quiet for the past few days—but one can never tell. Sometimes we think it is peaceful, when all of a sudden shells begin to rain around us and then we know war is on. The Germans, however, do not really have the materiel that we have—and seem to be short of everything from machines to men. We are just sweating out the end of this mess and hope it comes very soon. One of these days I am going to wake up to find war ended—wouldn't it be great.

Received a letter from Mrs. Crowell addressed to Shelby. I lost her address so when you write her next please thank her for the letter and tell her where I am. It was nice of her to remember me.

It's really a wonder how we can go without the comforts of home that we thought were indispensable. We just carry along the clothes on our back and a jacket to sleep on—no baths—canned rations, and always the shovel. No *punee* (couch), no washbasins, no hot food. I have met Italian families of the better class here who have lost everything but the clothes on their back, with no immediate sight of food, no clothes, no shoes—just life. And yet they keep going. It must be tough, and sometimes I admire their stoicism. I guess I told you about that night I was taking refuge in a building from some heavy shelling and this Italian mother came in scared to death and crying. I made some coffee for her and talked to her which must have helped her some. She was the wife of an Italian colonel—about fifty or so years of age and quite better class. Ever since then she has more or less adopted me as her son, whenever I am in the vicinity. Don't know where she is as we move along so fast but she was one of the people who lost everything she owned. What was not bombed out was stolen by the Germans.

My Italian is improving a little. In a few months I ought to be able to teach the darn language in Italy.

Did you read the article in the *Reader's Digest* on Naples City [about] panic and famine? In the short time I was there, one could easily see how true the article is. Just imagine what is going to happen to the rest of Europe when the war is over. These Italians expect America not only to feed them but to rebuild the darn place for them—they must think America is in this for humanitarian purposes. They should suffer through this themselves and perhaps they will eventually learn that warmongering does not pay. Old Mousso should rebuild it for them, and there is a lot of rebuilding to do.

Passed through a town not long ago which was nothing but rubble—and looked as if it was going to take years to rebuild the place. Multiply that by many times all over Europe, Russia, and England, and what an engineers' holiday it will be. What will this country do for an existence, with trade and industry wiped out. Surely they lived on imports; and how will they live? It is sad to see these little youngsters come to our kitchen and beg for *mangiari* (food to eat)—food, food, nothing but food. They havn't seen coffee, tea, and chocolate for four years, except [for] the Fascisti gang. They had everything.

The Germans, before leaving, had grabbed everything—even clothes, shoes, and jewelry. German mothers and sisters and sweethearts are probably wearing nice clothes today—stolen clothes from the backs of these disillusioned *paesans*. Just high-class robbery I call it. They steal the oxen to pull their artillery with. The Germans first had automobiles, then horses, and now oxen to maneuver around with. The more I come across German brutality, the less I like them and wish they were really wiped off of the map. They are really brutal—Dillinger in his heyday had nothing on these blood-thirsty heinies. Just hate to think of what would happen to Germany if the Russians ever got in there first—and perhaps it would be a good lesson for them to learn—to have whole villages of people lined up and mowed down like so much wheat.

Give my best regards to Shinso and the gang. Tell them I am OK and will be OK for the duration. Ask them to save their pin money for the day I come home and we all will have that chop suey dinner I dream about almost nightly. The last good chop suey I had was in Shinso's office, remember? Just before I left for the boat. If I knew it was going to be the last for this long, I would have eaten more. Please thank Kenneth Mau for his letter.

Haven't seen Takeshi as yet but presume he is OK. He has had many very, very close shaves, but guess God does take care of *nonki* (carefree) people like Tak and myself.

Love

Dad

July 25, 1944

Dear Mom:

Am living comparatively like a prince now in paradise—comparatively speaking, far away from the noise of cannon and the nervebreaking crash of shells—even if I am sleeping on the ground and in a tent, [and] eating sand with my food, this is the perfect life. Let us hope the war ends soon before we have to go back into it.

Am not too busy right now although we have to take care of a lot of odds and ends for the boys and plan on several services. Somehow the last few weeks have been just like a bad dream to me—and one does get to forget things so easily. We do miss the fellers that left us—but guess the full impact of it will not be felt until the time when we go home.

For the past few days I have been trying to locate German dead—and surprisingly have found that more Germans were killed in battle against us than our own losses. After two weeks any body isn't too beautiful to behold. Around the bodies sometimes are strewn pictures of home and mothers and brothers and children belonging to the German dead. Funny to think that one's enemy does have homes and mothers and all the little things in life that make it sentimental. Behind a gun they are devils. Last night I dreamed that I was writing a letter to one of the mothers of a German in which I said:

Dear mother of a German soldier: I saw your son's body today. He was lying in a hot sun, face black and unrecognizable except the golden lock of hair which must have rotted away from the scalp. Around him was strewn like leaves a whole folio of pictures, as if in his last moments he kept looking at them. There were pictures of himself in uniform, of a lady sitting by a window smiling which I presumed must have been you, and several pictures of a blond little feller like my own boy—so very fair and happy looking—which must have been his brother. The boys tell me that when your boy fell he cried "Mama," like all the German boys do. I expected them to cry "Heil Hitler," but no, they always cry for mama. It was one of these boys still little over fifteen who must have led some sixty Italian civilians and shot them—men and boys in cold-blooded murder—and left them screaming in one of the towns that we passed. It may have been your boy that a *paesan* lady told me raped her daughter and murdered the father. And yet he looked so young and sweet, your boy. Instead of bringing him up yourself, you gave him to Hitler. He became a fiend—and yet when he died he did not cry "Hitler," he cried "Mama." He really did not want Hitler—he wanted his mother from his childhood. But no, you sent him to the SS group and felt proud. He cried for his mother.

And this about rounds up my impressions of the enemy—probably coming from good clean backgrounds, but educated for murder by Hitler.

I think the thing that frightened me so much the first few days was the thought that so many were dying unnaturally. It unnerved me but gradually I am getting used to it. I suppose when I get to normal living, the peace of it will be hard to get back into again.

I picked up several steel helmets—have one here which I hope to send to Pete. It's a little large and perhaps should wait until I find a pretty good little one, but for the present Peter will have all kinds of fun strutting around with it—and bringing it to show-and-tell class. This helmet, I found next to a blond feller—young, sprawled like a marionette. We do find a lot of things but leave most of them strictly alone.

I have also a little elephant made in silver which I bought along the line somewhere which I ought to send home to you. It has a little story behind it, I am sure, as it belonged to one of these Facsisti fellers.

The Russians are really going like wildfire, aren't they? Hope they keep it up and the Allied invasion is making some headway.

This morning I watched the Italians threshing wheat. It is really a very agrarian country with wheat and corn and fruits aplenty. The farmers are the only ones that will not starve, I think.

Take care of yourself, Mom, and the children, I am quite worried over Jane's little cold and asthmatic cough. There is nothing so excruciating, I think, as asthma in youngsters.

My best regards to Margaret and family—and hope they are taking it well.

Love
Hiro

July 26, 1944
Dear Mom:

How be you. Tis pretty good here—that is, good because we are not too active at the present time. Saw Takeshi last night, and it was great to see him. When in battle, we don't get to see each other at all and worry no end over each other until we get to a place like this.

He stayed overnight with me, and I got one of the soldiers to play Hawaiian music for us. The moon was at the quarter, and all of us sat behind a haystack and sang songs of home and popular songs. It is nights like this I am sure that will be remembered by us more than the terrible things that we see. It's human nature to forget the bad things and only to remember the wonderful moments in life.

Lying in my slit trench I think of all kinds of things—and also of death. I wonder why life is so precious to us individually—some time or another we will all go beyond through sickness or old age. And yet, I wonder if I will fear death as much as I do in battle when old age comes. Perhaps death in a violent form makes us fear more—the thought that our body may lie in the hot sun and disintegrate more or less. I have seen so many German bodies in all states of decomposition—and if I can think of them only as physical matter, just a cold chemical body lying there, it would help. Somehow or another we always attach personalities to cadavers, and if one can get over that, it would be so much easier to face fear. Tak and I talked over these things and swapped experiences—each time my experiences get better and better I notice. Really, I am not in very much danger in comparison with line soldiers like Tak.

Tak has been in battle for over a year now. So far he has been extremely fortunate and [we] pray and hope that his luck holds out. He has had many narrow squeezes as do all the other fellers. Some of the stories they tell would make my hair stand on end if I were there. We joke and laugh over it now but when it's time to go in, I know that everything will be grim.

Yesterday, I went over to a *paesan's* home to arrange entertainment for our men. Before the war, [the family] used to be a theatrical group with musical comedies, etc. Among their repertoire they have a hula dance—with cellophane skirts and everything. However their interpretation of the hula consists mostly of hip movements and less hand movements, which affords us no end of fun. To see an Italian version of the hula so far away from home—

Don't worry about me—the war, we hope, will be over soon and we'll be home.

Love
Dad

August 1, 1944

Dear Mom:

Just a month to go before the date of my choice for the end of this phase of the war. Hope for once that my predictions come true.

Have been just resting for the past few days doing nothing but eating and sleeping. However, we know that sooner or later we will have to go back into the holocaust again, which strictly is *niente buona* (nothing good) as the *paesans* say. Getting so that I can carry on a pretty good conversation in Italian—at least the Italians understand my version of their lingo.

Am planning to go to Rome on pass sometime this week. It won't be much of a pass as I will have to visit the hospitals and make the rounds of them while I am there but it will be away from the immediate front line—and airplanes coming around at nights.

The Germans apparently don't have any planes that fly during the day. Haven't seen one since going into action here—that is, during the day, but they come around at night, one or two of them at a time. It would be a mess, however, if they came around during daylight.

Am sitting behind the same haystack as last week. It gives one a very pastoral feeling. The homes, as all over Italy, are made of bricks and mortar—thick walls that help quite a bit when one needs protection from things.

I had a very nice memorial service for the boys killed in action on Sunday. The news-photo man was here to take pictures so you will probably get pictures in the local papers of the service. I felt that it was impressive and well managed—somehow a minister always knows when his services go off well. Received many compliments on the service, which made me feel good. Each chaplain has his own service for his battalion.

I suppose Peter is having the time of his life this vacation. Keep an eye on him as he is rather active for a youngster and daring—don't like him to climb trees, if possible, or go swimming alone. Jane will be walking in a few months—will miss seeing her first steps and probably will miss her first words. Am worried about her asthmatic cough; asked the doctor about it and he said that it does not necessarily mean that she has asthma. Doc Ushiro, a Stanford graduate, and I usually run around together. We play cribbage nightly. At the present time, he is still only one game ahead of me.

Saw Ben yesterday and he is doing OK. Pete, too, is OK—he hasn't come around for quite some while but hope to see him as soon as opportunity allows.

This morning I plan to spend my time writing letters to the parents of the deceased. It is a tough job and don't know just what to say, and besides there are certain things one can say and one cannot. We cannot write directly to the parents but must send it through the War Department so that it will be quite late when they do receive the letters. I have to type my letters; my handwriting would be illegible. I wonder how long it takes before the War Department notifies the parents. They try to do it as soon as possible, but always check and recheck the list to make sure of no mistakes.

Yesterday I got up early in the morning and visited a hospital. Spent practically the whole day visiting different hospitals and then in the afternoon, late, Doc and I went to the village to buy some fish. If we only had some soy sauce here, it would be perfect. Guess I will ask Alice to send me some.

I am typing this letter sitting on a German helmet which I hope to send to Peter. I don't know whether the postal system will accept it or not but others are doing it OK. I tried to find a helmet with *SS* printed on the side but have had no luck so far—the SS is Hitler's personal troops made up of youngsters brought up under him. They are a tough, brutal group and really fiendish. However, caught alone, they cry. The boys tell me that these German soldiers all cry when caught, except the old-timers. See in the *Stars and Stripes*, our local paper, that they found some hundred or so bodies of women and children who were machine gunned by these Germans. Perhaps many of these atrocity stories may not be true but these have been verified by the authorities, and in one instance one of our boys saw the act. I often wonder how any man or a group of men could be so cruel.

I am frightened to death most of the time—and am getting so that just the mention of combat or returning to the lines stops my breath. Guess everybody else is that way, but the marvel is that we do go back and carry orders.

I remember that day we were bivouacked in a little valley and the Germans began to shell us. The whistle of the shells as they come nearer and nearer makes one believe that it is headed straight for the hole you are in. It starts with a faint whisper and goes stronger and stronger as it comes near and then breaks with a loud crash that pushes one's eardrums in. That's the day I had spent two hours digging a slit trench one foot [deep] before the shelling—and after fifteen minutes of the shelling had dug it down to five feet with my shoes, hands, fingers, and shovel. It's the same day my Jeep got shrapnel all over it and the tires were cut to pieces—luckily no one was in the Jeep. I came out of that slit trench with my clothes ringing wet from cold sweat. A few boys were wounded but not seriously. It is a funny thing—with all these shells and bullets and bombs and mines—the casualties are very low in comparison. I figure it takes thousands of shells to kill one man and the same for bullets—and then the wounded are more than ten times the [amount of the] killed, I suspect. Most of our wounds have been light wounds, although I have seen some that made me turn my face away. One does get used to blood after a while, I know, but I haven't as yet. I don't think it is the blood that gets me as much as the fact that I know all these boys and many of them are personal friends of mine.

Sometimes I go after bodies of men killed in action. We try to get the bodies buried as soon as possible and not have [them] laying in this hot climate too much. I got lost from the other officer who was leading the way and took the wrong direction when all of a sudden came the familiar whistle and a crack which made me beat a hasty retreat.

There are several shells that come. The large German guns which come whistling over and give you a couple of seconds to seek cover, the fast-shooting 88s that come so speedily that one doesn't know about it until it cracks, and the mortars which make no noise at all and just crack. The boys hate the mortars most, as [they] give them no warning—personally I would have no truck with [any] of them. Of course, the mines are terrible but I make it a policy not to travel on unknown roads or unswept roads and so far have had no trouble. The Nazis have booby-trapped several places but the *paesans* get hurt more than our men, as we are very careful about those things. But if we hate their artillery, the Germans must just die nine times when our artillery comes over. The Germans usually shoot *boom*, then a second, then *boom*, and so on, while our artillery go like machine guns and crack *boom boom boom* all at once and give them fifty times more than they give us. They are really afraid of our guns. And then we have planes which go out and scare the living daylights out of them. They don't seem to have any to spare on this front, it seems, but I wouldn't put too much faith in that thought.

Then the Germans shoot a lot of duds—one day I counted four duds in a row, which is really a soothing feeling to hear their gun go *boom* and a little plop on this end. The saboteurs in Germany are doing a pretty good job. It has saved many a life in Italy. Someday we will get a full story of these saboteurs. Feel that the Germans ought to crack up soon— and when the break comes, the war will end sudden-like. They can't stand up against such heavy pressure as we are giving them on three fronts—and one realizes that when one sees the kids we fight against—but behind a gun these kids are really tough.

A hug to the children and regards to Obachan.

Love
Hiro

August 13, 1944
Dear Peter:

Thank you for the letter you wrote; it was most interesting and fine. Yes, we have been in battle for a long time now—and am taking care of myself. Every time Daddy digs a foxhole, he digs one extra deep and [I] say to myself, "This is for Peter and Jane and Mom." Then once in a while German airplanes come over us at night and we dive into the foxhole, or many times they shoot [at] us with cannons and we dive into the foxhole. The most dangerous things in war are the cannons and mortars, then bombs and mines. Machine-gun bullets and rifle bullets are not too scary, as we can see the enemy, but not the others.

War is not like the movies you see. It is much more awful and dangerous than that, and very, very bad.

I am sending little Jane a little gift of a doll made in Italy with a Florentine dress and also a little rattler. Please tell Mommie about that—and also enclosing in this envelope a little piece of straw which I forgot to include in the other letter I wrote to Mom.

Mommie told me about your swimming lesson which you missed. Try hard to learn, and when I come home we will go swimming together almost every day. We will also build a nice large home of hollow tile, two stories high, with a room for Jane, and a study and science room for you. Wouldn't it be grand? We must have a large living room because Daddy likes large living rooms, and a large kitchen 'cause Mommie wants a large kitchen and a large bedroom. We will have an extra nice bedroom for Obachan, too, won't we?

Dollar was slightly wounded in one of the battles but now he is alright and will be out of the hospital very soon. He is a very brave soldier and knows that he will someday do many brave deeds with his machine gun. I see Takeshi once in a while and he always talks about his cousin with the same name—he is also a brave soldier and you can be proud of being his cousin.

Not long ago, Daddy was in action and a large cannon shell came booming down—Daddy jumped out of his Jeep and hid in a hole and the shell landed and nearly blew my Jeep to pieces. I know, though, that God is watching over me because I have such a nice family.

I am hoping that the war will be over by Xmas. Then we will have a nice Christmas together with real Christmas trees and lights and good food and everything. In war, we don't live in houses or tents—we just sleep where we find ourselves, in holes and in ditches—anywhere. We don't eat very much—only C and K rations, which do not taste good and [have] just a small portion. We don't change clothes for many days, and never take a bath for months. It is very dirty—after a week of fighting, our beards look like the one Santa Claus has on.

This is a tough war.

Daddy visited many Italian families. They do not have much to eat and go hungry most of the time. I bought a little toy for one of the little boys in a family. He had not received a toy for four years and his eyes shone, and he could not talk because he was so happy. He would not play with the toy because he said it was "too precious." They don't have any clothes to wear because there is no cloth in Italy—and the children go barefooted because there are no shoes. I think of you and Jane and say how lucky you all are in Hawaii. When you pray at night, perhaps it would be good to ask God to watch over the little children all over the world so that they may have food and clothes and toys, too, like you do.

Please tell Mommie that I received her letter of the 16th today. My letters home take only a few days, but letters from home do take a long, long time to get here. I also wrote to Dr. Dunstan concerning the new job I was planning on and hope that he will consider it.

And Peter, be a good boy. I know you are, and Mommie and Uncle Sambo write all kinds of good things about you. Maybe the next time you see Shinso, you can thank him for the glasses for me. I did not receive them yet—but hope to very soon. I use the dark glasses all the time, as this Italian sun really hurts the eyes.

Take care of yourself. Give Mommie and little Janie a big hug and kiss for Daddy. Please tell me how tall you are now. I have a stick with me all the time and measure it every time I get your height. By the time I come home, maybe I will have to look up at you to talk to you.

Bye.
Love
Daddy

August 14, 1944
Dear Mom:

Got your letter of the 21st today and it was grand. I am writing this from the same haystack—how I love it. Only I know one of these days, they are going to take me away from it and it won't be so *buona*. It's funny but by this time, we have forgotten the terror of combat—but know that as soon as we go in again, it'll all come back and maybe in double dose.

Haven't received Doc's letter as yet but please say that all I want after the war is a good dinner and a good session with him.

This afternoon I took a convoy of men to see the graves of their relatives, brothers, and cousins. The cemetery was beautifully laid, and we spent several hours stopping before the graves of our boys for prayer and meditation. There are so many of our close friends there, and as I knelt before each, somehow could not keep the tears from welling up in my eyes—each of them loving life, each of them laid so carefully so far from home. They had given the supreme sacrifice, and we who remain owe them a debt that we cannot ever repay. There was one boy who brought with him a little flower plant—a beautiful little thing which he got somewhere and carried so carefully to the cemetery. He laid the plant carefully over the mound and then came to ask me to read a passage of scripture and say a prayer over the grave of his pal. It was so touching, so sad. After that, I had a service in the cemetery—please assure the parents when you see any of them that I have given them all the devotion and care of our faith. We don't get to perform the funeral service as we are at the front all the time and the bodies are interned in the rear echelon. However, some chaplain takes care of the funeral services. We go back when we can to say a prayer for them. I left there with a lump in my throat, for many of these boys grew up with me in my boys clubs and my Sunday school.

Last evening I dropped in to see the Bellincioni family. They are very nice to me and hate to think of leaving them, for they have become very good friends of mine. The kids all tag along when I come. Had dinner with them, which the Italians usually eat so late. Their dinner consisted of a rice soup, vegetable salad, black bread, eggs, and raw bacon. It was very good finished off with wine. I told them it made me feel so happy, as it reminded me of my own home, with Father at the head and Mother at the other end, the children on one side with Grandma on the other side. They think I am the best man on earth and call me their pastor. What will their good priest think of that when he learns that they have adopted a protestant minister?

Am so glad that you are thinking seriously about rehabilitation because someone has to do it, someone who will not forget ever the sacrifice these kids made and the hell that they have gone through. As I sat in front of the grave today—some boy who had been so fine and so good, boys who had been my best in my clubs at home—I realize that my fight and my work is only beginning. There are many things to do yet.

Yes, I wish, too, that you were here with me, for it would give me greater courage and inspiration than ever. One night, or rather the night I met the Bellincionis in the old house, shells—large shells—dropped around us, each one capable of blowing each and every one of us to hell, and each splinter capable of cutting off our heads like so many chickens. I was scared. But just the knowledge that these people depended upon me for confidence helped a lot. I made coffee, and kept their spirits up some way or another. After the night of shelling was over, I was shaky and nervous. I often wondered why a shell did not land on us then.

Peter wrote me such a fine, brave letter. Tell him thanks. I miss the boy a lot, you know. Tell him that Daddy always takes extra precautions because of him.

By this time I know that casualty reports have come in—and you already know of some of our friends who have lost their sons. Such is war—and I know that it has hit you pretty closely, too. Please help these families in whatever way you can—a word of comfort and a word of courage that their son has given [his] life for an ideal, and [his] sacrifice would really be for nought unless they, too, kept the fight going, not at the battlefront but on the peace front. Tell them to be brave and courageous and have faith—this is not the end of their loved ones. Jesus has promised in St. John, chapter 14, that he was going to prepare mansions for those who follow. Faith—we need faith so much.

Tell Doc not to write me serious things—we want to laugh, we want cheer—something to keep our mind away from all this horror. I never enjoyed a letter so much as Sambo's—he gives me a kick and a lift every time.

Hope you got the pictures I sent you. They were taken at one of the places near here. I have gained a little in weight maybe, look a little rugged—but no difference. Of course if I did not shave, you would see big splotches of white hair in my beard, for the war has done that to me overnight almost.

See by the papers that the French front is traveling in leaps and in bounds and that Russia, too, is going great guns. I certainly wish them all the luck—the war couldn't end any sooner for us. They must really be going through a tough fight—much tougher than the ones we had gone through, although I don't know what could be tougher.

I do hope that Shinso's glasses arrive soon. Did he send it airmail? I am down to my last broken pair, and those sunglasses are just the thing for this place. I wear them all day and only resort to my regular glasses during the night—and sometimes don't use glasses at all.

Take care of yourself, Mom. I dream of home and you constantly. Of the little things that made home what it is—our dinner table with Peter kicking the chair and giving us his accounts of the day. Of the evenings on the *punee*—Peter, you, and I—of the afternoons at home in the yard and my promises to fix things later, always later or tomorrow. Don't get too old or gray or fat while I am away—I'd like to come home to see the same trim little wife I left. Or were you trim?

Say hello to Obachan for me and tell her that I really enjoy her letters and read them over every time, twice or more. She has really been grand—and I appreciate it no end.

Dollar is getting better—he had a very narrow escape but all in all certainly showed his courage and braveness. He will be with us soon. Toshi Anzai is not back—he had some trouble with his knee so may be out indefinitely. I am glad for him since at his age he can't do very much.

Yes, the 100th is doing a grand job. Understand there is an article in *Time* magazine in which the general of the division says that they are the best battalion in his whole division. These Hawaiian kids certainly made a name for themselves. They are brave and tough—and the unity is very good.

Kiss the children for me, will you?

Love
Dad

P.S. Did I stop to tell you? I love you.

October 22, 1944

Dear Mom:

Two months ago they said the war would be over by now but guess no one really knows and every guess is a bad one. My guess is now that the Germans will fight until the last man and child capable of pulling a trigger is killed or taken prisoner. They are tough customers and bad ones. Now in their desperation some of them are even shooting our wounded on litters, which shows how low they are really getting.

We have moved again and are ensconced in a French farmhouse. And gradually as we move farther east, I find that the people also speak Deutch, which is a great help to me, although we also find that the people are not as friendly. We got our first mail in several weeks today and I hit the jackpot with four letters from you scattered here and there, one written on the 25th of August and the last written on the 29th of September. Also got a letter from Ruth Takayesu—she writes so regularly—thank her for it, will you please, and when I last saw Ben, he asked me especially to write to you and tell you that he is OK but had no time to write to his parents. Saw Nobuo Hirotsu today; he came to service and so he, too, is OK. Horace's brother is OK. As he is in the artillery, there isn't very much to worry about him until we hit something really stubborn or the Jerries throw in a lot of planes. Got up early this morning and had services on the front and also with a few scattered here and there. It is always a risky business and I go out cautiously, as I always do. I was quite sure since Chaplain Yamada's close shave that people at home would have us mixed up. I have been rather fortunate lately, and I say it with knocking on wood, to have any shells that land near me duds, or land after I left the place or just before I came to a spot. Hope this luck holds out, although yesterday when I went out for the bodies there was certainly danger of one sort or another.

I enjoyed your letters so much. I think you have Peter's height mixed up since you said he was five foot one when I think you meant four foot one inches. He must be quite a man now and I am proud of him. Please thank Lieutenant Albers for the bars—guess I will receive them eventually.

Please, please tell Obachan not to work so hard but to take it easy. She must not worry about anything and try to gain weight if possible. I feel very responsible for her and do not want her to worry but take it easy. Being a captain now, this ought to be an order. Please thank her for the letter; it is always a boost to hear from her.

Please tell Peter not to try swimming without anyone older near him, as I am always worried about swimming in the Islands. Guess you must be quite busy with everything—don't overdo and take it easy. I will try myself to be very careful and not take too many chances.

The news today seems definitely good on all fronts. Guess from now on in, the Germans are really on the slide and ought to fold up as an organized strength soon, although I am afraid that there will be a lot of mopping up to do in Germany. As I come nearer to the border, I often think about Madame Schurer and her sons [about] whom she was so worried. Guess they are in the army and more than likely dead by this time, or wounded. The Germans are really getting a terrific licking on all fronts and it is really the best way to finish this phase of the war in a hurry.

Had three grand services today and the newsreel man came out with me and took pictures of me on the front talking to the boys and of services held in other places. Guess you might be able to see them some day. I gave as my home my Waipahu address, so perhaps Waipahu will have a chance to see their prodigal son in the pictures, so to speak.

This part of the war is tougher than we had in Italy, although Italy was plenty tough. The krauts are really desperate, although the way we take prisoners daily by the dozens, we wonder how desperate they are. Besides that, I figure our casualties are much lighter than theirs.

Tomorrow, if possible, I plan to comb over the combat areas passed over to look for wounded Jerries. After all, that is the only human thing to do. We take their dead out and bury them, too, although the frontline chaplains actually never do any burials.

Helen Oshiro, Mavis' younger sister, wrote me a letter today. She always writes regularly. Please thank the little girl for me, as I know she would appreciate hearing from me, but for the present am not able to write any more than to you.

Will write again when I can. If you don't hear from me for a long while you will understand because it is so difficult to write while in combat. Pray for an early peace and for our boys out in the cold and rain. And take care of yourself—love to the children.

Love

Dad

October 27, 1944

Dear Mom:

I swear when we build a home, I am going to insist on having a fireplace, even in Hawaii, so that I can soak in all the warmth that left my body during the past few days. The fighting is still going on fiercely, and sometimes [we] get insensible to things that were beautiful, and good. It's funny but when in rest, we only think of the funny incidents that happened during combat and forget or refuse to think of the horrors of it.

Had a pretty good sleep last night, although the Germans threw a lot of artillery around us—and several, I thought, were going to climb into bed with me. They come in with a resounding crash that scares one's life to the zero point—and then a few minutes later another would come. The idea is perhaps to keep a feller up all night, worrying. I did worry till about twelve and then dropped off into slumber.

According to the papers, the enemy we are fighting is the fanatical Herrenvolk army—boys and old men recruited within the last few weeks and given a rifle and a uniform. No wonder the uniforms of the prisoners we caught looked pretty clean and new, and the soldiers still nonshaving youngsters with fuzz still on their face. But they are fanatical and never give in—rather die than do it. How long will this sort of thing keep up?

It's a long way yet for us into German soil, and once we are in, no doubt have to keep a wary eye on the civilians as they must be really desperate.

Am still in this French peasant's home, where we moved in yesterday. I sleep on the floor in an unheated room—dirt and cobwebs all around me and the dank smell of mud whiffing me off to bed. Tis cold—and too near the enemy lines to give us any ease of feeling.

In one of the last homes I was in, the wife of the doctor gave me a woolen scarf, which helps a lot. That was a nice home, too, as I had a grand room to myself with enough protection above my head to give me a feeling of security and a nice basement to run into if the going got too tough.

Am enclosing the rest of the films taken in Italy. Doc Ushiro is the feller standing next to the poster which I carry around with me. I don't think I sent a picture of him back to you yet.

Guess the rainy season hereabouts is about over, but dark clouds seem to be the order as the sun hasn't peeped out for ages and it is becoming colder and colder. I hope to get paid in the next few days and, if so, will send home $160 to you. That ought to help with your Christmas expense. If I am not mistaken I did send home eighty dollars through the government in September—wonder if you got it as yet. If not, I will start an inquiry on it.

Take good care of yourself and don't worry about Dad.

Love
Dad

December 19, 1944

Dear Mom:

Here it is six days before Christmas and I am relieved of all the worrying over Christmas cards and things that used to clutter up my Christmases before, although I will have to think about answering all those people that wrote to me hence. Received several cards lately.

Last night I had a Christmas program for the children of this French community—about two hundred young kids and their parents. The boys scraped the bottom of their candy kits and donated enough candy to give each boy an armful. The kitchens made cakes and sandwiches with real meat for the filling, which is such a treat to the people here. We served hot cocoa and had a real grand party for the kids. The mothers surged into the line, too, for food is so precious here. The hall was packed. We put up a Christmas tree and the people decorated it and had the little town hall decorated the best as possible. It reminded one of the Christmases in some dinky, small town back home. We did not have a Santa Claus, as I understand the old feller is a religious character here and thus hated to hurt the old curé's (parish priest in France) feelings. The people came early and the old curé and the mayor came in, and this being the biggest event in their town's history beside the liberation, they bustled around and finally, after getting the minor riot settled, we began our program. First we had the GIs sing "Hark the Herald Angels Sing"—as the French do not know any American carols. Then the orchestra played some American jazz, which was perfect. In the middle of the orchestra program, our colonel comes in so the old curé insisted that we play the national anthem. We told him that one didn't do that in America but he insisted, so I bustled around looking for the music. Meanwhile the band began to play "Sweet Susie Brown" or something and the curé, not knowing the difference, made the French audience rise up at attention for "Sweet Susie Brown." Finally after about five minutes of that I got the curé straightened out on "Sweet Susie Brown" and the national anthem. After the orchestra pieces—we had a quartet sing "Silent Night" then a solo from one of our boys—then we sang "O Little Town of Bethlehem," then we turned the program over to the French kids and they really went to town singing folk songs to us. After that, a French civilian sang "Lilting Marseilles" very stirringly. It was quite alright. Then we passed out the gifts and candies and each child had more candy then he had seen since the German occupation. The kids were goggle-eyed and would have appreciated it more if they knew that the boys had given up a day's candy ration for them. Then we served the cocoa and sandwiches and these people ate well for the first time in a long while—for American white bread is considered a cake here in France. Thus went a nice program.

This afternoon I have to go into town to the Red Cross and practice [with] some forty French girls in carol singing and prepare for the boys' program. They don't know how to sing American carols and the French carols are not familiar to us. We are teaching them "Silent Night" and also "O Come All Ye Faithful," plus "White Christmas." So you see, I will have my hands full for the next few days. In the meanwhile, we are going to move again—so all in all it is going to be a busy Christmas anyway, without the usual gift wrapping and card sending.

On the way into town I am stopping for my pictures which I had taken in town and will send them to you. I have, or rather had, four enlargements made—one for you, Ets, Sam, and Kamejiu, and I think you will love the picture as it turned out rather well.

The boys in the battalion are so good to me. The other day when I went into town for the pictures the clerk said, "So, you're the chaplain." I said, "How do you know?" and the clerk said, "Some of the men were in here and said that you were the best dammed chaplain in the U.S. Army," which makes me feel so good. Of course, other outfits will swear to their chaplain similarly, too. The boys often get me some meat or something, so I take this to some French family and get them to cook it for me. They are more than pleased, as they get to eat meat, too, and so [I] have been eating very well since hitting this part of France. The people, however, seem so mercenary around here and methinks it is because the place is a tourist town.

Christmas this year is going to be a rather lonesome one but know that you at home will have a good Christmas. Don't worry about

Dad—he is OK so far and hope to keep OK. The work is dangerous and full of hardships and wonder often how I ever took it so well so far. The fear that grips you at times just about cramps one up—but [I] feel that I must keep on. No doubt I do not take half of the danger that others do, but I must keep up.

Today I am sending Peter a French helmet and an Italian helmet. His collection of helmets should be almost complete now, if I can find a British one and a Japanese helmet. There is also a Jerry cap enclosed. Wash it before using it.

I sent Peter a whole package full of stamps the other day. Hope you get it as I would like to have Peter have it for Christmas. However, doubt if it will go that fast. They are stamps of French colonies and some of Greece. The modern French stamps are difficult to find—guess I will have to buy some. I hope to send Dickie some, too, when I get around to it, but things are so dear here today I don't dare walk into a store. I have to go to the dentist tomorrow as I have chipped my front tooth a little, and then visit the hospital.

I am enclosing in envelope the photograph of myself which I will send to you enlarged tomorrow. I made some two dozen of these to send out to friends and people I owe things to. I will probably mail them to you and have you give it to them, as it would be easier that way.

Take care of yourself, Mom—Dad is OK. The war should be over within another few months and then we will have a grand homecoming. I haven't been away from home so long compared to some soldiers I know, and would rather be here in the thick of it than in some outpost living the life of Riley.

Love to the children and on Christmas morning, please give them an extra kiss from me. Love to Obachan and to you all.

Love
Dad

Chaplain Masao Yamada

442nd Regimental Combat Team

"DEAR A": LETTERS HOME

Chaplain Masao Yamada was one of three chaplains who provided spiritual guidance and support to the men in the 100th/442nd Regimental Combat Team. He was immensely proud of the nisei soldiers and their dedication to their country—a pride he shared in letters home to his wife, Ai.

October 22, 1943
Dear A,

Yesterday morning I began a letter, but had to leave it unfinished in camp. We went into camp just to meet and be in review for the assistant secretary of war, Mr. John McCloy.

It was a real big day. The officers had to be in their best—blouse and pinks. The men were in their best, also. The whole combat team passed in review. I stood on the line with the reviewing officers and had a very good view. As the men passed the stand, the assistant secretary of war commented on the troops most favorably. As they passed by, many a time my heart beat fast and I felt like weeping to see the gallant young men, eager and strong, looking forward to the day of battle. Oh, it made me feel proud and again sad to think one had to die to become the proof of loyalty. I know if the parents could have seen the whole team march by, they, too, would stand silently and weep. . . .

M.

May 1, 1944
Dear A,

May Day is lei day in Hawaii!

We were a happy group on board ship, singing our dear Hawaiian holiday anthem. Some of our men were ingenious. They made a lei out of orange skins—sliced nicely in thin strips, making a long continuous skin to hang on the neck. What humor our men could concoct.

Our day on the waters was uneventful in the sense that we anchored offshore without much movement, waiting for the others to fall in line. It was a good foretaste of the sea journey. It got our men acquainted with the ship, the salt air, and the crowded quarters.

After two nights in the harbor, May 3, we finally got underway. It was certainly a grand feeling. The men were certain; they were on the move. I discovered that the spirit of all was united, for now we knew that we could not do without each other! The sense of fellowship between the officers and the men has increased. They are fraternizing in a normal, natural way. As far as I can see, in an army such as ours, it is all to the good. We are not professional soldiers. We are in the army because we want to bring victory to our country. We are in for a mission and when it is over, return home!

M.

June 14, 1944
Dear A,

Since our training program is strenuous, I really have not found much inspiration to write. I should be more at ease, but too many things have taken place.

The excitement of meeting the 100th is not over. They are so battle hardened that we beginners feel green in their presence. I met Captain Takahashi and he is a great leader. His men adore his command. I have not met Sparky Matsunaga yet, but hope to soon. . . .

M.

July 28, 1944
Dear A,

Two letters, July 10 and July 13, came. Thanks!

Yesterday, we had a very impressive ceremony for the 100th Battalion citation. General Clark came and spoke to the whole regiment. He officially welcomed the 442nd, praised the good work of the green troops, and gave a boost to the 100th. The 100th deserved every bit of it. The citation was for the courageous work done in two towns—Belvedere and Suvereto.

The 442nd was in the same action. In one of the towns, I was in the town long before any of the 100th came in full force. I was with a small patrol walking leisurely and before we knew it, enemy rifles and machine guns fired. We were green then, and we did things that we will never do again.

That was the time I was told by Captain Takahashi to withdraw to the rear. He thought I was out too far forward for safety.

What the general of the Fifth Army said, however, was impressive. He gave credit to the AJAs for courage and loyalty. He made a good speech. The 100th Battalion was filmed. Colonel Charles W. Pence also spoke. It will appear in the newsreel one of these days. You won't see me. I'm too far in the rear. You won't see much of the faces, but it will give you an idea of how we look in combat areas.

The army now wants a lot of publicity. We have a reporter working with each battalion to give the fullest account of our team. Most of these reporters are from Hawaii. I hope the job will be done properly. It will be for the good of all our cause.

The Hawaiian atmosphere still prevails here. We have a sign on the beach—442nd Waikiki Beach. Every day, morning and afternoon, you can see our men swimming. I'm taking a swim every afternoon. So far, I was able to continue for four afternoons. It is the best exercise one can get here.

The other day I visited the 38th Evac. (Evacuation) Hospital. A good many of our men are in the hospital. Every ward has some of our 442nd. I also had dinner with the doctors. They all commented that our AJAs are excellent patients. They can "take it." The surgical officer, who did a lot of amputations, etc., asked me how our men could be so stoical. I had no answer but to say that's how they were trained at home.

They were also interested in Hawaii and Pearl Harbor. We had a grand time talking of Pearl Harbor and the AJAs. I'm sure any haole that comes in contact with an AJA will always be our friend. The chaplain, the doctors, all are quite well impressed with them.

There is no question now about the courage of our men. All the haole soldiers are spreading the stories for us. Even the rear echelon—the Quarter Master Corps, etc.—all show a good deal of respect for us. In due time, the 442nd will be outdoing the 100th.

The sad side of our team is that some of our officers can't do as well as the men. They sit in the rear and expect to accomplish their mission. It simply cannot be done. Leadership springs from a healthy respect of the heart. Unless one respects the other from within, there can be neither leader nor follower. Our AJAs can't stand an officer who shows cowardice. We do have a few who are not up to expectation. I wish something could be done about it, but you can't implant courage in a man's heart as you could some other vice and thought. Courage is a by-product of the sum total of one's training, thoughts, and beliefs. It is one's philosophy and faith that makes for courage or for cowardice.

I see how changed our officers are now in the field. They are no longer the haughty, proud, arrogant dictator-type of officers. At home, they expected to have their orders and their rank respected to almost the point of worship. Now only those who are inwardly strong, who are willing to lead their men have that spark of command in them. The men can rightfully love and follow only such. The others are now like empty, tinkling cymbals. They can't practice what they preached back home.

This Sunday we are holding special services for our real heroes. My battalion is 46. Hiro's is 70. My group is in better shape and has stood up better throughout the campaign. Hiro still has nine missing. I have all accounted for.

I'm trying to do in some ways more than I'm supposed to. During our worst days, Eddy Yamasaki and I carried out over twenty dead bodies. It was not a pleasant task, but since the officer in charge was afraid of his job, we did it. For it, however, all the men have shown their deepest respect. From it I have learned to brave any danger.

Goro Kashiwaeda, my Makaweli chairman, [and] Shin Sugawara, of Hanapepe, were two I recognized one night as I lifted them on my Jeep. My heart was sick to see such good people lost.

So far our Kona boys, Isami Hiraoka [and] Taketa are O.K. I see them often. In the 100th, I have seen Lieutenant Fujitani quite alive. There are several others, but I can't recall. . . .

Love to the Boys!

M.

October 30, 1944
Dear A,

After four days of fierce fighting, we are still pushing to get to the trapped battalion.

The cost has been high. I admire the courage and the discipline of our loyal men. They took their orders in stride without complaint and went into the volley of fire, with one spirit and one mind. Actually, those that saw the charge (our men call it the "banzai" charge) came home with a vivid and stirring account of our men unflinchingly charging on the double, falling under machine-gun fire, yet moving on as the ceaseless waves beat on a seashore.

I am spiritually low for once. My heart weeps with our men, especially with those who gave all. Never has any combat affected me so deeply as has this emergency mission. I am probably getting soft, but to me the price is too costly for our men. I feel this way because the burden is laid on the combat team when the rest of the 141st (Battalion, 36th Division) is not forced to take the same responsibility.

In spite of my personal lamentations, our men are facing their enemy with the courage that comes from the heart. When we complete this mission, which we will today or tomorrow, we will have written with our own blood another chapter in the story of our adventures in Democracy. . . .

M.

November 4, 1944
Dear A,

Your letter of Sept. 29th arrived. Some of the letters are slow, others pretty fast. The twenty-cent airmail doesn't make any appreciable difference. From now on, use six cents airmail and the result will be about the same.

The radio has broadcast the news of the lost battalion. Some of the men of the 141st spoke regarding their experiences—no food, enemy harassing, etc. But it did not say specifically that the 442nd sacrificed more than anyone else to save them.

Our men really don't care about the credit, but personally, I feel that such events are so rare and far between that our friends should utilize the news as "spot news." The cameraman was on the job and took some very exciting pictures—the charge, etc. I suppose the truth will come out probably in a month or a year from now.

In the meantime, our men are still courageously pushing forward. How they can stand fighting is creating serious comment from leaders of the haole groups. Some of them have asked me how we can keep our men pushing and fighting as we do.

I asked several of the men themselves. It is difficult to answer, but most of them agree on the following.

1. We are of one type—AJAs, so we have a common bond and a sense of social solidarity, a common unity.
2. They are strongly sensitive to the fact of doing their duty. They would go beyond their ordinary strength for their pride's sake! They would push to the last step to keep up their reputation!
3. They also go on due to a deep sense of loyalty to one another. When their pal is going on, they go on for each other's sake. Many times they fight on to be with their friends. Their sense of solidarity is oft times the basis of their unselfish, sacrificial output.

They started with the basic challenge: Are the AJAs loyal? By the time our men got into combat, they were psychologically determined to prove it by action and not by arguments. The 100th set the pace, did a good job, and now the 442nd is repeating the same output. The sense of being challenged started the ball rolling, but since they feel that their initial victory of loyalty has been won, the more personal angle is pushing them on or causing their break.

The proof is beginning to show. Up to now we had a very small portion of shell-shock cases. We are beginning to receive serious cases of shell shock in greater numbers. Many of them break down due to the loss of their best friends. In many cases when they see their buddies go, the going becomes a mental strain, and the enemy shelling becomes a mental disturbance of greater fear than usual. When shelling continues for days and nights, mental hope diminishes and the accumulation of fear increases in proportion to the degree hope vanishes. The result is finally a close call—a complete mental breakdown.

Those that were once wounded also have a difficult time adjusting themselves to combat. The fear of being hit again, the sense of suffering, the dread of physical pain, all sensitize the soldier mentally to avoid combat. Hence with the intense shell fire around, one normally more dreads the experience. If the fear continues long enough, one cracks up. It is one of those tragic episodes of combat.

I have seen a lot more haole boys come in shell-shocked. They cry, moan, and yell, and are almost impossible to control. A, relatively few of our men cry and are uncontrollable. Sometimes one [becomes] unconscious or forgets everything—just jumps or twists the body with every sharp sound about him.

To minister to the breaking soul is a difficult job. I can hardly say much or do much. The men are so stubborn until they really break down that a chaplain can do nothing when it happens. The observation, however, of the really strong and courageous being the true spiritual soul is inescapable and true.

We are in need of more spiritual food today than ever before. This second phase of our combat experience will be our test of the spirit more than any one item. A, do continue to pray for our courageous and conscientious souls. They fight on so honorably, one must admire them. Love to the boys.

M.

March 10, 1945

Dear A,

Our men are a puzzle to the nurses. Every one of them, when they are well enough, do everything to get out. Most of the nurses want to take care of our men.

The artillery boys are no longer part of our combat team. They are going into action again. We will be missing them and their excellent support. After all, they are very good as artillery men.

It seems that they will be in the final push to crush the Jerries. On the other hand, our task is still a mystery. We will soon be told of our mission.

The mainland nisei are no longer being trained as buddhaheads. They will be in all branches of the service and they will carry on their citizens' duty. The old Camp Shelby outfit has been disbanded, according to the news we received. It all points toward a hopeful outlook for us.

Many of our officers hope we will not be in a stiff struggle again. Our last officer was quite costly and an unforgettable experience. He may not be asked to spearhead again as we did before.

The wish in our hearts is like all combat soldiers—return home safely. Combat experience makes one see the dangers and the risks and after so much, it becomes a painful and heartrending effort. Our men, like other loyal, patient GIs, fight on, but I hope they can be spared of the heavy toll.

It may be that the leaders of Hawaii and the U.S. will consider our future. We hope a good remnant can be given an opportunity to blossom forth into full stature as American citizens. I'm sure they will make their real contribution in peacetime.

By God's grace, A, it is not impossible to have your hunch of meeting again come true. At least continue and hope for such a day.

For the next week or so, I will not be able to write regularly. Time will be scarce. Don't worry. Love to all.

M.

April 10, 1945
Dear A,

You must be anxious to hear from me. I could have written a few lines days ago, but the going was too exciting and epic-making. I couldn't resist walking about, taking in the battles.

We are again a "myth." We accomplished what a division had tried for several months. The news gave us full credit without mentioning our names. The return of our men to Italy therefore has been quite a significant event.

A, I trailed our men on the hills. A day before the attack, they marched with full field packs through the dark. Many fell off the trail, but kept going. Late the next day—evening—they began the historic attack. The hill was over 3,300 feet high. On a single trail, our boys marched in single file in total darkness. All night long, they kept moving and tried hard to get to the top by 5 A.M.

We were waiting at the foot of the hill. At ten to five, the guns, big and small, opened up. It was a beautiful sight. So many rounds were fired that the whole hillside was aflame with light and shell burst.

The hills were steep—similar to Waimea Canyon. Just imagine climbing the canyon-side from the river beds. That's what our boys had to do.

One boy slipped and fell almost a hundred feet. He was unconscious for a long while. He was the only casualty on the steep climb.

The attack was to start at 5, but our men did not get to the top until 6:30. One hour and a half lapsed and so our officers thought the Jerries would stop them.

Fortunately, no Jerries were up. They were fast asleep. When 1st Lieutenant Shoichi "Pop" Koizumi reached the top, only a guard was watching. They got rid of him. They came on the high point and saw little trouble, and the Jerries were all captured. It took only thirty minutes to capture the high peak commanding the rest of the terrain.

Our boys accomplished what was considered an impossible feat. I admit that if the guards were awake, we could never have done it. One machine gun could have stopped the whole column from reaching the top. Our boys made the grade and so we were rated as tops again.

We actually broke the defense line of the Jerries. From now on it is the old grind of pushing and pursuing the Jerries. Some of the high mountains will be hard to take, but otherwise we have them on the run.

A, our men are up to expectation. They are uncomplaining veterans. The new men are very enthusiastic and give the needed strength to the others. This spearheading business will make the men more conscious of their reputation and their future. This also will make the 442nd and the 100th a unit which will be a proud AJA outfit. . . .

A, keep praying and I'll be close to you in spirit. Love and plenty to you and the boys.

M.

April 11, 1945
Massa

Dear A,

The war news is encouraging. The Germans are on the run on all fronts. In the near future, we ought to know how the end will come. It is already conjectured that there may be no honorable end. If there is no government left to surrender, our task will be to keep fighting to the bitter end. That is what we hate to see. It would be easier on our men, morally and spiritually, to stop honorably. They will not be going on and on until we lose the goal. Yet A, we are, however, going to see this thing through.

The men are certainly in good condition; no matter what their task, uncomplainingly they push on and on and on. I can never stop admiring those youthful GIs whose strength seems inexhaustible.

They know from experience now that a man's will and heart has more power over the body. The fact our men can be acclaimed as good fighters is because they are believers in what they do. They have an understanding heart, a purpose driven by the long nights of challenge after December 7 to prove themselves! Oh, I wish we could be as determined to prove our sonship of God as we are trying to prove our loyalty to a country. . . .

A, keep your chin up. . . . Don't worry. Love to the boys.

M.

May 2, 1945
Dear Chaplain Yamada:

My mother received your very comforting letter dated the 14th with further reference to the death of her son, Pvt. Tom T. Nishimoto, ASN 36468457, Company L—442nd Infantry Regiment. She also has acknowledged your letter and in all probability by this time, you have received same.

Although we had been officially notified by the War Department of the death of their only son and my only brother, it was not until your letter was received that we found solace and comfort in knowing where he was killed, the circumstances leading up to his death, and his burial. It was gratifying to know that Protestant rites were performed at his burial as it is the religion of the family for generations. My father, mother, and I feel the loss of Tom deeply, much more than I express in words to you, for we were a very close family, but we knew that he has gone to meet his Maker and that he's no longer enduring the sufferings and miseries that wars bring. We are consoled, too, with the fact that he died for a valiant cause and for the country that he so loved—loved enough to have been willing to die [for], although I know that he wanted to live. Providence must [have] thought that more could be accomplished by his death.

Tom wrote often and spoke about how proud he was to be in a minor way affiliated with such a grand organization as the 442nd Infantry, and repeatedly stated that he hoped he could live up to the reputation built by veterans.

I am very desirous in securing his personal affects such as his wallet, one dog tag, if possible, personal clothing, pen, and other incidentals, and if you are able in some way to accumulate them, it would be appreciated.

My parents join me in thanking you sincerely, from the bottom of our hearts, for attending to our beloved Tom in his last moments, and we're praying for an early termination of the war so that the boys of the 442nd Infantry could return to their loved ones, although for us, it will be a lonely victory.

If there is anything I can do in return to your kindnesses, please do not hesitate to call on me.

Thank you again,

I am very sincerely yours,
Lily Nishimoto

Chaplain Israel Yost

100th Infantry Battalion

THE MAKING OF THE 100TH

The following is a speech that Chaplain Israel Yost delivered in June 1992 to veterans of the 100th Infantry Battalion at their fiftieth anniversary memorial service in Honolulu. Chaplain Yost, a Lutheran minister, provided spiritual guidance to the 100th Battalion soldiers during the war.

Today we remember something that happened fifty years ago: the formation of a provisional battalion of the United States Army, composed entirely of men of Japanese ancestry. All of us here today have been affected in some way by this remarkable part of our nation's military system. We have memories of these men; so many of them gave their lives in order that the battalion might prove the worth of Americans of Japanese ancestry. Before we consider anything else, let us pause in silence to remember those close to us who were killed in action or who died of wounds.

In like manner, let us also remember those who survived the war but whose wounds changed their lives as civilians. And let us also remember the next of kin of all who gave their lives for our sake.

Today we know that these heroes did not die in vain—for the accomplishments of the 100th Battalion changed our country for good; we who live now are indebted to those who died.

Today, let us also remember the many persons who did not die as soldiers but whose deeds helped to make the battalion record as we know it in history. In other words, let us remember all those who kept up the morale of the men in uniform: family, friends, government officials, Americans with ideals, American servicemen who were not of Japanese ancestry—indeed, a host of right-thinking men and women. And especially, let us remember today all those who had a part in the making of the 100th.

"The making of the 100th" is the theme of today's presentation.

From October 5, 1943, to August 15, 1945, I served as the chaplain of the One Puka Puka, observing daily the uniqueness of this outstanding combat unit. The only part of the 100th's wartime experience I did not participate in was the initial battle of late September 1943. Like the men of the battalion, I had come from North Africa to Salerno with the 34th Infantry Division—but with the combat engineers. I was reassigned to the 100th because I had asked to work with infantry troops.

I could have been the loneliest person in the outfit: I was not an AJA, not from Hawaii, had never been associated with any of its officers or men in any school, or church, or organization. I was without infantry training, and my motive for military service was not the same as theirs. Furthermore, I had been transferred from a unit where there were Lutherans and Pennsylvanians with whom I had just begun a satisfying relationship. I came as a stranger to a group of men about whom I knew almost nothing.

However, because of the fine qualities of the officers and men from day one, I was never lonely in the One Puka Puka. From the top officer to the shyest private, I was quickly accepted, as if I had grown up with them in the Islands. As time went on, I realized that this was the very assignment I would have chosen to take had I been given the choice. The 100th was rightly named: One hundred is the perfect score.

What was there about the 100th that enabled it to establish such an exceptional record among fighting units? From my point of view, I have been impressed by six favorable circumstances that combined to make the 100th unique in military history: 1) the Japanese heritage of its men; 2) the Hawaiian setting of its formation; 3) the American ideals of its wartime friends; 4) the U.S. Army's decisions; 5) its magnificent personnel, officers and men; and 6) the hand of God.

First, we recall the Japanese heritage of the men of the 100th. Their parents deserve high praise for influencing the nisei to accept the ideals of America. When people live close to the soil, they are not thinking warlike thoughts. They pass on to their children the respect for their neighbors and thankfulness for the good earth. I, as a seventh-generation German American, am proud of my farmer ancestors, Peter and Johannes, who, in 1738, came to Pennsylvania. Men of the 100th must write about or talk into cassettes about their foreign-born parents and their concern about America even when they could not become citizens. Senator Inouye has done as much in his autobiography.

As educated persons we ought also be aware of that part of Japanese heritage that is much like what we call "American." There were individuals in Japan who opposed the war. "The Case of General Yamashita" (a book review appearing in the fall 1991 issue of *Nikkei Heritage* from the National Japanese American Historical Society) contrasts the actions of an American general with those of a Japanese general, with the verdict of approval going to the enemy officer. Likewise, all Americans ought to know about Toyohiko Kagawa and his influence on affairs in Japan. We must remember that the 100th's beginnings go back to the parents of those who made up our battalion. Good ancestors produce good descendants.

Next, we recall the Hawaiian setting in which the 100th was formed. Even though the issei on the mainland were like the island issei in their attitudes about America, the One Puka Puka could not have happened on the East Coast.

As an outsider among the nisei, I learned much more about Hawaii than I did about Japan. This was not because everyone was hiding his Japanese background. Not at all—for I quickly learned that all were concerned about making a good record so that all Americans of Japanese ancestry would be accepted as fully American. Rather, it was because the Islanders were in culture Hawaiian, as were the Caucasian officers, the songs, the leis, the tales about school, the Hawaiian pidgin, the rivalry among those of the several islands.

In Hawaii, the AJAs found some acceptance; on the West Coast they found none. There were those in Hawaii who spoke up for the loyalty of Japanese Americans—even for service in the military. Later on, on the mainland, the Caucasian-Hawaiian officers saw to it that the nisei were accepted as first-class Americans.

The third circumstance that made possible a 100th Battalion (Separate) was the presence, at the right time and the right place, of

Americans who took seriously the ideals that make our country great; these persons believed in democracy—even in time of war.

Anyone who has read *Ambassadors in Arms* knows that the commanding officer of the battalion, Farrant L. Turner, understood his men, trusted them, and did all within his power to get for them their spot in history. He was ably supported by all his haole officers, not only those of the original unit, but also those who came in as replacements. I suspect that if I had not fit into his unit as a chaplain who accepted his boys, I would have been quickly replaced by someone else.

The unarmed men who left Hawaii on the SS *Maui* in June 1942 did not know that there was a general in high places who had not succumbed to the idea that Japanese Americans were untrustworthy. This was Mark Clark, who had advised against the removal of the issei and nisei from the West Coast and who would welcome them to fight under his command in Italy. Also, General Ryder of the 34th Division saw to it that the men of the 100th had the opportunity to prove themselves in combat, and he remained unchanged in his admiration of the One Puka Puka.

Had there not been those in positions of power willing to use the 100th in combat, there would not have been an opportunity to put down the racist feelings some felt against AJAs. On the honor roll of those who supported the 100th should also be inscribed the names of news reporters who broadcast the successes of our men.

The fourth circumstance at work in the making of the 100th was the army of which our men were a part. Even when its decisions did not seem to make much sense, they seemed to work in favor of the success of the battalion.

No one seemed to know just how to use the 1,432 men brought from Hawaii to the mainland, so they spent much more time being trained than other units of the army, preparing for winter combat as well as summer combat. There were two extra companies, making the battalion overstrength. We had overqualified men because none of the AJAs were to be assigned to regular army units. Had it not been for the prompt action of Turner, the men would have been branded as second-class soldiers in the South. All of this was the result of the segregation of the nisei by the army as part of the government's actions.

All that the army did only served to prepare the 100th for its outstanding role after it was sent into combat. Everyone was well trained and knew well all others in the platoon and company. All felt they could trust their replacements (for the extra companies were so used later on). There was time to build up morale during the many months of training. Because of segregation the AJAs could be identified, and this increased the desire on the part of all to prove once and for all that the nisei were loyal citizens of the United States.

Here, let me interject a special note. When I first joined the unit, I was made aware of one company commander who seemed gruff and complaining much of the time. To get to know him better, I marched beside him as we advanced into fighting positions. I quickly learned why he was upset; he wanted to fight in the Pacific theater because if we did not fight against the Japanese, after the war some would say that AJAs fought against Caucasians but would not fight against their own kind. We know that his fears were groundless, for today we know the story of the men in the Military Intelligence Service who fought in the Pacific. We must make sure that their story is made known in the history books.

What if the army in North Africa had assigned the 100th to patrol the supply route from Casablanca to Oran instead of using us as combat troops? This is explained on page 121 of *Ambassadors in Arms*. What kind of a military record could have been made with such an assignment? What if the army had assigned the 100th to anything less than use in the toughest of the battles of the campaigns in Italy and France? It was the army, through its generals, who gave the One Puka Puka the opportunity to prove its worth. This was costly in terms of KIAs and MIAs, but it was precisely what the men themselves wanted from the military.

The army permitted the 100th to keep its special designation when it became a part of the 442nd Regimental Combat Team—we were never its First Battalion in name, even though we were in reality.

The nisei were never given a choice as to how they would serve their country; army service was the only field (apart from Intelligence) where they could serve. The 100th must acknowledge its debt to the United States Army, even when its decisions were made for the wrong reasons.

A truly important circumstance, the fifth in my list, that made the 100th what it became was the abundance of magnificent individuals serving in its ranks, both nisei and others. As we remember our comrades, I will name only one—the others shall remain anonymous—and he is Captain Kometani. I call him the "nonofficer officer" because he was as much an enlisted man as he was an officer. He was dentist, swimming coach, morale officer, medic, and litter bearer. He was the first person in the 100th I met, and we became close friends, especially as we two carried the wounded to the forward aid station. In the book I typed up about my experience as chaplain of the 100th, written for my children, I included the following story:

Komi and I and a medic returning from rest camp walked toward the forward area to go to the forward aid station. When we came to a section of the trail under observation by the enemy, we decided to cross the open spot individually so that we would attract less attention and not be fired at. I went first, got to the rendezvous, and waited for Komi. After an interval of time, he arrived. The two of us sat in a sheltered place and waited for the enlisted man to join us. After some time I became alarmed because the medic did not catch up with us. Komi suggested that we wait a bit longer before checking to see if he might have been injured—we could not see far down the trail.

After quite some time Komi said, "I don't think he's coming, Chaplain. I thought when we started out that he looked scared. I'm not surprised that he hasn't come."

"But that's bad for him," I replied. "He can be court-martialed for not obeying orders, for not coming back into combat."

"No, Chaplain, that won't happen. When we get to the aid station I'll phone back to the rear and have them reassign him to some duty back there. He's been in combat too long as a company aid man. He just can't take it any longer."

And that is just the way the matter was handled. No one was wiser except the three of us involved. The soldier had already given all he could for the war effort; he no longer had the spirit to keep on pushing himself. Those of us who were healthy and with high morale were able to carry on in his stead, just as he would have done for us had the circumstances been reversed.

However, the incident just related may be misinterpreted if the situation of the GI is emphasized instead of the compassion of Kometani. Let me relate a story about myself: The day before Christmas of 1943, when the 100th was resting in tents, a message from the regimental colonel was relayed to me. I was to spend the day working as the graves registration officer. I had already planned the whole day with chores for observing Christmas. I told our headquarters officers I would not obey the colonel because my duties as chaplain came first. I returned to my tent, expecting to be disciplined. Instead, our staff assigned a sergeant to take over my assignment so that I was free to work as I saw fit. In addition, I was given orders to take several days of leave after Christmas at an officer's rest camp in Naples. The colonel never learned how the One Puka Puka covered for their chaplain's refusal to obey his command. When I was the one in trouble, compassion was shown for me. In the One Puka Puka, we not only were good soldiers; we also were compassionate brothers, one to another.

I remember an AJA lieutenant who commanded a mortar platoon; he always carried the mortar base plate himself, although that was not his job. Then there was the soldier who told me he was so upset by the death of a friend at the hands of the Germans that he would no longer take prisoners. A day or two later, I stepped out of the aid station to watch a file of prisoners of war coming under guard from the front. Their guard at the rear was the same soldier who had said, "No more prisoners." When he got close to me, he looked up and said quietly, "Chaplain, you can't kick a man when he's down."

Another day, not being careful, I set off an enemy mine. Although I was only scratched by a fragment, another GI was hurt more seriously. The next day the sergeant in charge of the mine platoon came to me, quite perturbed. He said, "Chaplain, don't ever again go into a mined area without me. If you want to pick up a dead buddy, that's fine, but don't go into a minefield without me." A short time later I had him check out a field where a dead enemy lay; his sweeper detected a mine close to the body. He saved me from death or serious injury.

The men of the 100th were magnificent individuals. We know that about the many who received medals for heroism, but we don't know as much about others who, in their own ways, were also outstanding as soldiers and outstanding as concerned persons. What a group to work with!

I suspect that many of these men, if asked why they were so magnificent, would be bashful about such praise, and I suspect that many of them would point out that they had loved ones at home who faithfully wrote to them, sent packages to them, and yes, prayed for them. Parents, sweethearts, wives, members of their extended families, and good friends—a host of caring persons kept up their morale as month was succeeded by month and war dragged on. In my own case, I counted on the almost-daily letters from my wife—and I saved them up and got them home—I still have them. And there were others, too, who I knew were supporting me and praying for me. When we remember today the heroes of the 100th, we must also remember their support groups back home.

At this fiftieth anniversary reunion we should be aware of another group of magnificent persons within our ranks—the replacements from the 442nd's First Battalion. If these officers and men had not fit so well into the One Puka Puka, the story of the 100th after Cassino would not have been possible. We compliment these replacements for their part in our ongoing history.

Another special note: We must not forget our comrades who, as prisoners of war, were forced to live through seemingly endless days, until the war ended.

There remains yet one other circumstance, the sixth, that played a part in the making of the 100th. It has to do with God.

I am a Christian, and as such I believe in a heavenly Father who is concerned about all his creations and especially about those made in his image. Furthermore, I am a Christian who has felt the call to become a preacher of his work and a pastor commissioned to work with his people. Early in my life as a pastor I was influenced by one Bible verse in particular, Romans 8:28: "And we know that all things work together for the good to them that love God, to them who are called according to his purpose." When I entered military service in 1943 it was that I might follow God's call, do His will, and serve His people. I believe that I became chaplain of the 100th because God wanted me in this position and being chaplain would work for my good as well as the good of those I was to serve.

Looking back at history, Christians might well come to the conclusion that somehow God was concerned about the making of the 100th—for Christians do not believe that chance rules our lives, but that God does. I am not talking about God being the God of the United States, or of the U.S. Army, or of an ethnic group. What I am saying is that the story of the "ambassadors in arms" has the marks of God's intervention for good in our lives.

I know that my life—including the months I spent with the 100th—has been in the hands of God. I would urge all Christians who have served in the 100th to consider that they, too, have been in the hand of God. Perhaps others of differing faiths may also be able to see the supernatural in the record of the One Puka Puka.

When I had finished writing this address, I looked over its main points and discovered my speech can be summarized as an acrostic using the word *Hawaii*: the six favorable circumstances in the making of the 100th were

H –the Hand of God
A –Ancestors from Japan
W –Wartime friends with American ideals
A –Army input
I –the Island setting
I –Individuals with magnificent personalities

I cannot imagine that ever again will there be such a piece of history as that written by all the persons, military and civilian, who had a part in the saga of the 100th Infantry Battalion. I am thankful to God and to all of you for the opportunity to have been a part of it.

Katsumi "Doc" Kometani

100th Infantry Battalion

LETTERS FROM THE FRONT: LETTERS HOME

The following letters were sent home to family members by Captain Katsumi Kometani, who served as morale officer for the 100th Infantry Battalion. Kometani was a dentist by training. Since a dentist was hardly essential personnel for a combat unit, Kometani, who was respected in Hawaii's AJA community, was given the role of morale officer.

Here is a sampling of letters he sent home to his wife, Yaeko, and his three children, Franklin, James, and baby daughter, Carol.

To Yaeko Kometani

October 25, 1943
My dearest Mom:
 The first thing is that we are all well, although we must admit that

it has been a tough week. From time to time the War Department will release different news of the boys, so save the clippings when you come across any. Some news may be pleasant while others may not be, but we must learn to take the bitter with the sweet. Without question, the boys are doing a swell job and you should all be proud of them. These boys will carry on their shoulders the responsibilities placed on them by the country and will share every bit of the burden placed on them.

Love,
Daddy

December 9, 1943
My dearest Mom,

Your letters of Oct. 25, 28, and 31 arrived—V-mail (short for "victory mail"; letters were photo-copied in reduced size for compactness)—and was certainly good to hear from you. You can't write very much in V-mail, but you can write oftener. The news of Joe's death must be a blow to his family, but they can be proud of his work and his sacrifice. Greater love hath no man than that he laid down his life for his friends and country. We are all proud of Joe. The anxiety for the home folks is great, probably greater than ours, as you await news every day, so we try to write whenever possible to let you know all's well thus far. The work is hard but we are happy because we know there is an end and that our end means righteousness and freedom for you and the kids. Our goal is not blind and every hardship means [we're] a little closer to our goal and home. It's going to be a great day when it's over.

Love,
Daddy

December 19, 1943
My dearest Mom,

Often wonder that it is going to be a sad Christmas and New Year's at many homes—but when you consider the existing conditions and the deeds of our boys, we still have many things to be thankful for. Whatever you do, don't worry, as we are not taking this life as a matter of course and are doing our share. Mrs. Joe Takata wrote me a very nice letter and thanked me, but certainly I have done so little that it should be forgotten. I'm dropping her a line soon. We are now resting and taking it easy and the boys are relaxing. It's good to feel this way. Miss you and the children, especially Carol, who is growing up and [is] probably [at] the cutest time. Imagine, she won't remember Daddy's face when I get home, but hope I won't spoil her.

> Love to you all,
> Daddy

October 6 (no year)
My dearest Mom,
 Just to let you know that we are all well and today resting after a strenuous week. This is the greatest experience any man can have, and instead of the feeling that perhaps we were in the wrong era of hardships and conflicts, maybe it is a privilege that only comes to a certain generation; especially, it is a test for us to be able to give to our country when it really needs manpower.

> Love,
> Daddy

October 21 (no year)
My dearest Mom,
 It has been a busy day—with continuous goings [-on], but the realization that the inward flesh of war is not pleasant and kind is getting stronger. May war end soon, but only after our principle for which we are fighting is completely attained. Today has been very memorable. Hoping that there will not be another day to overshadow this. Keep this letter and when we meet, I'll give some interesting accounts which could not be told in mail.

> Love,
> Daddy

To Franklin Kometani

November 13, 1943
Dear Franky Boy,
 There are many interesting things and sights in this country, but that is for the day when Daddy comes home and we all sit around and talk story. However, I'd like to tell you that we can't bathe like you, and today, after quite some time, we had a short clean up. It is getting cold, so we keep every available clothes on. At night we wear all our clothes, includ-

ing shoes, so you can imagine it is not so comfortable. Two days ago, we had some candy and fig bars and cookies, those that are not given to us by the army. Even cookies and fig bars are a treat, but the best is bread when we can have it. Outside of these rest times, we eat can rations. Like fig bars, each man gets a few, so you see we don't live like you all. The children that we see have not seen candy for many months and whenever they see an American soldier, they yell for candy, *calamel*, which is "candy" in Italian. In fact, they have very little to eat after the Germans get through with them. Children run around without shoes, and bread (brown) is their chief diet. As for you all, you must not waste [food] and remember that every little bit must be saved. Under separate cover, I'm sending you a letter of commendation that I received from our commanding officer today, and it is something you will be proud of some day. I want you to keep it and hold it for me. It will be in my record in the army, and I know Mom and you all will be proud.

Good luck, boy.
Daddy

To James Kometani

October 10 (no year)
Dear Jimmy,

It is good to hear that you are getting along like a big man, working hard to help Mama. Always remember that Daddy is always thinking of you. Take care of Carol and listen to Franklin and I know you will always be a good boy.

Love to you,
Daddy

To Carol Kometani

(no date)
My dear Baby:

Here's a Christmas and a New Year's greetings to you and Mama and the two boys. Daddy has a little souvenir which I'm trying to send you. It's a little novelty because it comes from so far away. Tell Franky and Jimmy to be good boys and Daddy will try to get them something when it is possible. The stores are very poor and they don't have very many things, so we can't buy anything. Be a good girl and Daddy will come back soon. Tell Mama not to worry as things are shaping [up] well. Also, give all our friends my holiday greetings.

Love,
Daddy

November 25, 1943
From somewhere in Italy to you a Merry Christmas and a happy new year . . .

My dear Carol, Jimmy, and Franky Boy,
In about a month and a half, Christmas and New Year's will be here. This is the second Xmas and New Year's away from all of you. I miss you all and I know you miss me, too. But somewhere in Italy, a job must be done and I am here doing my share, not only for my country but for all of you. When this letter and greeting reaches you, remember there are many thousands of our boys away from home just like Daddy, fighting for our country. They are doing a good job. Remember all of them in your prayers. It is my sincere hope that when the next holiday season comes, we will be all together as one big and happy family. Until then, be good and help Mama more than ever. Take care of your health. Be good to others. Please give Uncle John and his family, and Babasan and Jiisan, Fujisue and his family, Uncle Kotogi, and our family my greetings. Take care of Mom and you all give my greetings to her.

Love to you all,
Daddy

Hoichi Kubo

Military Intelligence Service

IF I AM FILIAL . . .

I was drafted into the U.S. Army in June of 1941, five months before Japan's attack on Pearl Harbor. After being inducted, I was assigned to the 298th Infantry Regiment and underwent thirteen weeks of infantry basic training at Schofield Barracks. Because of the chemistry courses I had taken for my agriculture major at the University of Hawaii, I was assigned to the medical detachment.

When the war began, the 298th and 299th National Guard units were activated. Both units included many nisei from Hawaii who had been drafted into the U.S. Army as early as a year before the attack on Pearl Harbor. We were renamed the Hawaiian Provisional Infantry Battalion just before we left Hawaii for the mainland on June 5, 1942. One thousand four hundred thirty-two of us boarded the SS *Maui* that night and sailed out of Honolulu. We had no idea where we were headed. Some people say we were ordered to the mainland because of concern about the Battle of Midway.

Our destination turned out to be Oakland, California, and eventually Camp McCoy, Wisconsin. When we arrived in Oakland, we were told our new name, the 100th Infantry Battalion (Separate). The 100th Battalion left Oakland in several trains for the five-day trip to Camp McCoy, where we would receive more infantry training. I remember that the window shades were drawn.

While at Camp McCoy, we were visited by language evaluators from the Military Intelligence Service Language School at Camp Savage, Minnesota. They had come to recruit linguists for the Pacific theater. I tried to *fail* the test because I wanted to go to Europe with the 100th Battalion, but my military records showed that I had studied Japanese at the middle-school level. They knew that I was fairly fluent in Japanese, so I was ordered to the Military Intelligence Service Language School.

As a youngster, I had attended Japanese-language school at the Hongwanji every day after English-language school and on Saturdays. My parents wouldn't have had it any other way.

My father was from Hiroshima and my mother's parents were from Kumamoto. I was born in 1919 in Puukolii, Lahaina, Maui. I attended school in Lahaina until the eighth grade. In the ninth grade, I transferred to Central Intermediate School in Honolulu and then graduated from McKinley High School.

I distinctly remember that in February 1935, the fiftieth anniversary of the arrival in Hawaii of Japanese immigrants, the Japanese Consul General reminded Japanese American students like me that we were American citizens, not Japanese citizens.

I attended the University of Hawaii from 1938 to 1941, majoring in agriculture. I also took a year of Japanese. I had taken Junior ROTC at McKinley High School and two years of ROTC at the University of Hawaii, which was required.

I guess the combination of my education and experiences made me a natural target for the MIS recruiters. Although I could read all of the materials, I played a cat-and-mouse game with the faculty. As my barrack's senior noncommissioned officer, I took care of my men because I didn't have to study.

A language team was formed in June 1943 following our graduation from the language school. Tim Ohta was our team leader; the members were Dick Kishiue, Richard Moritsugu, Jack Tanimoto, Frank Mori, Joe Fujino, Larry Saito, William Nuno, Roy Higashi, and me. We sailed for Honolulu in September 1943. When we arrived, we were assigned to the Joint Intelligence Center, Pacific Ocean Area, although we didn't know it. Our team was sent to Schofield Barracks and attached to the 27th Infantry Division, a National Guard unit from New York.

I participated in the invasion of Makin Island in the Gilbert Islands in November 1943, and of Majuro in the Marshall Islands in January 1944.

In June I was assigned to 3rd Battalion of the 105th Infantry Regiment, which participated in "Operation Forager," the invasion of Saipan by the 5th Amphibious Corps.

I was searching caves on the island, urging the occupants to surrender, which many civilians did. The 27th Infantry Division pushed up the center of the island, suffering heavy casualties. It was truly "Death Valley." The division finally reached the west coast, pinching out the 2nd Marine Division at the Tanapag Plain.

In early July, a Japanese civilian who had been taken prisoner was brought to Jack Tanimoto and me. The prisoner was a civilian employee of the Japanese navy. He told us that a *gyokusai* had been ordered for the night of July 7th, which coincided with Tanabata, the "festival of the weaver." Literally translated, *gyokusai* means "smashing the jewel." It was not a banzai charge, but rather an attack by all surviving forces intent on annihilating the enemy—in other words, "death with honor."

The prisoner was forwarded to Lt. Ben Hazard and Dick Kishiue at their prisoner-of-war collecting point at Tanapag Harbor and interrogated further. The information about the *gyokusai* date was telephoned to the Division G-2, who alerted Maj. Gen. George W. Griner, then commanding general of the 27th Infantry Division. He, in turn, alerted the 5th Amphibious Corps Headquarters.

On the afternoon of July 7th, I found a Japanese enlisted man in a culvert. He repeated the same story as the civilian captured earlier, saying that the attack would be at 8 P.M. Maj. Malcolm M. Jameson, the regimental S-2, ordered me to bring the prisoner to regimental headquarters for further interrogation before forwarding him to Lieutenant Hazard and Dick Kishiue.

They obtained the same information and immediately telephoned the division. The *gyokusai* was scheduled for midnight, however. The Japanese had lost all communication equipment, so the units were widely scattered. They had to be contacted by runners. The 27th Division was firing at the routes to their line of departure. Thus, the assembling of the Japanese was delayed several hours.

At 4 A.M. on July 8, 1944, the Japanese launched their attack. There were between four thousand and six thousand men. While the 1st and 2nd Battalions of 105th Infantry Regiment killed more men than the casualties they incurred, they were finally whittled down. The Japanese broke through, only to find our regimental headquarters blocking their way. I joined the cooks, clerks, mechanics, and headquarters personnel in fighting as infantry to stem the Japanese.

At least twenty Japanese, led by an officer, reached the small creek bank just above the Japanese naval base. The base was located above Tanapag Harbor. They were cut down by a marine machine-gun crew covering the bridge. Ben and Dick and their thirteen military police supported the marines. This may have been the deepest penetration of the *gyokusai*.

Of the fifty-two officers and more than one thousand enlisted men from the 1st and 2nd Battalions who were either killed or wounded on Saipan, it is not known how many were actually casualties of that night. Both battalions were below strength due to casualties. The 1st and 2nd Battalions and Headquarters Company were awarded the Presidential Unit Citation.

Saipan was declared secure on July 9, 1944. The 27th Infantry Division remained behind to mop up. Linguists with the line regiments were charged with trying to persuade civilians to come out of the caves and surrender, for there were still many Japanese soldiers among the civilians.

On July 23rd, a platoon of the 105th Infantry Regiment discovered a cave in the cliffs south of Marpi Point. During the mop-up operation, two civilians climbed up to the edge of the cliff with their hands raised in surrender. They were Okinawans who had been brought to Saipan to work on the sugar plantations. More than a hundred civilians—men, women, and children—were being held captive by Japanese soldiers in a large cave at the base of the cliff. I reported this to 1st Lt. Roger Peyre of K Company, 3rd Battalion.

I tried to convince the two Okinawans to return to the cave where the Japanese soldiers were holding the civilians. They refused, fearing the Japanese soldiers. I decided to go down into the cave. With a forty-five caliber under my fatigue jacket, I slid down the rope near the mouth of the cave. I disappeared from sight at ten o'clock and walked about seventy-five yards through light jungle growth. Rounding a point, I found myself facing eight Japanese soldiers with their rifles aimed at me. They were surprised to see a Japanese wearing an American uniform. They may not have fired at me because of that. I took off my helmet and began talking with them.

"You're a spy," the sergeant shouted. "I am an American," I replied. "My ancestors fought with the 5th (Hiroshima) Division and the 6th (Kumamoto) Division, and distinguished themselves in the Russo-Japanese War. I am here to take out the noncombatants."

Hearing this, the Japanese soldiers allowed me to enter the cave. They were preparing a pot of rice, so I handed over my K rations as my contribution to the meal.

The Japanese demanded to know how I, of Japanese ancestry, could serve the United States. I responded: "*Ko naran to hosseba chu naran. Chu naran to hosseba ko naran* (If I am filial, I cannot serve the emperor. If I serve the emperor, I cannot be filial)." The soldiers clearly understood the quote I had cited by one of Japan's most renown warriors, Taira no Shigemori.

"You are the sons of Japanese parents. You were born in Japan and fight for your country, Japan. I also am the son of Japanese parents, but I was born in the United States. The United States is my country, and I fight for it. The United States has honored me by making me a sergeant. I do not come here to discuss that you give yourselves up. I wish that you devote your consideration to releasing the civilians whom you are holding captive."

For more than an hour, I pleaded for the civilians, especially the children. Finally, the Japanese sergeant told me to return to my unit; they would make a decision.

The civilians began climbing up the rope at about 2 P.M.—122 men, women, and children . . . and at the end of the rope, the eight Japanese soldiers without weapons.

A 105th Regimental officer asked Lieutenant Peyre for a report of what had taken place. At that moment, from across the valley, a Japanese soldier shot at Lieutenant Peyre, killing him. His body fell to the valley floor.

I was angry! I yelled at the Japanese who came out of the cave. "Someone has shot the man who saved all your lives! Is there not one of you a *bushi* (warrior)? Four young men from the Okinawa-ken *shonen-dan* (youth unit) climbed back down the cliff and recovered Lieutenant Peyre's body.

I learned forty years later that Lieutenant Hazard had obtained sworn statements from the eight Japanese military personnel and from several civilians who were in the cave. My Distinguished Service Cross might not have been possible without them.

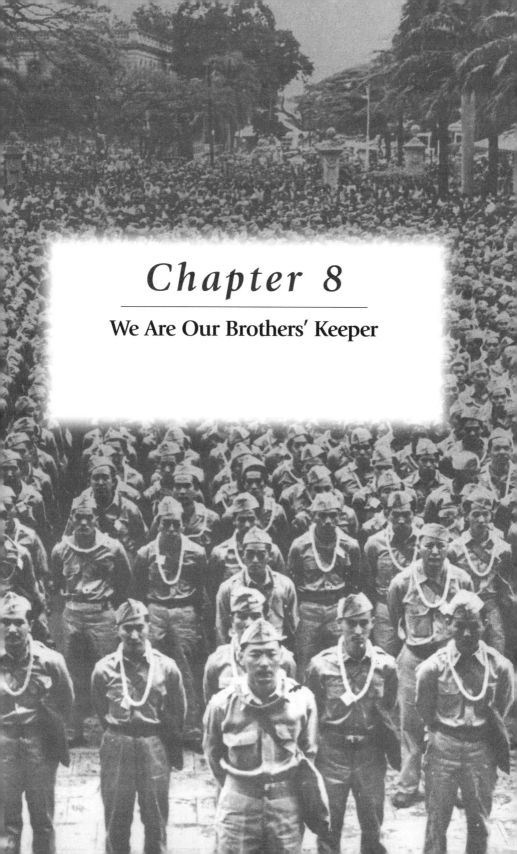

Chapter 8

We Are Our Brothers' Keeper

Edward Ichiyama

442nd Regimental Combat Team

SUNKEN EYES AT DACHAU

In mid-March 1945 the 522nd Field Artillery Battalion (FABN), of which I was a member, crossed the Saar River, near Saarbrucken, and entered Germany. We had been detached from the 442nd Regimental Combat Team and sent to Germany. The 442nd had returned to Italy after the "Champagne campaign" in the French Maritime Alps.

For a moment after we crossed over into Germany, I found myself literally and figuratively in another world, a world that had fascinated me as a youngster growing up in Hawaii, mesmerized by library books that swept me away to distant lands. Before my eyes appeared common German names like "Schneider," printed in bold Gothic lettering. Time stood still, and history and geography came alive in visions of medieval castles and other ancient Gothic architecture. Albeit short-lived, it was an exhilarating experience that I remember to this day.

The German army had made a hasty retreat into the interior section of Germany following the Allied invasion of their country. We were moving so fast behind them that we sometimes had to move our bulky howitzers several times a day. That meant uncoupling them, digging new trenches for gun pits, and so forth, to prepare the howitzers for firing.

As we approached the vicinity of the snow-covered fields of Dachau, Germany, in late April 1945 we unexpectedly witnessed a most gruesome and pitiful sight: hundreds upon hundreds of emaciated, gaunt, malnourished people in black-and-white prison clothing. Their eyes were sunken and their cheeks hollow. They were living skeletons, wandering aimlessly about the countryside.

Many were sprawled on the snow-covered ground, unable to walk another step. We saw several prisoners shred what appeared to be either a dead horse or cow and eat the raw flesh. "Who are these people and what are they doing here?" we asked each other.

Regardless, we tried to help them as much as possible, offering them whatever food, clothing, water, and medicine we had, and words of kindness, comfort, and compassion. In their faces we saw appreciation, for they had been subjugated by their German captors for weeks, months, perhaps even years.

There were a few English-speaking prisoners with whom we spoke. We learned that many of the prisoners were Jewish; others were political prisoners. They had been housed in a number of slave camps scattered throughout the Dachau area. The prisoners had been forced to work in a number of factories, including ammunition- and airplane-production houses.

As the Allied forces approached these camps, the German guards had herded the prisoners out of the compounds and started them on a "death march" of sorts toward the hinterlands of Germany. As the Allies came closer, the German guards fled, abandoning their prisoners. These were the prisoners we had stumbled upon.

Historians hold different theories regarding the forced march. Some believe the prisoners were being marched to the mountains near the Swiss border, where the Nazis had planned to take their last stand. The prisoners were to be used as their labor force in building the fortification. Others say the prisoners were removed from the camp to conceal any human evidence of the existence of a concentration camp. Still others believe that the Jewish prisoners were being marched to the Swiss border, where the Swiss government was to mediate an exchange of prisoners: Jewish prisoners for German POWs held by the Allies.

That afternoon, after we had pitched our tents, many of us

entered one of the nearby camps, which, by then, was deserted. There were many such camps in the Dachau area. Upon entering the compound, we were overpowered by the stench of feces, urine, and decaying matter. It was unbearable beyond description. I quickly ran out after a few minutes, wretching.

Several of my comrades with stronger constitutions bravely wandered about the compound. They observed what appeared to be huge ovens. Beside them were several fifty-gallon drums filled with what they believed to be ashes that were still warm. Some of the braver souls even wandered behind the compound, where they saw what they thought was cord wood stacked on a railroad flatbed. Upon closer scrutiny, they found that it was not cord wood but human corpses.

One of the greatest ironies of World War II occurred there at Dachau, Germany, when members of a persecuted minority, Japanese Americans, many whose families were interned by their own government, reached out to members of another persecuted minority, the Jewish people of Europe. These two minority groups were victims of the most blatant disregard for civil liberties and human rights ever perpetrated by a government against its people—one for being of Japanese ancestry, the other for being of the Jewish faith.

Our involvement with the Dachau holocaust survivors did not end in April 1945. In September 1994 several members of the 522nd FABN met with Jewish holocaust survivors and members of the Jewish community in Tokyo, Japan, who were observing Sukkoth, or Thanksgiving. They were honoring the memory of Senpo Sugihara, the Japanese diplomat who risked his professional career by defying an order from the Japanese government to cease issuing transit visas to Jews. Sugihara issued visas to approximately six thousand Jews in 1941.

We, too, were there to honor Mr. Sugihara for his humanitarian deed. Had it not been for his benevolence, the "Sugihara Jews" might have suffered the same fate as other holocaust victims. During the ceremony, the 522 Field Artillery Battalion was honored also for helping the Dachau survivors. The meeting was particularly heartwarming because I was able to meet a Dachau survivor whom we had helped in April 1945.

Solly Ganor, an Israeli writer, publicly acknowledged being saved from death by members of the 522nd FABN. A seventeen-year-old Lithuanian Jew in 1945, he recounted the following scene for me while we were in Japan in 1994.

Starving, emaciated, and physically unable to move much, he remembered that he was sitting in the snow in the vicinity of Dachau, near death. Suddenly, a Jeep carrying American soldiers drove up. He was taken aback, for these soldiers had Oriental faces. They stopped and talked to him. In the process, he learned that they were with the 522nd Field Artillery Battalion. They were there to help him.

The 522nd FABN soldiers helped the weakened youth to their Jeep and then drove him to the bivouac area where Headquarters Battery was stationed. There, the soldiers nursed Solly until he regained his strength. Solly recounted this experience with the 522nd in his book, *Light One Candle*, which he published in 1995.

Is Solly Ganor's story stranger than fiction? Why was he singled out and helped when there were many others like him, possibly in worse condition? I believe it was fate that brought us together.

In December 1939 Solly Ganor, then eleven years old, invited Senpo Sugihara, a total stranger, to his home to spend Hanukkah, the holiest of Jewish holy holidays, with his family. Mr. Sugihara, a newly arrived Japanese diplomat in Lithuania, was so impressed with Solly's hospitality that he accepted the invitation. The two, an eleven-year-old Lithuanian Jew and a distinguished Japanese diplomat, became fast friends. Perhaps it was Solly's gesture of kindness that inspired Mr. Sugihara to reciprocate by issuing six thousand visas to Polish Jews. This made it possible for them to travel safely through Russia, then to Japan, and ultimately to safety in Shanghai.

Unfortunately, Solly Ganor was a Lithuanian Jew. Since Russia had occupied Lithuania, the issuance of transit visas to Lithuanian Jews through Russia was forbidden. The Ganor family was instead sent to Dachau.

Although Mr. Sugihara, a humanitarian, saved six thousand strangers, he was unable to save his young friend. But in a strange twist of fate, Solly Ganor was rescued by Mr. Sugihara's "cousins"—Japanese American members of the 522nd Field Artillery Battalion.

I am frequently asked by schools and community groups to share some of my World War II experiences. Oftentimes, someone in the audience will ask, "Did the Holocaust really happen?" My answer to them is simple and straight-forward: Although it is difficult for rational men and women to associate the atrocities of Dachau with an enlightened society like the German republic, the Holocaust did, indeed, happen. I know it did . . . because I was there.

Tadashi Tojo

442nd Regimental Combat Team

DACHAU, 1945: WHAT HAVE WE LEARNED?

My experience with the Holocaust concentration camps in the Dachau region took place sometime between April 20 and 28, 1945.

Throughout the campaign in Italy, France, and Germany, I was part of a forward observation team usually made up of Lt. Albert Binotti, Thomas Mayeda, and Robert Sugai. The field observers worked with the 442nd Infantry unit up front and provided them with artillery cover and backup for all their missions. Sugai and I had worked as a radio communication team in our basic training days at Camp Shelby. This teamwork continued through the Italian, French, and German campaigns up to our final days at Bertchestgarten in May 1945.

On the day we stumbled upon one of the Dachau concentration camps, we had no idea that camps like these even existed during the war. Sugai and I were on an M-35 reconnaissance vehicle. I remember that the battle lines changed rapidly, even day-to-day.

I do not remember how Sugai and I were separated from our scout corporal, Tom Mayeda, who was with our lieutenant, the forward observer. On our mission with the tank and infantry group that day, we stumbled onto a huge barbed-wire encampment with a double-lock gate. The roadway leading to the camp looked like a swamp. I learned later that it was a moat, covered with overgrown brush. After discovering the camp, we backed out and let the lead tank destroyer, which was much larger, break into the compound. Prisoners in tattered striped uniforms came out of the barracks.

Most of the people appeared to be walking zombies. They were expressionless and disoriented, shuffling out of their compounds, walking about aimlessly. An American GI threw them a chocolate or fruit bar. One of the prisoners picked it up and took a bite of it, only to throw up. Someone wisely yelled that we shouldn't feed the prisoners, who were starved and emaciated beyond help. I saw a medic attempt to administer intravenous feeding to one of the prisoners, but he had great difficulty locating a blood vessel to start the procedure.

Sometime later, when returning to the Battery area, I saw many prisoners drinking from the irrigation ditches. Others were ravenously feasting on the raw meat of draft horses killed during the battle. To me, these were the more fortunate ones: At least, they were able to move about and had command of themselves; these people were able to stomach their food.

People have asked me how I feel about what I saw and experienced that day more than a half century ago. What can I say? I saw, firsthand, the horror of a Dachau concentration camp and the destruction and killing of World War II. I have read about the unspeakable horrors visited upon human beings in Korea, Vietnam, the Middle East, and am aware that a small but ominous group called "skinheads" appears intent on repeating the inhumane treatment and ultimate genocide of nonwhite people, both here in the mainland United States and again in Germany.

I believe that every nation that participated in World War II is responsible for the human suffering and the grievous hurt that followed it. To me, when and where this inhumanity will end remains the paramount question.

The words of wisdom by Eugene O'Neill sum it up best for me: "There is no present or future—only the past, happening over and over again—now."

Takejiro Higa
Military Intelligence Service

THE SPIRIT OF A THREE-YEAR-OLD CHILD

Mitsugo no tamashi hyaku made . . . the spirit of a three-year-old
child will last a hundred years.

Few people can appreciate the meaning behind those words in the same
way I do.

I was one of more than a dozen Japanese American soldiers who
were involved in the Battle of Okinawa in 1945. Some historians have
described it as the cruelest battle of the Pacific. More than twelve thousand
Americans and about ninety-five thousand Japanese were killed. About
sixty thousand were Okinawan civilians.

The Battle of Okinawa pitted my two homelands against each other.

I was born in Waipahu. When I was two, my mother took me, my
brother, Warren, who was five, and our eight-year-old sister, Yuriko, to
Okinawa to meet our paternal grandparents. My father stayed in Hawaii

because he had to run our family store in Waipahu. Three years later he came to Okinawa to take all of us back to Hawaii.

But when he arrived at my grandparents' home in Shimabuku Village, my mother was really sick, so she couldn't travel. My father didn't want to leave her, but he had to go back to Hawaii. So my parents decided that only Yuriko and Warren would return with him to Hawaii. I was only five at the time and still needed my mother's care, so I stayed in Okinawa with her. We lived with my grandparents.

When I was eleven, Papa died of a heart attack in Hawaii. My grandpa died that same year. A year later, I lost my grandma, and a few months after that, Mama died. I was twelve years old when I became an orphan in Okinawa.

My father's younger brother and his wife took me in and supported me until I finished the eighth grade. They were very kind-hearted people. At the age of fourteen, I began working for my uncle, doing a variety of jobs.

As my sixteenth birthday approached, I began thinking seriously about going back to Hawaii. Japan had begun recruiting strong, healthy young men, aged sixteen to nineteen, whom they sent to Manchuria for the Man Mo Kaitaku Seishonen Gyudan, or Manchuria Mongolia Development Young People Service Corps. These paramilitary "volunteers" worked in large-scale farming projects, producing food for Japan. In the event of war or an emergency, these young men were to be used as Japan's first line of defense.

When I turned sixteen in April 1939, I wrote to my sister in Hawaii and asked her to sponsor my return before the Japanese army grabbed me. I didn't want to go to Manchuria. If I had to leave Okinawa, I'd rather go back to Hawaii where Warren and Yuriko and my other relatives were.

That July, fourteen years after leaving Hawaii as a baby, I went "home."

I enrolled in schools that specialized in teaching English to students who had just arrived from Japan. I had such a hard time learning English that, several times, I thought seriously about going back to Okinawa. My sister urged me to buckle down and keep trying. It was a good thing I took her advice and stayed in Hawaii. Otherwise, who knows what might have happened to me.

Less than three years after I returned, Japan and America were at war.

In early 1943, I volunteered for the 442nd Regimental Combat Team. I had reservations, because I couldn't speak English very well. My brother, Warren, had also volunteered. He was accepted, but I wasn't.

Several months after the 442nd left for training at Camp Shelby, I received a letter from the War Department, informing me of their plans to form a special unit of Japanese-language soldiers, the Military Intelligence Service, to serve in the Pacific war front. They asked whether I was willing to serve.

It put me in terrible turmoil psychologically, because if the unit was to be made up of Japanese-speaking Americans of Japanese ancestry, it was understood I'd be sent to the Pacific war front. What if I came face-to-face with someone I knew—a relative, a classmate? It might not happen, but it was possible. I felt torn between that fear and my desire to serve my country. After thinking about it for several days, I decided to volunteer for the MIS. This time, I was selected.

When I reported for my interview with the FBI and Army Intelligence, they seemed to know more about me than I knew about myself—and I was a "Mr. Nobody," just another kid that came from Japan a couple of years before the war.

I was accepted into the MIS and sent to Camp Savage in Minnesota, where I underwent eight months of language training. There were 239 of us in that first group of MIS volunteers from Hawaii. We studied not only the language but technical and military terminology based on a Japanese Military Academy textbook. I graduated in July 1943.

While at Camp Savage, I had been writing to my brother, Warren, who was in basic training with the 442nd at Camp Shelby in Mississippi. I wrote about the good life we had in Minnesota and about how wonderful it was to have fresh milk and eggs for breakfast. Compared to Mississippi, life in Minnesota was much, much better.

Warren was hooked. When a recruiter from Camp Savage went to Shelby to recruit more nisei for the language school, Warren volunteered. He finished basic training at Shelby and then came to Minnesota to begin his language training.

Meanwhile, I was sent to Camp Blanding, Florida, for basic training. Because of the urgent need for interpreters in the Pacific, our basic training was pared down from the normal sixteen weeks to an accelerated eight weeks.

My sister put in a request to the War Department that I be assigned to my brother's team. We had to get the War Department's approval. The department had stopped letting family members serve together after five brothers serving on the same cruiser were killed when it was torpedoed in the South Pacific.

In my case, Yuriko wanted me to be with Warren because of my lack of proficiency in English. She felt that two brothers serving together would cover each other and help each other. The War Department approved my sister's request.

Warren and I came back to Hawaii in the summer of 1944 and were assigned to the 96th Infantry Division. After two weeks of jungle training on Oahu, we were sent overseas.

We were on our way to Yap Island when we learned that it had been secured. Our division was then diverted to Gen. Douglas MacArthur's headquarters in New Guinea and then sent to Leyte Island in the Philippines.

About a month later, I was ordered to report to the G-2 Photo Interpreters Section. The captain said he heard that I had lived in Okinawa for many years. He wanted to know what area. I told him and pointed to the general area of my grandfather's village in Nakagusuku.

Next he pulled out an aerial photo of Okinawa's capital, Naha. At first I couldn't recognize it: It was completely destroyed. On October 10, 1944, navy carriers had launched an extensive bombing raid of Okinawa. Large aerial photographs of the island were shot after the raid.

The captain then pulled out another photo. I recognized it immediately as my grandfather's village, Shimabuku, which, up until five years earlier, had been my home. It was the northernmost village in the area known as Nakagusuku.

My hair stood up! For awhile I couldn't even open my mouth; I was so choked up.

I looked at the photo through a special three-dimensional lens capable of picking up minute details. I instantly recognized my grandpa's home and from there, finger-traced all of my relatives' houses. I was relieved to see that their homes were intact.

The captain then pulled out a shot of a typical country hillside in Okinawa. I looked at it and then looked back at the captain with a "So what?" look on my face. "Godammit, look carefully!" he shouted. "We think the whole island is fortified!"

The captain had mistaken traditional Okinawan burial tombs for fortifications. I suddenly realized the wrong impression the captain and other intelligence officers had and, afterward, gave the officers a crash course in Okinawan culture. I explained that Okinawans view their burial tomb as their final resting place, so they try to build them on a hillside with a good view, overlooking the ocean. I also explained that the crater-like holes that intelligence officers had observed in the corners of fields were composting pits used by farmers, not machine-gun nests.

From that time on, the captain said, "Sergeant Higa, you're going to assist us right through from here." I was sworn to secrecy. When I returned to division headquarters later, my brother asked me what I had done during the day. "Don't ask me, because I've been told not to say anything," I told him.

I didn't know it at the time, but Warren had informally volunteered my knowledge of Okinawa to the division brass in the event of an Okinawa invasion.

All the signs—the aerial photos, the questions—pointed to an Okinawa invasion. I knew of the plans at least five months before the actual strike. The only thing I didn't know was the landing date. I think I was of some help to corps headquarters because the area in which they landed was about a mile from where I had grown up.

It was a horrible feeling. Ever since the first day I saw the pictures, every night I dreamed about my relatives. Every night . . . never miss. I dreamed about my uncle, my cousins, and even my schoolmates.

As an American soldier, I had a duty to perform. I didn't want to harm the Uchinanchu (Okinawan) people, but I didn't know how I could avoid that without violating the military code of conduct. Deep inside, I was torn. It's a feeling hard to describe. Unless you yourself experience it, you can't appreciate it.

Anyway, by late December, Leyte had been secured. In March 1945 our division boarded a troopship. On our second day out, we were told our destination: Okinawa.

Quite often I was called to the radio shack to translate radio transmissions picked up from Okinawa. Most of the time they were music programs with some Okinawan language sprinkled in the broadcast.

The Okinawa offensive, which was code-named "Operation Iceberg," began on April 1, 1945. Early that morning, all of us soldiers lined up on the deck.

When the outline of Okinawa came up on the horizon, I recognized the hills instantly. I couldn't help but choke up. Only five years had passed since I left Okinawa, and my heart felt like it was being pulled in opposite directions. I was an American GI; I had a duty to perform, and yet, I had cultural and family ties to Okinawa. I was really torn between loyalty and patriotism versus personal feeling. . . . I can tell you I had tears in my eyes.

It was different for my brother, Warren. Yes, he's Uchinanchu and his ancestral roots are in Okinawa. But he had never established an emotional attachment to Okinawa because he was there for only three years. Although I've been back in Hawaii over fifty years, even to this day, the little country roads and small ditches and taro patches that I played in in Okinawa seem more like a real homeland to me than Honolulu.

There's an old Japanese saying: "*Mitsugo no tamashi hyaku made . . .* the spirit of a three-year-old child will last a hundred years." What you learn in your small-kid time, you'll never forget.

Because of my firsthand knowledge of the area and the Okinawan dialect, I was assigned to the division's advanced unit. We landed at the Chatan beachhead on the western side of the island.

I still remember what I saw when we landed—farmhouses all on fire, farm animals all over the place, all dead, some of them still burning. We began moving toward higher ground. While walking along a narrow road, I suddenly saw something move in a small roadside dugout. My heart stopped beating. I jumped back and took cover. Slowly I began walking toward the dugout. With my carbine trained, I shouted, "Come out, whoever you are! Come out!"

I was so scared I can't even remember whether I spoke English, Japanese, or Okinawan. I meant to speak Uchinaguchi (Okinawan dialect), but I have a feeling it was a mixture of everything—and maybe even some pidgin.

There was no response to my order, so I began squeezing the trigger. Suddenly, I saw a thin human leg appear. "*Njiti mensoree* (come out, please)!" I ordered in Uchinaguchi.

An old woman crawled out from the dugout. She was thin and frail, and her clothing was covered with dirt. There was a little girl with her, about five or six years old—her granddaughter, I later learned. I began questioning the old woman. She said her family had escaped to the north, but because of her weak leg, she had remained behind with her granddaughter.

I recommended that they be taken to a civilian refugee camp. To this day, I'm so glad that I didn't pull the trigger. At point-blank range, I wouldn't have missed. If I had shot that old lady, I think I'd go crazy, knowing that she was a civilian.

I have tried locating the granddaughter, who by now would be in her sixties. The old woman has probably died by now. In all probability, the granddaughter may have been the first Okinawan civilian prisoner.

Soon after arriving at Chatan, what I hoped would never happen, did.

My former teacher, Shunsho Nakamura, had been caught while scurrying around, looking for potatoes to eat. Sensei was sent to a civilian refugee center. However, because of his tall, conditioned physique, they thought he might be a Japanese soldier trying to pass himself off as a civilian, so they sent me to interrogate this prisoner.

I recognized him instantly; after all, he was my teacher for seventh and eighth grade. I looked at him, "Sensei . . ." He turned around and looked at me. He recognized me immediately. *"Ah, kimi ka* (oh, it's you)!" Both of us got so choked up. I told the escort officer that Nakamura was indeed a teacher, not a Japanese soldier, and that he should be allowed to remain at the refugee camp.

Our division continued to advance. For the first three days, we set up camp inside an Okinawan *kaaminafuu ufaka,* a turtle-back burial tomb. The concrete tomb offered lots of protection. In no time, captured documents began arriving. I was assigned to translate some Japanese maps. I worked around the clock for three days straight without any sleep, burning a gas lantern at night. A dark curtain concealed our location from the enemy. Lined up behind us were *jiishigaami,* ceramic containers which held the bones of the deceased. I felt really uneasy about working in someone's final resting place.

The Japanese didn't put up much resistance in the first two days of the invasion. Okinawa took a beating because one Japanese military division had been pulled out and sent to Formosa. That left Okinawa underdefended.

By the end of the second day, Okinawa was cut completely in half. The marines went north and the army headed south. In two weeks, our division lost about a third of its combat strength. The Japanese lost about the same number. Nakamura *sensei* later told me that although the Battle of Okinawa lasted three months, the Japanese army was effective for only about fifty days of the entire battle. The Japanese troops were pushed back to the south after their line at Shuri, Okinawa's ancient capital, had been broken.

Our headquarters was moved one last time, to Onaha. In May, shortly before Okinawa was secured, two prisoners were brought in. Their uniforms were all torn up and they were hungry. I was ordered to interrogate them. I offered them some biscuits and D rations, which is a hard chocolate candy bar equivalent to a complete meal.

The prisoners refused to eat. "Why won't you eat?" I asked. They said they thought the rations contained poison. *"Bakayaro* (Fools)!" I shouted at them. Then I began nibbling at the candy bar to show them that it was okay. Relieved to see me eating the candy bar, they began gobbling it down.

The two men had been captured in a cave. When they refused to come out after repeated calls from American soldiers, the engineers had sealed the cave and planted dynamite. The two frantically dug themselves out. The American soldiers were waiting when they surfaced. The men surrendered and were brought to headquarters.

After giving them time to compose themselves, I began to interrogate them. Their answers to my question about the school they had attended, Kishaba Shogakko, made my ears perk up, because I had attended the same school.

Without revealing my identity, I started asking more specific questions, drawing on my memories of school. Each response led me to believe that these guys were my classmates. Finally, I asked them whether they knew Nakamura *sensei*. They were shocked. How could this American GI possibly know Nakamura *sensei*? I looked them square in the eye and said, "I'm an American Military Intelligence Service language-school graduate, noncommissioned officer. I know everything about you guys, so don't lie to me."

I decided to put them through one final test. "Do you remember one of your classmates named Takejiro Higa from Shimabuku?" I asked. They were shocked.

"How do you know him?" they asked. "I told you," I said. "I know everything about you guys. Don't lie to me."

One prisoner said he heard Takejiro Higa had gone back to Hawaii. They hadn't seen each other for so long and didn't know where he was, nor if they would recognize him today.

By then I was positive that they were my old classmates. I looked at them straight in the face, and in Okinawa-go (Okinawan dialect), said, "Godammit, don't you recognize your own classmate?" They looked up, shocked beyond belief, and began crying.

"Why are you crying?" I asked.

They said they were crying because they were relieved. After answering my questions, they'd thought they would be no longer useful and would be executed.

"Now, knowing that our own classmate is on the other side, we believe our lives will be spared. That's why we're crying, because we're happy," one guy said.

I couldn't restrain my emotions any longer. The three of us grabbed each other's shoulders and had a good cry. I still get chickenskin whenever I think about that incident. Unfortunately, I never saw those two guys again. I wish I could remember their names. So far, I haven't been able to track them down.

For the remainder of the Okinawa offensive, I interrogated suspected imposters at the civilian compound at Sashiki-Chinen. One of them was a Japanese colonel, and I think that incident really shows how valuable my personal knowledge of Okinawa was to America.

I nabbed the colonel after his claim that he was from Yamachi Village turned out to be full of inconsistencies. I knew because I had grown up in Shimabuku Village, which is next to Yamachi Village.

In Uchinaguchi, I asked him, "Who the hell are you?" He was stuck: He couldn't understand a word of what I had said. I then proceeded to tear his story apart.

"Ah, shimatta (dammit)!" he said. He thought he would get better treatment in a civilian refugee camp than in an army POW camp. He might have gotten through had I not been assigned to interrogate him. Then again, if the colonel claimed to have been from a village I wasn't familiar with, I might not have detected his charade.

I remained in Okinawa for the duration of the Battle of Okinawa, which ended in early August. My division, the 96th, was then returned to the Philippines. On our way there, we learned of the bombing of Hiroshima and Nagasaki, which ended the war. We reached Mindoro on August 15, the day Japan surrendered.

My brother had accumulated enough points to be discharged immediately. I didn't have enough points yet, so I was sent to Korea, where I interrogated Japanese evacuees for almost four months. I wanted to stay in Okinawa and serve with the occupational forces, but my request was denied because the 96th Division was being withdrawn.

The Okinawa I left behind when I boarded the transport ship to go to the Philippines in 1945 was very different from my memories of Okinawa in 1939 when I left as a teenager. Everything was burned out, especially in the South. . . . The worst ground battle of World War II took place in Okinawa. Just about everything was busted up. You couldn't recognize anything.

And there were changes from 1945, when the war ended, to 1965, when I went to Okinawa for the first time since the end of the war. The landmarks were all different. What I had seen as targets twenty years earlier were gone.

I didn't get to see Nakamura *sensei*, whom I had interrogated, until my first visit to Okinawa in 1965. Now, whenever I go to Okinawa, I visit Sensei. He's in his eighties, but he is still healthy and alert. I take a bottle of whiskey when I go. We have oodles of things to talk about. In my case, a bond that was formed in childhood and strengthened during the war remains strong.

In 1995, the fiftieth anniversary of the end of World War II, I heard that there was going to be a big memorial service in Okinawa to honor the memory of all the people who died in the Battle of Okinawa: American military, Japanese military, and Okinawan civilians. From the moment I heard about the memorial service, I knew I wanted to go and pay my respects to those who had died. It turned out to be a very, very special trip.

Nakamura *sensei* had told me numerous times during my visits to Okinawa after the war that many Okinawans hiding in caves were saved because of the nisei linguists. But I had never heard it with my own ears, until I went to Okinawa for that fiftieth anniversary memorial service in 1995.

Shortly after arriving in Okinawa, I was interviewed by Miwa Saito, a reporter for the *Ryukyu Shimpo,* one of the daily newspapers. She wanted to know about my experiences as an American soldier in Okinawa during the war. Soon after the article was published, Saito-san received a call from a woman named Toyo Tawada, who said she wanted to meet me.

Mrs. Tawada said she had thought about me for a long time before deciding to contact Saito-san. She told Saito-san, "My life was saved by this person, but at that time, because of the education we received, I remember I reacted very strongly against him. I am truly sorry for that."

On April 6, 1945, Mrs. Tawada, who was a young woman at the time, about twenty years old, was with about two hundred people hiding in the cave near Futenma. She told Saito-san that if I hadn't come to their cave, everybody inside would have committed suicide. The young people, including herself, refused to go out. Finally, some of the older people encouraged them to take a chance. "We were saved, but I remember that I threw very strong words at him," she told Saito-san.

She said she remembered my calling them out in Uchinaguchi. She heard me tell them my name, Higa. "He saved so many people's lives. I owe Mr. Higa for the life I enjoy today," she told Saito-san. She said that for a long time, she had wanted to meet me—and we finally did meet fifty years later. That's the first time that anybody has thanked me face-to-face, has said that because of my continuous urging, they came out.

I always tried to gain the trust of the civilians by introducing myself, telling them that I was Uchinanchu, just like them. I told them my name and my parents' and grandparents' names. I told them that my parents and grandparents were from Shimabuku Village. I told them that I was a nisei who was born in Hawaii, but that I grew up in Okinawa. I always spoke in the Okinawan language and tried to assure them that they would be treated well if they came out. That was my main point, to make them feel at ease, knowing that an Uchinaa (Okinawan) boy was out there.

When I look back on that experience now, more than fifty years later, I really feel that my approach made a difference. I see it in people like Mrs. Tawada; she's living proof. She said they were all ready to commit suicide. They all had hand grenades.

When I met with Mrs. Tawada in Okinawa, she brought along her daughter, who sat beside her mother. She, too, thanked me. "Because of you, I'm also here," she said.

I told them, "Thank you. Up to now, my only thought was I hoped I was of some help." Hearing from someone directly that I had been of help meant so much to me, but when the daughter told me that she was alive because of my help, wow, that hit me even harder.

During that trip, I also met up with some 96th Division veterans at a reception. They had been part of the invasion forces that landed on Okinawa in April 1945. I didn't know them back then, but because we came from the same division, at that reception we established an instant rapport.

During the reception, a former Japanese officer got up on the stage and asked whether any of the Americans in the audience had fought at a particular spot in Okinawa, which he named. Several hands went up. The response gave me chickenskin. He called them up front and, shaking hands, said, "I was there and you folks fought gallantly. We all had a duty to perform at that time, even though when we think about it, it's so silly now. We have become friends. . . ."

That really hit me—a very touching scene. Yesterday's enemy shaking hands today, and each pledging to work for peace.

Today, there's hardly any trace of the bloody battle that took place in Okinawa a half century ago, which surprised many of the veterans— most of them were returning for the first time since the war ended. It was just unreal to them. Every one of them had nothing but praise for the tremendous recovery and reconstruction, because when they left Okinawa, hell, the whole place was just burned-out villages and countryside.

Shimajiri, the southern part of the main island, suffered the most damage. It was totally rebuilt and is today not only the most populated section of Okinawa, but the center of business and government as well.

That's a tribute to the spirit of the Okinawan people. American aid was tremendous, but that alone wasn't enough. The bottom line is that the people themselves worked hard and rebuilt.

I'm relieved that Shimabuku Village, where I grew up, was spared massive casualties. Hawaii had a lot to do with that. In the early 1900s, many of the village people came to Hawaii to work on the sugar plantations. When their contract was over, many went back to Shimabuku Village. Although it was very limited, I feel that their exposure to the English language during those few years made the difference between life and death for them.

My parents' village had so many people who returned to Okinawa from Hawaii; they could speak broken English. They understood the Americans. When the GIs told them, "Come out, come out," they came out, and they knew that Americans were not savage—not like the others who had been brainwashed by the Japanese military to believe.

From the time I made my decision to go into the Military Intelligence Service, I was always afraid that I would meet, face-to-face, a relative or friend that I had known while growing up. So I really had serious reservations about serving in the Asia/Pacific theater. But, in time, I realized how valuable my knowledge of the Okinawan language and culture were from a humanitarian standpoint.

I have only one regret about Okinawa. If the Uchinanchu had believed in us just a little bit more and followed our pleas, we could have saved a lot more people. But, then again, I realize how badly brainwashed the Okinawan civilians had been—and I know I have to let that go.

When I look back on the war, actually, I'm glad I was sent to the Pacific war front—and to Okinawa. Innocent people were killed; that's war. But if my personal knowledge of Japanese and also Okinawan language and culture saved even one life, I'm content.

I feel at peace with myself regarding my wartime experiences. By using the Japanese-English dictionary, notebook, portable megaphone, and my mouth, I fully discharged my obligation as a U.S. citizen, and at the same time, I was able to help the people I grew up among. The bottom line is, I was able to serve both sides without firing a shot. For that, I'm very happy.

In a way, I went to war—and found peace.

Governor George R. Ariyoshi

Military Intelligence Service

IN THE SPIRIT OF *OKAGE SAMA DE*

My father was lean and muscular, and he was known in his younger days for his skill as a sumo wrestler. When I was a boy, I always saw him as strong and self-assured. He guided me with a sense of confidence and certainty. When I grew up I was amazed to learn how difficult his life had been. He was born in a small village in the prefecture of Fukuoka, Japan. Although he was an excellent student, he only went to school through the third grade. When he was young he went to sea. When he arrived in Hawaii, he liked what he saw and jumped ship. As a result, he struggled not only with being an immigrant who spoke little English, but also with being an illegal alien. During World War II, he lived with the expectation that he would be interned.

In the ancient sport of sumo, wrestlers are given special names. His sumo name was "Yahata Yama," and for many years he was known casually by this name, not Ariyoshi. The first year I was to campaign, which was thirty-five years after his arrival in Hawaii, I was surprised to hear people greet him as "Yahata."

We moved a lot, but I remember best our two-room place at the corner of Smith and Pauahi streets in Chinatown, just above Honolulu Harbor. One of those rooms was a dining room, living room, and a bedroom as well. In Japanese style, the dining table was low and we sat on mats on the floor while we ate. At bedtime, the table was rolled away and our futon bedding was unrolled onto the mat floor.

Papa often worked on the waterfront as a stevedore. He also got work as a stone mason. But he had an entrepreneurial streak. He contracted to supply gravel to road builders, and he quarried the rock, which required the blasting of dynamite. He didn't want to ask anybody else to do it, so he learned to blast the dynamite himself. He also made tofu and sold it, and he eventually opened a dry-cleaning shop in lower Kalihi. He was also to become a campaigner with seemingly boundless reserves of energy.

My mother was from Kumamoto Prefecture, which is next to Fukuoka in southwestern Japan. Like my father, she had only an elementary-school education. Also like my father, she had an amazing way of seeing the bright side of things when she might have despaired. Because our family shared a communal kitchen, she usually got up at four-thirty to start the day's cooking. When she cooked our favorite dishes, she would announce she wasn't hungry. In fact, she said she did not care for a particular dish, and she would pass her share on to us. At the time I thought it strange that she did not care for such delicious food, and it was not until long afterward that I saw through her little story.

My parents' idea of opportunity was the opportunity to work hard, be free to improve their lot in life, and raise a family. I was born in 1926, the first of six children. I had one brother and four sisters. Although our two rooms were on the second floor of a rough-board building, I never thought of our place as a tenement, nor did I think of ourselves as poor.

We had a positive sense of our neighborhood, our schools, and of Hawaii itself. Family life sheltered us, and within this nurturing environment we practiced discipline willingly and happily. We were free to venture out, but I adhered to the boundaries set by my parents. My mother wanted to know what I was doing, so I always told her, "Okaasan (Mother), I'm going to such-and-such a place." If I was going to some other place afterward, I would go back and tell her where I would be next, so she always knew where I was. From that point of view, I was quite protected. We were a tightly knit family, and my parents were totally in control, yet I didn't feel I was being deprived of freedom.

I was constantly told there was a right path, and there was no question that I was to follow it. My father was always saying to me, "Do the things that are right. Never mind what happens." I should add that he often told me, "Be number one. Be the best."

His beliefs were derived from a code that was both an inner code and a community code. The two ran together so harmoniously as to be almost one and the same. What you knew to be right came from within, yet it was intertwined with the individual doing right in the eyes of others. He used the Japanese word *otagai*, referring to the deep Japanese sense of mutual obligation. He used the words *okage sama de*, an expression of appreciation for the support and assistance of others, which is sometimes translated as, "I am what I am because of you."

He would say, "Remember to be considerate of other people. Be grateful that you can get help from other people. Acknowledge others. Be humble, because many other people help make things possible for you."

The essence of my father's thinking accompanied me through my career and into the governorship. In my role as governor, I began using some of the Japanese words my father had used to explain my beliefs. *Okage sama de*, because of your shadow which falls on me, because of your help, because of you, I am what I am. I reminded myself of that idea often, and I tried to nurture that attitude in others. We are extensions of one another, and we are beholden to one another. . . .

When my father arrived here in 1919, a significant number of Japanese were leaving the relatively harsh conditions of the plantations for life in Honolulu. At this distance in time from my childhood, I can see how my life was influenced by the fact that my father tried his hand at many things, but never plantation life. I did not experience the racial stratification of the plantation, nor the wounded feelings that sometimes resulted. We lived among all sorts of people. Many were of Japanese ancestry, but there were many others of widely varying backgrounds.

Because my father worked at a variety of jobs, I went to school in several parts of the island. I went to kindergarten in the Waialae area, east of Honolulu. I went to the first grade on the Windward side of Oahu in the country, at Laie School. There were all kinds of children there, and my experience of the idyllic outdoor environment would later influence one of my major efforts as governor. I then went to elementary school near downtown in the Palama neighborhood, which today is a sort of legendary place for bringing different immigrant groups and Native Hawaiians together. I played with kids of varied backgrounds without giving much thought to our diversity, because we readily did things together. We had our scraps, but our problems were minor. The first day at Palama, a bully grabbed me by the shirt. He wanted me to know he was the "bull" of the school, as the saying went: I took a poke at him. We lived in Chinatown during my intermediate school days until the war broke out.

Within our family centered environment, institutions of Japanese community life were mingled with the institutions of American life. Public school was by far our most important experience, and it took the biggest share of every day. Like most of the new Japanese generation, I went to Japanese-language school after public school was over. We had to wait for language class to start, and the class itself went on for an hour. By the time we got home, it was around five o'clock.

I participated in both the Young Buddhist Association and the Young Men's Christian Association. The YMCA played a vital role in providing opportunities for people to develop their bodies and learn to get along with others. I took part in the swimming program at the Nuuanu Y, and later I belonged to a YMCA club. After that I became a "High Y" advisor. I was forever being inspired by other people, and I thought in my own little way I could help inspire people as a junior leader in the Y.

Life was distinctly simpler than today. Options were fewer, and choices were easier to make. Opportunity lay in education. The basic education provided for us was adequate and, for me, fulfilling. I had good teachers. Although some people talk about how limited our school opportunities were then, our teachers taught us reading, writing, and mathematics. The basics are very important, and that's why I feel strongly about our school system today—what it can be and what it ought to be. If only we could acknowledge to our teachers—as we did then—that they make such a difference, and acknowledge also that the all-important process of education happens only in the classroom between teacher and student.

People have stories about their favorite teachers. I had a teacher who has influenced me all of my life. Mrs. Margaret Hamada was my core studies teacher for two periods a day when I went to Central Intermediate, which is the school directly above today's downtown. I was her student for three years, and during those years I addressed the question of what I wanted to be when I grew up. At first I thought I might like to be a journalist. I was a reporter on the school newspaper, which really interested me, but Mrs. Hamada encouraged me to look at my options. She guided me into making an appointment with a lawyer, Arthur Trask, a member of a well-known Hawaiian family. I decided lawyers help people in trouble, and that was what I wanted to do. I was in the eighth grade when I embraced law as my goal. From that moment I never wavered in my intense desire to become a lawyer.

In my excitement I told my father. He often had said to me, "I can give you money, but you can spend it all. If I help you get an education, it will be with you forever." He was extremely happy to hear about my plan. In Japanese he told me, "*Hadaka ni nattemo,*" meaning that even if he had to go naked, he would make my schooling possible. He was saying he literally would give me the shirt off his back, to which he added: "Go for it." *Gambatte.*

The fact that we had no money did not seem to be a barrier, but I had a barrier of a different kind. I had a speech defect: I lisped. I had experienced this problem in elementary school, and it was still with me at Central Intermediate—a heavy lisp. Sometimes I stuttered. I would think about sound production so much that oftentimes I would forget what I wanted to say. When I decided I wanted to become a lawyer, I talked about my speech problem with Mrs. Hamada. I told her I could become a lawyer only if I learned to speak properly. Mrs. Hamada was not a speech pathologist, but she did everything she could to help. On weekends, she had me come by her classroom on the excuse of helping her with chores. I would do a few little tasks and then she would have me read aloud to her. She also encouraged me to enter oratory contests.

We had a student court at Central Intermediate, and she helped me become a defense lawyer. After I left Central, she came to the Oahu finals of one of the oratorical contests where I represented McKinley High School. She said she couldn't believe I was the same George Ariyoshi she had first met. When I became governor more than a quarter century later, Mrs. Hamada was there. Her selfless gifts lent a special meaning to the phrase *okage sama de.*

I should mention one other educator from my childhood, Dr. Miles Cary, who was the principal of my alma mater, McKinley High School. Dr. Cary is an important figure in the experience of the second generation of Japanese Americans because of his passionate dedication to the ideals of progressive education. He was at McKinley High during the first several months of my first year, which happened to be the autumn of 1941. In my limited contact with him, he projected an excitement about what others saw as ordinary. Every time you saw him he would say, "What a beautiful day! Isn't this a nice day?"

He was like my mother in the way he seemed to be saying that life was good and precious. Miles Cary made you feel there was something so exciting about any given moment that you wanted to do something with it. You wanted to do something with yourself. After the war started, Dr. Cary went off to the mainland. It was a mark of his deep commitment to Americans of Japanese ancestry (AJAs) that he spent a year of the war developing education programs in a mainland internment camp.

Obviously, not everyone in those early days had the qualities of the various people who inspired me, but today I am struck by the depth of commitment and durable values of those who helped me grow up. We in Hawaii were a long way from becoming the "last among equals," but in those sheltered days before the war, I think you could see the foundation of an American society that would one day be first in its serious dedication to equality.

By the standard of the many tales about December 7, 1941, mine is remarkable mainly for the calmness and clarity of my parents. In the early Sunday morning of December 7th, I went to Hongwanji Buddhist Sunday school on Fort Street downtown. We went early to be the first on the Ping-Pong table, so we got there by seven-fifteen or so. I was in the basement, and I actually heard some noise coming from above, but our Ping-Pong continued and then we had Sunday school. I walked home down Fort Street to our place on Smith Street, and when I got home my parents told me that Japan had attacked Pearl Harbor.

My mother told us all the things we needed to do, and she was quite an organizer. She had started to get canned foods and blankets together for each of us, in case we had to evacuate. She made each of us a bag, so we could take what we needed wherever we had to go. For the moment, as it turned out, we stayed where we were, but a little later we had to move out of our place in Chinatown by order of the martial law government. Everyone of Japanese ancestry near the harbor was required to move, as well as everyone near military installations. Many years later this forced move became an issue for which AJA people sought reparations. Compared to the suffering of those who were interned and relocated during the war, it was a minor thing for us. My family was used to moving, and we took it in stride. We went up into Manoa Valley to live with our cousins, who had a banana farm.

I enjoyed the farm life, and I enjoyed my cousins. We did not lack for opportunities to learn how to work. When I was fifteen, I cut *kiawe* trees along the Waianae-Nanakuli coast with a hand ax to clear a field in case of fire in the event of a Japanese invasion. During the rest of my high-school years, I went out to work in the pineapple and sugar fields to keep the plantations going. Our work was well organized, and we didn't mind it. We were paid fifty cents an hour.

The summer I was seventeen, I went to work in the pineapple cannery, which then was standard fare for kids in Honolulu. The first year, I worked in the storage warehouses of Dole Cannery. The cans were carted to us on pallets, and our job was to stack them up and store them away while they cooled. Then we would get an order from the labelling department saying they needed so many cans, and we would hop to it. We carted the order to the quality-control testers, who checked to see that the cans of fruit were in perfect condition. The best quality controllers could tell if there was a flaw merely by tapping the can with a tiny metal device. The next summer I went to work for the California Packing Company as a timekeeper for the contract trimmers. This was a privileged position for a seventeen-year-old.

I was just young enough to miss the brunt of World War II. I was drafted just as the war in Europe ended. While I was taking my basic training, the war with Japan ended. From basic training, I was sent to the Military Intelligence Service Language School at Fort Snelling, where many young men from Hawaii had trained. The role of Hawaii's Americans of Japanese ancestry in the MIS had been pioneered by several people, including Masaji Marumoto, a Harvard-educated attorney and later associate justice of the Hawaii Supreme Court. Such other well-known people as Ralph Yempuku and Ted Tsukiyama were lifted from the army training camps, trained in language school, and sent to the Pacific, where they played roles in intelligence-gathering and interpreting. The MIS people were widely scattered by the nature of the work, much of which was classified until the 1970s. As a result, the MIS did not develop the group cohesion or gain the public attention of the famous nisei army units, the 100th Battalion and the 442nd Regimental Combat Team. The work of the MIS was nonetheless dramatic. They saved many lives, and General Douglas MacArthur gave them credit for helping to shorten the war.

I was shipped to occupied Japan, where I spent most of my time in the ruins of Tokyo. The first Japanese person I really had a chance to talk to was a shoeshine boy at the NYK Shipping Lines Building, where I was stationed. He was seven. He told me about the suffering and the lack of food. My next meal I put some bread and jelly and butter together and wrapped it in a napkin. We were prohibited from passing food to the Japanese people, but I felt so sorry for the boy that I ignored the regulation. He put the sandwich in his box.

I asked him, "Why are you putting the sandwich away? Aren't you hungry?" He told me he was extremely hungry.

"But," he said, "I want to take this home for Mariko."

"Who is she?" I asked.

"My three-year-old sister," he said.

Every chance I got, I went into the Post Exchange and bought hamburgers, one for myself and one for the shoeshine boy. I was aware that I had relatives in Fukuoka and Kumamoto, but I was in Japan only a few months and had no opportunity to travel the country. I would have to wait for the discovery of much of my parents' homeland. I got my discharge as quickly as I could. I had dreamed about law school, and I was eager to pursue my dream.

When I got back to Hawaii, the veterans were streaming in, and the drinking and partying were getting into full swing. I thought if I got into that, I might get lost. I wanted to go to the University of Michigan at Ann Arbor because their law school had a good reputation, and I left for Michigan without applying, let alone being accepted. Once I was there, I was told that out-of-state registration was closed but registration was still open at Michigan State in East Lansing. I did my undergraduate work at Michigan State, studied hard, and gained acceptance to the University of Michigan Law School. I enjoyed my time there. Again, I had no sense of being treated differently. On the contrary, I enjoyed the fact that Hawaii had a reputation even then for people of different racial backgrounds coming together and living harmoniously.

In 1951, just before my last year of law school, my father told me about being a merchant seaman and jumping ship and living all his adult years in Hawaii as an illegal alien. I was flabbergasted. I said, "Papa, weren't you concerned during the war that they were going to come and pick you up?" He told me, yes, he was, that he had assumed it, but it never came to pass.

In 1952, Congress passed the Walter-McCarran Act, amending the U.S. immigration law. It allowed people who could prove continuous residence since 1924 to become legal residents. In general, the Walter-McCarran Act was a step forward, in that it defined legal rights for Japanese immigrants in America, although its quota system was severely weighted against immigration from Asia. When I came home after graduation, the first thing I did after passing the Hawaii Bar was to use the Walter-McCarran Act. I legalized my father's resident status in the United States. After that he did not need to worry. For the first time, he held a passport, which allowed him to leave Hawaii and return to Hawaii. Thereafter he took many trips to Japan.

Fujio Takaki

Military Intelligence Service

THE MAIZURU TREES OF ALOHA

On December 7, 1941, I was a civilian working as a mechanic at Pearl Harbor. As I watched the Japanese planes bomb Pearl Harbor, I had mixed emotions. As an American, I was very angry. And yet, being of Japanese ancestry, I felt very sad. I was also very concerned about my family, for they had returned to Japan to live after having immigrated to Hawaii, where I was born.

As the bombs fell around me, I saw a Japanese plane crash into the waters off Pearl Harbor. A navy officer and I jumped into a rescue boat and headed toward the wreckage. I spotted the pilot amidst the wreckage and debris in the water. When we got close to him, the pilot slipped out of his jacket and sank to his death, leaving his flight jacket and helmet floating. I noticed some Japanese characters on them, but I couldn't read them. I often wondered who the pilot was and what the Japanese characters meant.

A few weeks later, I was ordered to work as a machinist at Wheeler Air Force Base.

In 1944, I volunteered for the U.S. Army. I was prepared to go to war against my ancestral homeland, and the country where others in my family lived.

As a Japanese-speaking American, the army decided that I was a potentially valuable asset to the war effort. I was sent to Camp Savage in Minnesota to begin Military Intelligence Service training. There, I learned to read and write Japanese, and in time, I was able to answer my question from three years earlier regarding the identity of the pilot who had drowned at Pearl Harbor. He was Chief Petty Officer Asahi. He had been listed as "missing" among the Japanese attack force.

Upon completion of language training at Camp Savage, I was assigned to Camp Rich, Minnesota, where I underwent counterintelligence training at a top secret school.

I completed my training and was then dispatched to U.S.-occupied Guam, where I remained with other intelligence personnel until the end of the war. We were then sent to Japan, where we worked out of General MacArthur's headquarters in Tokyo.

I was subsequently assigned to Okayama Prefecture to do military intelligence work, and then transferred to Sasebo. There, my duties included interrogating and debriefing returning Japanese prisoners of war who had been held captive in the U.S.S.R.

During this time I visited my family, who lived in Iwakuni City. The war had taken its toll on them. I found their home in shambles. Life was doubly hard for them in postwar Japan. As a machinist, I had saved quite a bit of money, so I offered to pay for the repairs to their home.

However, my mother politely refused my offer, saying she did not want what she felt was preferential treatment. Instead, she encouraged me to do something for all the people of Japan.

Shortly after my visit with my family, I was assigned to Maizuru City in Kyoto Fu, which, at the time, was being used as a navy port. The entire city was devastated from the bombing and other effects of the war. It was a very bleak and depressing sight.

In Maizuru City, I worked as a Military Intelligence Service officer, interrogating repatriates from Siberia and gathering information about postwar activities there. While screening the Japanese repatriates, I was surprised to learn that my younger brother, Hideo, whom I had not seen in fifteen years, was in a group returning from Nakhodka. I watched him disembark from a repatriation ship from a distance, knowing that Soviet agents might have him under surveillance. Finally, later, when he was about to leave Maizuru, I introduced myself to him and urged him to hurry home to Yamaguchi, where our parents were waiting for his return.

Based on information gathered during our interviews with Japanese POWs returning from Siberia, we were ready to produce a large map of Siberia—its cities, industrial centers, railway and highway networks, and so forth. Since we didn't have any equipment to produce the maps, I approached Mr. Shukichi Sakomizu, an executive with Iino Kaiun Company, a large shipping company. He kindly accommodated my request to use his company's equipment.

Eventually, Mr. Shukichi Sakomizu and I became very good friends; I even married his daughter, who, many years later, has retired from teaching Japanese language at the University of Hawaii.

On one occasion, I told Mr. Sakomizu about my visit with my family and about my mother's refusal of help from me. I told him also about her request that I instead do something to help all of the people of Japan.

After thinking long and hard about her request, I decided to plant some cherry trees in Maizuru City, for I had been so captivated by their beauty when I first arrived in Japan. In the aftermath of the war, there was so little greenery left in this once-beautiful city. I shared my wish to plant the trees with Mr. Sakomizu.

In training at Camp Savage and Camp Rich, I had seen only black-and-white photographs of Japan: They weren't very impressive. That changed the moment I saw the cherry blossoms with my own eyes. It was quite a contrast to the black-and-white photographs. What I saw—the beautiful cherry blossoms in bloom against the backdrop of a war-ravaged city—made a lasting impression on me.

I had no idea of how to get the seedlings or where to plant them, or, for that matter, whether the people of Maizuru even wanted cherry blossom trees around their city. I hoped they would. Mr. Sakomizu liked the idea so much that he immediately volunteered to assist me. With my savings, and Mr. Sakomizu's help, I was able to purchase one hundred seedlings from Ikeda in Hyogo Prefecture. Mr. Sakomizu arranged to transfer them by rail to Maizuru City.

Before the seedlings arrived, however, I was assigned to another area of operations, so I wasn't able to witness their arrival. Prior to my departure, though, I met with several other MIS members who were stationed in Maizuru City and asked them to help plant the trees. They liked the idea so much that they donated money from their monthly activities pool, to which each person contributed from their pay. With my savings and contributions from Mr. Sakomizu's shipping company, they were able to plant several hundred trees in and around the city.

Today, situated behind Maizuru Station is a small hill by the name of Kyoraku Park. Planted in and around the park are the cherry trees I envisioned some fifty years ago. The trees are big and healthy now. The people of Maizuru City erected a large stone monument in the center of Kyoraku Park, which they dedicated to the lasting friendship between the people of the United States and Japan. Inscribed on the monument is the story of these "trees of aloha."

Every year, the people of Maizuru City celebrate this wonderful gift and the continuing friendship they represent with a festival. The years since the war had passed so quickly that, unfortunately, I had never returned to Maizuru City to see what had become of the seedlings . . . until April of 1994.

That year, the people of Maizuru City invited me and my wife to participate in their cherry-blossom festival. They honored me and other members of the MIS who had been stationed there. The following day, which happened to be my seventy-sixth birthday, the mayor of Maizuru City hosted a party in my honor.

In the years after the war, I had never told anyone about my involvement in the planting of the cherry-blossom trees, for I wasn't looking for recognition. I wanted only to help bring a smile to the faces of the good people of Maizuru City and to share with them a gesture of peace and aloha.

Kan Tagami

Military Intelligence Service

A CONVERSATION WITH THE EMPEROR

My parents came from Hiroshima, Japan, and settled in Selma, California, where I was born in 1918. Selma was a rural farming community near Fresno. As a child, I remember the discrimination people of Asian ancestry experienced. In 1928, when I was ten years old, my parents sent me to Japan to live with my grandparents. I lived there for four years.

I was drafted into the U.S. Army in February 1941 and assigned to the 7th Infantry Division, 6th Army, under the command of Gen. Joseph Stilwell. I learned of the December 7, 1941, attack on Pearl Harbor while standing guard duty on the waterfront in San Francisco.

I'll never forget an incident that happened two months later, in February 1942, while guarding the Union Pacific Railroad in Utah. I was ordered to surrender my rifle and bayonet because I was of Japanese ancestry.

The nisei in the 6th Army were eventually shipped out to Camp Crowder, Missouri. I was sent to Military Intelligence School at Camp

Savage, Minnesota, where I did so well in language school that after graduating I was retained as an instructor for two subsequent classes.

In July 1944 I was appointed to lead an eighteen-man language team assigned to the 124th Cavalry Regiment. We were shipped off to the India-Burma theater. My unit became part of the Mars Task Force at Myitkina. Our mission was to infiltrate and harass the enemy behind their lines and it culminated in the battle to secure Lashio, the key terminal along the Burma Road. I received a field commission during that assignment.

I later led a language team to Rangoon and assisted the British army with the Japanese surrender at Kuala Lumpur and Singapore. After Japan's surrender, I stayed on and served with the occupation forces in Japan until 1951. My military career ended in 1961 when I retired from the Counterintelligence Corps (CIC) at the rank of major.

The highlight of my twenty-year military career was the five years I served as Gen. Douglas MacArthur's personal interpreter in Japan. The job resulted in my most memorable assignment ever: a one-on-one meeting with Emperor Hirohito following Japan's surrender.

When I arrived in Japan, I didn't have a specific assignment: My responsibilities were rather general. I was told to report to GHQ, which meant I would be serving in ATIS—the Allied Translator and Interpreter Section. I only spent about a week there.

One day, while talking with Shiro Omata, who worked in the office of the commander-in-chief, he told me that he was leaving and asked whether I was interested in the job. "What job?" I asked.

"Interpreter for MacArthur," Shiro replied. I told him that I didn't have an assignment yet, so I was interested. Shiro offered to put my name in the pool for consideration, and I was eventually selected.

My first job as MacArthur's personal interpreter involved a visit by the *shugi-in gichoo*, or lower Diet chairman. He had come to pay his respects to MacArthur after the election. At the time, I hadn't yet met or even seen General MacArthur.

I walked in and "Old Mac" came out to greet Mr. Matsuoka from the Diet. "How are you, Mr. Matsuoka? Sit here," he said. Mr. Matsuoka began speaking, so I translated his message. He said he had just been elected chairman and had come to pay his respects to the commander. General MacArthur told him that his responsibilities were very important. He added, however, that he had no say in what Mr. Matsuoka did because he had been elected by the Japanese people. The two men exchanged pleasantries and then Mr. Matsuoka stood to leave. Something seemed to be bothering him still, so he sat down again and began speaking to General MacArthur.

Japanese Eyes . . . American Heart

He said he was worried that Japan had no way of defending itself now that a "no war" clause was in effect. How could Japan save itself in the event of an invasion?

General MacArthur pointed out that the citizens of Japan had approved the constitution. He added, however, that the constitution could always be amended to improve it, as the United States Constitution had been with twenty-one amendments. There were really two options, the general explained: Amend the constitution, or revise it completely. "The people have the power to do it. I won't oppose anything like that," General MacArthur said.

Mr. Matsuoka was so moved by the general's response that he began to sob. He was very worried about Japan's national defense. General MacArthur was really surprised. He had never seen a Japanese man cry. We waited until Mr. Matsuoka settled down, and then the general wished him good luck. Mr. Matsuoka thanked him and then General MacArthur asked me to escort him out.

After that, we were called upon by many Japanese leaders, including Prime Ministers Ashida, and Yoshida.

Prime Minister Yoshida was very appreciative of my cooperation. One day, his aide came to see me. "Lieutenant Tagami, do you think it's wise for Prime Minister Yoshida to ask to see MacArthur by himself?" I told him that I had no objections as long he could speak English. He said the official request would come from Prime Minister Yoshida. In a way, I was relieved, because I could just imagine the amount of overtime I would have to put in for that session.

One officer, General Whitney of GHQ's Government Section, was not happy about Prime Minister Yoshida having seen the general by himself.

Thereafter, I interpreted for Yoshida several times. From the first time, everything was fine. I didn't have a problem with his flowery language.

MacArthur was really the right person for the job. He didn't interfere unless there was trouble. He let the Japanese police and other officials do what they had to do. Americans probably didn't like that, but the Japanese liked him because he kept his distance. He left them alone.

I was with MacArthur from December 1945 until April 1951, when he was fired. In fact, he and I were fired together. The general told me that he was leaving and then asked me where I wanted to go. I told him I had no idea—only that I was leaving. "Let my senior aide know where you want to go. We'll make sure you get there," the general told me.

I later requested assignment with the Counterintelligence Corps in Baltimore, and General MacArthur did indeed push it through for me.

A lot of pressure was put on the emperor by the American media following Japan's defeat and during the occupation of Japan. The media wanted to show the American public how the emperor's family lived, and they would invade the imperial residence, set up their cameras, and begin taking pictures.

Some of them wanted to photograph every aspect of the emperor's life. In some instances, the American media contacted the Foreign Ministry directly for clearance. The ministry then proposed it to the *kunaicho*, the Imperial Household Ministry. In those days, when the Foreign Ministry suggested something, it meant something.

One day, General MacArthur was told by our own liaison with the Imperial Ministry that the *March of Times* and others had made a request through the Foreign Ministry. I had been out golfing that day. When I returned, there was a message from Colonel Laurence E. Bunker to report to the office immediately.

I arrived at the office at about seven P.M. and found Colonel Bunker, senior aide-de-camp, still at work. "Kan, do you mind going to the imperial household right away?" "No, I have my pass, so I'll go," I answered. He said he would call the ceremonial head of the imperial household, the *shikibu gashira*, to set up a personal meeting for me with the emperor. Not with anybody else, just myself. He said General MacArthur wanted the emperor to know that there was no pressure from headquarters for him to grant requests from the media if he felt it infringed on his privacy. General MacArthur believed the emperor had the same right to privacy as any other Japanese citizen. If the emperor refused the request from the American media, General MacArthur would back him up. The general was very angry that Americans would do such a thing to the emperor, and he would not bow to any pressure to open up the Imperial Ministry against the emperor's wishes. That is what I was told to communicate to the emperor.

When I arrived, I was met by an official. "Do I sign something now?" I asked. "This is an unofficial visit. You just walk in by yourself," he said, directing me to the door. "Aren't any of you coming with me?" I asked. "No," he replied, adding, "Personal. Just you and the emperor. That's what it's going to be." "Any restrictions?" I asked. "No, just go in there and give your message."

The room was small with only a few pieces of furniture: a small round table, a chair for the emperor, and one for me. As I walked in and sat down, my mind flashed back to my days as a grammar-school student in Kaita Ichi Machi, when Emperor Hirohito was *sessho no miya*, or prince regent.

The Taisho Emperor was still in power, but he was ill, so Hirohito had already assumed the responsibilities of the emperor.

The *sessho no miya denka* was on his way back from Kure Naval Base. He was scheduled to transfer to the Hon-sen, the main line at Kaita Ichi Machi. All of the schoolchildren were called out to the railroad station and lined up. We waited patiently as the Kure-sen train slowly pulled in. The future emperor and his attendant disembarked from the train.

I remember hearing the order: "*Saikeirei . . .*" which meant we were to bow our head and not look up. I couldn't resist the temptation, and as he passed before me, I lifted my head and looked at him.

Within minutes, he boarded the Hon-sen and was gone. There I was, a child, not allowed to even set eyes upon him. And here I was, some twenty years later, sitting directly across from him, the leader of Japan's eighty million people.

Many people had seen the emperor, but always among others. How many people could say they had had a private audience with him one-on-one. This Kaita Ichi student, now a U.S. Army first lieutenant, thought that was quite an honor, and I was very proud of myself.

The emperor walked in alone. We bowed to each other. He shook my hand, and then we sat down.

One thing I noticed was that he never addressed me as "first lieutenant" or "lieutenant"—only as "Tagami."

"*Tagami no otoo-san, okaa-san wa dochira kara desu ka* (What part of Japan did your parents come from)?" I told him that they were from Hiroshima and added, "*Watakushi mo Nihon ni sukoshi orimashita* (I was in Japan a little while myself)." "*De, kyo wa gokuroo san desu* (Thank you for your efforts today)," he said. I replied, "*Maa, gensui wa hijyo ni shimpai shite imasu* (General MacArthur is very worried about you)." I continued, "There has been a lot of pressure on you from *kunaisho* and *gaimusho* to open up your household to the media so they can get a good picture of you and an interview." "Yes, there was a request. I'm worried about that, too," he said. "What should I do? How should I react?"

I explained to him how General MacArthur felt about the emperor's role. I told him that the right of an individual to maintain his privacy was one of the most sacred things the general advocated. I also told him that if someone tried to force him to do something he did not want to do, that General MacArthur would back him up.

"General MacArthur told me to tell you that if you want to stand strong and say 'no,' he agrees with you. General MacArthur wants you to understand that. You have the full rights of a Japanese citizen. No one can make you do anything. I am very sorry that this happened, but I understand there is some pressure."

"I will do what is appropriate," the emperor said. He didn't say "yes" or "no." "That is all I have to say," I said. "*Watakushi no ninmu wa owarimashita* (I have now completed my assignment)."

The emperor then relaxed. "*Anatagata no shigoto Nihongo de iroiro seifu no shigoto o tasukete itadakimashite hontooni arigatoo gozai masu* (Your language abilities have made the government's work much easier. Thank you very much)."

Then the emperor said something I thought was quite profound. "The nisei are the bridge across our two countries." He said he hoped that we would do just as well in the years to come. "Thank you," I said. I didn't feel it was my place to sit and chit-chat, so I bid him good night and left.

In retrospect, I never imagined that such a meeting would ever take place—me, meeting the emperor, one-to-one, in a closed room. Being able to talk with him was quite an adventure. I don't think it will ever happen again, but back then, it was an era in which something like that was possible, and I was very impressed.

The first thing I did after arriving home was report to the office. "Everything is alright," I told General MacArthur. "Oh, good, good, good," he said.

That is one example of some of the things that went on, unofficially. General MacArthur was very strict about Americans and occupation personnel taking advantage of their position and imposing on the Japanese people. He would not allow that kind of thing. He emphasized to us that regardless of whether they were good or bad, whether or not they had started the war and fought the war—the emperor was the only one in Japan who could keep Japan stable. His mere presence created a calming atmosphere that could prevent violence.

That is why I was impressed with General MacArthur's feelings for the imperial household and his courage to fight anything that would infringe upon it. He understood the people and how they revered the emperor. He understood how that reverence could impact the American occupation. General MacArthur really was the right man for the job.

Kenneth K. Inada

442nd Regimental Combat Team

HUMANITY IN ACTION

The fiftieth anniversary of the end of World War II brought back many long-forgotten—and, perhaps, suppressed—memories of experiences and exploits in our tender years. Many of them are bitter and sweet in the same moment. The brutality, cruelty, and senselessness of war have been well documented by the media and in various publications and videos. In fact, perhaps there has been an overkill of this discussion.

My first taste—or, sight, more specifically—of battle came while walking in single file along the road to Bruyeres. Near the town, I spotted a pale hand with elbow down, lying on the roadside like a broken piece of a vase. It was obviously the result of a direct hit by an artillery shell or perhaps a barrage of shells. I cringed momentarily, wondering what happened to the rest of the body. As the battle progressed, I would encounter more gruesome scenes, especially during the nightmarish yard-by-yard struggle to rescue the "Lost Battalion" of the Texas 36th Division.

My recollections of humanity in action are drawn from events following the liberation of Bruyeres.

We advanced on the left side of the town, clearing machine-gun nests and bunkers along the way. I still remember seeing the landmark water tower high on the hill to the right. We advanced steadily and came to the edge of the rather thin forest. It overlooked a grass-covered ravine where a single-track rail ran from left to right, passing a cluster of farmhouses nearby. We later learned that the houses were being used as unit headquarters by the Germans. We dug our foxholes quietly since the Germans were unaware of our presence.

We awoke to a beautiful Sunday morning. The sun was out and the verdant Vosges Mountains were in their finest in the cool autumn surroundings.

Suddenly, from the left, we heard the bouncy whistling of a song. Someone passed on word that the tune was coming from a young German soldier on a bicycle. He leisurely rode his bicycle in the middle of the track, his pouch and rifle slung across his shoulders. The young soldier was apparently signaling his arrival to his headquarters in the farmhouses.

There were at least two platoons of us at the edge of the forest, facing the tracks, barely fifty yards away. He would have been a perfect clay pigeon.

"Let's get him when he's right in front of us," someone suggested. The platoon sergeant, I believe it was, added, "Wait until I give the signal."

We waited with rifles at the ready. Within seconds, the command came. "Fire!" As expected, all hell broke loose with a thunderous volume of fire. I pressed my trigger, but my eyes were riveted on the German. He hopped off his bike, flung it and his rifle away, and took off like a scared jackrabbit toward the farmhouses and safety.

We all burst out in laughter. None of us had ever thought of gunning him down in cold blood. Perhaps another situation might have prompted us to take more brutal action. But this time, we had not the slightest thought of harming him. Our shots were all *around* him, not *at* him. A big bang, for sure, but a hollow one, nevertheless. I felt good inside about having spared the life of that soldier—and so did everyone else, I'm sure.

After that incident, the enemy seemed to be on the run. Our artillery began shelling the dense mountain forest across the tracks at will. The firepower was awesome. After a day or so, we could easily see the bald areas of the mountain where huge trees had toppled over in pronounced ways. With signs that the enemy was in full retreat, we were signaled to cross the tracks in pursuit.

As we entered the forest, we immediately came under heavy fire from the well-hidden machine-gun positions. Our squad concentrated on one of them halfway up the hill. We succeeded in routing the occupants, who, except for one wounded soldier still in the bunker, fled up and over the hill.

Our squad was within ten yards of the dugout and ready for the final assault. Suddenly, we heard the cry of the wounded German soldier, his voice revealing excruciating pain. Within seconds, a huge German sergeant appeared from the hilltop clearance. He ran down the hill, jumped into the dugout, and immediately lifted his wounded buddy on his back. Piggybacking him, they raced up the hill, step-by-step, and disappeared.

We were all lying flat on the ground, triggers at the ready, as we observed this uncommon scene. No one in our squad had the heart to destroy that easy moving target. The piggyback trudge up the hill took several minutes, but it seemed like an eternity. I looked at my buddies around me. We were engrossed in silence—a silence with complete understanding of the human situation.

Like gallant samurais imbued with bushido, we could not strike an enemy in the back. Could it be that we were trained to fight a thousand battles but still held in reservation an expression for that one finest rare moment? I often wondered about the nascent power we possess.

These two events, only days apart, have haunted me throughout my life. This is the first time I have written about them. Some who were witness to them—or to similar incidents on other occasions—will undoubtedly recall with anxiety that such things do happen, despite the ugliness of war.

For me, the war thrust forward experiences that made me become a real human being. I relish those experiences, for I believe that they are the foundations for human relationships that transcend our cultural differences.

The war matured us in unexpected ways, nourishing us in richer and more profound ways. But we have been notoriously reticent, not speaking out like veterans all over the world. I have learned also that this silence is a mature one that adds character to any culture.

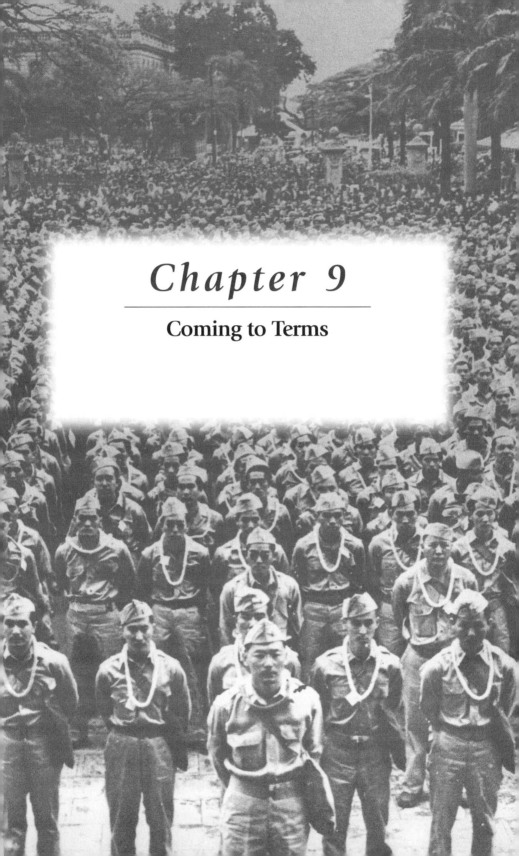

Chapter 9

Coming to Terms

Emperor Hirohito

FELLOW CITIZENS OF JAPAN. . .

The following surrender message, signed by Emperor Hirohito, Premier Suzuki, and various cabinet members, was delivered to the Japanese people at 12 P.M. on August 15, 1945, by the emperor.

After analyzing the present condition of Japan and the world situation, I am forced to accept the Allied terms of surrender in order to further save the Japanese nation. I am opposed to the further unnecessary destruction of Japan. Despite the combined efforts of the army and navy, and my work during the past four years, luck was against us and we are forced to concede victory to the enemy. The atomic bomb has demolished our cities and slaughtered our people. For the sake of my ancestors and from the standpoint of human culture and civilization, I cannot permit the further destruction of our people and our country. I deeply sympathize for the friendly nations of Japan and for the bereaved families of those who lost their sons in the front or those who died at their posts in their homeland. I advise the people to retain their integrity and to prevent being branded as outcasts in this world. Fellow citizens of Japan, please follow my advice.

Sohei Yamate

Military Intelligence Service

ON THE WAY TO SUGAMO PRISON

In 1943 I volunteered for the U.S. Army out of patriotism and love for my country, the United States of America. I think today's youngsters would find that statement strange and hard to accept.

While growing up on Kauai, my teachers had played a very important role in my life. During my first five years of public school, I had teachers who were either Chinese, Portuguese, Japanese, Hawaiian, or Caucasian—or combinations thereof. We were taught to get along with each other, to express ourselves, and to appreciate our democratic form of government.

On the other hand, the Japanese-language school I attended was regimented, full of propaganda from Japan, and a place where students were physically beaten. Thus, when World War II broke out in 1941, I was eager to defend my country against the Japanese.

I still remember the date I volunteered for the army: December 7, 1943. Three months later, in February of 1944, I was one of 310 volunteers from Hawaii who began Military Intelligence Service language training at Camp Savage in Minnesota. I had volunteered for the 442nd when the call for volunteers was issued, but I was turned down because I was underage.

My friends were surprised that I had volunteered to become an interpreter—and had been accepted. The mainlanders in training with us referred to themselves as "Japanese Americans," or "nisei," while we from Hawaii called ourselves "Americans of Japanese ancestry." In fact, the word *nisei* puzzled us because we had not heard it commonly used. Our public-school teachers had referred to us simply as "Americans."

Although I had completed up to the eighth grade in Japanese school, like others in the lowest section at Camp Savage, I found the lessons hard. In order to keep up and pass, we studied on weekends, and even in the latrine after lights out.

After language training, we were sent to Fort McClellan for basic training. One day, a camouflaged sedan pulled up in front of our squad. Out stepped Chief of Staff Gen. George C. Marshall. As we stood at attention, the general asked our cadre if we were being readied for Europe. The sergeant replied that we were being sent to the Pacific. The general was surprised. "I didn't know these men were going to the Pacific war," he said.

The irony of that remark hit us hard because just a month earlier, Marshall's second-in-command, G-2 Gen. Clayton Bissell had announced to us: "I bring you greetings from the chief of staff, General Marshall." Evidently, the right hand did not communicate with the left.

When our training was over, our detachment headed for the China-Burma-India (CBI) theater of operations, via a two-month ocean trip around Australia to India and a freezing flight over the Himalayas to Kunming, China.

Each of us was assigned to an old-timer. I was assigned to veteran Sgt. Kenji Yasui, already well known for his outstanding courage. He had photos of himself in Japanese army uniforms and was known to go in and out of enemy lines.

In Burma, American troops approaching the Irawaddy River had encountered hostile gunfire from a small island in the river. Yasui volunteered to get the enemy to surrender. With a Caucasian officer and a Pfc. in tow, he stripped off his clothes and waded toward the island. In flawless Japanese, Yasui announced that he was Colonel Yamamoto of the Japanese Imperial Army, now working with the Americans because Japan had lost the war. One of the Japanese officers doubted him and rushed toward the Americans while pulling the pin from his grenade. The grenade exploded in his hands, killing the Japanese officer on the spot. Yasui escaped unharmed.

Regaining his composure, he ordered the Japanese to surrender. He then ordered them to row him across the river. Almost single-handedly, Yasui had captured seventeen enemy soldiers. For his valor, he was awarded the Silver Star. Yasui later told me that an officer just handed him the medal. Knowing his colorful vocabulary and his attitude toward officers, I can understand why. He probably wouldn't have shown up for the ceremony, anyway. Kenji Yasui was indeed a nonconformist; he listened to no one.

In the spring of 1945 while attached to the Chinese Combat Command, we set out to interrogate about one hundred eighty Japanese soldiers who had been captured outside of Chih Kiang. We traveled for two weeks—by truck convoy, wood-burning train, and rafts. Interior China was extremely mountainous and we were always either climbing or descending mountains. The POWs we interrogated were a sorry sight. They were stragglers who had not heard from anyone in Japan for three years.

The big surprise proved to be one of the officers in the Chinese army, which was holding the prisoners. He was a former Japanese soldier who had deserted to the other side. We were skeptical of him at first—until we met up with other Japanese deserters. I was able to practice my Japanese with them. From them, we learned of the cruel treatment of Chinese civilians by Japanese soldiers. Discipline was tough in the Japanese army. The phrase "man's inhumanity to man" often came to mind when we heard their accounts.

We used these "new Chinese" to put *furikana* (Japanese alphabets) on the kanji, which sped up our reading of the documents. One of our *kibei* spot-checked their furikana and was sufficiently satisfied with their abilities. If any of our *sensei* back home—John Aiso, Shig Kihara, or Minoru Shinoda—had heard about our methods, they would surely have demanded that we commit hara-kiri.

At our headquarters in Kunming, I had a chance to work in the war room. The early MIS men, probably John Burden's group, had done a superb job of putting together a book that identified almost every Japanese unit in China. Listed were the names of the officers, noncommissioned personnel, and, in some cases, even the privates. If we had a Japanese soldier in our capture and he told us about his unit, we knew immediately who his senior officers were and what part of Japan they were from. The team members who worked on that top secret book deserve a special citation.

Interestingly, at home in Hawaii, the MIS men of Japanese ancestry could not enter Pearl Harbor, even though they carried important documents about the Japanese. In Kunming, someone had forgotten to clear our Caucasian officers, so they could not enter the war room. We enjoyed reminding our officers that they were "security risks."

On the ship crossing the Pacific, I had met a Chinese air force pilot. We became friends and kept in touch. In one of my letters, I had written that I was stationed in Nanning. He wrote back, saying his brother was stationed nearby. When the war ended, I was assigned to Canton, where his brother contacted me and invited me to his headquarters.

He turned out to be the commanding general for the entire Southeast China region. What an experience that turned out to be! He presented me with a Japanese sword and made me an honorary officer in the Chinese army. Our lieutenant, Akiji Yoshimura, couldn't believe the scene of my arrival to the unit, accompanied by the Chinese general and his aides.

Prior to leaving for Canton, we had flown in a cub plane from Nanning to Fort Bayard in Kwang Chowwan, formerly leased to France, where we attended an informal surrender ceremony of Japanese troops to the Chinese army. All we did was observe; no words were spoken. Couriers with written instructions in Chinese were utilized. We thought that our group was headed for Hainan Island. That was not to be, however.

We returned to Kunming just in time to witness the start of the Cultural Revolution. We passed through Shanghai on our way to Japan but did not see any visible damage in Shanghai. Everything seemed normal; the stores were selling their wares. From what I saw, the last two years of the war in China had been quiet. The Chinese had not battled the Japanese. The press seemed to have been doing most of the fighting with their stories.

The rumor or standing joke at that time to explain the busy Kunming Airport was that the planes landed with U.S. money and flew out with the same money, to deposit in U.S. banks for the "fat cats."

At Sugamo Prison

In Japan, we joined up with ATIS (Allied Translator and Interpreter Section). The officer in charge of assignments was Lt. George Sonoda. When he asked whether any of us had worked with POWs, someone mentioned my name. I later learned that I had "volunteered" to go to Sugamo Prison, along with another Hawaii interpreter, Kazuto Okamura.

The prison was located in Ikebukuro, Tokyo, where the Sunshine City Prince Hotel stands today. At the time, Sugamo was the only large concrete building left standing in the area, which had otherwise been completely destroyed. A few smokestacks could be seen here and there, but like most of Tokyo, there was little else.

Sugamo Prison was a beehive of activity, as the facility had just begun to receive war criminals. Okamura and I were the only interpreters, so we didn't have much time to goof off. Our job was to process the POWs: fingerprint them, gather personal information on their next of kin, send them off for delousing, and so forth. I processed most of the major war criminals.

We were on call in case the prisoners became ill. Former Japanese Premier Kuniaki Koiso became ill one night, so I took the doctor in to check him. The doctor, a curious fellow, questioned Koiso about his role in the war. When asked why he did nothing to try to end the war, he replied that he was powerless: a group of active admirals and generals had dictated all the moves, while he, being retired, did not wield any power.

When Gen. Masaharu Honma arrived at Sugamo, his six-foot-tall stature surprised me. Col. Robert Hardy, the prison commandant, came out personally to greet him. The two officers had apparently known each other before the war. General Honma had attended Oxford University and spoke fluent English. His amiable nature facilitated my conversation with him. In one of our talks, the general recalled a scenic train ride he had taken along the Monongahela River in Pennsylvania.

General Honma was held responsible for the Bataan Death March and for the actions of his men. He was taken from Sugamo to the Philippines, where he was tried, convicted, and sentenced to death by firing squad.

Marquis Koichi Kido, the emperor's closest advisor, was also escorted into the prison. He provided information on the emperor, revealing how well-informed Japan's ruler had been on the status of the war. He said that in the spring of 1945, Japan had sent diplomats to Russia to help them negotiate peace with the United States. Russia, however, did not acknowledge the diplomats. Japan realized then that the Russians were involved with the Allies and that it was only a matter of time before they would launch an attack against the Axis.

All of the war criminals had been instructed to report to the prison by a certain date. To our surprise, everyone surrendered as scheduled. One day, we learned that Prince Fumimaro "Butch" Konoye would be coming to Sugamo. (The prince had acquired the nickname while attending an American Ivy League college prior to the war.) There were also rumors circulating that the emperor himself might come to Sugamo. We knew that Gen. Douglas MacArthur's decree had kept the emperor on his throne. With Marquis Kido already in, and Prince Konoye scheduled to arrive—the two individuals closest to the emperor—I was looking forward to processing the "Big One" himself. However, Prince Konoye committed suicide the night before he was to report to Sugamo. That put an end to the rumor, and the "Big One" was a no-show.

Japan's ambassador to Italy, Toshio Shiratori, also spent time at Sugamo. He, along with Prince Konoye and others, had worked on the Axis treaty involving Japan, Germany, and Italy. Ambassador Shiratori understood English well, as did ambassador to Germany, Hiroshi Oshima, who turned out to be a rather ornery individual.

Upon arriving, Ambassador Oshima demanded that he be interviewed by a ranking officer. Okamura and I, the two interpreters, were the ranking noncoms. I made it perfectly clear to Ambassador Oshima that I did not care about rank and protocol. With a guard standing behind me, I told Oshima that he had to do as I said.

"Your country lost the war and you are a prisoner," I said. Eventually, we got along without further problems.

When Gen. Hideki Tojo came to the prison, he was greeted by a hoard of reporters and photographers. The general was still recovering from a botched suicide attempt a month earlier. The .32-caliber bullet had just missed his heart.

I met General Tojo at the gate and escorted him to the processing room. He was barely five feet tall. I noted his wound and was struck by the demeanor of this defeated man. He listened to my instructions. After he had been deloused, I took him to see the medic, Dr. Lloyd Edwards, a native of St. Paul, Minnesota, whose home was only about a mile from Fort Snelling.

The two men smiled and shook hands. They had met earlier. Dr. Edwards had been among the physicians who had worked to save Tojo's life following his suicide attempt. The doctor had his moment in the sun when *Life* magazine published a photo of him holding a stethoscope to the general's chest. In later years, I visited Doc many times at his Minnesota home, where we often reminisced about the picture and Sugamo Prison.

General Tojo's family was permitted to visit him in prison. Colonel Hardy requested that I sit in during their visits. They were to have no physical contact and were not allowed to exchange gifts. The door was to remain open and a guard was posted outside. Seating arrangements called for the general to sit at one end of the table while members of his family sat at the other end. I was seated in the middle. They could converse freely and had unlimited visits.

The general's wife and children were cordial and soft-spoken. They seemed surprised at my age. From time to time, a question or two was directed at me.

We always feared that the general would make another suicide attempt. One day I told General Tojo, "Don't try to commit suicide because Colonel Hardy will hold me responsible." On several occasions, he reassured me, "Don't worry, Sergeant. I won't commit suicide."

One day, unaware that others were within earshot, he repeated that statement. It amused everyone—even our Colonel Hardy. General Tojo said he was prepared to accept full responsibility for the war. He declared that the war-crimes trial was one of "victor over loser." I know that General Tojo realized fully that Japan had lost the war when he heard me speak Japanese. My Japanese was so bad he couldn't believe that I could be of Japanese ancestry.

The Filipino prisoners, many of whom were leaders and officials in their government, had been brought to Sugamo from the Philippines. They were never tried or punished, however, because with the stroke of a pen, General MacArthur sent them all back to lead their country again.

Overall, the prisoners at Sugamo were treated well. Unlike the Japanese-run POW camps, there were no beatings or physical torture. A liaison team from the Japanese government came to check on the prisoners. The government provided for them and even dispatched cooks. Still, we treated the prisoners like prisoners whose country had lost the war, They behaved accordingly and obeyed our orders. We were in Japan as conquerors, not liberators.

While at Sugamo, I read a number of affidavits written by American POWs regarding their treatment at the hands of their Japanese captors. In most of these camps, the interpreters were English-speaking Japanese American civilians who had been stranded in Japan, or stranded Japanese Americans who had been drafted into the army. How these people treated the American POWs would tell a revealing story about their true feelings for the United States.

Our replacements—six GIs fresh from the States who outranked Okamura and me—arrived in late December of 1945. The time had come for us to go home. I left Sugamo in January 1946. At the time, all of the major and minor war criminals were being held there. I was gone by the time they received their sentences.

In recent years I have read materials written about individuals at Sugamo. I don't know how these writers got their information because security at the prison was extremely tight—and tightened even more as the war-crimes trial got underway.

To my relief, my Japanese-language skills were never really tested. Someone—a *kibei* or a Russian civilian—was always there to help me. At times, I can hardly believe that at the young age of twenty, I was handing out orders to former generals, admirals, ambassadors, and prime ministers. Given my Hawaiian upbringing, I was never good at honorifics.

Ted T. Tsukiyama

442nd Regimental Combat Team/
Military Intelligence Service

AN AMERICAN—NOT A JAPANESE LIVING IN AMERICA

Most nisei grew up in a bicultural home environment that oftentimes found their American upbringing competing—and at times, even in conflict—with their Japanese culture. However, any such conflict was minimized in the case of my family, where the process of "Americanization" was much stronger.

My father, Seinosuke Tsukiyama, immigrated to Hawaii from Japan in 1911 to work as a merchant. He was originally from Tokyo, where he had graduated from Keio University. My mother, Yoshiko Kagawa, was raised in Kagawa *ken* and educated at the Ferris Seminary in Yokohama.

I was born in Honolulu, Hawaii, in 1920 and grew up in Kaimuki. There were five children in our family: three girls and two boys. We grew up in a bilingual home environment; both of my parents spoke and wrote English. All of us kids completed public school and went on to graduate from either a college or university. We also attended Japanese-language school for an hour every day, which even after ten years of attendance was equivalent to only *shogakko*, or elementary-school level of proficiency. Although living in America, most issei parents, including my own, insisted that their children be exposed to Japanese culture and language.

Despite such a bicultural environment and upbringing, I never had any question or problem regarding my identity. There was no doubt in my mind that I was an American of Japanese ancestry—not a Japanese living in America. I knew where my loyalty lay and never hesitated nor regretted volunteering—at least three times—to serve my country during World War II.

I was in my junior year at the University of Hawaii when World War II broke out. Growing up in Hawaii in the twenty years before World War II was hard for anyone of Japanese ancestry. The strength and solidarity demonstrated by Japanese sugar workers in the 1909 and 1920 sugar strikes had generated great fear of and animosity against the Japanese by those who controlled Hawaii's economy and government. The Japanese, who comprised 40 percent of Hawaii's population at the time, were considered a political, military, and economic threat to Hawaii. The U.S. military in Hawaii even suspected and doubted the loyalty of American-born nisei, resulting in many investigations and intense surveillance of the Japanese in Hawaii between 1920 and 1941, just as relations between Japan and the United States were deteriorating.

The military's suspicion, fear, and prejudice against the Japanese was only made worse by Japan's military invasion of China and Manchuria beginning in 1931 and the brutality and atrocities committed by Japanese soldiers against the Chinese and Manchukuoans. As political tensions between Japan and the United States heightened between 1939 and 1941, the nisei became acutely aware that everyone of Japanese ancestry was "on the spot" and "under the gun" as a highly distrusted racial minority. With Japan as the potential enemy in mind, some Americans asked Japanese Americans, "Who you goin' shoot, them or us?"

I think all nisei felt it extremely imperative that we convincingly demonstrate our loyalty to America in the event of war with Japan. That moment arrived December 7, 1941, when Japan attacked Pearl Harbor.

I spent all of World War II, beginning with the Pearl Harbor attack, with five different paramilitary and military units. In all, I volunteered to serve three times.

As a member of the University of Hawaii ROTC unit, I reported for duty during the Pearl Harbor attack. The ROTC was converted into the Hawaii Territorial Guard, which guarded important buildings and installations in Honolulu until January 19, 1942, when all nisei soldiers were discharged because of our race. On February 25, 1942, 170 of the discharged nisei volunteered for a civilian labor battalion, which became known as the Varsity Victory Volunteers (VVV).

We served in the VVV until January 1943. A month later, I volunteered for the 442nd Regimental Combat Team and trained with the 522nd Field Artillery Battalion at Camp Shelby, Mississippi. Six months later, in August 1943, I was transferred to Military Intelligence School at Camp Savage, Minnesota, where I was trained in signal intelligence. From March 1944 until the end of the war, I worked with the 10th Army Air Force, stationed in India and Burma, doing radio-intercept work and translating intercepted communications from the Japanese army air force in Burma.

America's war with Japan in World War II has been described as a ferocious clash of cultures. The bushido code that dictated the Japanese soldier's view of surrender or capture by the enemy as the ultimate disgrace drove Japanese soldiers to treat surrendering enemy prisoners with bestial inhumanity. They also fought tenaciously until death rather than surrender. This happened at Tarawa, Saipan, Iwo Jima, and Okinawa, where there were mass suicides—an incomprehensible act to the traditional Western mind.

And yet to the nisei, who had grown up with the heroic tale of "Bakudan San Yushi" (which probably accounted for the three banzai charges by the 100th/442nd during World War II), and exposed to the concept of *Yamato damashii*, the fanatical psyche and mindset of the Japanese soldier was no mystery. We nisei understood the nationalistic and militaristic propaganda of military-controlled Japan during its invasion and conquest of Nanking and Manchuria in the 1930s.

When I heard that it was Japan that had attacked us at Pearl Harbor, I vowed I would punch, kick, and beat up the first Japanese soldier I encountered for all the pain, sorrow, and suffering Japan was inflicting on innocent and blameless Japanese in America, like my parents, just because they were of the same race. I nursed and harbored that hatred for the Japanese soldier throughout my war experiences.

Finally, four years later in Burma, I had a chance to visit a Japanese prisoner-of-war stockade, where I vowed to take revenge for all of the suffering they had caused. As we entered the stockade, all of the Japanese POWs jumped up and bowed low to us. Instead of the "proud and superb fighting-machine Japanese soldier" we had been taught to fear and hate, I saw only young, bewildered, *inaka* (rural), underaged youth who looked more like beaten dogs, terrified of being tortured or shot by Americans, as they had been taught. They had probably been drafted to fill the depleted ranks of a desperate Japan army, fighting a war in which they did not believe.

When I saw these miserable creatures, all of the pent-up anger and hatred I had felt for the Japanese soldier melted away. I suddenly realized that they personally bore no fault or responsibility for their country's war, and that they were themselves unwilling participants and victims and captives of Japan's militaristic ambitions and fervor. There were millions of ordinary people in Japan who were similarly victimized by their own misguided military leadership and who endured great pain and suffering during that experience. I learned that there are no true winners in war.

Today I bear no hatred or ill will for the Japanese people. Actually, I feel sorry for all the *kuroo* (hardship) and suffering they endured during World War II. But I detest Japan's military leaders—men like Sadao Araki, Korechika Anami, Hideki Tojo, and others—who spread the destruction and suffering of war to many nations and their people prior to and during World War II. I can never forget nor forgive them.

After Japan's attack on Pearl Harbor, almost all nisei, if given a choice in the matter, would have preferred to fight the Japanese rather than German Nazis. That would have more dramatically and conclusively answered the question, "Who you goin' shoot?"

Over six thousand MIS nisei linguists willingly did so, without question or reservation. They compiled an impressive record and contributed significantly to Japan's early defeat. But they were forced to operate under a veil of secrecy for security reasons throughout their war service. Only in the last ten to fifteen years has their story been told.

And so it is primarily the magnificent fighting record of the 100th/442nd—the most decorated unit for its size and length of combat in World War II—that we have had to rely on to conclusively establish and prove the Americanism of the nisei.

Many years later that realization struck me like a bolt of lightning as I rode a bus through northeastern France, headed for Switzerland. When the bus driver pointed out the Vosges Mountains to our right, my heart leaped when I saw those forested mountains a scant mile away. The names of Bruyeres, Belmont, La Houssiere, and Biffontaine came to mind—military shrines standing in muted silence of the sacrifices endured by the 100th/442nd on a frigid October in 1944, when the regiment was decimated to less than half its normal size in less than three weeks of fighting. We passed just above Epinal, an American military cemetery where many of the white crosses bear Japanese surnames. The white crosses at Epinal were among the nearly eight hundred that once filled European cemeteries bearing the names of 100th/442nd comrades before they were returned to their families in Hawaii.

As I recalled the names and faces of some of those comrades who never returned, the words from John McCrae's poem, "In Flanders Fields," came back to me, like a voice speaking from the graves, conveying a universal message from the fallen soldier. It had deep meaning in World War I when it was composed—and still does today.

In Flanders Fields the poppies blow
Between the crosses, row on row,
That mark our place; and in the sky
The larks, still bravely singing, fly
Scarce heard amid the guns below.

We are the Dead. Short days ago
We lived, felt dawn, saw sunset glow,
Loved and were loved, and now we lie
In Flanders Fields.

Take up our quarrel with the foe:
To you, from failing hand we throw
The torch; be yours to hold it high.
If ye break faith with us who die
We shall not sleep, though poppies grow
In Flanders Fields.

The blood our men shed in the ultimate dedication to country was red—just as red as the blood of any other fallen American hero. And I know that because of those eight hundred white crosses with Japanese names, people no longer ask, "Who you goin' shoot?"

Because of them, we all can hold our heads up . . . as Americans!

George Akita

Military Intelligence Service

SHARED ETHNICITY

Former Governor George R. Ariyoshi and I, even at age seventy at the time of this writing, are still the youngest contributors to this volume. We were drafted the same day in June 1945, took basic and language training, and shipped off together to Japan in August 1946. The only time we fired a rifle was at the rifle range in Texas. Still, we had been drafted when the Pacific War was still on and were being trained to take part in the invasion of Japan.

I speak only for myself, but I had mixed feelings about my role in the Pacific War. I suspect that the nisei who fought in Europe were not weighed down by the sense of ambiguity I felt. I say this because I shared their sense of certitude when it came to the European theater, as my oratorical contest speech makes clear. Moreover, the unease that I experienced did not come from a sense of divided loyalty between the country of my birth and that of my parents. Indeed, I had volunteered for the U.S. Army language school when I was a senior in high school with my father's written permission, which was required for those under eighteen years of age. I remember clearly going to the adult section of the Nuuanu YMCA to take a preliminary Japanese-language test, which I proceeded to fail miserably.

The ambiguity I felt stemmed in part, I believe, from the internalization of Japanese values taught to us by our parents and by Japanese-language school staff. We were told incessantly that these were "good" and "positive" values that would guide us throughout our lives. Japan, of course, was the source of these values. But in truth, the men who fought in Europe had taken these values with them.

Gene Castagnetti, director of the National Cemetery of the Pacific, on the occasion of the fiftieth annual memorial service for the 100th Battalion, spoke of the battalion's achievements that came from "hard work and character," "cohesion," and "discipline," and then pointed to "unit cohesiveness," that undergird of the unit's combat success. He rightly observed that they "would not allow themselves to bring shame upon their families." Hard work, character, cohesion, discipline, and avoidance of shame are precisely those values impressed upon us as we were growing up.

My mixed feelings came also from the undeniable and inescapable fact of shared ethnicity with the Japanese who were our enemies. I suspect that apart from the sense of humaneness that they possessed in abundance, the motive impelling interpreters such as Hideto Kono (on Iwo Jima) and Takejiro Higa (on Okinawa) to go that extra mile to persuade Japanese civilians and soldiers to emerge from their caves was this sense of shared ethnicity. They both recall—and a moral judgment is not in any way implied here—that their Caucasian comrades-in-arms were inclined to more quickly seal the caves—this to save American lives—than they had been.

This sense of shared ethnicity came to me in two stark and unforgettable moments in Japan. The first occurred on the train taking us newly arrived from Yokohama to Camp Zama, then the Fourth Replacement Depot. As the train wound slowly through the countryside, children appeared alongside the train, imploring: "GI, GI, *chokoletto* (chocolate), chewing *gamu* (gum), *kyande* (candy), *cigaretto* (cigarette)."

I can still recall vividly the thought that had flashed through my mind: "It easily could have been me begging for the goodies. What roll of the dice made my parents emigrate from Japan to Hawaii, thus sparing me the fate that had visited these children?"

The second instance occurred on a chilly, late fall evening in 1946. My mother's relatives took me to pay respects at the grave of her parents. I only felt a vague sense of connectedness with them, but the thought that matters would have been so different had not my parents emigrated to Hawaii remains strongly in my memory. The poignancy of that moment was heightened by my recollection of the words of my father that he was the last of the line since his family had been at the epicenter of the bomb that fell on Hiroshima.

We are but one generation removed from the Japanese in Japan, so I can understand and have come to grips with my ambiguous feelings in the same way that I can understand the feelings of Irish American Catholics who are five or six generations removed, but who still reach out unashamedly and unapologetically to those in Northern Ireland.

Joe H. Shimamura
442nd Regimental Combat Team

SANJI AND ME

I was recovering from my shoulder injury at Halloran General Hospital in Staten Island, New York. One day the hospital ship came in. Most of the boats came into Halloran, and from there the injured men were sent out to different hospitals.

On this particular day, I had gone to lunch and was headed back to my ward when I saw a guy with a 442nd patch. I went up to him and asked, "Excuse me, did you just come in?" "Yeah, we just came in today," he said.

I introduced myself and then asked, "By the way, what company were you in?" He looked at me, hesitated, and said, "I was in K Company." That hit me because I was in K Company. The guy was a Hawaii boy, but I didn't know him. By my expression he could tell that I was wondering about him, so he explained that he was a replacement.

I was curious so I continued to ask him questions. "By the way, as far as you know, did any of the 'original' guys come back with you?" He said one guy from K Company came back—a guy named Sanji Kimoto. "Oh, Sanji came back with you? Do you mind if I wait with you, because I want to go see Sanji."

Sanji was a Big Island boy. He and I were in the same platoon but in different squads.

I didn't know what kind of condition he was in when I followed the replacement into the ward. The guy never told me that Sanji was blind. When I walked in, I saw Sanji sitting on the bed; his eyes and everything looked normal. He was facing in my direction, just like he was looking at me.

I called out, "Eh, Kimo!"—we called him Kimo. "Who dat?" he called out. He was looking at me and asking, "Who dat?" I said, "God damn, whatsa matter with you, only sit down! You don't even recognize me!"

That's when I realized that the guy had forgotten to tell me that Sanji could not see. He poked me to point out that Sanji was blind. I wanted to tell him, "Why you tell me now, you knucklehead?!"

I sat down with Sanji. Our conversation turned serious. "Eh, what's the matter?" I asked. He said things started getting fuzzy just before he was supposed to come home.

Sanji had gotten shot in the back early in combat—that was June or July 1944, sometime around there, in Italy—but he had seemed okay. The winter had come and he had gotten through it okay. But while waiting to come home, he noticed his eyesight fading. The bullet must have hit his optic nerve.

We continued to talk. He said they were going to send him to Valley Forge Hospital in Pennsylvania to give him his final check, to see if anything could be done. "Okay, Sanji, you keep in contact. I'll give you my address; you write me so I know where you stay."

Sanji went on to Valley Forge. I got a letter from him. He said nothing could be done, so they were going to send him to a school for the blind in Connecticut. I wrote right back and asked him to give me the address to the school for the blind that he was going to. I didn't tell him why. I figured he would be lonely, so I planned to go see him.

Sanji and I were in different squads, but we got to be close after he came into the hospital, because he didn't know anybody. Anyway, they sent him to a school for the blind in Connecticut.

One weekend I decided to go visit him, so I caught the train and went. When I arrived, the sergeant told me Sanji would be coming out from a particular door, so I was to watch for him. I waited and he came out of the door. The buggah started walking, no cane or anything. He walked to the flagpole, made a left turn, and came straight to me. "Joe!" "Eh, Sanji! Howzit?" "Eh, thanks for coming up," he said. "Eh, brah, I going spend the weekend here with you, you know." "No problem there," he said. "Let's go up to my room."

Once we got settled, he said, "Okay, let's go drink beer." I just followed him, straight to the PX. We had a good time, drinking and talking story. That night I slept there. He was so happy.

Walter "Biffa" Moriguchi
100th Infantry Battalion

LUCKY WE CAME BACK

February 8, 1944. I got wounded that morning, just below my right knee on the shinbone. We were someplace just before Cassino, on a mountain that was terraced. We couldn't go anyplace; the Germans had us pinned down. After that, I spent three-and-a-half years in six hospitals until I finally told the doctors to cut my leg off.

After I got shot—I think the bullet came from a machine pistol—a medic gave me first aid to stop the bleeding. Then Doc Kometani came to tell me that they couldn't get me out yet because "It's not a serious wound." There was another guy with a head wound that they considered serious, and me, nothing, so I had to wait for the litter bearers, who could come only when it was dark. I waited thirty-six hours. I felt completely helpless.

They took me to a field hospital. The medic there said, "You got a million-dollar wound—you're going home." But first I had to go to the hospitals: Casserta, then a hospital in Africa, then I returned to the States on D day, June 6, 1944. I went to Charleston, South Carolina, then to

Rhoads General Hospital in Utica, New York. They had a special orthopedic department for the war-wounded. I was there for two years. Then the hospital closed, so I was transferred to Fort Dix, New Jersey, in 1946.

All during this time I was using crutches. The wound never really healed. They tried to cover it up with skin grafts, by taking skin from the thigh of my good leg. Two to three weeks after the operation, I would wake up with a high fever. They would cut at the edge of the graft, discharge the pus, then wait again. I don't remember how many times they tried to graft the skin.

When I was in New York, I had a good time. As long as I wasn't scheduled for surgery, I got a pass every weekend and I went to the city. I would meet friends—everybody came out on the weekend—went to see shows, the USO, Yankee games. That was good: Our uniform was our ticket.

Then I was transferred to Walter Reed Army Hospital in Washington, D.C. When they told me that I might have to be in the hospital for two to three more years, I told them to "cut the damn thing off." They cut just above the knee. Then I went to rehab.

In July 1947 I got a medical discharge. They gave me my artificial leg—in those days they were made of leather—but the upper muscles of my leg were atrophied after not using them for so long, so I just used crutches.

I got a chance to come home in November 1944. They couldn't do anything more with my leg, so they gave me a medical pass. I bummed rides all the way from New York to Hawaii. I got home the day before Thanksgiving and returned to the hospital at the end of December. When I came home after the amputation, my parents saw me in crutches. They accepted the situation.

Yeah, I could walk and do whatever I wanted to do, so I was okay. I didn't realize that as I got older, it would be harder to move around, but that happens even if you have two legs.

Boy, there sure have been a lot of changes—nowadays, the wheelchairs are light, you can even fold them up. When I was in the hospital, they were big chairs with high backs, wooden and woven. Now we have special reserved parking, and even the toilets have those grab-bars, which makes it easier for us.

When I first came back, I didn't think of myself as handicapped. In fact, I used to tell those other guys in the hospital, "What the hell are you crying for? Lucky you never come back in a box!" No kidding, we real lucky we came back!

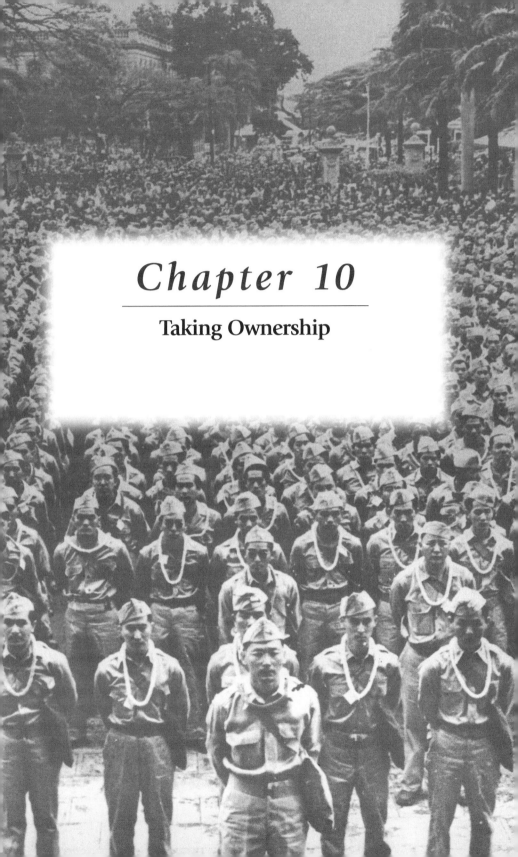

Chapter 10

Taking Ownership

Joseph R. Itagaki

442nd Regimental Combat Team

THE DREAM FOR TOMORROW

The following is an exchange of wartime letters between Staff Sgt. Joseph Itagaki, who served with Service Company of the 442nd Regimental Combat Team, and Charles R. Hemenway, then president of Hawaiian Trust Co.

Hemenway served on the University of Hawaii Board of Regents from 1910 to 1940. As a regent, he befriended many Japanese American students. Although Hemenway was not in a position to make decisions, he used his influence as a respected business and civic leader to persuade the FBI and later the World War II military government to oppose mass internment of Hawaii's Japanese Americans following Japan's attack on Pearl Harbor.

Hemenway never failed to voice his trust and faith in Japanese Americans, particularly the nisei soldiers from Hawaii.

Although a busy executive, he took a personal interest in the Hawaii boys—even writing to them on the battlefields of Europe, encouraging them and praising them for their courage and loyalty.

One of the soldiers with whom he corresponded was Staff Sergeant Itagaki, who many knew as "Kemoo," manager of the Kemoo Farms restaurant in Wahiawa. At age thirty-six, Itagaki was the oldest AJA to volunteer for the 442nd—and the first to step forward from his home district of Wahiawa. He was also the first Oahu AJA to take the oath of induction. The content of Itagaki's letters to Hemenway reflect his maturity.

From the 442nd's days in training at Camp Shelby, Itagaki served as mess sergeant for Service Company, utilizing his experience as a restaurant manager. His service won him a Bronze Star for meritorius achievement in the support of combat operations.

October 5, 1944

My dear Itagaki:

I appreciated very much receiving from Delegate Joseph R. Farrington a copy of the letter which he received from you. It is one of the best letters which I have seen from any of the men in service and I cannot compliment you too highly, not only for its substance but for its form. It contains, to me, the very good news that at least the strong feelings which existed between the local men and those from the mainland have been practically wiped out. I have felt that this would be sure to occur with a growing understanding of each other and so it is particularly gratifying to know that it actually has happened.

The men from the mainland, just like the men from here, of course, were largely influenced by the environments in which they grew up and lived, and we all ought to have the deepest possible sympathy for these men, particularly those from the West Coast, who were so outrageously treated for no cause whatsoever except for the accident of race. While we are very far from perfect here, yet at least for many years we have lived in a friendly, understanding, and tolerant community. All of us, therefore, ought to stand ready, as you say you are, to give every possible help that we can to these young men from the mainland, many of whom have this difficult task of adjustment after the fighting in Europe is over.

I agree with Mr. Farrington that there is a growing understanding and a better understanding on the part of a great many people on the mainland. I think the prejudice is disappearing slowly, but nevertheless steadily, in most parts of the country. It is, however, still strong on the Pacific Coast and particularly in California, and that is where a great many of the men now in uniform came from. That is the state which they have a right to call home and to which, no doubt, many of them will want to return.

I agree with you that it is our business as well as theirs to carry on this fight against racial intolerance and to support them in every way within our power. I feel that the pattern of living in Hawaii is one which the entire country may well adopt, not that it is by any means perfect but because it is better insofar as racial prejudice is concerned than the pattern of life in most other parts of the country.

I am sharing your letter with the members of the Emergency Service Committee and I feel sure that they will be in agreement with you.

It looks now as if you may spend another winter away from home, which is a matter of deep regret to many of us who had hoped that our boys could come home in the relatively near future. I certainly hope that you are not kept on garrison duty after the fighting is over. That duty could be better performed by many units which have not had the strain of your unusual combat experience.

My aloha goes to all in the 442nd, together with my hope that the end will come before too long.

Very sincerely,
C. R. Hemenway

October 25, 1944
Somewhere in France

My dear Mr. Hemenway:

Your gracious and kind letter of October fifth just reached me. To say that I am grateful for the many nice compliments you pay me for my letter to Delegate Farrington would only be to emphasize the obvious.

Particularly pleasing to me is your comment that you too believe that the problem of the mainland Japanese Americans directly concerns us in Hawaii and that all of us ought to stand ready to give them every possible aid both now and after the war. Delegate Farrington is correct when he states that the general feeling toward those of Japanese ancestry has improved tremendously, especially since the exploits of the 442nd Combat Team have received such widespread and favorable attention. On the other hand, as you point out, feeling is still strong on the West Coast, specifically in the state of California.

The problem, then, it seems to me, is to win over the Californians. And that, from their long history of race bigotry and prejudice, will be a difficult nut to crack. I am in perfect agreement with you that the pattern of living in Hawaii, though not perfect, is far better than that of any other part of the United States and right well be adopted by the rest of the country without fear.

What we have in Hawaii, I believe, is not race tolerance, but racial goodwill. For tolerance in the common understanding of the word suggests a superior magnanimously consenting to permit an inferior to exist. In the Islands, we enjoy a sort of friendly semifamily relationship in which every race and racial extraction understands and appreciates the others, or at least attempts to do so. We also recognize the family obligation that every member must be given his chance to success, that is to say that the welfare of all is dependent upon the status of the poorest. That, to me, is the secret of Hawaii's success with the complex problems of race; our very approach suggests application of the Golden Rule and not one of toleration for expediency's sake alone.

That such goodwill has continued to exist in the Islands through all the changing circumstances of war is indeed a tribute to our leaders and our people. The enlightened guidance of such men as you and Delegate Farrington, though often unappreciated, has contributed much to the spirit of the comity which exists back "home."

This may be an appropriate time for our "happy" way of life to be introduced to the mainland. With so many servicemen from the States enjoying the hospitality of our shores, perhaps it is not too much to expect them to return to their homes, if they can bear to leave Alohaland, and preach the gospel of live and let live.

But I am afraid that this is not enough. What our fellow Japanese Americans need is quick and tangible action as to their postwar world. Will they, for example, be permitted to return to their homes in California? And if they were "evacuated" for military reasons, should they not receive some sort of compensation for their losses sustained through cooperation with the government? Buildings and land taken over by the government for military reasons have netted handsome profits to most of those who were so "fortunate."

Whether you agree with any of the above or not is immaterial; what is material is whether men of your influence in Hawaii are willing to use your good offices with those in high places of responsibility to see that Americans of Japanese ancestry are given an equal opportunity with other Americans in making their own destiny, whether that be in Los Angeles or Chicago. From what I know now of the mainland Japanese American, and from the way they fight in battle, I can say that they are not seeking special privileges or favors. All they ask for is the same chance as that given any other American. From there on out, it is their own fight, though it remains our responsibility to see to it that those who desire to do them harm through underhanded or un-American means will be thwarted.

I believe that we in Hawaii, of all ancestries, owe at least that much to our fighting comrades and their families behind barbed wires, to do our little bit to see to it that they are given the same chance as we ourselves would want to make our own way in the postwar world.

Though some small personal differences may remain between a few of our island volunteers and a few of those from the mainland, by and large our relations are now most cordial and respectful. This afternoon I saw a striking example of how far we have gone in this regard. An island boy who used to hate his first sergeant, a mainlander, with a vengeance while in Camp Shelby now idolizes him as the "best damn sergeant in the whole army," while his first sergeant affectionately calls this Hawaiian lad "the most underrated man in the combat team." And that, in greater or lesser degree, typifies the new spirit of our unit.

This same duo told of a platoon sergeant, a mainland boy, who was probably the most hated *kotonk* in Camp Shelby but who was the best-loved and most respected man in his company in Italy and France. As he risked his life to save an injured lad from Kona, he was wounded. Two boys from Hawaii volunteered to bring him back to safety for treatment. Discarding their rifles, they went out with a litter and a white flag to rescue their beloved platoon sergeant. While returning with him on the litter, all three were shot and killed by a German sniper. The men in his platoon, Hawaiian and mainland, were so incensed at this action that they charged up a hill where a company of Germans were entrenched and killed fifty, wounded some ten who were taken to Allied aid stations for treatment, and captured twenty, including a captain and his whole command post.

The men from the Islands and the men from the States are now a real team, a team which will do more than its share to help the United States win the war.

Last night, after our first tour of duty in France, we were relieved. Though the terrain and weather were more formidable than anything we experienced in Italy, in the space of less than a week our boys had stormed and taken several hills which other regiments had unsuccessfully tried to take several times previously. We also liberated a great communications center which controls the main highways into Germany proper and a ridgeline which dominates the entire valley. I wish that censorship would permit me to name our locality and this particular action, but since I cannot, suffice it to say that our boys are again the talk of their sector and the toast of the division.

It is rainy and cold here, and our boys are suffering tremendously. They are always soaking wet, for they must not only fight through this autumn rainy season but also sleep at nights in slit trenches half-filled with cold water. But they are the same fine group of fellows who volunteered over a year ago from Hawaii; they still can laugh and joke and kid each other. So you can tell the folks back there that the morale is high and their courage an inspiration to all about them. They are a real credit to all Hawaii, and to all America.

The eerie whistle of German artillery landing close by, and the carefully concealed candlelight with which I can see well enough to type this out for you on this captured fascist typewriter, make me miss Hawaii and all it means to me more than usual. So, it is with these thoughts of home and you good people back there who are doing your bit to make our lot a little happier and a little easier that I conclude this letter; again thanking you for writing me and wishing you and yours the season's greetings. Aloha.

Gratefully yours,
Joe Itagaki

April 25, 1945
My dear Itagaki:

Your letter enclosing copy of the *Stars and Stripes* came through in exactly two weeks, which is a very surprisingly short time, and I appreciate very much your thoughtfulness in sending me the copy of the paper and also enjoyed getting your good letter. The paper is starting on its way around a good many who are just as interested as I am in our boys in Italy. The picture on the front page is not only interesting but is really quite amusing. It almost looks as though the smallest man in the regiment had been chosen as one of the guards for the prisoners who are being taken into the stockade.

Delegate Farrington not only wrote me a long letter giving an account of his visit to the 442nd but also talked with me concerning it while he was here. Of course, he also talked to many others. He seems to be particularly impressed with the unanimity of opinion among all of the commanding officers with whom he came in contact, from General Clark down, that the boys from Hawaii have made a remarkable and an outstanding record. Of course, this is not surprising to me nor to many others here, but it cannot help but be surprising to a good many mainlanders and unfortunately, there are some here who ought to know better.

I had hoped that you would not be called on for any more frontline spearhead service, but this perhaps was a selfish way of looking at it and to be chosen to break the stalemate shows a confidence of those in command as well as the unusual qualities of this unit. I hope that you won't have to be called on to walk over the Alps. According to the morning dispatches, the enemy in Italy is already demoralized and quite rapid advances appear to have been made. I hope that the cost to you is not too great. We had noted the fact that you had lost your artillery unit because it has been mentioned in some dispatches in connection with the advance of the 7th Army. Possibly you will meet again on top of the Alps.

I certainly will be very glad to do all that I can to see that your son is admitted to the university this coming fall and I feel reasonably sure that he will be, assuming, of course, that he passes the entrance requirements, which I have no doubt that he will do. I hope that he will not be called into service too soon and that the need for calling additional men will be over before they get around to him.

Our best regards and aloha go with this letter to you and to all the others in your unit.

Very sincerely,
C. R. Hemenway

P.S. I wish I could meet with one of your "sizzling" steaks again!

June 3, 1945
Ghedi Airport, Italy

Dear Mr. Hemenway:

Thank you so much for your welcome letter of recent date. It is good to know that my son is doing so splendidly in school, but it is even better to know that you were kind enough to look into the matter for me. I shall be ever grateful.

Now that the war in Europe is won, all of us are thinking of home. We have done our part, and we are most anxious to return to our friends and loved ones, to take up again the threads of life in the Hawaii we love. No one, unless he has gone through what we have, can begin to appreciate our longing for the dear things of life. And now that we have come through the hell and the fire, we are even more anxious to return and see if the things we fought for are still the same—the friendly life, the happy associations, the unbounded opportunities, the charm of home.

Perhaps it is my age, but the memories of Hawaii and my life there are more vivid today than ever before. And there is no gain saying that I have missed my wife and son, not to mention all of you who are so much a part of my life in Alohaland.

Nowadays, our favorite pastime is counting points, to see whether we have the minimum of eighty-five to be considered for redeployment. Most of the original members of the 100th Battalion have totals running into the hundred plus. And we from Hawaii in the original 442nd have been fortunate enough to have our training period in Camp Shelby, Mississippi, classified as overseas time. Naturally, many of us are on the borderline, that is to say that our aggregate points total less than the necessary eighty-five. I, for example, have some eighty-three points. Since my captain has recommended me for an award, I am hopeful that I shall have the minimum number soon.

Most of us, both from Hawaii and the mainland, had high hopes that our unit would be returned to the States as a unit and that we could be demobilized as one group. But this seems out of the question now, for daily a selected few are leaving for the United States and soon a large group of replacements are due here. We have fought through so much together that we have an esprit de corps second to none. How wonderful it could be if only we could be together to our last days as a unit, instead of straggling off one by one like strangers hurrying home.

Our present mission as a regiment is to process German prisoners. Thus far, almost a hundred thousand have passed through this station. As you can gather, we are bivouacked in pup tents out on the hot and dusty flats of an airport, halfway between Milan and Verona.

Our life is not hard, but it is discouraging—for the heat and the dust, not to mention the spit and polish now demanded of us—is difficult to be happy about. While we were in combat, we didn't mind these things, but now we are thinking so much of home that we tend to be irritable and quarrelsome.

But the important thing is that the war is won over here. And we have contributed our small share to that victory, can be proud of that victory, [and] can be proud of our part. And we who have been fortunate enough to have gone through the battles without injury, let alone without being killed, should be doubly grateful. Though we are humble in the thought that our buddies are no longer with us, we are happy that we have survived.

In the not too distant future, I am hoping that I shall be walking down the gangplank in Honolulu, that I shall be removing my ODs and GIs for the last time, that I shall be a "civilian" again in the kind of world we and millions of others have fought for, and are still fighting for in the Pacific.

Till that happy day,

Aloha,
Joe Itagaki

Governor George R. Ariyoshi

Military Intelligence Service

JOURNEY TO WASHINGTON PLACE

*The following submission by former Governor George R. Ariyoshi
is excerpted from his autobiography,* With an Obligation to All.

A Democratic Revolution

In today's social and political climate, people often seem to feel their lives
are out of control. People talk about trying desperately to gain power,
about empowerment, and "organizing." You also hear it said, "Why both-
er? My vote doesn't count." There is an intense frustration with the democratic process. You hear it said of people in office, "They're all a bunch of
crooks." This is frightening, because it suggests people are retreating from
the best form of government ever devised.

I had a very different experience, because I was fortunate to become
part of the Democratic Party campaign of 1954, an event which has been
elevated to a mythical level in Hawaii's history. I had been back from law
school only a short time, and I was troubled by what I was seeing from my

vantage point as a young attorney. I had grown up with my pleasant idea of Hawaii, and I had gone off to the army and college without experiencing any negative incidents. But when I returned to Hawaii as an attorney I realized there was a subtle but seemingly immovable barrier above me—above "us." We could expect to go only so far. Your success did not depend on what you knew, or how capable you were, but on who you knew. I was dismayed, because this was not what I had been led to expect of Hawaii.

The controlling group often has been described as a white oligarchy, but such a description is too simplistic. It was a plantation-based society that did not exist for the benefit of the common man, but for the benefit of the owners. It excluded the great majority of people of talent and dedication from its rewards, merely because of the circumstances of birth and economics. This great majority included virtually all non-white people. Caucasians who were outside the controlling group—who were not well-connected—were often kept from advancing as well.

In the making of modern Hawaii, the year 1954 is always described as a great turning point, but that description is the result of hindsight and the writing of history. As the election season approached, there was—to my knowledge—no great sense of change in the making. In people's memory, Hawaii had always been run by the Republican Party.

The Republican Party was the party of those who had overthrown the Hawaiian Kingdom and then participated in annexing Hawaii to the United States. The Republican Party usually elected Hawaii's non-voting delegate to Congress, and it controlled the Territorial Legislature. The Republican Party stage-managed who would be appointed governor of Hawaii under Republican presidents of the United States. Under Democratic presidents, the same privileged circles seemed to have considerable influence as well, if less directly. Even the appointed Democratic governors were on the conservative side. They did little or nothing to nurture the growth of a grassroots Democratic Party.

There were some courageous Democrats of that time who fought lonely battles. We owe a debt to them, but they consistently squabbled among themselves and fell short, and Hawaii went on year after year as a U.S. territory, denied statehood and dominated by this web of political and economic interests.

I got involved in my first political meeting through a personal friend from boyhood, Tom Ebesu. Tom invited me to go with him to the Nuuanu YMCA, which was a fitting place to get together, because some of us had grown up attending programs at that "Y." I remember clearly that the meeting was held only three days before the close of filings for the primary election of 1954. This was remarkable because it shows how spontaneous our actions really were.

Tom Ebesu said he wanted me to meet Jack Burns, the former policeman who had become chairman of the Democratic Party. Burns was to become a towering figure in the history of Hawaii, and my life was to become slowly enmeshed with his, but at the time I was merely a young person just out of school. I was twenty-eight years old. Burns had worked most of his adult life as a policeman, and in 1954 he was forty-five.

In the meeting, Burns asked me a lot of questions about what I saw going on in Hawaii. I told him I did not like the way opportunity was controlled by the select few. I said not everyone was being treated fairly. I said it wasn't how good you were at doing something, but who you knew. I said this problem wasn't limited to the Orientals or any particular racial group. It applied to the Caucasian person as well, because the Big Five controlled Hawaii, and you could only advance if you were "in" with them.

At a certain point in the meeting, Jack Burns looked my way and said, "You should run for office."

I thought he was talking to someone else. I turned around to see if there was someone behind me, but no one was there. He fixed me with a look and said, "You should run for office."

My response was, "I'm too young. Nobody knows who I am."

He said, "It's not the age. It's the heart. It's how you feel."

He was insistent. "Run for office this year, and there'll be some other people running with you." He was clear about not waiting.

I went home. The next day, Tom Ebesu came back with nomination papers, and all the required number of signatures were on it. He said, "Let's go file." I was shocked. I told him, "Tom, I'm not prepared for this."

Tom suggested we talk. We went to Ala Moana Park and bought a plate lunch, and we sat looking out at the ocean. We sat for about three hours and talked about our childhood and growing up, and about how nice it would be if we could have the kind of Hawaii as adults that we experienced when we were youngsters. We talked about things that needed to be done to create a better future.

When we finished, Tom said again, "Let's go file the papers."

By now this was the next to the last day to file, but I asked Tom for one more day. In my conversations with my parents, they encouraged me to run. If I wanted to do it, they thought there was a place for me. My parents told me not to be concerned about being too young, or lacking experience. They said, "It is not age, but it is how a person is, and what a person does." The next day Tom came back again, and I agreed. We filed the papers at nearly the last possible moment. . . .

On election night, I was one of twenty-two Democrats who took over the thirty-member Territorial House. We even defeated Hiram Fong, the incumbent House Speaker, in what would be the only electoral loss of his lifetime. We gained control of the Senate as well, by a margin of nine to six. When I looked around, I saw people who were to become nationally and internationally known. Others were to serve admirably and well with only modest recognition, but they were mainstays in the process of changing Hawaii.

Many of these new legislators were veterans. World War II—war in general—is an awful tragedy, but it had helped catalyze this great change. If something good can grow from tragedy, it happened here in Hawaii. For the first time, the majority of people had a true voice in their government, and a new direction was set for Hawaii.

I was the youngest among those who won office. But this wasn't an issue. I was grounded in a sense of what I wanted to happen in our community, and there were a lot of people who wanted to go in more or less the same direction I did. . . .

With Jack Burns

In 1969, between Christmas and New Year's, several people called on me to discuss running for lieutenant governor. One was Bert Kobayashi, who by then had been Burns' attorney general for two terms of office. The second was Eddie DeMello of the ILWU. The third was a man named Nelson Prather, a lobbyist for the sugar industry.

I was surprised. I had never thought about such a thing. My first response was, "How does Governor Burns feel about this idea?"

They told me, "You'll get a call from him."

They had no sooner left my office than the telephone rang, and the governor asked if I would join him early the next morning at Washington Place. Over breakfast he reiterated what Bert Kobayashi had said, that he wanted me to run for lieutenant governor. I told him that running for higher office was not something I had given much thought to. I said I already had put in many years in the Senate. I was thinking about one more term, which would give me twenty years in the Legislature. By then I would have done my part, and I would become a private citizen.

The governor said he wasn't thinking so much about who would run with him in 1970, but who would succeed him in 1974. He kept on talking about 1974. I kept telling him, "Governor, I'm having a hard time thinking about 1970. Please don't ask me about 1974."

He said, "Okay, as long as you don't say no for now."

Fifteen years had gone by since Governor Burns had recruited me to run for the Legislature. He had not only taken an interest in me but in my father. I had been inspired by the way he handled the Statehood Bill in Congress. As Ways and Means chairman I had taken some criticism to pass a budget that stayed within what the State could afford. I had taken a lot of criticism over the Maryland Bill, saving him the problem of vetoing it.

However, I was by no means a part of Burns' inner circle. My closest link to him was Bert Kobayashi. Bert and I had tried to mediate the conflict between Burns and Gill in 1956, and after Burns won the governorship, the first person he brought into his cabinet was Bert Kobayashi, even though Bert was not a member of his political circle.

I think my connection with Bert played a role in the governor's assessment of me, because Bert was a fair-minded person who focused on getting things done. Bert's job as attorney general was crucial because the Democratic agenda was to break up the interlocking boards of directors of the Big Five companies. Within the small group that historically had controlled Hawaii, influential directors from one of the companies would sit on the boards of other companies, and vice versa. Bert had actually worked for one of the companies and had decided that his opportunities were limited, so he might have relished hauling the boards of the Big Five into a bitter, humiliating court battle. Instead he negotiated an agreement that led the companies to abandon their interlocking directorates without going to court. It saved taxpayer money, and it also prevented further ill will.

This approach was typical of Bert, and such moves became a trademark of the Burns Administration. After years of conflict, this constructive approach created a consensus over what kind of place Hawaii should be. The very word "consensus" took on a special meaning.

As a key aspect of building the consensus, Bert served as Burns' mediator in labor negotiations. Hawaii had a history of economically disastrous strikes, and Burns, wanting to change this long pattern, kept his finger on the pulse of labor negotiations. He commanded the respect of labor, and also of business, which was glad to learn he was not anti-business. At the right moment, often at literally the last hour before midnight, Bert Kobayashi would step in, using Burns' immense prestige to pull out a settlement.

While I think my association with Bert Kobayashi helped me in the eyes of Burns, I believe it was the governor who came up with the idea of me running with him, because he was so ready to talk about the idea in detail—as if he had developed it himself, and not borrowed it.

Beyond the narrow question of how Burns came to ask me to run, I now can see how conflicts within our society, and within the Democratic Party itself, had been building up for many years to set the scene for our breakfast meeting.

John Burns was born in 1909, which made him seventeen years my senior. He had grown up as a *haole* boy in the local neighborhood of

Kalihi, the oldest of four children, raised by a devoutly Catholic mother. Jack Burns understood viscerally what other liberal Caucasians understood in perhaps a less basic way. He understood how hard life had been in Hawaii for the great majority of people, how limited opportunity had been, how hurtful discrimination was, and how people were held back if they were not among the privileged few.

Burns joined the Honolulu Police Department in the 1930s as a way of supporting his own growing family, and in the hope it was a system in which a person rose on ability rather than through social contacts. As the war with Japan threatened, he was assigned to head something called the Espionage Bureau of the Honolulu Police Department. In that capacity he worked with the federal government's intelligence agencies on the question of whether people of Japanese ancestry in Hawaii would be loyal to America in the event of war. As a result of his ease of communication with Hawaii's people, Burns knew that we who were of Japanese ancestry were overwhelmingly loyal to America and to American ideals. Burns knew this from experience, and he knew it in his heart. He played a unique role because he addressed the question of loyalty as a Hawaii resident at a time when the national government was looking at us all with such intense suspicion.

When I got involved in the Democratic Party in 1954, there were some older Japanese who still believed that Burns had spied against the Japanese. They said he was an *inu*, a dog. When I think about the things that happened, I know this whispering against Burns was wrong, and that in a real sense he had put himself on the line for people of Japanese ancestry.

He had to have had a real conviction to speak up for AJAs at that time. After he had assured everyone that the AJAs were completely loyal to the United States, what if there had been some kind of incident? He would have been held responsible.

After the shock of the Pearl Harbor attack, Burns was involved in helping maintain morale within the Japanese community, and then with organizing the 442nd Regimental Combat Team. As the war went on, he worked with a circle of associates who began to map out how the Democratic Party could be a vehicle for transforming Hawaii. . . .

The idea of breaking barriers, which originally had motivated me, was an inseparable part of my considerations. The new State of Hawaii had produced United States representatives and senators of Caucasian, Chinese and Japanese ancestry, reflecting our diversity. But only Caucasians had been governor. Lately a writer has described as ironic the fact that Burns as a white person led the 1954 movement, while most of the votes came from nonwhites. My own view is that sometimes it is easier for somebody else to tell you that you or your group can do better than you're doing. It carries more weight if someone from another group makes the case, because it is not as likely to be dismissed as biased. Burns tended to validate us. . . .

Burns thought it was important to break the barrier, not just for the Japanese but for all minority groups. I think he felt that if I could become governor then a lot of people would be able to say, "We can take off all the constraints. We can dream, and we can feel that Hawaii is the place where we have unlimited opportunities, a place we can become anything we want to become."

Burns felt that if we did not make the breakthrough, there might never be a governor of non-white minority background. He told me how badly he had wanted Mitsuyuki Kido to become lieutenant governor so that Kido could move on to become governor. Because that didn't work out, Burns felt that perhaps 1970 was the opportunity for me to move up to lieutenant governor and then look at the governorship in 1974.

Some people asked, "Why Ariyoshi?" When people look back, I may seem like a logical choice, but it was not that simple at the time. A person such as Mits Kido had been through the inner workings of the war experience while I was a teenager enjoying life at McKinley High. Kido was of an earlier generation. By several years, I had missed the experience of the 442nd with which Burns was so heavily identified. The 442nd group had been preoccupied with the issue of loyalty, and their legend revolved around that theme. As a result of the war, they developed a tremendous cohesion and direction. I felt my own experience was inferior to theirs, and what they had endured. I felt a great debt to them and what they had done to make things easier for those of us who followed. At the same time, I was different from them. I was the youngest of the 1954 group, and I had to be myself.

I announced my candidacy in early May, after the Legislature adjourned and just as the campaign season was starting. I made it clear I was not in this merely for my own sake, but I was supporting Jack Burns for re-election. By July, my campaign group had organized a big fund-raising dinner that really got the energy going in my campaign. When it was my turn to speak at the dinner I addressed my children, Lynn, Ryozo and Donn. At the time they were nine, eleven, and thirteen. I was concerned that they be part of the campaign and also that they understand the pending change in our family life. I told them they were fortunate to grow up in a community that is committed to human dignity, "where there is equality of opportunity, and where you can dream, and dreams become real if we work for them."

Many people did not like to remember that "we didn't always have equality of opportunities, and people were not always advanced in business on the basis of their abilities."

I said if any single individual deserved credit for the great changes that had occurred in Hawaii it was John A. Burns. I believed deeply in what I said, and people caught the spirit of my conviction. Through this speech, which I repeated many times through the campaign, I tried to get the longer and most pertinent span of history clarified in people's thinking. . . .

In 1971, a few days after my forty-fifth birthday, my father said to me in Japanese, "Oh, you've become a man now." It is kind of odd to hear that translated into English, but I knew it was a pronouncement of his confidence in me. He used the words *"ichinin mai ni natta,"* meaning I had become a full person, that I had reached my potential and had become an adult in a real sense. He said I would continue to grow, that I had a great deal more to learn and do and accomplish, but he was satisfied. My father was also saying he was convinced that the next time around I was going to become governor.

My birthday is on March 12, and I think we had our conversation shortly after that, on March 14. He usually did not go to Japan until around June, but that year he went right after our conversation, because his brother was having his sixtieth birthday party and wanted him there. Papa caught a cold. It got much worse, and he was put in Kumamoto University Hospital. My mother called me to come see him. When I got there the doctor told me it was too bad I had come so far. He wanted me to understand my father would probably not know I had come.

When I went in there, my mother told my father that I had come. I bent over and said, "Papa, can you hear me?" He gasped and said yes, *hai.* He put his arms up and put his hands around my neck, and he pulled me toward him.

The doctor was watching. He said, "You must be very close to your father. If I had not seen it I would not have believed he could do that."

A trade mission from Hawaii was headed for Tokyo. The governor was to have headed it but could not, so he had asked me to do so. I told my mother I was going to cancel my involvement with the trade mission, but she insisted that I not. She said, "You're not a private person now. You're a public person. I understand that, and Papa understands that, and if he felt that because of his condition he kept you from discharging your public responsibilities, he would feel terrible. You've got to go."

I went to Tokyo to meet the group as they came into the airport, and I was with them for the business meetings. Then my mother called me to tell me that my father was not doing well at all. I couldn't get a flight out, so I took the train. A distant relative met me at the station and told me that my father had passed on. Later he said when he saw the reaction on my face he felt terrible, and that he never wanted such a responsibility again. When I saw my mother in Kumamoto, I started to say, "I shouldn't have gone," but she stopped me. "Don't say that. You did the right thing," she said.

We brought my father's body back to Hawaii and held his funeral services here. When he first had seen Hawaii he had said, "This is nice; I think I'll stay," and his life turned out to be an amazing saga. . . .

As the year went on it became obvious that Governor Burns' illness was incurable, and I officially became acting governor on his behalf.

At the point I became acting governor, the Democratic Party had been the dominant party for twenty years. The election season approached, and there was a lot of shifting around and vying for position. Uncertainty was in the air. The *Hawaii Observer* described the Democratic goals of 1954 as being either "accomplished, forgotten or discredited," and the Democratic Party as being splintered into a half-dozen groups. I could count at least six different campaign groups myself.

Elements of the Burns group supported me, but others were slow to come around. Some turned away. . . . More fundamentally, I realized Jack Burns, in his wisdom, felt I ought to develop my own campaign and my own strength instead of relying on his group. I think he was concerned that if I relied on his group I would not develop my own adequately, and I would not be as strong as I needed to be. I concentrated on improving my own statewide group, and I thought of getting volunteers from the Burns group as a bonus. . . .

As the first governor of Japanese ancestry, I felt a special obligation, and sometimes a special burden. From my background, I think you can see how the concept of *haji* (shame) came in. In Japanese terms, it was my job to avoid failure, to not bring shame on the family or on our heritage. I had to do well not only for my own sake, but for the sake of many others.

On election nights, Jean and I had always watched television at home to get a feel for what was happening so we could be prepared when we went to headquarters. That 1974 election, when I knew I was going to be okay, I went to the Kuakini Hospital to see Governor Burns. I walked in and said, "I think things are going to be okay, Governor, and I want to thank you very much."

He said, "Don't thank me. I want to thank you for making my dreams come true."

When he was taken home to his place in Kailua, I would go to see him. Mrs. Burns took me aside and said she was no longer going to send him back to the hospital. She was going to keep him at home and let him go with dignity. She recalled all the times I had been to Washington Place for dinner as lieutenant governor, and the peace of mind he had gotten from having me on the job.

In those last days, Governor Burns couldn't talk much, and we never talked business, but I experienced the deep feeling that existed between us. He had been born into an almost feudal plantation society. He had played a central role in transforming it into the most shining example of fair play and democracy. When he was asked to name the most important achievement of his administration, he ignored all of his administrative and legislative achievements and focused instead on a letter he had written early in his first term. The Pacific Club, a symbol of the old order, had invited him to be a member, and Burns had written to them courteously declining. He said he could not think of such a thing until it opened its doors to all races. About a year later the letter came out in the newspaper. Suddenly the club's racial policy was reversed, as if life in Hawaii had changed forever.

John Burns had vision. He had a passionate concern for correcting injustice. He taught us, above everything else, the worth and dignity of every human being. He saw in all of us the gleam of hidden treasure. He reminded us that we are all the equal children of a Divine Creator. He stood up courageously in the panic of 1941 when people of Japanese ancestry were in the greatest jeopardy, and he took pride in seeing a person of Japanese ancestry becoming governor. He passed away at the age of sixty-six on April 5, 1975. . . .

Our Next Step

Across the years, I personally have retained an inner feeling of excitement which, thankfully, has never deserted me. I think I inherited Papa's energy and Mother's perpetual optimism. I was supported by my wife and children, and motivated by them. If they had not supported me, I could not have served, but they made it easy for me. I experienced my time in office without letdown or fatigue, without burnout or despair.

I had that one extraordinary moment, alone at my desk, in my last night as governor, when I felt so totally drained. After a night's sleep, I was up and running again. To have joined with thousands of other people in transforming Hawaii from a politically backward territory to a progressive, multiracial state, has been rewarding beyond imagination. I do believe this most essential accomplishment of the Democratic Party is a beacon that lights up American democracy and can be seen around the world.

But our obligation to the future compels us to not rest on past accomplishments. We have new challenges to meet, and we must get on with the process. *Otagai*. We are obligated to one another. *Okage sama de*. We are what we are because of one another. To see things whole, to go for the long term, to act as stewards—these are the things that are most important, when all is said and done.

Mike N. Tokunaga
100th Infantry Battalion

BUILDING BEHIND THE SCENES

The following narrative by Cynthia Oshiro of the Social Science Research Institute's Center for Oral History is based on a 1989 oral history interview with Mike Tokunaga. The interview was conducted by Daniel W. Tuttle, Jr., and Larry Meacham for the Hawaii Political History Documentation Project.

Childhood in Lahaina

My dad, Nobumi Tokunaga, came from Japan and went directly to work at Pioneer Mill Company in Lahaina, Maui, where he met and married my mother.

I was considered a "downtown boy" because we lived close to Lahaina town. If you lived in Mill Camp, which was primarily a Japanese community, you were known as a "Mill Camp boy" or "Pump Camp boy."

There was also a Portuguese community called Luna Camp. Most of the *lunas* (foremen) were Portuguese.

There was a mixture of people in Lahaina. After all, it was the capital of Hawaii during the Hawaiian monarchy. There were a lot of Portuguese, Hawaiians, and Chinese. When I went to school, we had a good mixture of students at Lahainaluna High School. I think that's why I grew up getting along with Hawaiians, Chinese, and all kinds of ethnic groups.

After graduating from high school in 1939, I wanted to go to the University of Hawaii. My parents told me they couldn't afford it, so I told them that I was going to work for two years and then go to the university with the money I earned.

The first year, I worked in the fields, cutting cane, doing *hapai ko* (carrying cane), and cutting grass. In the morning, everybody started at one end of the field. I let the guys on both sides of me go ahead, so they would cut the cane on the bank. Then, when I went, three-fourths of the cane was already cut.

One day, I was goldbricking and sharpening my cane knife. All of a sudden, I got a swift kick in my *okole* (buttocks). It was a real hard kick, like I would kick a mad dog. I stood up and turned around. There was the assistant manager, Harry Taylor.

"If you do that to me again, I'll wrap this cane knife around your neck," I told him. He backed off and took off. I think he could see in my face that I really meant it.

Another time, we were assigned to cut the cane in front of the cane grab—that's the machine that picks up the cane and puts it in the car. We were supposed to be between the tractor and the grab, cutting the cane not pulled out by the grab. It was a very dangerous job.

I told my friend, Takao Okamitsu, "Eh, let's get out of here." So we walked out. We refused to do that kind of dangerous job.

The next day, Harry Taylor came down to the mill at four o'clock in the morning when we reported to work. "You and Okamitsu, we're going to give you separate jobs." They assigned us to unload the mud press—the mud that came out of the mill that they dumped way out in the valley. You couldn't talk to anybody because there was nobody out there except the mynah birds.

In June of 1941 I got a draft notice, telling me to stand by because I might be going into the army in July. They didn't take me in July, but rather in November 1941. I thought I was drafted because I was such a Bolshevik on the plantation. I thought the plantation manager, John T. Moir,

Jr., wanted to get rid of me, and hoped that I would never come back to Lahaina again.

Basic Training

We were training as recruits at Schofield in the U.S. Army infantry. When the war broke out on December 7th, I didn't even know how to shoot a rifle.

I recall one incident about two o'clock in the morning. Somebody came into our tent and took our rifles and ammunition away. There were about nine hundred Japanese boys; the total complement at "tent city" at the time was about twelve hundred.

The next morning, the colonel called us together and apologized. He said the reason they took the rifles and ammunition away was because they heard rumors that the Japanese were going to riot in Honolulu, and they weren't sure what we were going to do.

In February of 1942, some of us got shipped to Maui, some got shipped to Hilo, and some to Kauai. I was in the contingent that was sent to Maui. I was assigned to A Company of the 299th, a National Guard outfit.

There was a group on the *Royal T. Frank*, a small transport. The *Royal T. Frank* was pulling a barge loaded with petroleum and building materials and other stuff. The transport landed in Kahului and the Maui contingent all got off. The boat left Kahului that night and continued on around Hana, bound for Hilo.

Just outside of Hana, the *Royal T. Frank* was torpedoed by a Japanese submarine. Twenty-nine men were killed in the sinking of the *Royal T. Frank*. We saw the survivors at Camp Paukukalo. They told us how they got hit.

In February 1942 I went home on my first pass. To my surprise, I found that a picture of President Franklin Delano Roosevelt was now where Emperor Hirohito's picture had been before. I asked my dad, "What did you do with the emperor's picture? Did you burn it?" "The emperor is hiding behind Roosevelt," he said with a chuckle. He had the emperor's picture in back of Roosevelt's picture.

I laughed. But, think about it; my dad was a first-generation Japanese from Japan. When the war broke out, some of his best friends, who were connected with the church, got interned. I think deep down, he was still loyal to Japan. He wouldn't say it, but that was my suspicion anyway.

We patrolled the shores and also went on patrol up to Haleakala. We were waiting for the Japanese to land, but nothing happened.

In June of 1942, all the Japanese boys were told to report to Camp Paukukalo. When we reported to the camp, they told us that they were going to form the 100th Infantry Battalion as a separate unit.

We were shipped to Schofield Barracks to form the 100th Infantry Battalion. Many of the draftees were members of the Asahis baseball team. Consequently, when we went to Camp McCoy in Wisconsin, we had a good baseball team because so many of the Asahis players were on our team.

Going down to Mississippi was a cultural shock. On my first pass, Jimmy Yoshida and I went to a theater in Hattiesburg, which was a small town. A black girl said, "You all buy your ticket on the other side." That's when I realized that we weren't considered "black." So I went over to the other side where the haole girl was selling tickets and bought our tickets from her.

When we started going up the stairway, the head usher called us and said, "You cannot go up there." "Why?" I asked. "That's 'N----- heaven.' That's only for n------." I was twenty-two years old, and that was the first time in my life that I realized what "N----- heaven" meant. When I went downstairs, I looked upstairs at the balcony. All I could see were black faces.

Another incident happened in New Orleans. There were always two lines at the bus stop: one for blacks and one for whites. I was the first guy in the white line, catching the bus back to Camp Shelby. An old black woman—she must have been about seventy or eighty years old—was standing in the black line. When the bus stopped and the door opened in front of her, she tried to get on. The bus driver, who was white, came out and pushed her to the ground. "Let the white people in first," he said. I grabbed the bus driver by the shirt and dragged him out of the bus. Six of us kicked the hell out of him for knocking that poor black woman down.

When I got back to camp, our colonel got the whole battalion together. "I want to warn you guys—you cannot change the mores of the South. You got to live with it," he said.

Combat in Italy

We went by convoy from New York to Oran, North Africa. There, we were told that we were being attached to the 34th Division, the Red Bull Division. From North Africa, we went to Salerno, Italy, where we landed in September 1943.

The Germans were always up in the hills, looking down on us. Consequently, we had to go up after them. From, I would say, the third day in Italy, they put us up on the front, and we started getting involved in combat. The most fierce fighting we did in our first months in Italy was in an area called Alife.

We were attacking the German line when all of a sudden, two Germans opened fire on us with a machine gun. They missed me but hit two guys behind me. I saw the Germans running, so I ran for their machine-gun nest. I turned the German machine gun around and tried firing. It was jammed! No wonder the two guys had taken off.

From behind the house, another German took a shot at me with a machine pistol, which is like a tommy gun. He split my helmet and grazed my cheek. He had me pinned down; I didn't know what to do. All of a sudden, my Hawaiian ingenuity started working. I picked up a stone and threw it at him, figuring he would duck, thinking it was a hand grenade. When he ducked, I jumped out and ran into the bushes. The crazy guy stuck his head out again, so I hit him—and from only about thirty yards.

A tank came into the gully and stopped with its motor running. I called for Masao Awakuni, our bazooka man. I loaded the bazooka and told him to shoot through the bushes. Awakuni put the bazooka down. "What's the matter?" I asked. "My glasses, it's all fogged up," he said. He put his bazooka down, and got his dirty, old GI handkerchief, wiped his glasses, and put them back on. Then he picked up his bazooka and hit the tank, knocking it out.

The same thing happened with another tank in Cassino. The tank came for him, and like a turkey, he showed his head. When he moved, the tank fired in his direction. From his second position, he hit the tank on its track. This tank was medium-sized, but still a bigger tank than the first one. But he couldn't knock the tracks out. We yelled at him to hit the underside of the tank, where there was a lot of oil and excess gas. Sure enough, the second shell set the tank on fire, and the Germans started coming out of the tank. He got a Distinguished Service Cross for that, but I think he deserved the Congressional Medal of Honor.

My company, Charlie Company, started off in Salerno with about two hundred three boys. By the time we got to Cassino, we had about one hundred twenty-six. When we went up on Cassino to take the monastery, the brass told us that we had to pull back because the Allied forces were going to bomb the monastery. On the day we pulled back, twenty-three of us walked back. Most of the others were wounded.

Return to Hawaii

On my way back to Hawaii, I was sent to Camp Beale, outside of Sacramento, waiting for shipment back to Hawaii. Three of us on a pass went to San Francisco. We went to the opera house because I heard that they were having a meeting to organize the United Nations.

The colonel in charge of security took us up through the side entrance and sat us right up front. We watched the proceedings. I remember Edward Reilly Stettinius, the silver-haired man representing the United States.

After that, we went to a bar. I don't drink, but two of my friends wanted to have a beer. But nobody would serve us. I asked the bartender, "Eh, how about some service?" The guy said, "We don't serve Japs in this bar."

I saw red. I picked up the chair and threw it at him. He ducked. There was a big glass mirror behind him and the chair shattered the glass mirror. My friends picked up their chairs and started breaking things and throwing them through the front window. I told them, "Eh, wait, wait, wait. Let's get out of here," so we got out. We had just come from a function where we were treated like first-class citizens, and now we were being treated like third-class citizens.

I was in the contingent that came back in driblets. We didn't come back in a big group. Two or three days after we came home, the war in Japan ended. Consequently, they sent us out on pass, so we went to Maui and came back thirty days later. We were discharged in September of 1945.

That same month, I went to see Dr. Bruce E. White at the University of Hawaii, because I wanted to go back to school immediately. He suggested instead that I take some night courses at McKinley High School and get into the habit of sitting down and studying. Thus I started the University of Hawaii in February of 1946.

Building the Democratic Party

In 1950, Dan Aoki and I were cochairmen for the Japanese circus, sponsored by the 442nd Veterans Club and Club 100. One day Dan said, "Come on, I'll take you to talk to Jack Burns." Jack Burns was civil defense director in Mayor Johnny Wilson's administration. His office was in the basement of city hall.

One of the first things Jack Burns asked me was whether I was a plantation boy. "Yeah, I'm a plantation boy," I said. He asked, "You feel you getting equal treatment in this community?" "No," I told him. "If you want to get treated like a first-class citizen, play politics," he told me. So I asked him, "How am I going to get treated like a first-class citizen if I play politics?"

"Whether elected or not, if you belong to the Democratic Party and get into a position of power, you don't have to go after them. They will come looking for you, and they will socialize with you and start talking to you." So I told Jack Burns, "It's a deal. I'd like to get into a position where they come looking for me."

Dan Aoki started working among the 442nd boys, and I started working among the 100th. The 100th Infantry Battalion boys were older, and the older Japanese boys were generally Republicans, like Wilfred Tsukiyama, Joe Itagaki. The younger ones, where Dan Aoki was organizing, were ripe for the picking, because they had never played politics. Before they left for the war, politics meant nothing.

We started organizing among groups first. We even moved into the Parent-Teacher Association (PTA). We went to their convention, trying to recruit Democrats.

Through the 442nd and the 100th, we contacted boys on the neighbor islands. We had no problem there. I think on the neighbor islands, mostly, when the boys decided to run, they had to check with the ILWU (International Longshoremen's and Warehousemen's Union) because they had to get ILWU support to get elected.

Burns concentrated on the fourth and fifth districts on Oahu, especially the fourth district, where Dan Inouye, Masato Doi, Sparky Matsunaga, Russell Kono, Anna Kahanamoku, Herman Lum, and Willie Crozier ran in 1954. He wanted to take that because it was a Republican stronghold. The only Republican that survived in that one was Hebden Porteus.

Burns worked on the fifth district, and, again, was trying to get veterans, AJAs, and lawyers to run. George Ariyoshi was one of them. My good friend, Charlie Kauhane, a perennial candidate, also ran. I forget who the others were. Patsy Mink ran in the following election, 1956.

In '54, nobody gave Burns a chance of winning against Betty Farrington for delegate to Congress. Even I wasn't convinced that Burns could win. But as we worked on the campaign and went to the rallies, we kind of got a feeling that Burns was picking up.

About two weeks before the general election, we ran out of money, completely out. So Dan Aoki and I went down to see Jack Hall, who was regional director of the ILWU. We told him that we wanted three thousand dollars from the ILWU.

Jack Hall said, "If I'm going to give you three thousand dollars, I might as well take the three thousand, throw it in the toilet bowl, and flush it." He says, "I'll never get it back and Jack is not going to win."

We never got the three thousand dollars, but he promised us that he would put ads in the papers worth about fifteen hundred dollars. We told him that we didn't want the ILWU label on the ad, because an ILWU label would only solicit votes from ILWU members, and we already had those votes. We needed votes from outsiders or independents. Jack Hall, being a good union man, put the two ads in with the union label on it. We lost by 890 votes. It was the first and last time I cried in a political campaign.

I started working at the Hawaii Government Employees Association (HGEA) in 1956. Dan Aoki and I went there and applied for jobs. Through some of our friends on the board of directors, we got jobs. Besides doing HGEA work, we were always campaigning. We were real political animals.

In 1956, Burns ran for delegate for the third time. Dan and I got Charlie Kendall, who was the executive director of the HGEA, to endorse

Burns. Kendall and Burns were both from Kailua and they belonged to the same Lions Club. After that, HGEA endorsed Burns all the time.

When campaign time heated up, Charlie Kendall would close his eyes, and Dan Aoki and I would go down to the headquarters and work like dogs. It was a good job for political contacts, because we were always meeting and talking to people. We would find out if they were willing to come down to the campaign headquarters to work, or to go house-to-house, or ask some of our business associates to raise money for us.

If they said, "No, we cannot come to the office, but we'll talk to people," we gave them an eight-by-fourteen-inch sheet that said, "We, the undersigned, will vote for Burns," with their name, address, and phone number. We started accumulating that over the years. I think Governor John Waihee had something like forty-five thousand names in the computer.

Representative Edith Green, a Democrat from Oregon, helped us that election. She sent us a Drew Pearson article that said that Betty Farrington was very happy when the statehood bill was recommitted. We printed one hundred fifty thousand copies of the article and mailed it all over. I think that's what did it in the 1956 election, because Burns won by more than fifteen thousand votes.

When we got statehood in 1959, Dan Aoki was the first one to call and tell me about the vote results. He told me to get ready for the statehood elections.

We all wanted Burns to go for the U.S. Senate. We figured that was the easiest race, especially Dan Aoki and me, because we were the campaign managers. But after a meeting of about eighteen of us at Herman Lemke's office at which we all gave our opinion, Jack Burns finally came out and said he was going to run for governor. He said, "I thank you guys all for your opinion. I'm going to run for the governorship because if you want to build the Democratic Party up, we gotta take the governorship."

About two weeks before the general election, Republican candidate William Quinn promised that the state of Hawaii would sell an acre of land for fifty dollars to every citizen in the state who wanted a piece of land. It was named the "Second Mahele" after the Great Mahele, the 1848 division of Hawaii lands. The land-hungry citizens of Hawaii believed his campaign promise, and Quinn won by forty-one hundred votes.

But the bill didn't pass, so in the '62 gubernatorial elections, we used that: "What happened to the Second Mahele?" We beat Quinn by thirty-two thousand votes.

One day, Vance Middlesworth from Dole Pineapple Company called me up. "Mike, I want you to arrange a meeting between Jack Burns and Malcolm MacNaughton." MacNaughton was the president of Castle & Cooke.

I think people in the Big Five were afraid of Jack Burns. They thought he was so prounion that he was out to get the sugar companies. But Burns was smarter than that. The sugar companies were the lifeblood of the state of Hawaii, and at least at that time, the biggest industry. He was not going to do anything to get the sugar plantations to go down. That's essentially what he told MacNaughton. They were good friends after that.

When we were organizing the cabinet, very early, Jack Burns said, "I want Dan Aoki in my office." When it came to me, I told Burns, "I don't want to work in your office because you're going to use me as a 'no' man"—you know, "anytime you want to say 'no' to somebody, you're going to say, 'Go see Mike Tokunaga.' "

I told him to put me anyplace—not as a director, but as a deputy director. I wound up with Sidney Hashimoto, whom he appointed as director of the Department of Regulatory Agencies.

In the 1966 race, Burns wanted Kenny Brown for his lieutenant governor. Later on, he felt that besides Elmer Cravalho, Kenny Brown would make the best governor. I think in the back of Burns' mind, he did not want to see Tom Gill become governor. I think he thought Gill would be too prolabor and that industry and labor would drift further and further apart.

In the primary, Tom Gill smashed Kenny Brown. I was appointed liaison with Gill's campaign. I was in constant contact with Gill's campaign; we tried to coordinate everything. We never had the two going to the same rally. We struggled through the campaign with the candidates not talking to each other. In spite of that, Burns and Gill were elected.

In the 1970 campaign, which pitted Governor Burns against Lieutenant Governor Gill, I was disabled. I'd had a heart attack in 1967, and Dan Aoki didn't want to be campaign manager all by himself. Up until the 1966 election—from '54 to '66—Dan Aoki and I used to be cocampaign managers.

In the 1970 campaign, we pulled in Bob Oshiro. We told Bob, "You run the campaign." He said okay. He ran a winning campaign. I think we spent close to two million dollars.

In the 1974 campaign, way back in June, Burns had called Dan Aoki and me and told us to organize the campaign for George Ariyoshi for governor. Fortunately, Tom Gill and Frank Fasi decided to run against George Ariyoshi in the primary. Gill and Fasi split the Democratic votes, and George Ariyoshi walked in.

In October, just before the end of his term, Burns had cancer surgery. As it turned out, he died in December, the month his term was to have ended.

I decided to retire in December of 1985. In November, a month before I planned to retire, John Waihee asked me if I would support him for governor.

I told Waihee, "Do me a favor. Take Dan Aoki and Don Horio, Governor Burns' press secretary, to lunch, and ask them personally to help you." They had lunch, and about three days later, Dan Aoki called me up and said, "Eh, we're going to go Waihee." I told him, "Okay, Boss."

Dan was heavily involved in Waihee's campaign until he died suddenly on June 11, Kamehameha Day, 1986. About a week later, at the headquarters, Bob Oshiro called a meeting. "Mike, I want you to give a very emotional speech to the boys about Dan Aoki."

I got up there and told the boys how hard Dan Aoki had worked and what a great politician he was, that he had committed himself to supporting John Waihee, that he worked like hell, and that he died with his boots on. John Waihee was in Bob Oshiro's office and he heard that.

I never go down to the headquarters on election night; I always watch the returns on my TV at home. I noticed that on election night, when Waihee won, he dedicated his victory to Dan Aoki.

If you look at the history of the Democratic Party, I think it's coming to the end of the rule. Not so much the House and the Senate, but the major positions. I think in the old days, if you take the Nadao Yoshinagas, and the John Ushijimas, and the Kazuhisa Abes, and Nelson Dois, throughout the state, these people in the 1950s and '60s had a common purpose, because they were of plantation stock, and they wanted equality. And they worked for equality; they improved the educational system. Now I kind of sense that the Democratic Party is getting splintered, and it looks like everybody is out for himself.

Robert T. Sato

100th Infantry Battalion

ISSEI AND CITIZENSHIP: PROUD AMERICANS

Why do people want to become U.S. citizens? The answer is simple. They want to enjoy the advantages of citizenship in this great country.

In 1790, Congress had limited the right to naturalization to whites only. Most of the issei came here to work for the sugar plantations and endured many difficult years, both socially and physically. The plantation work was hard and sometimes brutal. In spite of adverse circumstances, they worked diligently for the future, and most important, *kodomo no tame ni* (for the sake of the children). For more than a generation, they were still refused citizenship.

It was not until 1952 that issei were permitted to become American citizens. Thanks to the passage of the Walter-McCarran Act in 1952, not only issei but many other nationalities became proud Americans. Today, approximately one hundred twenty-five thousand persons become United States citizens annually. Naturalized citizens of the United States cannot become president or vice president, but they have all the other rights and duties of people born as United States citizens. Applicants must prove that they have lived by generally accepted moral standards for the last five years.

By the end of 1953, many issei took exams and happily became citizens of the United States. There is no doubt in my mind that these issei looked forward to becoming citizens of this great country, the land of plenty. Whenever I say "*Shiminken omedeto* (Congratulations on your citizenship)!" to these new citizens, they reply without hesitation, "100 *butai*, 442 *butai, tsuyaku butai no okage desu* (Thanks to the 100th Infantry Battalion, 442nd Regimental Combat Team, Military Intelligence Service)."

I wish our fallen comrades could have heard their kind words. Their expressions of gratitude inspired me to teach the citizenship course at the McKinley Community School for Adults. Approximately sixteen hundred have attended my class, and practically all of them passed the exams and became American citizens. Teaching the citizenship course was the best decision I ever made.

I remained true to Club 100's motto: "For Continuing Service."

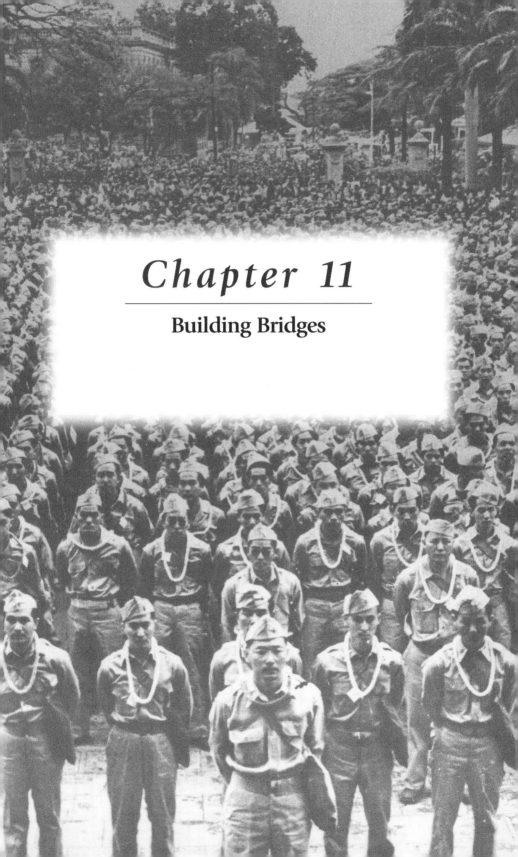

Chapter 11

Building Bridges

Kaoru Yonezawa

100th Infantry Battalion

SERVING FOR TWO

I first met Sgt. Gary Hisaoka when we shared a pup tent in our early E Company days. We had lots of time to talk back then. We talked about our plans for when we got back to civilian life.

Gary wanted so much to help the community. He said to me, "If I am killed and cannot go back, you do my share." We agreed that we would do each other's share if one of us somehow did not make it back. He also asked me to tell his younger sister to continue her education in his place, so his ten thousand dollar life insurance went to her education. I don't know if he somehow knew that he wasn't going to make it back.

After two or three big battles, we were sent in on the battle for Cassino. The shape of the mountain had changed because of all the bombing. Charlie Company, which we had been transferred to from E Company, decreased from 135 men to 78. That's how many men we lost. Our battalion commander, Maj. James Lovell, was hospitalized because he was injured in an earlier battle. Since he couldn't see his soldiers, he left the hospital and took over the command at the front line, even though he was not fully recovered. This made us very happy. Lovell took his gun and led the way up Mount Cassino, dragging his injured legs.

Although Major Lovell was a Caucasian, he had worked in Hawaii, so he understood us. We did everything together.

At night, our squad was ordered to scout the enemy territory, which we did, returning around midnight. It started to rain so we dug a trench. By this time we were good at digging trenches. By using a small scoop, we could make a hole big enough so that we could hide ourselves. We brought a door from a bombed-out farmhouse, put it on top of the trench, put sand on the door, and slept under it. We thought that it would prevent the Germans' fireworks—like small metal cannon fragments—from falling on us. We were tired, so we fell asleep immediately in the trench, which was already filling with rain.

In the morning, the Germans, who were watching us with binoculars from the top of the mountain, started their attack on us. Their first cannon shot exploded near us, burying my trench with sand. I lost consciousness and was buried alive. I don't know what happened after that.

Someone told me later that when the heavy gunfire ceased, my sergeant, Gary Hisaoka, went looking for me. He found my legs sticking out from the ground and touched them. Since they were still warm, he screamed, "Yone is still alive! Give me a hand!" and got others to help dig me out. After a rest, I walked slowly up to the battalion headquarters and they sent me to the nearest MASH (Mobile Army Surgical Hospital) hospital to check out the pain in my spine, which they said was due to being crushed by the weight of the soil. Thanks to Hisaoka, Richard Miyao, Yoshito Morikawa, Masaru Nanbara, Lefty Kimura, and other war buddies, my life was saved.

After I recovered, I rejoined the unit and met up with Sergeant Hisaoka again. The 133rd Infantry Regiment had asked each platoon to send a man for guard duty. Hisaoka sent me so that I could take it easy for awhile. I was on guard duty until C Company needed me to fill in for the casualties.

One of my first assignments was with a reconnaissance patrol with Yoshito Morikawa near the Arno River. After we returned, Morikawa came down with pneumonia. I never saw him again. Hisaoka assigned me to the kitchen area of C Company. Just before Anzio, we were joined by the 442nd Regimental Combat Team. Our fighting strength had been reduced due to casualties, so I was glad the 442nd boys came to join us.

When we arrived at the Anzio beachhead, we were in a rest area. At that time, all the leaders went to the Mussolini Canal for reconnaissance. I was on guard duty at the time. Lieutenant Norman C. Mitchell came to tell me that a sad thing happened. The only one killed on that patrol was Sgt. Gary Hisaoka. We all felt very sad. I lost not only a good friend but someone who was like my older brother. He gave me so much good advice.

Today I carry Gary's picture—the same one for over fifty years—in my wallet, so no matter where I go, Gary is with me and can enjoy whatever it is I'm doing. When I go to Japan, I take his picture out and say, "Gary, we're in Japan now."

Because of Gary and the C Company boys, I came back to Hawaii alive. Because of my promise to Gary, I got involved in doing volunteer work. But I felt I had to do the work of two people—his share and my share.

After I came home in September 1945, I helped out the Kumamoto Kenjin Kai, our prefectural group, made up of families whose ancestors came to Hawaii from Kumamoto Prefecture in Japan as immigrants. In 1958 the United Japanese Society of Hawaii (UJSH) was organized. I was on the original board of directors. I served off and on with the UJSH until my retirement from Lewers & Cooke in 1978. After my retirement, I began to devote more time to UJSH.

Besides the usual things that nonprofit cultural groups do, the UJSH provides greeters for Japanese naval cadets visiting Hawaii. They usually come about twice a year, so we have a group go out to meet them and set up refreshments and entertainment. The Japanese Defense Force also holds a maneuver in Hawaii every year, so I get involved with that, too. Although we aren't in a war situation now, I remember how it was for me to be a soldier in the army in a foreign country, so far away from family and friends. Having lived in Japan and being able to speak the language, I can relate to the young cadets.

On November 2, 1996, the government of Japan awarded me an Imperial Decoration, the "Order of the Sacred Treasure Gold and Silver Ray 5th Class," for my volunteer work in promoting goodwill between Japan and the United States of America. Of course, Gary was "with" me at the ceremony, because it was really he who had earned it. I know that if I hadn't made it back and Gary did, he would have carried out the promise we made to each other.

Don Seki

442nd Regimental Combat Team

MISSION ACCOMPLISHED

A native of Hawaii, I volunteered for the 442nd Regimental Combat Team in March 1943. I remained with the "Go for Broke" regiment from training at Camp Shelby to battle in Europe, where I fought in Italy and France until I was seriously wounded.

I was wounded on November 4, 1944, during a fierce battle that took place somewhere between the towns of Biffontaine and Bruyeres in the Vosges Mountains of northeastern France. During the battle, I was hit in my left arm above the elbow by harassing machine-gun fire. It shattered that part of my arm completely, so much so that only skin held together the lower part of my arm to the upper part.

My platoon sergeant, Bill Oshiro, and others in my squad assisted me until I could be sent to the field hospital. They amputated my arm above the elbow because only flesh and skin were left hanging.

Three days later, I was approached by a lieutenant colonel who was a doctor. He presented me the Purple Heart. I was in such pain and confusion, and feeling so miserable that I felt like telling him to "can" the medal.

About a week later, I was sent to a hospital in Aix, France, where I was confined for the next two weeks. What I really wanted to do was go home to my family, but that was not to happen for quite a while because the war was still going strong and transportation to the United States had been curtailed.

By then, my arm was in a cast, which was attached to a traction machine so the skin could be pulled downward. They needed some extra skin to stitch around the stub. I was nicknamed "Papoose" because of all the different bandages and casts I had on my arm.

Us buddhaheads were treated well in the hospitals. I think we were able to withstand more pain than many of the other men, and that was appreciated by the hospital staff. At least, that was my experience . . . and my observation.

Sometime in late November or early December 1944, I was shipped from Aix to Marseille, France for the start of my trip back to the good ole U.S.A.

We boarded a troopship. Because of German submarines in the area, we traveled cautiously through the seas. To get back to the United States, we first sailed along the Mediterranean coast to Oran in North Africa. From there, we sailed across the Atlantic to Newport News in Virginia.

I was very disappointed with our route as I had wanted to see the Statue of Liberty and New York City. Unfortunately, because of the wandering German submarines—the "wolf packs"—we were forced to take the southern route. At that time, the wolf packs were busy destroying our ships throughout the North Atlantic. Some had even been spotted along the Eastern Seaboard.

My next hospital stay was in Richmond, Virginia, at McGuire Army General Hospital, where I spent another week recuperating before being flown to Hill Field, Utah.

In Utah, I was hospitalized at Bushnell Army General Hospital in Brigham City, which is located about sixty miles north of Salt Lake City. There, I had three or four more operations to help prepare my arm for the next step: being fitted with a prosthesis, which, in my case, was a hook.

There were other arm amputees at the hospital. We were all taught how to use our prosthesis. We also took part in various forms of therapy: chow class, horseback riding, swimming, trout fishing, and others—all of them aimed at teaching us how to manipulate the prosthesis so we could be independent and do just about anything by ourselves.

As I was being transferred from one hospital to the next, I kept thinking that if I could only go home to my family in Hawaii, I would get well a lot faster. I was so homesick for Hawaii and my family that some days I would just stay in bed.

As soon as I'd had the last of my operations and finished my physical therapy classes, I began to use my two good legs to move about the hospital. My problem was my upper extremity, while most of the 100th Battalion and 442nd patients in this hospital were being treated for injuries to their lower extremities. Most of the nisei patients were bedridden or had just had surgery. Being ambulatory, I got to know, or at least meet, most of the 100th and 442nd men who were confined at Bushnell.

I also became friends with Sadayuki Hino, a nisei soldier who had served in the Brazilian army as part of the Allied forces. Sadayuki was a double amputee: He had lost both legs. He could only speak Japanese and Portuguese—no English—so he was happy to have me for company and we quickly became friends.

Hospitalized AJA soldiers like me were very grateful to the Japanese Americans who traveled long distances—from Ogden, Salt Lake City, Provo, and Brigham City—to visit us in the hospital. They were very hospitable and so kind to us, sometimes inviting us to their homes and to various activities and parties. It was heartwarming, as many of us were very homesick for our families.

After nine months at the hospital, I was fitted with a permanent prosthesis. It was hard leaving Bushnell because of the kindness of Utah's Japanese people. I always think of them when I hear the song, "I Left My Heart in San Francisco," which I retitled to, "I Left My Sugar in Salt Lake City."

In the fall of 1945 I was transferred to Letterman General Hospital in the Presidio in San Francisco, where I was fitted with another arm. By then I fully realized that I could not "grow" a real arm, so I worked hard to get this one to fit correctly. It took about six weeks before I began to adjust to it and to feel comfortable with it. Finally, my release was approved by the Board of Doctors. I was free to go home!

Two days after the doctors' final approval, I was bused to Pittsburgh, California, a replacement depot situated about fifteen miles east of San Francisco. I stayed there for about three days, then took a bus to San Rafael, north of the Golden Gate Bridge, where I reported to Hamilton Field, an army air force base.

More than a year and five hospitals later, I was finally on my way home. The final leg of my trip was an eleven-hour plane ride to Hickam

Field in Honolulu. I begin to feel much better the moment the plane touched down. I was home! I then boarded yet another bus for a quick trip to Tripler Army General Hospital in Honolulu, where I was awarded the Ruptured Duck Pin. Two weeks later, in December 1946, I received my formal discharge from the service. I was ready to begin a new life as a civilian.

In June of 1978, my wife and I took a tour of South America. While on the tour, I began thinking about Sadayuki Hino, the Japanese Brazilian soldier I had met in the hospital in Utah. I had not seen him since leaving Bushnell Hospital in Utah.

There wasn't much I remembered about him—only that he had served in the Brazilian Infantry Regiment, that he had fought in Italy with the Allied forces, been raised in Brazil by Japanese parents, and, of course, that he spoke no English.

While touring Rio de Janeiro in Brazil, we asked Japanese business people in stores and restaurants if they knew of Sadayuki Hino. But, no luck.

It finally dawned on me one day to find out whether there was a veteran's organization in the city. I managed to ask this question by writing a note in English. Fortunately, some Brazilians could read English, even if they could not speak it. We were in luck; there was a veterans organization. We inquired at their clubhouse and were given Sadayuki's address and home phone number in Sao Paulo, which was the next stop on our itinerary.

As soon as we reached Sao Paulo, I called Sadayuki's home. Speaking in Japanese, I asked to speak to my World War II friend, Sadayuki. They told me he had died about five years earlier. Ironically, on that very same day that I called, the Hino family was holding a special service for Sadayuki's mother, who had passed away forty-nine days earlier. I never got to see Sadayuki again, or to meet his mother. But I was content in knowing that I had accomplished my mission in South America.

Ben H. Tamashiro

100th Infantry Battalion

TOMOSU HIRAHARA RESTS AT EPINAL

100th Infantry Battalion veteran Ben Tamashiro shared this story at Club 100th's fortieth anniversary closing banquet on July 4, 1982.

After a long series of injustices, the American colonists went to war against the British. On this day, July 4, 1776, 206 years ago, the Second Continental Congress officially declared the independence of the United States of America.

But the path to independence is strewn with the lives of patriots. Our time was forty years ago.

Most of the boys who were killed in the war are buried in cemeteries near home. A few still lie overseas. One of them is Staff Sgt. Tomosu Hirahara, B Company. He rests in France in the Epinal National Memorial Cemetery, just outside of Bruyeres. He was killed October 15, 1944, the first day of the battle for Bruyeres. That was a little over two years after the 100th had left the States for overseas duty.

Just before leaving, Tomosu had a chance to call his elder brother, Tom, who was in one of the military camps in the East. Tom caught a bus and arrived at Camp Kilmer as the men of the 100th were boarding trains for the ride to Brooklyn. Tomosu was at the head of his section, going aboard, when Tom came running up the station platform. Tomosu broke stride for just an instant. There was no time for even an embrace, just for a clasp of hands. As the hands separated, Tomosu called out, "I think this is the last time we'll see each other alive."

How is it that Tomosu still lies in Epinal? I asked the question when I visited the Epinal cemetery many years ago. But it was only recently that I came to understand why.

Bruyeres is a small town in the northeast corner of France, just this side of the German border. When France fell to the German onslaught in June 1940, Bruyeres fell under the absolute control of the invaders, for it was a strategic communications and transportation center. Four years later, another military force came to fight over the town: the 100th/442nd.

In the forest above Bruyeres is an impressive memorial to the nisei soldier. A modest one is set in the woods above Biffontaine where the "Lost Battalion" was trapped for a week until rescued by the 100th/442nd. The memorials were erected by an appreciative people in memory of the men who gave their lives fighting there.

But the memorials also stand for something else. After being under stern military control for years, here came a bunch of loose and easy-going Americans—nisei GIs—total strangers to the French, who carried on airs of being liberators, or conquerors, or rescuers. Yet their modest mannerisms and their attitude toward the townspeople restored the citizens' faith in humanity. They were, once again, masters of their own free will. That is the other side of those memorials.

When the French people looked about them, they saw in Tomosu Hirahara's grave another symbol of that transformation, a representation of all that was beautiful in the nisei, who had helped them regain their sense of dignity. So they asked Tomosu's family if they would kindly leave him there with them; they said they would take good care of him.

That request, however, nearly tore the Hirahara family in two. One group wanted to bring him home; the other wanted to accede to the wishes of the French people. It was a time when those who had been killed in action were being brought home to Hawaii. The side of the family arguing for Tomosu's return was rightfully concerned that if he did not return with the rest, friends and others would wonder about his death.

Within the family group, Tom had been closest to Tomosu; he adored his kid brother. Now, that last handshake at the train station and Tomosu's parting words were all that were left. And when Tom came upon

Tomosu Hirahara's final resting place at the Epinal American Military Cemetery in northeastern France. Inset: Tomosu Hirahara, who served with the 100th Infantry Battalion, was killed in action near Bruyeres on October 15, 1944. The cemetery is located a few miles from Bruyeres.

Tomosu's grave at Epinal, somehow, his heart told him that this is where Tomosu himself would have chosen to rest.

So there he lies—one grave among the thousands of beautiful marble crosses, row after row, in Epinal cemetery—a bridge of sorts between people halfway around the world.

Tomosu was the youngest in a large family of ten. His eldest sister, Mrs. Shizue Masutani, is here with us today. So is his brother Ronald and another sister Mrs. Helen Morita and her daughters, Mrs. Dale Evans and Mrs. Momie Bradley and her husband.

I share with you this account of Tomosu, just one of hundreds of such personal narratives, because in time, the greater glory of the 100th may come to be not the circumstances under which it was formed, or the heroism and sacrifices of its members, or even the test of Americanism—but rather the fact that they were out to do a job the best way they knew how . . . and in the doing, reaffirmed a truth about independence, about themselves, about all of us: That under our skin, we are brothers all.

U.S. Senator Spark M. Matsunaga
100th Infantry Battalion/Military Intelligence Service

REDEDICATION

> *The late U.S. Senator Spark M. Matsunaga, a 100th Battalion*
> *and Military Intelligence Service veteran, delivered the following*
> *Memorial Day address at the Fairmount Cemetery in Denver,*
> *Colorado, on May 30, 1968.*

We assemble here today, as thousands of Americans are assembling at other cemeteries throughout the country, in remembrance of sons, fathers, neighbors, and friends who, while serving in the armed forces of the United States, laid down their lives that this nation might live. We honor especially here at this cemetery the memory of some seventy-six Americans of Japanese ancestry who, in accordance with the principles upon which this nation was founded and nurtured, responded bravely and willingly when duty demanded the payment of the supreme sacrifice. It is an undeniable fact that although these fallen heroes paid the highest price of citizenship, many of them while living bore a greater burden as

Americans because of their ancestry. It was a burden which many others in this assembly shared with those in whose memory this beautiful and impressive edifice was erected.

I speak of the period which immediately followed the bombing of Pearl Harbor on December 7, 1941. Each of us of Japanese ancestry has his own individual memory of that period. No doubt, some of us endured greater hardship and sacrifice than did others. But regardless of the weight of that burden, it can be said of all of us that because we carried it well, we are today enjoying a better life.

My own memories of this period are sharp and clear. It is as if many of the events had occurred only yesterday instead of a quarter of a century ago. I am told that this is a sign of advancing age—when events of the distant past are recalled with greater clarity than more recent happenings. If this is true, then I for one would not mind growing old. I would want to continue to recall vividly the things which have instilled in me—and I hope they have in you—a better appreciation of our American way of life.

As a child in school, I was taught that under our system of society all men are created equal, endowed with certain inalienable rights, that among these are life, liberty, and the pursuit of happiness. I was taught that as an American, regardless of race, color, or national origin, I could aspire to the highest office in this land. This I believed as a child, and of its truth I am convinced as a man.

This belief, however, was not without severe testing during the period shortly after December 7, 1941. I had earlier volunteered for military service and was serving with the Hawaii National Guard, which had been federalized. When invasion was believed imminent, all Americans, regardless of race, stood side by side in beach dugouts and trenches, fully prepared to repel the enemy.

After the battle of Midway, however, when invasion of the Hawaiian Islands by the enemy became a remote matter, our fellow Americans suddenly turned to us of Japanese ancestry and looked at us with a suspicious eye, almost as if to say, "Why, he's a Jap."

It was shortly thereafter that all of us of Japanese ancestry who were in American uniform were given orders to turn in all our arms and ammunition and were corralled at Schofield Barracks, an army post located about twenty-two miles northwest of Honolulu.

Before we had any chance to bid good-bye to our loved ones, we found ourselves onboard a troopship, sailing for God-knew-where. Speculation was rife that we were headed for a concentration camp.

Upon landing at Oakland, California, we immediately boarded a train awaiting us there. From there on, it was a secret move into the hinterland. When the train finally came to a grinding halt after several days of travel, one of the first things we saw was a barbed-wire enclosure. Our suspicions developed into an abyss of despair. The pessimists were right; we were headed for a concentration camp, we thought.

We soon learned that our destination was Camp McCoy, Wisconsin. We were joined in Wisconsin by Japanese Americans from other parts of the United States. The barbed-wire fences, we subsequently discovered, enclosed prisoners of war, including two Japanese naval men who were captured in a two-man submarine off Waimanalo Beach on the island of Oahu, Hawaii. We were not placed behind the fences, but speculation again arose as to what was in store for us. Inasmuch as we were initially named a provisional battalion, we once more pictured ourselves as a battalion of forced labor.

As time went on, we were put through close-order drills and trained with wooden guns. Letters were written home, telling our folks back home what a wonderful time we were having and of the wonderful and cordial reception the people of Wisconsin were giving us.

We wrote home also of our great desire for combat duty to prove our loyalty to the United States. It was not known to us then that our letters were being censored by higher authority. We learned subsequently that because of the tenor of our letters, the War Department had decided to give us our chance.

Our guns were returned to us, and we were told that we were going to be prepared for combat duty. The atmosphere in our camp was a joyous one. Grown-up men leaped for joy upon learning that they were finally to be given the chance on the field of battle to prove their loyalty to the land of their birth and the ideal that was embodied in America.

It was with this spirit that the men of the 442nd Regimental Combat Team and the 100th Infantry Battalion, of which I was a member, fought and died in World War II and carved for themselves an indelible niche in modern world history. When the peace was won, they had amassed for themselves, among other awards, seven Presidential Unit Citations, a Congressional Medal of Honor, fifty-two Distinguished Service Crosses, five hundred sixty Silver Star Medals, more than four thousand Bronze Star Medals with more than twelve thousand Oak Leaf Clusters to them. General Mark Clark described them as "the most fightingest and most highly decorated units in the entire military history of the United States."

It has been said by wiser men than I that soldiers at the battlefront frequently don't know what they are fighting for and that they fight because they are forced to do so by the circumstances in which they find themselves. It early became clear, however, that men of the 100th Battalion and the 442nd Regimental Combat Team *did* know what they were fighting for; they were fighting to preserve and to prove their loyalty to the American ideal.

It is true that, like other soldiers overseas, many of them at times expressed skepticism. They were skeptical because even while they were engaged in mortal combat, news used to reach them about Private Matsuda, a veteran of the 100th Infantry Battalion, who had been returned to the continental United States because of wounds suffered in battle, and who, while wearing a Purple Heart and walking on crutches, was thrown out of a barbershop because he wore a Japanese face; and about Sergeant Frank Hachiya, a winner of the Distinguished Service Cross, whose name was taken off the Honor Roll at Hood River, Oregon, because his name was Japanese. And we had learned of the evacuation of 120,000 Americans of Japanese ancestry and their parents who had been uprooted from their homes along the West Coast and thrown into so-called relocation camps, which in essence were concentration camps, complete with barbed-wire fences and armed guards. Many of the Gold Star Mothers who are with us today bore a heavy double burden: personal hardship in a concentration camp and the loss of a son in the military service of his country.

If ever any group of Americans had been driven to a point of despair and rebellion, it was the Japanese Americans in World War II. They would have been justified in the eyes of the world to turn against the country which they called their own. But they did not! Why? Because even in the height of adversity, they had faith in the American dream, in this thing we call "American Democracy." Every man in the Japanese American combat units was imbued so deeply with the spirit of serving this ideal that he was willing to die while so doing—men like my messenger, Private Yasuo Kawano, who in his last few words on Earth told me, in effect, "Well, Lieutenant, I know I'm going to die, but I have no regrets. I have every faith that because of us who die, those of us who will survive, and our folks back home will be recognized as true Americans and will live a better life."

That that faith was not misplaced is abundantly in evidence, for Americans of Japanese ancestry today enjoy a much better life than they ever did before World War II. I for one would not be enjoying the high position of a member of Congress, the highest legislative body in the United States, had it not been for the supreme sacrifice of men like Kawano. I am sure that many of our men who fought in Korea and Vietnam died with the same faith in our system of American Democracy.

"What then is this great thing called American Democracy?" we might ask. Admittedly, as we look about in this country today, we can point to the ghettos of our cities, to the pockets of poverty, and to the racial strife that goes on, and rightfully inquire, "Is this the American Democracy we are trying to preserve? Is this the American way of life we wish to perpetuate?"

There is no question that our American system today is not without its shortcomings. We know this, and we know, too, that it is not the system that is at fault, but some of our own citizens who have failed to live up to the requirements of the system.

Whether they are conscious of it or not, most of the three billion people in this world today are striving for a common goal: a life worthy of their dignity as human beings. Most of them have not gone to the extent of naming this way of life. We Americans call it "democracy." The great upsurge of desire for democracy which we are now witnessing throughout the world is of utmost importance to us because our nation has been the proving ground of democracy for 192 years. We must not let it fail, and we who bore arms to defend it and we who spent weeks and months and years behind the barbed-wire fences of United States relocation camps must assume the responsibility of seeing to it that it does not fail.

Ours is a comparatively young nation—and a dynamic one. We believe in progressing toward the American ideal, and while change does not necessarily mean progress, progress necessarily involves change. The public demonstrations against established authority and the clamor for a change of order which we are today witnessing in the forms of college campus uprisings, Poor People's marches, and urban civil disorders represent an impatience with the rate of progress. It certainly is not a sign of weakness in our democratic principles and institutions, as some would have us believe. It is a part of our seeking and finding, of establishing and implementing lasting solutions to the domestic problems of America— the growing pains of a dynamic society.

We Americans who were the victims of earlier growing pains in our nation's history, can attest to the rewards of patience, faith, and hope. Ours is a story that needs to be told and retold, for it is a story which can inspire other Americans of other minority groups to exercise the same patience, and have the same faith and hope to live through their difficult times.

The English historian Arnold Toynbee has said, "By what we do and by what we leave undone, each of us has a genuine effect on history. Each of us makes a difference, and each of us is responsible for the difference that he makes. We have to take this responsibility of ours to heart. Democracy will not work unless we do."

If we are to give any real meaning to our observance of this national Memorial Day, we must here resolve as individual citizens that the story of the heroic dead whom we honor shall not lay buried with the dead, but will be kept alive to inspire the poor, the downtrodden, and the disillusioned to rise above social injustices. We must resolve not only to make ourselves, but to help others, to become better Americans in a greater America for a safer world.

Edward Ichiyama

442nd Regimental Combat Team

PATRIOTS STILL

From Aiea to Alaska, Northern California to New York, six hundred World War II AJA veterans and their spouses assembled at Central Union Church in the predawn darkness of September 2, 1995. They were gathered to answer their country's call to serve one last time.

These warriors—once patriots—were patriots still. They were there to participate in the international commemoration of the end of World War II.

President Clinton and the defense ministers of roughly thirty Allied nations journeyed to Hawaii for the activities. The core events of the V-J (victory over Japan) Day observance were a morning memorial service on September 2nd at the National Cemetery of the Pacific and a veterans parade through Waikiki later that afternoon.

Iwao Yokooji, a veteran of both the 442nd and the Military Intelligence Service, chaired the preprogram wreath-laying ceremony. I served with Iwao on the Commemoration Committee. We both felt it imperative that the local veterans groups, particularly the AJA veterans groups, participate in the event. This concern was noted early in the planning because national veterans organizations such as the American Legion, Veterans of Foreign Wars, and Disabled American Veterans were not fully participating in our V-J Day activities due to schedule conflicts.

Thus it became incumbent upon the AJAs, the largest organized veterans group in Hawaii, to demonstrate their commitment to our country. This we did. We did not fail our state of Hawaii, or our country. Above all, we did not fail ourselves, because we served once again with pride, distinction, and honor.

The Punchbowl ceremony, which boasted a distinctive Hawaii flavor, was a shining moment for all AJA veterans. Iwao began at ground zero with no wreaths and ended up with eighty-two, which provided a beautiful backdrop for President Clinton's special wreath.

The Punchbowl ceremony was especially significant for Americans of Japanese ancestry, and particularly MIS veterans, because the Buddhist invocation offered prior to President Clinton's address was delivered by Rev. Yoshiaki Fujitani, himself an MIS veteran.

Some three hundred fifty veterans participated in the afternoon parade. Those able to march the parade route did; others hopped on one of the four trolleys proudly identified with a big "AJA Veterans" banner on its side.

As we marched down Kalakaua Avenue, we were energized by the accolades of the crowd. Did any of us who experienced the euphoria of that moment not manifest a tinge of pride?

Prior to the parade, several people had asked me why the AJA veterans were parading as a unit rather than mingling with other World War II veterans.

I replied simply that we began as a segregated unit fifty years ago—not by choice, but by military order. Thus we became a symbol of a failed democracy. It was very important, therefore, that we maintain and preserve our unique identity as a reminder to all of the fragility of democracy and the importance of being vigilant.

Edward Ichiyama

442nd Regimental Combat Team

THICKER THAN BLOOD

It is often said that the bonds of friendship and camaraderie born in battle are sometimes even more intense than the blood relationship between siblings. In this excerpt from a eulogy delivered at the 1997 funeral of 442nd veteran Henry Tetsuo Kobayashi, fellow 442nd veteran Edward Ichiyama recalled the special friendship Henry shared with two army buddies—ties that began with war and continued for more than fifty years.

Henry was doubly blessed, because in addition to his family's support, he received the support and help of many others. Although Henry was not a rich man in the material sense, he was rich in other ways, surrounded by friendship, love, and respect.

For the last ten years that Henry was completely incapacitated, Tsuneshi Maruo, one of Henry's closest army buddies, unfailingly visited him about twice a month. During his visits, Tsuneshi would give Henry a shave and a haircut, which undoubtedly made him comfortable. While doing his chores, Tsuneshi would constantly talk and joke with Henry, knowing all the while that he was unable to respond. The only signs of recognition and appreciation that Tsuneshi received was the slight squeezing of his hand by Henry when Tsuneshi shook his hand. This was sufficient reward for Tsuneshi.

Gilbert Nishimi, another of Henry's army buddies, visited him almost weekly for the past ten years. Gilbert, who does not drive, rode the bus from Ewa Beach to Manoa, a distance of about thirty miles requiring numerous transfers. This was a time-consuming task; nevertheless, Gilbert cheerfully spent the necessary time and energy to visit his sick friend.

The friendship, love, and respect of Tsuneshi, Gilbert, and others could not be bought. They had to be earned, and Henry did, a thousand-fold, by extending his friendship and support to others while he was able to do so.

The powerful camaraderie of ex-warriors of C Battery, 522nd Field Artillery Battalion, was spawned more than fifty years ago in the heat, misery, and insect-infested fields and woods of Mississippi. It was further strengthened in the rainy and muddy battlefields of Italy. And finally, it was inextricably bonded and welded in the snow, and icy cold, bloody battlefields of France and Germany.

Aloha means a great many things: hello, goodbye, love, respect . . . giving of one's self. This evening, please allow me to use *aloha* in the latter context: of love, respect, and of giving of one's self. As all of us Hawaiians know, the greatest compliment one Hawaiian can pay to another is to say, "I have much aloha for you."

That is our sentiment this evening, for we have much, much aloha for our buddy Henry. In a sense, we are simply giving back the aloha spirit, that intangible and undefinable phenomenon which Henry so nobly embodied and embraced during his lifetime. *Mahalo*, Henry . . . for the many fond memories you left with us. This legacy will be cherished by all. And finally, aloha . . . aloha *pumehana* (with fond aloha) my dear comrade on your forthcoming journey, this time into the hereafter of eternal peace.

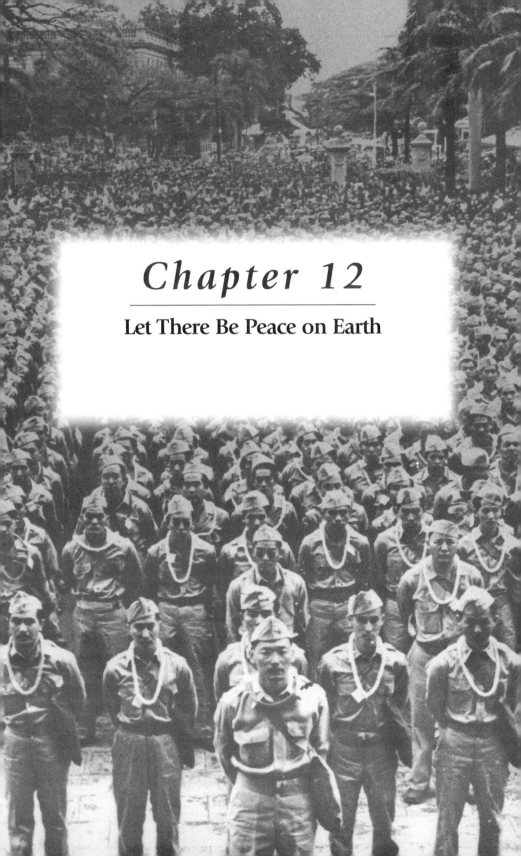

Chapter 12

Let There Be Peace on Earth

U.S. Senator Spark M. Matsunaga

100th Infantry Battalion/Military Intelligence Service

WE MUST TEACH OUR CHILDREN TO WANT PEACE

The following is an excerpt from a composition written by Spark Matsunaga for an English class while a student at the University of Hawaii in 1938. Matsunaga served with the 100th Infantry Batallion and the Military Intelligence Service following the outbreak of World War II. He later distinguished himself as a United States senator.

Wants are the drives of all human action. If we want peace we must educate people to want peace. We must replace attitudes favorable to war with attitudes opposed to war. Parents should protect the child from experiences with materials of warfare. Teachers should let the generals fall into the background and bring into the foreground leaders in social reform as heroes. We must help our young men to see that there are other types of bravery than that which is displayed on the battlefield.

If in our teaching we emphasize the life and work of our great contributors instead of our great destroyers, people will come to realize that moral courage is bravery of the highest type, and America will be called the Champion of Peace.

Epilogue

Bishop Ryokan Ara

THE LIGHT FROM ONE CORNER . . .

It has been over twenty years since I arrived in these Islands to establish the first postwar overseas mission of Tendai, the oldest of the Japanese Buddhist sects. Although there were many Japanese Buddhists in Hawaii, it was difficult for me to attract and establish a congregation, for most of the people had already affiliated with one of the sects that had come to Hawaii earlier.

In assessing the situation, I came to realize that a sizable congregation need not be the only goal of my mission. I could work toward keeping Buddhism a viable religion in Hawaii and America, regardless of sect, by nurturing and sharing its basic philosophy and culture. I saw my mission as one of transcending sectarian Buddhism, and even involving other religions that exist here.

Having determined this, I became increasingly involved in the community, while continuing my Tendai activities. In cooperation with the University of Hawaii, I commissioned an English translation of

Shikyogi. Also published were a number of outstanding treatises on Buddhism by American scholars. I am continuing to work with the university on translations of the *Makashikan* and *Tendai Shoshikan*, the original Zen texts.

In the community, I established the Hawaii Bijitsukan (Hawaii art academy), Hawaii Gakuen (Japanese-language school), and Ichigukai (a service organization meaning "one corner," or "one-nook society"). These organizations have afforded me the opportunity to work with various segments of the Japanese community.

I became acquainted with a group of *nikkei* (person of Japanese ancestry born outside of Japan) leaders who participated in the Ichigukai: The members were Christians as well as Buddhists. Some of the Buddhists belonged to other sects: Jodo Shinshu, Shingon, and so forth. Together, we established the Hawaii Japanese Immigrant History Center.

One of our goals was to preserve the stories of the issei immigrants. As we discussed the scope and methodology of the project, we also studied its financial aspect. We wanted to interview the immigrants on video but were concerned about the four thousand dollar cost of the equipment. It was at this juncture that one of the members, Mr. Masayuki Tokioka, offered to donate the necessary funds. He referred to a Buddhist lesson I frequently shared, extolling the greatness of the person who "lights up one corner of the world."

The name of the organization, Ichigukai, comes from this lesson. Similarly, the Bible in Matthew 5:11 says, "Let your light so shine before men." Aren't they referring to the same idea? What a beautiful example of the commonality of the teachings!

Over a period of ten years, we interviewed issei immigrants on videotape. Each interview lasted about an hour. In 1985, on the occasion of the one hundredth anniversary of the arrival of Japanese contract immigrants to Hawaii, we presented one hundred tapes to the Bishop Museum for preservation and to be used for research purposes.

Often heard in the interviews were statements such as, "Although our earlier years were difficult ones, our lives are now comfortable and fulfilling. We are fortunate. Much of this is due to our sons, our nisei boys' actions in the service of their country, America, and their efforts toward a new Hawaii in the postwar era." As soldiers they fought to win the war, and as civilians continued to fight for a better Hawaii.

They utilized the GI Bill of Rights to go to college and to professional schools. Returning as lawyers, doctors, educators, businessmen, and economists, they participated, often as leaders, in the building of a Hawaii in which each person, regardless of race or creed, would have equal opportunities and the right to a life of his choice.

One of the major obstacles was statehood, which became a reality in 1959. The nisei thus were the beam of light to focus on equal opportunities for all. The light lit in one corner, Hawaii, sent its rays throughout the United States of America.

Who were these nisei soldiers? Why did they fight? These questions came to mind as I read and talked with them about their experiences.

Photos of them as young soldiers evoked in my mind the statue of Asura at Kofukuji in Nara. In this figure, Asura is depicted as a personification of different forces of life: Its three faces, six arms, and body express warlike fierceness, compassion, and action.

The nisei, too, were young and innocent, but full of determination as they went into battle, mowing down the enemy with machine-gun fire and grenades, or gathering information behind enemy lines. Where did that determination and spirit come from?

I quote from a Buddhist parable in the *Tannisho*, a collection of sayings of Shinran Shonin, founder of Jodo Shin Sect:

> *Shinran: "Would you do anything I asked of you?"*
> *Yuien (disciple): "Of course I would!"*
> *Shinran: "Then, go out and kill a thousand men."*
> *Yuien: "I can't do that. I can't even kill a single person."*

This exchange reveals that we act in a particular manner because of the causes there. Even if we don't want to kill, we would, subject to causes and conditions. There is something more in our makeup that compels us to go forth.

What was the karma that compelled these filial, gentle, and cheerful young nisei men to go into battle? There are many publications that chronicle the men's experiences in battle, but very few explore how the nisei soldiers were affected—their beliefs, feelings, and thoughts. I felt that they were worthy and needed to be recorded so that all may fathom the depth and significance of their participation.

The fiftieth anniversary of the end of World War II gave me the incentive and the opportunity to attempt to document the personal aspect of the nisei soldier's wartime experiences. However, as an outsider—as well as a Buddhist priest—I wondered how many of the nisei soldiers, many of whom were Christians, would respond to my queries. Fifty years had passed and the courageous soldiers had aged. Generally, when asked about their heroic actions, these "quiet Americans" responded with a smile and very little talk.

I discussed my ideas with a few nisei leaders: Mr. Hideto Kono, former director of the Hawaii State Department of Planning and

Economic Development; Rev. Yoshiaki Fujitani, former bishop of the Honpa Hongwanji Mission of Hawaii; and Dr. Robert Sakai and Dr. George Akita, both emeritus professors of history at the University of Hawaii. These men had all served America as soldiers and, subsequently, had contributed to the development of today's Hawaii. Fortunately, each saw the need and committed himself to the project.

Just as we started on the project, a shocking dissertation, "Dispelling the Nisei Myth," appeared in a local English-language newspaper. Written by a sansei working on her doctorate in political science, the article questioned the authenticity of some of the well-publicized stories of the wartime nisei, such as the freeing of Jews from the Dachau concentration camp in Germany, and the idea of having fought for the sake of the children (kodomo no tame ni). This sansei feared that these accounts created a "mythical" image of the nisei as "perfect" human beings. She also felt that discussing their wartime exploits glorified war.

The veterans responded by asking themselves whether the sacrifices as well as the significance of their endeavors would dissolve into myths for succeeding generations. Are there factors spiritually sustaining for the younger people in those experiences that we consider to be negative ones? Is it not imperative that we bring to light much that we have not talked about, except among ourselves, while we are still able to do so? Wouldn't written records of things not said before be of value? Should we do so kodomo no tame ni, for the sake of the children, so they might realize that many of the rights and opportunities they enjoy now were not heaven bequeathed, but won through the outstanding performance and sacrifices of the nisei.

Facing these questions, the nisei and I have collected testimonies, diaries, and other materials, many of which contain soul-bearing statements and insights, agonies as well as dreams. Some of them have been included in this book. We have many others, but they must await a subsequent publication.

Fifty years after the war, the erstwhile young soldiers, when queried about their wartime experiences, respond, "Yamato damashii!" Discriminated against, their rights and responsibilities of citizenship taken away, their properties seized, their "Yamato spirit" has still survived.

So Proudly We Hail:
Honor Roll of World War II
Americans of Japanese Ancestry

The following are enlisted men and officers of the 100th Infantry Battalion, 442nd Regimental Combat Team, Military Intelligence Service, and 1399th Engineer Construction Battalion who lost their lives in World War II. They were either killed in action, died as prisoners of war, or succumbed to injuries sustained in battle or in a catastrophic accident, such as a plane or Jeep crash. Although every effort was made to confirm each name through a variety of sources, it is by no means the definitive list of World War II AJA casualties.

It is to these men — most of them Americans of Japanese ancestry, but a few non-AJAs as well — that we dedicate Japanese Eyes . . . American Heart.

Chester Abe ☆ Matsuei Ajitomi ☆ Tokio Ajitomi ☆ John Akimoto ☆ Victor Akimoto ☆ Hideo Akiyama ☆ Zentaro Akiyama ☆ Nobuo Amakawa ☆ Daniel Anderson ☆ James H. Anzai ☆ Yoshiharu N. Aoyama ☆ Harold Jentoku Arakawa ☆ James Yasushi Arakawa ☆ Masashi Araki ☆ Yasuhira Arata ☆ Frank N. Arikawa ☆ Hiroaki Arita ☆ Ralph Yukio Asai ☆ Reginald M. Asato ☆ Shotaro Harry Asato ☆ Kenneth Iwao Asaumi ☆ Shigeo Ashikawa ☆ Daniel Den Betsui ☆ James Boodry ☆ Howard Vernon Burt ☆ Joseph L. Byrne ☆ Henry Matsuo Chibana ☆ Giichi Chinen ☆ Jenhatsu Chinen ☆ Onso Chinen ☆ Danny Kiyoshi Choriki ☆ Cloudy Gary Conner, Jr. ☆ Walter Crone ☆ Niroku Dochin ☆ Haruo Doi ☆ Kenneth E. Eaton ☆ Tetsu Ebata ☆ William Kazuhiko Eji ☆ George Eki ☆ Hiroo H. Endo ☆ Masaharu "Mac" Endo ☆ Robert T. Endo ☆ Kaname Enomoto ☆ Kiyozo Enomoto ☆ Ralph B. Ensminger ☆ Harold C. Ethridge ☆ Charles O.

Farnum, Jr. ✦ Fred H. Fritzmeier ✦ Abe M. Fuji ✦ Masao Fujii ✦ Richard Toshio Fujii ✦ Yutaka Fujii ✦ Jitsuro Fujikawa ✦ Masaki Fujikawa ✦ Hideo Fujiki ✦ Toshiaki Fujimoto ✦ Shigeto Fujimuro ✦ Noboru Fujinaka ✦ Yasuo Fujino ✦ Yoshimi Fujino ✦ Shisuke Wendell Joe Fujioka ✦ Teruo Fujioka ✦ Teruo "Ted" Fujioka ✦ Sadami Fujita ✦ Ross Kameo Fujitani ✦ Takeo Fujiyama ✦ Akira Fukeda ✦ Shigeo Frank Fukuba ✦ Masami Fukugawa ✦ Herbert Masano Fukuhara ✦ Edwin Yukio Fukui ✦ Roy Shizuto Fukumoto ✦ Ichiji Fukumura ✦ Chester Takumi Fukunaga ✦ Arthur M. Fukuoka ✦ Katsumi Fukushima ✦ Kaoru Fukuyama ✦ George Funai ✦ Stanley Kazuto Funai ✦ Ichiji Furuihara ✦ Satoshi Furukawa ✦ Tatsumi Furukawa ✦ Tsuyoshi Furukawa ✦ Kenneth Kenzo Furukido ✦ Henry T. Furushiro ✦ Mitsuo Furuuchi ✦ George Futamata ✦ Shigeto Edward Fuyumuro ✦ Roland Joseph Gagnon ✦ Seikichi Ganeko ✦ Sol Harold Gleicher ✦ Hiroshi Goda ✦ Ralph Masao Goshikoma ✦ Kazuo Goya ✦ Yeiko Goya ✦ George Gushiken ✦ Frank Hachiya ✦ Victor K. Hada ✦ Hatsuji Hadano ✦ Eiichi F. Haita ✦ Tom S. Haji ✦ Tetsuo Hamada ✦ Katsuyoshi Hamamoto ✦ Seiichi Hamamoto ✦ Fred Yeiso Hamanaka ✦ Clifford H. Hana ✦ Richard Shintaro Hanaumi ✦ Tamotsu Hanida ✦ Charles Kiyoshi Harada ✦ John Y. Harano ✦ Kiyoshi Hasegawa ✦ Mikio Hasemoto ✦ Henry S. Hashida ✦ Denis Masato Hashimoto ✦ John Hashimoto ✦ Hisao Hashizume ✦ Masao Hatanaka ✦ Kunio Hattori ✦ Harry Minoru Hayakawa ✦ Makoto Hayama ✦ Stanley K. Hayami ✦ Donald Shiro Hayashi ✦ Joe Hayashi ✦ Robert N. Hayashi ✦ Tadao Hayashi ✦ Torao Hayashi ✦ Henry Yuzo Hayashida ✦ Hideyuki Hayashida ✦ Robert Hempstead ✦ Eiji Hidaka ✦ Charles Seigi Higa ✦ Eddie Kamechu Higa ✦ Katsumori Paul Higa ✦ Masao Higa ✦ Takemitsu Higa ✦ Toshio Higa ✦ Wilson Eiki Higa ✦ Yeiko Higa ✦ Bert Kenji "Smiles" Higashi ✦ Harold Tanoshi Higashi ✦ James Tetsuo Higashi ✦ Masami Harold Higuchi ✦ Harry Nobuo Hikichi ✦ Tomosu Hirahara ✦

Mitsuo Hiraki ✮ Kazuo Lawrence Hiramatsu ✮ Hiroyuki Hiramoto ✮ John Hirano ✮ Robert Rikio Hirano ✮ Genichi William Hiraoka ✮ Satoru Hiraoka ✮ George Hirata ✮ Gerome Mitsuo Hirata ✮ Himeo Hiratani ✮ Yasuo Hirayama ✮ Yutaka Hirayama ✮ Masao Hisano ✮ Gary Tsuruo Hisaoka ✮ Yeiichi Hiyama ✮ Richard Minoru Honda ✮ Hitoshi Honemura ✮ Kay I. Horiba ✮ James George Joji Horinouchi ✮ Paul Horinouchi ✮ Kazuo Horiuchi ✮ Robert S. Hoshino ✮ Earl Hosoda ✮ Max M. Hosoda, Jr. ✮ Kihachiro J. Hotta ✮ Toshio Hozaki ✮ Leon I. Hunt ✮ Kenichi Ichimura ✮ Edward Yukio Ide ✮ Shigeo Igarashi ✮ Kiyoshi Iguchi ✮ Masao Iha ✮ Kazuo Ihara ✮ Martin Minoru Iida ✮ George T. Ikeda ✮ George Tsuyoshi Ikeda ✮ Isamu Ikeda ✮ Masao Ikeda ✮ Roy Y. Ikeda ✮ William Yoshio Ikeda ✮ Lloyd Ikefugi ✮ Henry Shinkichi Ikehara ✮ Kikuchiro Dick Ikehara ✮ Haruyoshi Ikemoto ✮ James Shiro Ikeno ✮ Tomio Imai ✮ William I. Imamoto ✮ Larry Mitsuru Imamura ✮ Susumu Imano ✮ William Shunichi Imoto ✮ Thomas Takashi Inada ✮ Ben Masaki Inakazu ✮ Masami Inatsu ✮ Kazuyoshi Inouye ✮ Masato Inouye ✮ Minoru Inouye ✮ Masaji Irie ✮ Tadayoshi Iriguchi ✮ Mitsuo M. Iseri ✮ Haruo Ishida ✮ Minoru Ishida ✮ George Fukumi Ishii ✮ Masayuki Ishii ✮ Richard Hichiiro Ishii ✮ Walter Shinichi Ishiki ✮ Akira Ishimoto ✮ Kosaku Isobe ✮ Hachiro Ito ✮ Takashi Ito ✮ Tetsuo Ito ✮ Robert Kumao Iwahiro ✮ Hisashi Iwai ✮ Yoshio Iwamasa ✮ Lawrence Tsuyoshi Iwamoto ✮ Henry S. Izumizaki ✮ Thomas Munemasa Jichaku ✮ Katsui Jinnohara ✮ John A. "Jack" Johnson ✮ Chitoshi Walter Kadooka ✮ Joe Yazuru Kadoyama ✮ Yasuo Kagawa ✮ James Junichi Kagihara ✮ Tsugito Kajikawa ✮ Nobuo Kajiwara ✮ Fred Yoshito Kameda ✮ Bob T. Kameoka ✮ Shinobu Kametani ✮ Mitsuo Kami ✮ Shizuto Kamikawa ✮ James J. Kanada ✮ Walter Etsutoshi Kanaya ✮ John S. Kanazawa ✮ Frank Kanda ✮ Takezo Kanda ✮ Takeo Kaneichi ✮ Katsuhiro Kanemitsu ✮ Seichi Kaneshiro ✮ Yasuo Kaneshiro ✮ Isamu Kanetani ✮ Yasuo Kanmotsu ✮ Tom T. Kanno

✯ Akira Kanzaki ✯ James Karatsu ✯ Haruo Karimoto ✯ Kenneth Goro Kashiwaeda ✯ Yoshitaka Kataoka ✯ Noritada Katayama ✯ Joseph Kato ✯ Kenji Kato ✯ Yoshio Kato ✯ Masaichi Charles Katsuda ✯ John R. Kawaguchi ✯ Richard Hiroo Kawahara ✯ Tetsuro Kawakami ✯ Haruo Kawamoto ✯ Sadao Kawamoto ✯ Toshio Kawamoto ✯ Yutaka Kawamoto ✯ Kikumatsu Frank Kawanishi ✯ Cike C. Kawano ✯ George Kawano ✯ Tetsuo Kawano ✯ Yasuo Kawano ✯ Albert Goro Kawata ✯ Satoshi Kaya ✯ Stephen Mitsugi Kaya ✯ Yasuo Kenmotsu ✯ Lewis Key ✯ Tadashi Kijima ✯ Leo T. Kikuchi ✯ Matsuichi Kimura ✯ Paul Kimura, Jr. ✯ Tsuguo Kimura ✯ Shomatsu E. Kina ✯ Francis T. Kinoshita ✯ Mamoru Kinoshita ✯ Richard Kunito Kinoshita ✯ Joseph Kinyone ✯ Toshio Kirito ✯ Robert T. Kishi ✯ Roy Kitagawa ✯ Paul T. Kitsuse ✯ Ronald Shigeo Kiyabu ✯ John Kiyono ✯ Edward Yorio Kiyota ✯ Kiichi Koda ✯ Sadaichi Kohara ✯ Sadamu Koito ✯ Hayato Koizumi ✯ Shaw Kojaku ✯ Tadashi Kojima ✯ Nobuo Kokame ✯ James Kameo Komatsu ✯ Katsuto Komatsu ✯ Fred Hajime Komeda ✯ Nobuo Komoto ✯ Harushi "Blackie" Kondo ✯ Henry H. Kondo ✯ Herbert Y. Kondo ✯ Howard N. Kondo ✯ Jimmie Korubu ✯ Seichi Kotsubo ✯ Shigeo Kuba ✯ Tadashi Kubo ✯ Yoshio Kubo ✯ James Kiyoshi Kubokawa ✯ Mitsuharu Kuboyama ✯ Thomas T. Kuge ✯ Isamu Kunimatsu ✯ Katsugi Kuranishi ✯ Jerry Sadayoshi Kuraoka ✯ Minoru Kurata ✯ Ichiji Herbert Kuroda ✯ Robert Toshio Kuroda ✯ Ben Satoshi Kurokawa ✯ Shosei Kutaka ✯ Masaji Howard Kutara ✯ Joseph Takeo Kuwada ✯ Sunao Thomas Kuwahara ✯ John Kyono ✯ William Laffin ✯ Clarence E. Lang ✯ Leonard Hideo Luna ✯ Harry F. Madokoro ✯ Saburo Maehara ✯ Richard Keiji Magarifuji ✯ Matsutada Makishi ✯ Seiso James Mana ✯ Ben F. Masaoka ✯ Kay Kiyoshi Masaoka ✯ Masatomo Masa Mashita ✯ Dick Z. Masuda ✯ Eso Masuda ✯ Kazuo Masuda ✯ Yoshito Masuda ✯ George A. Masumoto ✯ Noriyuki Masumoto ✯ Lawrence Kidan Masumura ✯ Kiyoshi Masunaga ✯ Peter S. Masuoka ✯ Zen M.

Matari ✯ Carl Goro Matsuda ✯ Masao Matsui ✯ Hiroshi Matsukawa ✯ Isamie Matsukawa ✯ Dick Yoshio Matsumoto ✯ Goro Matsumoto ✯ Kiyuichi Matsumoto ✯ Sadao Matsumoto ✯ Tommy Tomio Matsumoto ✯ Renkichi Matsumura ✯ Kaname Matsunaga ✯ Satoshi Matsuoka ✯ Kazuo Matsushima ✯ Shizuo John Matsushita ✯ George M. Mayeda ✯ Thomas Tsutomo Durham Mekata ✯ Katsuaki Miho ✯ Yoshio Minami ✯ Isamu Minatodani ✯ Tom T. Misumi ✯ Kazuo Mitani ✯ Kazuo Mito ✯ Jack E. Miura ✯ Larry Nagao Miura ✯ Toshio Miura ✯ Charles M. Miyabe ✯ Masayoshi Miyagi ✯ Masayuki John Miyaguchi ✯ Tetsuo Miyake ✯ James Hideo Miyamoto ✯ Thomas Tokuyoshi Miyamoto ✯ Yasuo Miyamoto ✯ George Suetomo Miyaoka ✯ Isami Miyasato ✯ Tamotsu Miyata ✯ Tokio Miyazono ✯ Tsuyoshi Miyoga ✯ Mitsuru E. Miyoko ✯ Noboru Miyoko ✯ Timothy Mizokami ✯ William S. Mizukami ✯ Larry Tamotsu Mizumoto ✯ Morio Mizumoto ✯ Terry Yukitaka Mizutari ✯ Henry Teruya Mochizuki ✯ Edward Moran ✯ Kiyoto Mori ✯ Haluto Moriguchi ✯ Rokuro Moriguchi ✯ Arthur Akira Morihara ✯ Roy T. Morihiro ✯ Haruto Morikawa ✯ Hiromu Morikawa ✯ Toshiaki Morimoto ✯ Harold Hisao Morisaki ✯ Joseph Morishige ✯ Takeo Morishita ✯ Iwao Morita ✯ George Kaoru Moriwaki ✯ David L. Moseley ✯ Hiroshi Motoishi ✯ Wilfred Masao Motokane ✯ Susumu Motonaga ✯ Susumu Motoyama ✯ Hachiro Mukai ✯ Sadao S. Munemori ✯ Isamu Murakami ✯ Kiyoshi Murakami ✯ Sakae Murakami ✯ Tadataka Murakami ✯ Toshio Murakami ✯ Masaru Muramoto ✯ Kiyoshi K. Muranaga ✯ Richard Kano Murashige ✯ Robert Shigeru Murata ✯ Larry H. Muronaka ✯ Mitsugi Muronaka ✯ Roy I. Naemura ✯ Grover Kazutomi Nagaji ✯ Hiroshi Nagami ✯ Setsuo Nagano ✯ Martin Mitsuyoshi Naganuma ✯ Goichi Nagao ✯ Hitoshi Nagaoka ✯ Hideo Nagata ✯ Jim Nagata ✯ Taichi Nagata ✯ Fumitake Nagato ✯ Kaoru Naito ✯ Hitoshi Najita ✯ Masaru Nakagaki ✯ Hirao Emil Nakagawa ✯ Shoichi Nakahara ✯ Hitoshi Nakai ✯ Masao Roland

Nakama ✴ Shigenori Nakama ✴ Shinyei Nakamine ✴ Joe K. Nakamoto ✴ Seichi Nakamoto ✴ Edward Etsuzo Nakamura ✴ George I. Nakamura ✴ George S. Nakamura ✴ Henry Yoshio "Hank" Nakamura ✴ John M. Nakamura ✴ Kosei Nakamura ✴ Masaki Nakamura ✴ Ned T. Nakamura ✴ Tadao Nakamura ✴ William K. Nakamura ✴ Yoshimitsu Nakamura ✴ Masao Nakanishi ✴ Tsutomu Nakano ✴ Robert K. Nakasaki ✴ Raito R. Nakashima ✴ Donald Takashi Nakauye ✴ Minoru Nakayama ✴ Saburo Benny Nakazato ✴ John T. Narimatsu ✴ Yutaka Nezu ✴ Shigeto Niide ✴ Edward Joseph Nilges ✴ Ban Ninomiya ✴ Takao T. Ninomiya ✴ Chikao Nishi ✴ Takanori A. Nishi ✴ Kazuo Nishihara ✴ Akio Nishikawa ✴ Joe M. Nishimoto ✴ Tom T. Nishimoto ✴ Shigeki Nishimura ✴ Wilfred Katsuyuki "Kats" Nishimura ✴ Charles Jun Nishishita ✴ Chieto Nishitani ✴ Taro Nishitani ✴ Sueo Noda ✴ Yoshito Noritake ✴ Albert Yoshio "Al" Nozaki ✴ Tadashi Nozaki ✴ Alfred Shizuo Nozawa ✴ Toshio Numa ✴ Masayoshi Oba ✴ Sanichi George Oba ✴ Stanley T. Oba ✴ Larry Mitsuru Ochiai ✴ Benjamin F. Ogata ✴ Fred S. Ogata ✴ Masaru Ogata ✴ Masayoshi Ogata ✴ Tsugio Ogata ✴ Edward Ogawa ✴ John N. Ogawa ✴ Sadao Ogawa ✴ Yoshio W. Ogomori ✴ Abraham G. Ohama ✴ Arnold Ohki ✴ Shigeo Oikawa ✴ Teiji "Tag" Oishi ✴ Akira Ojiri ✴ John T. Okada ✴ Donald Mitsumi Okamoto ✴ James S. Okamoto ✴ James Takashi Okamoto ✴ Ralph Sueo Okamoto ✴ Tomiso Okamoto ✴ Isao Okazaki ✴ Takaaki Okazaki ✴ Katsu Okida ✴ Richard Masao Okimoto ✴ Seiei Okuma ✴ Toyokazu Okumura ✴ Susumu Okura ✴ Henry E. Oliver ✴ George Omokawa ✴ Kenneth Omura ✴ Takeyasu Thomas Onaga ✴ Satoru Onodera ✴ Lloyd M. Onoye ✴ Choyei Oshiro ✴ Kenneth Chiyokiyo Oshiro ✴ Sam Yasuichi Oshiro ✴ Seikichi Oshiro ✴ Wallace Hideo Oshiro ✴ Yeishin Oshiro ✴ Randall Masakatsu Ota ✴ Roy Ota ✴ Tadashi Otaguro ✴ Masanao Russell Otake ✴ Douglas Otani ✴ Kazuo Otani ✴ Akira R. Otsubo ✴ Jiro Otsuka ✴ Harumatsu Oyabu ✴ Francis

Kiichi Oyakawa ✯ Robert Yukio Ozaki ✯ George Yoshio Ozawa ✯ Francis J. Perras ✯ Roy T. Peterson ✯ Neill M. Ray ✯ Masatsugu Riyu ✯ Ben Rogers, Jr. ✯ Herbert Kazuo Sadayasu ✯ Yohei Sagami ✯ Thomas T. Sagimori ✯ Atsuo Sahara ✯ Masami Saiki ✯ Calvin T. Saito ✯ Chuji Saito ✯ George S. Saito ✯ Kinji Saito ✯ Masuto Sakado ✯ Richard Motoji Sakai ✯ Yoshinori Sakai ✯ Atsushi Sakamoto ✯ Louis Kahaulelio Sakamoto ✯ Masa Sakamoto ✯ Noboru Sakamoto ✯ Robert Isao Sakamoto ✯ Uichi Willie Sakamoto ✯ Todd T. Sakohira ✯ George S. Sameshima ✯ Uetaro Sanmonji ✯ Yoshio Fred Sasaki ✯ Toshio Sasano ✯ Itsumu Sasaoka ✯ Saburo Sato ✯ Shin Sato ✯ Shukichi Sato ✯ Tadao Sato ✯ Takeo Sato ✯ Yukio Sato ✯ George K. Sawada ✯ Kurt E. Schemel ✯ Toll Seiki ✯ Koichi Kenneth Sekimura ✯ Hihumi Seshiki ✯ George Mitsuru Shibata ✯ Kenneth K. "Gus" Shibata ✯ Masao F. Shigemura ✯ Hideo Shigeta ✯ Masao Shigezane ✯ Takeshi Shigihara ✯ Ted Takao Shikiya ✯ Roy Kokichi Shimabuku ✯ Hideo Shimabukuro ✯ Tomoaki Shimabukuro ✯ George M. Shimada ✯ Akira R. Shimatsu ✯ Gordon Satoru Shimizu ✯ Jimmy T. Shimizu ✯ Takeo Shimizu ✯ Takeo Shintani ✯ Joe A. Shiomichi ✯ Roy R. Shiozawa ✯ Kiyoshi J. Shiramizu ✯ Kizo Shirokane ✯ Henry Masayuki Shiyama ✯ Toshiaki Shoji ✯ Masaru Sogi ✯ Yeishun Soken ✯ David Isami Suda ✯ Sadami R. Sueoka ✯ Theodore Teruo Sueoka ✯ Shinichi Sugahara ✯ Kenji Sugawara ✯ Hiroshi Sugiyama ✯ Itsuo Sugiyama ✯ Togo S. Sugiyama ✯ Michiru Sumida ✯ Albert Mitsuo Sunada ✯ Nobuyuki Suwa ✯ George W. Suyama ✯ Jiro Suzawa ✯ Takashi Suzuki ✯ Edward H. Sweitzer ✯ Teruo Tabata ✯ Shigeo Tabuchi ✯ Yoshio Tagami ✯ Hitoshi Bob Taguchi ✯ Cooper T. Tahara ✯ George Yeiichi Tahira ✯ Masaru Taira ✯ Seitoku Taira ✯ Boon E. Takagi ✯ Itsuo Takahashi ✯ Iwao A. Takahashi ✯ Mon Takahashi ✯ Thomas T. Takao ✯ Ronald Kotaru Takara ✯ Gordon Kiyoshi Takasaki ✯ Katsumi L. Takasugi ✯ Shigeo Joe Takata ✯ John Nobuo Takayama ✯ Yoshito Jack Takayama ✯ Masaharu Takeba ✯

Shoichi J. Takehara ✷ Yoshinobu Takei ✷ Haruo Takemoto ✷ Iwao Takemoto ✷ Tami Takemoto ✷ Tooru Takenaka ✷ Robert Masaru Takeo ✷ Jimmy Taketa ✷ Shigeto Taketa ✷ William H. Taketa ✷ Tadashi T. Takeuchi ✷ Kenji Takubo ✷ Kunio Douglas Tamanaha ✷ Masao H. Tamanaha ✷ Thomas Tamotsu Tamashiro ✷ Masaru Tamura ✷ Toyoshi Tamura ✷ Kei Tanahashi ✷ Harley Tanaka ✷ Jack Manabu Tanaka ✷ Jiro Tanaka ✷ John T. Tanaka ✷ John Y. Tanaka ✷ Keichi Tanaka ✷ Ko Tanaka ✷ Matsusaburo Tanaka ✷ Saburo Tanamachi ✷ Larry Tadayuki Tanimoto ✷ Teruto Tanimoto ✷ Yukio E. Tanimoto ✷ Mitsuo Tanji ✷ Katsushi Tanouye ✷ Ted T. Tanouye ✷ Haruyoshi H. Tateyama ✷ George Tatsumi ✷ Masaru Tengan ✷ Yoshio Tengwan ✷ Henry Mamoru Terada ✷ Ted Akira Teramae ✷ Lloyd Masato Teramoto ✷ Shizuo Teramoto ✷ Herman Takeyoshi Teruya ✷ Kenkichi Kenneth Teruya ✷ Michio Teshima ✷ Theodore T. Tezuka ✷ Shiro Togo ✷ Clifford Toshikazu Tokunaga ✷ Hidetoshi Tokusato ✷ H. H. Tokushima ✷ Patrick Mitsuru Tokushima ✷ Minoru Tokuyama ✷ Tsugiyasu Toma ✷ Yasukichi Jerry Toma ✷ Calvin Tetsuo Tomikawa ✷ Hiroichi Tomita ✷ Isami Tomita ✷ Nobuaki Tomita ✷ Taro Tonai ✷ Minoru Tosaka ✷ Richard Kanse Toyama ✷ Shinsuke Toyama ✷ Shichizo Toyota ✷ Daniel Tsukamoto ✷ Ichiro Tsukano ✷ Kenichi Tsumaki ✷ Bertram Akira Tsunematsu ✷ Kazumi Tsutsui ✷ Yasuji M. Uchima ✷ James Koichi Uejo ✷ Kazumi Uemoto ✷ Howard Mitsuru Urabe ✷ Moriichi Uyeda ✷ Theodore "Ted" Toshiyuki Uyeno ✷ Daniel Matayoshi Wada ✷ Kenneth Yoshikazu Wasada ✷ Shigeo Wasano ✷ Hiroshi Watanabe ✷ Kiyotoshi Watanabe ✷ Theodore H. "Ted" Watanabe ✷ James Wheatley ✷ Floyd Earl White, Jr. ✷ Steve Seiki Yagi ✷ Hideo Yamada ✷ Raymond Tsukasa Yamada ✷ Torao Yamamizu ✷ Fred M. Yamamoto ✷ George Ikuo Yamamoto ✷ John H. Yamamoto ✷ Masaru Yamamoto ✷ Takeo Yamamoto ✷ Thomas Isamu Yamanaga ✷ Tsutomu Yamaoka ✷ Harry Shizuo Yamasaki ✷ Gordon Kenshi Yamashiro ✷ Lei

Seijiro Yamashiro ✶ Kazuo "Red" Yamashita ✶ Setsuro Yamashita ✶ Chiyoaki Jerry Yamauchi ✶ Gordon Yamaura ✶ Fred S. Yasuda ✶ Joe R. Yasuda ✶ Arata Yasuhira ✶ Hideo Yasui ✶ Yoji O. Yasui ✶ Mitsuru Yeto ✶ Matsuichi Yogi ✶ Hideo Fuku Yonamine ✶ Hitoshi Yonemura ✶ Kenjiro Yoshida ✶ Minoru Yoshida ✶ Yoshiharu Edward Yoshida ✶ Mitsuichi Yoshigai ✶ Toraichi Yoshihara ✶ Jacob Yoshio Yoshimura ✶ Minoru Yoshimura ✶ Saburo Yoshimura ✶ Akira Yoshinaga ✶ Isami Yoshioka ✶ Tatsuo Yoshizaki ✶ Shiyoji Yunoki

The Contributors

George Akita (Military Intelligence Service) is professor emeritus of Japanese history at the University of Hawaii at Manoa. For the last decade, Akita has been spending much of his time in Japan, transcribing and translating the sosho-written (flowing script calligraphy) letters and documents of the Meiji and Taisho era political leaders which are housed in the National Diet Library in Tokyo. The transcribed documents will be published in Japan by Akita and Japanese scholars. They are an important part of a major political history on the Meiji and Taisho eras which Akita is writing.

Stanley M. Akita (100th Infantry Battalion) was one of only a handful of sansei who served in World War II. Akita was in the first group of 442nd volunteers sent into combat to replenish the injury-plagued 100th Battalion. Akita worked for the Department of Transportation as an engineer in the Highways Division. He retired from the state in 1978. Akita and his wife, Yukie—a native of Mountain View, Hawaii—are the parents of two adult daughters and have one grandson.

Governor George R. Ariyoshi (Military Intelligence Service) was elected America's first governor of Asian ancestry in 1974, after serving a year as acting governor during the term of the late Governor John A. Burns. Ariyoshi served until 1986, an unprecedented three terms. Governor Ariyoshi's political career spanned more than three decades, beginning with his election to the territorial House of Representatives and culminating with his election as governor. Since retiring from political office, he has shared his time with a number of community and business organizations, serving as chairman of the board of governors of the East-West Center, president of the Center for International Commercial Dispute Resolution and honorary co-chair of the Japanese American National Museum, among others. He was also appointed to the President's Advisory Committee on Trade Policy and Negotiations and to the board of the Public Broadcasting Service (PBS). Governor Ariyoshi is president of Prince Resorts Hawaii; a partner with Cole, Gilburne, Goldhaber and Ariyoshi; and Of Counsel with the law firm of Watanabe, Ing and Kawashima. He holds honorary doctorate degrees from a number of international universities. The Governor was awarded the Grand Cordon of the Sacred Treasure, First Class by the Government of Japan in 1985, and the Emperor's Silver Cup in 1987. Governor Ariyoshi and his wife, Jean, have three adult children and one grandchild. The birth of his grandson, Sky, inspired the Governor to write his autobiography, *With Obligation to All*, which was published by the Ariyoshi Foundation in 1997.

Lyn Crost was a reporter for the Associated Press in Washington, D.C., prior to signing on with the *Honolulu Star-Bulletin* as its European war correspondent. A magna cum laude graduate of Boston University, she covered the 100th Infantry Battalion and the 442nd Regimental Combat Team on the frontlines. After the war, Crost served as the Star-Bulletin's Washington correspondent before joining the administration of President Dwight D. Eisenhower. The members of Club 100 recognized Crost for her many contributions to perpetuating their legacy by naming her an honorary member of the organization. Crost maintained close ties with many in the Japanese American community in Hawaii as well as on the Mainland. In 1994, she fulfilled her long-held goal of sharing the story of the 100th Infantry Battalion, 442nd Regimental Combat Team and the Military Intelligence Service with mainstream America with the publication of her book, *Honor by Fire: Japanese Americans at War in Europe and the Pacific*. Crost died in 1997 in Washington, D.C., where she and her husband, Dr. Thomas Stern, had resided.

Mrs. Kikuyo Fujimoto and her husband, Hikosuke, sent two sons off to war: Kunio, who was drafted into the 100th Infantry Battalion, and Hikoso, who volunteered for the 442nd Regimental Combat Team. Mr. Fujimoto worked as a steward to Hawaii's last reigning monarch, Queen Lili'uokalani, until her passing. He later found work as a butcher at the Moana Surfrider and Royal Hawaiian hotels. Mrs. Fujimoto worked as a housekeeper at the Royal Hawaiian Hotel. A widow since 1959, Mrs. Fujimoto will celebrate her one hundredth birthday this October. She has five children, ten grandchildren, seventeen great-grandchildren, and five great-great grandchildren.

Yoshiaki Fujitani (Military Intelligence Service) completed his sophomore year at the University of Hawaii after the war and then transferred to the University of Chicago, where he earned his master's degree. Fujitani also did post-graduate work in Buddhism at Kyoto University and Ryukoku University. He was ordained a Jodo Shinshu (Pure Land Buddhism) priest in 1955. Two decades later, he was elected Bishop of the Honpa Hongwanji Mission of Hawaii, serving until 1987, when he was appointed director of the Buddhist Study Center. A former police chaplain, Fujitani is president of the Institute for Religion and Social Change. He serves on the boards of the Samaritan Counseling Center of Hawaii, American Civil Liberties Union, and the Military Intelligence Service Veterans Club. He has been honored for his many contributions to the community by the McKinley High School Alumni Association, Honpa Hongwanji Mission of Hawaii, and the Samaritan Counseling Center of Hawaii. Fujitani and his wife, Tomi, are the parents of three adult children.

Takejiro Higa (Military Intelligence Service), who lived in Okinawa until just before the outbreak of World War II, completed high school in Hawaii after the war. He graduated from the University of Hawaii and then went to work as an agent for the Internal Revenue Service, from which he retired in 1990. Higa remains active with Hawaii's Okinawan community, Jikoen Hongwanji Mission, and the MIS Veterans Club. He continues to travel to Okinawa, where he visits with his former teacher. Higa and his wife, Ruby, have two adult sons and one granddaughter.

Chaplain Hiro Higuchi (442nd Regimental Combat Team), who had already graduated from Oberlin College in Ohio before the war, ministered to the 442nd soldiers on the battlefields of Europe. He returned to Oberlin for graduate studies in theology after the war. Chaplain Higuchi served as a minister in Waimea, Kauai, and at the Waipahu Community, Pearl City Community, and Manoa Valley churches, all of which he was instrumental in constructing. The highly respected minister also supported the communities in which he provided spiritual guidance, mobilizing the Waimea community to build a swimming pool, and the Lions Club to construct a visitor pavilion at the Waimano Training School and Hospital in Pearl City. He also served as chaplain of Oahu Prison in 1955. Higuchi and his wife, Hisako, raised two children: son Peter and daughter Jane. Chaplain Higuchi maintained close ties with the boys in the 442nd until his passing in 1981.

Jesse M. Hirata (100th Infantry Battalion) worked as a laundry supervisor at a Sand Island dry cleaning business before starting his own in 1948. He retired from the business in 1983 and embarked on a new career as a tour guide and later a handyman. He recently turned over the business, "Nandemo Yaru Ya," to his son. These days, Hirata spends much of his time leading Jehovah's Witness Bible study groups.

Edward Ichiyama (442nd Regimental Combat Team) worked for the Social Security Administration for nearly thirty years—the last ten overseeing Hawaii, Guam, American Samoa, and Saipan as Pacific area manager. While working at the administration's headquarters in Baltimore, Maryland, he earned his law degree by attending night classes at the University of Maryland law school. Ichiyama entered private practice after retiring from the Social Security Administration. In 1995 he served on a state committee to commemorate the fiftieth anniversary of the end of World War II. Ichiyama coordinated participation by AJA veterans in the historic event. Of late, he has been coordinating military upgrades for recipients of the army's Distinguished Service Cross. Ichiyama and his wife, Connie—who was interned during World War II—are often asked to share their wartime experiences with high school and college students.

Kenneth Inada (442nd Regimental Combat Team) retired in 1997 from State University of New York at Buffalo, where he had been a professor of philosophy since 1969. Inada began his teaching career at the University of Hawaii at Manoa in 1960 after receiving his doctorate in Indian and Buddhist philosophy from the University of Tokyo. While at State University, he was recognized as a Distinguished Service Professor, a rank above full professor. Last year Inada and his wife, Masako, retired to Henderson, Nevada, where he continues his research, writing and editing of Chinese and Japanese Buddhist texts for the Numata Center for Buddhist Translation and Research in Berkeley, California. Kenneth and Masako Inada are the parents of an adult son.

U.S. Senator Daniel Inouye (442nd Regimental Combat Team) returned to Hawaii as a highly decorated U.S. Army captain—his dream of becoming a surgeon dashed after losing his right arm in combat. He enrolled at the University of Hawaii, where he met and married Margaret Awamura. Inouye earned his law degree from George Washington University law school in Washington, D.C. The Inouyes returned to Hawaii, where the future senator was hired in 1953 as a deputy prosecutor with the City and County of Honolulu. Inouye first ran for elective office in 1954, leading the ticket in a race for territorial House of Representatives. In 1958 he was elected to the territorial Senate. A year later, Inouye became Hawaii's first elected member of the U.S. House of Representatives. In 1962 he challenged the son of a prominent Hawaii Republican for the U.S. Senate and won, capturing nearly seventy percent of the vote. The senator has risen to national prominence over the years, delivering the keynote address at the 1968 Democratic National Convention and serving as co-chair of the 1984 convention. He also served as a member of the Senate Watergate Committee in 1973 and 1974. Senator and Mrs. Inouye have an adult son.

Joseph R. Itagaki (442nd Regimental Combat Team) returned to managing the Kemoo Farms restaurant in Wahiawa after the war. In 1950, he became owner and manager of the Kewalo Inn restaurant. Itagaki also ran for political office as a Republican in 1946 and was elected to the territorial House of Representatives and to the territorial Senate in 1951. Itagaki was involved in a number of civic and community organizations, including the 442nd Veterans Club and the Rotary Club of West Honolulu. He had two sons.

Warren Iwai (100th Infantry Battalion), a St. Louis College graduate, worked for the federal government for thirty years, most of them as an Internal Revenue Service agent in the Honolulu office. Now retired, he enjoys golfing, raising orchids, and traveling. Warren and Betty Iwai raised four daughters and have five grandchildren.

Seiso Kamishita (100th Infantry Battalion) worked as a mechanic on Guam for a year following his discharge from the army. After returning to Hawaii, he worked as an automotive equipment inspector for the U.S. Army at Fort Shafter and later at Schofield Barracks. He retired after thirty-five years of service with the federal government. Kamishita remains active with Club 100's Baker and Rural chapters. He and his wife, Kay, have three daughters and five grandchildren.

Robert N. Katayama (442nd Regimental Combat Team) began his college education at the University of Hawaii after the war. He graduated from Yale and George Washington law schools. Katayama was recalled to active duty during the Korean War and later served as Staff Judge Advocate during the Vietnam War. He was a partner and is presently Of Counselor with the law firm of Carlsmith Ball Wichman Case & Ichiki. He is also honorary chairman of Kapolei Golf Course and president of Kapolei Holding Corporation. Katayama is actively involved in the Japanese American community, serving as president of the 442nd Veterans Club; trustee of the 442nd Regimental Combat Team Foundation; president of the Oahu AJA Veterans Council in 1997; governor of the National Japanese American Memorial Foundation; and director of the Japanese Cultural Center of Hawaii. The father of three adult children and a widower for many years, Katayama recently wed Jeanne Nakamura, the widow of a fellow 442nd veteran.

Minoru Kishaba (442nd Regimental Combat Team) and his wife, Molly, relocated to California in 1954. Lahaina-born "Chappie" Kishaba retired from Rockwell International after 21 years as an electronic technician, and then returned to work for another nine years as a test engineer for Northrup Corporation. The Kishabas have three adult children and one grandson. They reside in La Mirada, California, where they keep busy with their family and support their church.

Katsumi Kometani (100th Infantry Battalion), a dentist by profession, was a member of the territory's wartime Emergency Service Committee. He was in his mid-thirties when he volunteered to serve as the 100th's morale officer, rising to the rank of captain in the 100th. Kometani resumed his dental practice after the war, retiring in 1972. He served on numerous boards and commissions, held leadership positions with nonprofit organizations such as the Boy Scouts of America, and served on the board of directors of several corporations. At one point, Kometani also owned the Asahis baseball team. He received an imperial decoration from the Government of Japan and was also honored with the USC Alumni Merit Award by the University of Southern California, from which he earned his degree as a doctor of dental surgery. Kometani and his wife, Yaeko, raised four children. Dr. Kometani passed away in 1979.

Hideto Kono (442nd Regimental Combat Team and Military Intelligence Service), who chaired the Hawaii Nikkei History Editorial Board, was director of Hawaii's Department of Planning and Economic Development (forerunner of the Department of Business, Economic Development and Tourism) from 1974 to 1983. He was appointed to the post by Governor George Ariyoshi. Kono was later appointed president of the Japan-America Institute of Management Science (JAIMS). He served as chairman of the board of the Japanese Cultural Center of Hawaii in 1991-92. Prior to entering government and public service, Kono headed Castle & Cooke East Asia, Ltd., based in Tokyo. Kono and his wife, Fannie, have four adult children and eight grandchildren.

Hoichi Kubo (100th Infantry Battalion and Military Intelligence Service) learned the grocery business in Minnesota before returning to Hawaii after the war. Back in the islands, he worked for a company that serviced Hawaii wholesalers. Kubo later relocated to San Jose, California, where he and his brothers operated the Aloha Supermarket for twenty years. He retired in 1984. Kubo and his wife, Mary, have two adult children: their daughter is a schoolteacher, and their son is a retired navy captain who graduated from the U.S. Naval Academy at Annapolis. Hoichi Kubo died in February of this year.

Henry S. Kuniyuki (442nd Regimental Combat Team) worked as a veterans employment representative and unit chief for the territorial and later state Department of Labor and Industrial Relations. He was also state director of the U.S. Labor Department's Veterans Employment and Training Service with jurisdiction over the state of Hawaii and the territory of Guam. He retired from the post in 1981 after twenty years of service. Kuniyuki served as 1994-95 president of the 442nd Veterans Club and earlier this year chaired the Brothers in Valor monument project, which was dedicated at Fort DeRussy. Kuniyuki is currently president and chief executive officer of Kuniyuki Brothers, Inc.

U.S. Senator Spark M. Matsunaga (100th Infantry Battalion and Military Intelligence Service), who was twice wounded in battle, was assigned to the Military Intelligence Service Language School at Fort Snelling, Minnesota, from October 1944 until July 1945. He served in a number of positions, including company commander. The Senator earned his law degree from Harvard Law School and was admitted to the Hawaii Bar in 1952. He served as an assistant prosecutor with the City and County of Honolulu. Matsunaga was elected to the territorial House of Representatives in 1954 and re-elected in 1956 and 1958. He served in the U.S. House of Representatives from 1962 to 1976. Matsunaga was elected to the U.S. Senate in 1976 and re-elected in 1982 and 1988. Senator Matsunaga, who served as president of Club 100 from 1953 to 1954, was instrumental in the passage of the Civil Rights Act of 1988, often referred to as the redress bill, which he introduced as H.R. 442. The Senator also played a major role in the establishment of the Matsunaga Institute for Peace at the University of Hawaii. Senator Matsunaga and his wife, Helene, raised five children and have seven grandchildren. Sparky Matsunaga died in office in 1990.

Michael Miyatake (442nd Regimental Combat Team and Military Intelligence Service), who was commissioned a second lieutenant just before the end of the war, was discharged from the military in October 1945. He returned to Puna and subsequently enrolled at the University of Hawaii, specializing in industrial relations. Miyatake was recalled to active duty in 1950, during the Korean War, and served until 1953. He returned to the university and earned his bachelor's degree in business administration the following year. Miyatake worked for the U.S. Customs Service, from which he retired in 1974.

Tom Mizuno (442nd Regimental Combat Team) played baseball for the AJA and Hawaii leagues prior to being drafted into the 442nd. He settled on the Big Island of Hawaii with his wife, Mildred, after the war. Mizuno worked for the Hawaiian Agricultural Company and coached baseball at Pahala High School. He later worked for Hawaii County's Department of Parks and Recreation before getting into the auto sales business, from which he retired. He remains active in Hilo's 442nd Veterans Club and is a member of the Disabled American Veterans. Mizuno and his wife, Betty, have four children, nine grandchildren and three great-grandchildren.

Walter "Biffa" Moriguchi (100th Infantry Battalion) returned to work in the service department at Universal Motors in Honolulu in 1948 following his release from Walter Reed Army Hospital. He and his wife, Chieko, raised three children, have nine grandchildren, and are excitedly awaiting the birth of their first great-grandchild this year.

Tsutomu Tom Nagata (100th Infantry Battalion) recovered from wounds he suffered near Cassino, Italy, and returned to his native Maui after the war. Nagata worked for the U.S. Postal Service, from which he retired in 1980. He and his wife, Fumiko, have three children and six grandchildren. In his retirement, Nagata enjoys traveling and short line fishing.

Raymond R. Nosaka (100th Infantry Battalion) attended engineering school in San Francisco and the University of Hawaii after being discharged from the army. He worked as an agent with the Internal Revenue Service for more than twenty years before joining the Veterans Administration as a counselor. He also worked as a social worker with the state Department of Social Services. A flyweight boxing champion at Camp Shelby and a barefoot football and softball player and bowler in his younger years, Nosaka's interest these days are more musical, playing his guitar and *ukulele* and singing. He is a former president of Club 100 and Baker Chapter. Nosaka and his wife, Aki, have three adult children.

Ronald Oba (442nd Regimental Combat Team) enjoyed a long career in the health care industry, which included a tenure as chief operating officer of Kuakini Hospital and administrator of Hilo Hospital on the Big Island of Hawaii. Oba served as president of the 442nd Veterans Club in 1992 and 1993, the fiftieth anniversary of the formation of the unit. He also authored a book on his army company titled, *The Men of Company F.* In 1995 he served as Hawaii coordinator for a homecoming trip to Camp Shelby, Mississippi. Oba also coauthored *The 'Ole Man—Father Kenneth A. Bray,* on the life of the beloved Iolani School football coach. Oba and his wife, Michi, reside in Aiea.

Tokuji Ono (100th Infantry Battalion) resumed his career in education after the war, initially as a classroom teacher and later as a school administrator. He served as principal at Waimea High and Elementary School on Kauai and at Kailua, Washington and Kalakaua intermediate schools. Ono retired from the Department of Education in 1974 and worked part-time as a tour guide. These days, he can be found pulling grounds maintenance duties at his son-in-law's office building. Ono and his wife, Toshiko, are the parents of three adult children and grandparents to four grandchildren.

Robert K. Sakai (Military Intelligence Service) was discharged from the army in February 1947. He continued his study of Asian history, earning his doctorate in history from Harvard University in 1953. Sakai taught at the University of Nebraska at Lincoln for fifteen years, rising from an assistant professor of history to chair of the department. He joined the University of Hawaii at Manoa in 1966 as a professor of Japanese history, retiring in 1984 as professor emeritus of history. During his tenure at UH, he also served as curator of the Gannett Fellows Program for Journalists (since renamed the Freedom Forum Fellows Program).

Sakai has published extensively on the Satsuma Clan and the Ryukyu Islands and has lectured at prestigious universities in Japan. He served as 1996-98 president of the Japan-America Society of Hawaii and is involved in numerous community and educational programs, among them the Crown Prince Akihito Scholarship Committee, the Joseph Heco Society, and the Japanese Cultural Center of Hawaii. In 1985, Sakai was awarded the Third Order of the Sacred Treasure by the Government of Japan.

Richard M. Sakakida (Military Intelligence Service) was finally reunited with his family in December 1945. A career military officer, he returned to the Philippines for two years after the war and then spent nineteen years in Japan, several of them as part of the Occupation forces. Sakakida was commissioned a lieutenant in the U.S. Army. In 1948 he transferred to the air force, from which he retired in 1975 at the rank of lieutenant colonel. Throughout his life, Sakakida suffered recurring pain from the torture he had endured. Sworn to secrecy, he kept his experiences a secret for more than twenty years. In July 1988, Sakakida was inducted into the Military Intelligence Hall of Fame at Fort Huachuca in Arizona. Sakakida's experiences as an American spy are detailed in Wayne Kiyosaki's 1995 book, *A Spy in Their Midst*. Sakakida and his wife, Cherry, resided in Fremont, California, where he died in 1996. As he requested, Sakakida was laid to rest in his native Hawaii at the National Memorial Cemetery of the Pacific at Punchbowl.

Samuel Sasai (442nd Regimental Combat Team) returned from the war and earned both his bachelor of science degree in economics and his master's in business administration from the Wharton School of Finance and Commerce at the University of Pennsylvania. Sasai retired from the Bank of Hawaii in 1983 after thirty-two years of service. He remains active with the 442nd's Headquarters Company, Third Battalion. Sasai and his wife, Michie, have two adult sons.

Robert Sato (100th Infantry Battalion) worked as a censor supervisor for the U.S. government in Tokyo after the war. He earned his bachelor's degree in international relations from Bradley University in Peoria, Illinois, where he was a champion chess player. Sato also did post graduate work at Mexico City College. He was previously assistant vice president and director of public relations for Manoa Finance. Sato taught citizenship classes in McKinley High School's adult education program. He and his wife, Kazue, raised two daughters, both of whom are active members of the Sons and Daughters of the 100th Infantry Battalion. Bob Sato guarded second base in the Makule Softball League until 1995 when he hung up his cleats, capping a sixty-year career.

Don Seki (442nd Regimental Combat Team) visited his parents in Tokyo after being discharged from Tripler Hospital in December 1946. They had returned to Japan in 1941. Seki joined a group of 100th Battalion and 442nd veterans who had signed on in early 1947 to supervise the construction of Tachikawa Air Base. He returned to Hawaii later that year and went on to investigate job opportunities in California. Seki worked at the U.S. Naval shipyard at Terminal Island in Long Beach for twenty-six years, retiring in 1977. He and his wife, Sumiko, are the parents of four children and have two grandsons.

Joe Shimamura (442nd Regimental Combat Team) was eighteen years old and had just graduated from Farrington High School when he volunteered for the 442nd. He served with K Company. Shimamura returned to Hawaii after receiving a medical discharge for an injured shoulder. He attended the Chicago College of Optometry in Illinois and then opened his own optometric practice in Hawaii. He made it his livelihood for thirty-two years. Shimamura and his wife, Mildred, have four grown children and four grandchildren.

Adam A. "Bud" Smyser was a journalist with the *Honolulu Star-Bulletin* for 37 years before retiring in 1983 as editorial page editor. A native of Pennsylvania, he first came to Hawaii as a U.S. Navy officer during World War II. Smyser returned to the Islands after the war and made it his home. As a journalist, he has been a witness to virtually every turn in Hawaii's history in the last fifty years. Since retiring, Smyser has written a column for the Star-Bulletin titled "Hawaii's World." Hawaii's World War II soldiers of Japanese ancestry have been the subject of many of his columns. Smyser, an honorary member of Club 100, has received numerous awards for journalism. In 1997 he was appointed to the Governor's Blue Ribbon Panel on Living and Dying with Dignity.

Kan Tagami (Military Intelligence Service) was sent to Tokyo with the Occupation forces after the war. He served as General Douglas MacArthur's personal interpreter until MacArthur was relieved of duty as commander in chief in April 1951. Tagami earned his bachelor's degree from the University of Maryland in 1954. He made the military his career, retiring at the rank of major after twenty years of service. Tagami and his wife Sadae were married in Tokyo in 1947. They have five children.

Sakae Takahashi (100th Infantry Battalion) was discharged from the army in 1946 at the rank of major. He went on to earn his law degree from Rutgers University. Takahashi served as deputy city and county attorney from 1949 to 1950, when he was elected to the Honolulu Board of Supervisors (forerunner of today's Honolulu City Council). He was also appointed territorial treasurer and later elected territorial and state senator. In 1954, Takahashi helped organize and establish Central Pacific Bank. He chaired the bank's board of directors from 1972 to 1989 and served on the boards of several other Hawaii businesses. Takahashi and his wife, Bette, have four grown children. He is an active member of Club 100, the Hawaii Army Museum Society, and the Japanese Cultural Center of Hawaii.

Fujio Takaki (Military Intelligence Service), who served with the Counterintelligence Corps (CIC) during the occupation of Japan, remained with CIC after returning to Hawaii. From 1964 to 1966, he was the CIC's liaison with the FBI in New York City. Takaki retired from military service in 1967, ending his 23-

year military career with a tour of duty in Vietnam. After returning to civilian life, he worked as a maintenance supervisor for Kahala Mall, from which he retired in 1987. In April 1994 Takaki returned to Maizuru City with his wife, Cecilia, for the first time since the war and saw what had become of the seedlings he had been instrumental in planting in Kyoraku Park after the war. The Takakis have four adult children and two grandchildren.

Ben Tamashiro (100th Infantry Battalion) returned to Hawaii in July 1944 after twice being injured in Italy. Following his discharge, he worked as a supply clerk at the Ordnance Depot at Fort Shafter. Tamashiro was a military plans officer when he retired in 1976. He and his wife, Gloria, are the parents of five daughters and have seven grandchildren. In their retirement, the husband and wife duo embarked on a new career—as actors. They have been featured in Kumu Kahua Theatre productions and in television commercials as Bank of Hawaii's folksy husband and wife team, "Harry and Myra." An avid reader and writer, Tamashiro volunteers his time with the U.S. Army Museum Society, Japanese Cultural Center of Hawaii, and the Manoa Valley Church. He is often called upon to speak on his World War II experiences by schools and the University of Hawaii.

Tadashi Tojo (442nd Regimental Combat Team) attended Michigan State University before returning to Hawaii, where he started a poultry farm in Waianae. A few years later, he went to work for Governor George Ariyoshi, chairing the state's Agricultural Coordinating Committee. He continued in the post in Governor John Waihee's administration. Tojo then joined the University of Hawaii, working in the Agricultural Extension Service, from which he retired in 1995. In his retirement, Tojo does volunteer work and also enjoys the company of his 442nd buddies. He and his wife, Harriet, are the parents of three children and have two grandchildren.

Mike Tokunaga (100th Infantry Battalion) returned to Hawaii and finally enrolled at the University of Hawaii, graduating in three years. He worked for the Hawaii Government Employees Association (HGEA) before joining the administration of the late Governor John Burns, and subsequently, Governor George Ariyoshi. The Lahaina-born Tokunaga joined the Democratic Party in its fledgling years and became a trusted advisor to the party and its top office holders. After retiring in 1986, he got more actively involved in perpetuating the legacy of the World War II nisei soldiers by sharing his experiences with university and high school students. Mike and Betty Tokunaga raised three adult children and have five grandchildren.

John Tsukano (442nd Regimental Combat Team and 100th Infantry Battalion) was in the first group of 442nd soldiers sent to replenish the injury-plagued 100th Battalion. A native of Puunene, Maui and a graduate of Baldwin High School, Tsukano attended the University of Hawaii after the war. He worked in the entertainment and visitor industries for many years prior to retiring. In 1985, he published Bridge of Love, a highly acclaimed book on the World War II experiences of Hawaii's Japanese Americans. Tsukano's contribution to *Japanese Eyes . . . American Heart*, was excerpted and re-edited from *Bridge of Love*. Tsukano has two adult sons, John and Tod. He and his wife, Judy, reside in Kaneohe.

Conrad Tsukayama (100th Infantry Battalion) was discharged from the army at the rank of first lieutenant. He resumed his military career with the Hawaii National Guard, helping to establish Hawaii's air defense system. He retired as a lieutenant colonel. Tsukayama subsequently worked for the U.S. Property and Fiscal Office, which was responsible for distributing equipment to the National Guard. He retired in 1976 after more than twenty-five years of service. Tsukayama remains an active member of Club 100's Dog Chapter. He and his wife, Yoshi, raised four boys and have seven grandchildren.

Ted Tsukiyama (442nd Regimental Combat Team and Military Intelligence Service) returned to the University of Hawaii after the war and completed his final year in college at Indiana University. He earned his law degree from Yale Law School in 1950 and was admitted to the Hawaii Bar that same year. Early in his legal career, Tsukiyama worked with attorney Masaji Marumoto, who was subsequently appointed associate justice of the Hawaii Supreme Court. An arbitrator for forty years, he has issued hundreds of arbitration decisions. Tsukiyama serves as historian for the Varsity Victory Volunteers, 442nd Veterans Club and the MIS Veterans Club and is a trustee for the 442nd Regimental Combat Team Foundation. An avid bonsai hobbyist, Tsukiyama is also coordinator of the Japanese Cultural Center of Hawaii's Oral History Committee and an active member of Harris United Methodist Church. Ted and his wife, Fuku, are the parents of three adult children and have four grandchildren.

Albert Farrant Turner is the son of Lieutenant Colonel Farrant L. "Old Man" Turner, first commanding officer of the 100th Infantry Battalion. "Bert" Turner was a student at Punahou School when the Hawaiian Provisional Infantry Battalion shipped out of Hawaii in June 1942. He and his mother sailed to the West Coast with the AJA soldiers. He spent many weekends at Camp McCoy, watching the 100th boys play sports. Bert Turner served in the Air Corps during World War II. He also received an appointment to the U.S. military academy at West Point and served in the Korean War. Bert Turner retired from the military as a full colonel in 1971. He retired earlier this year as vice president of Greig Associates. Turner and his wife, Vonnie, have three adult children and six grandchildren.

Ernest Uno (442nd Regimental Combat Team), who volunteered for the 442nd from the Amache concentration camp, earned his bachelor's degree from Whittier College in 1950. He made the YMCA his career, working for "Y" organizations in California, Washington state and Hawaii. His career with the YMCA spanned three decades. Uno and his wife, Grace, raised three children. An ordained deacon in the Episcopal Church, Uno currently serves as chaplain of the 442nd Veterans Club. He also volunteers his time with the St. Francis Hospice program and with the U.S. Department of Veterans Affairs.

Chaplain Masao Yamada (442nd Regimental Combat Team), who studied theology at Auburn Theological Seminary in Auburn, New York, and at Andover-Newton Theological Seminary in Boston, Massachusetts, took a half-year sabbatical from the ministry to help organize the 442nd Veterans Club. He resumed his United Church of Christ ministry in 1946, serving as the first nisei pastor of the Church of the Holy Cross in Hilo until 1955. While living in Hilo, he was instrumental in establishing the Hilo campus of the University of Hawaii. The 442nd chaplain was an orchid hobbyist who was honored by having an orchid named after him. He and his wife, Ai, had three sons, six grandchildren and six great-grandchildren. Chaplain Yamada died in 1984.

Ben I. Yamamoto (100th Infantry Battalion and Military Intelligence Service) was in the first group of 100th Battalion soldiers selected for the Military Intelligence Service Language School. Yamamoto returned to Hawaii after the war and attended the University of Hawaii. He eventually took over his father's gas station and car repair business. The business has since closed, but Yamamoto continues to manage the property, which his family still owns. Ben Yamamoto and his wife, Constance, are the parents of two adult children and have three grandchildren and one great-grandchild.

Sohei Yamate (Military Intelligence Service), who swam and fished while growing up on Kauai, served his country in the China-Burma-India theater of operations. He earned his bachelor's degree from the University of Hawaii and his master's in retailing from Simmons College in Boston. Yamate spent most of his career working as an investment counselor. He previously served as president of the MIS Veterans Club in Honolulu and the Military Interpreters Club of Hilo. He and his wife, Margaret, have an adult daughter who lives on the Mainland.

Kaoru Yonezawa (100th Infantry Battalion), who served in E and C companies during the war, returned to work at Lewers & Cooke following his discharge from the army. He retired from the *kamaaina* company in 1978 after more than thirty-three years of service. Yonezawa was a volunteer calligraphy instructor for the Japanese Cultural Center of Hawaii. He continues to volunteer his time with the United Japanese Society of Hawaii and enjoys singing *karaoke* in his free time.

Chaplain Israel Yost (100th Infantry Battalion) joined the 100th about a month after it entered combat in Italy. The Lutheran minister was twenty-seven years old at the time and the father of two; his second child was born two weeks after Yost went overseas. The Yosts lived in Hawaii for a time after the war before resettling on the Mainland. In 1983, Club 100 members raised more than $8,400 to fly Yost and his wife to Hawaii to be a part of the unit's 40th anniversary celebration. The Yosts now reside in Pennsylvania.

Index

Abe, Sgt. Masao, 130

Aiso, John, 180, 330

AJA (Americans of Japanese Ancestry), 53, 329. *See also* Japanese Americans; nisei

Akins, Capt. Tom, 223

Akita, George, 411; diary entries on Pearl Harbor attack, 36–44; essay on patriotism and civic duty, 24–25; on nisei biculturalism, 340–342

Akita, Stanley M.: POW experience of, 203–218

Akiyama, Hideo, 80

Aleutian Islands: documents from, 178; invasion of, 8

Allied Translator and Interpreter Section (ATIS), 100, 171, 331

Allied Translator Service (ATS), 316

Amache (Colorado) Relocation Center, 138, 142, 220

Americans of Japanese Ancestry (AJA), 53, 329. *See also* Japanese Americans; nisei

Anami, Korechika (Japanese general), 338

Anchan (Hajime Akita) (elder brother of George Akita), 43

Andersen, Col. Wilhelm A., 152

Anderson, Gen. Michael, 188

Anderson, Lt. Daniel, 188

Angaur Island. *See* Palau Islands

Anti-Tank Company (Platoon), of 442nd RCT, 5, 6, 88, 113

Anzai, Toshi, 234, 249

Anzio (Italy): 100th Infantry Battalion at, 61, 75, 80, 203, 386–387; 442nd RCT at, 88

Aoki, Dan, 375–379

Aomori (Japan), 81st Infantry Division at, 132–133

Ara, Bsp. Ryokan, 409–412

Araki, Sadao (Japanese general), 338

Ariyoshi, George R., 340, 376, 378; autobiographical essay by, 359–369; on *okage sama de,* 303–310, 369

Arizona, USS, 55

Army Corps of Engineers, U.S., 219, 231

Asahi, Chief Petty Officer, 311, 312

Asai, Ralph, 62

Ashida, Hitoshi (Japanese prime minister), 317

ATIS (Allied Translator and Interpreter Section), 100, 171, 331

ATS (Allied Translator Service), 316

Awakuni, Masao, 374

Ball, Joseph (U.S. senator from Minnesota), 134

Bataan (Philippines), 163, 332

Bello (a scout), 195

Belmont (France), liberation of, 6, 225, 338

Belvedere, liberation of, 257

Biffontaine (France), liberation of,

4, 6, 113, 116, 198, 204–205, 338, 388

Binotti, Lt. Albert, 289

Bissell, Gen. Clayton, 329

Bronze Star Medals: for 100th Infantry Battalion, 4, 397; for 442nd RCT, 6, 352, 397; for MIS, 169

Brown, Kenny, 378

Bruyeres (France), liberation of, 4, 6, 90, 113, 114, 195, 203–204, 321–322, 338, 388, 392, 393

Bunker, Col. Laurence E., 318

Burden, John, 330

Burma, 8, 316, 329–330, 337–338

Burns, John A. ("Jack"), 361, 362–368, 375, 376–379

bushido (warrior spirit), 20, 86, 140, 165, 282, 323, 337

Bushnell Army General Hospital, 389–390

Byron Hot Springs (California), POW camp at, 178–179

Camp Beale (California), 374

Camp Blanding (Florida), training at, 127–128, 293

Camp Crowder (Missouri), 315

Camp Fannin (Texas), training at, 220

Camp McCoy (Wisconsin), training at, 3–4, 22–25, 57–59, 79, 153, 155, 178, 279, 373, 397

Camp Paukukalo (Hawaii), 372

Camp Rich (Minnesota), counter-intelligence training at, 312

Camp Ritchie (Maryland), military intelligence training at, 67, 68, 99

Camp Savage (Minnesota), military intelligence training at, 7, 59, 97–98, 126–127, 140, 178,

279, 293, 312, 315–316, 329, 337

Camp Shelby (Mississippi), training at, 4, 5, 25–26, 59–60, 69–70, 75, 79, 87–88, 103, 116, 117, 140–142, 171, 201–202, 203, 223, 233, 235, 293, 337, 352, 358, 373, 388

Camp Zama (Japan), 341

Cannon Company, of 442nd RCT, 5

Carlesso, Serge, 195

Carr, Ralph, 220

Cary, Dr. Miles E., 102, 307

Castagnetti, Gene, 341

Certain, Capt. Jack, 226

China-Burma-India (CBI) theater of operations, 329. *See also* Burma

Chinese Combat Command, 330

Chinese Cultural Revolution, 331

Ching, Hung Wai, 96, 97

Chojin, Sgt. Shinso, 130

Chong, Patrick, 36

Chong, Kim Fan (a schoolteacher at Central Intermediate School), 41

chugi (loyalty), 84, 92

Civil Rights Act of 1988, 148

Clark, Gen. Mark, 5, 6, 76, 221, 257, 268, 356, 397

Clinton, Bill, 401, 402

Club 100: anniversary banquets of, 108, 392; circus sponsorship by, 375; funding of, 24, 153; motto of, 24

Collin, Dr. Raymond, 195

Confucian ethics. See *shunshin* (ethics, moral training)

Congress, U.S.: declaration of war by, 38, 39, 41, 111

Congressional Medals of Honor:

for 100th Infantry Battalion, 4,
397; for 442nd RCT, 6, 397
Corps of Intelligence Police (COP),
167
Corregidor (Philippines), American
defeat at, 163–164
Counterintelligence Corps (CIC),
316, 318
Cravalho, Elmer, 378
Crost, Lyn: on 100th Infantry
Battalion's reputation, 73–76
Crozier, Willie, 376
Crystal City (Texas) relocation cen-
ter , 142–143
Cunningham, Brig. Gen., 173, 174

Dachau (Germany) concentra-
tion camp, liberation of, 6,
285–288, 289–290, 411
DeMello, Eddie, 362
Dickey, Maj. Joseph K., 181
Distinguished Service Crosses: for
100th Infantry Battalion, 4, 74,
159, 374, 397; for 442nd RCT,
6, 397; for MIS, 282
Division Commendations, 4
Dobashi, Frank, 224
dog-bait training, 155–157
Doi, Masato, 376
Drahon, Jean, 195
Dykes, E. B. (a schoolteacher), 122
dysentery, 171, 175, 221

Ebesu, Tom, 360–361
Edwards, Annette, 126
Edwards, Lloyd, 333
81st Infantry "Wildcat" Division,
128–129, 131, 132
Eniwetok, 8
Epinal (France), American military cemetery at, 338–339,
392–394

Executive Order 9066 (for the
internment of Japanese Americans), 137, 147

Farrington, Betty, 352, 353, 356,
376, 377
Fasi, Frank, 378
FFI (Freedom Fighters of the Interior), 195
1536th Dump Truck Company, 9,
229
1525th Base Equipment Company,
9, 229
5th Amphibious Corps, 182, 280
Fifth Army, U.S.: 100th/442nd RCT
attached to, 4, 5–6, 27,
221–222
Finch, Earl, 68, 233
1st Marine Division, 129
Fisher, Lt. Ralph, 127–128
517th Parachute Infantry Regiment,
114
522nd Field Artillery Battalion
(FABN), 5, 6, 285–288, 337,
404
Fong, Hiram, 361–362
Fort Belvoir (Virginia), 222
Fort Dix (New Jersey), 347
Fort Lewis (Washington), 128, 169
Fort McClellan (Alabama), 329
Fort Meade (Maryland), 220, 221
Fort Snelling (Minnesota), military
intelligence training at, 7, 98,
128, 142, 178, 180, 309
442nd Infantry Regiment, 5
442nd Regimental Combat Team
(RCT): battle cry of, 6; commendations awarded, 6, 76,
352, 389, 397; deployment of,
53, 88, 142, 221–222, 228;
description of, 5–6; formation
of, xii, 5, 33, 87, 115, 139,

364; 100th Infantry Battalion attached to, 4, 5, 65, 75, 110, 269, 386; recruitment for, 125, 139; training of, 5, 51–53, 69–70, 75, 87–88, 116, 140–142, 171, 203, 223, 233, 256, 293, 337, 352, 358, 388

442nd Veterans Club, 147, 375

14th Japanese Army Headquarters (Manila), 167

Freedom Fighters of the Interior (FFI), 195

Fujimoto, Hikoso, 108

Fujimoto, Hikosuke, 107

Fujimoto, Kikuyo: on issei attitudes, 107–109

Fujimoto, Kunio, 108

Fujino, Joe, 279

Fujitani, Aiko Furukawa, 95

Fujitani, Lt., 258

Fujitani, Rev. Kodo, 95, 96, 98, 101

Fujitani, Rev. Yoshiaki, 402, 411; on nisei soldiers, 94–102

Fukuda, Maj. Mitsuyoshi, 76

Furukawa, Shite (grandmother of Y. Fujitani), 100

G-2 Photo Interpreters Section, 294

gaman (perseverance, endurance), 89, 91, 166

ganbari (perseverance), 84, 89

Ganor, Solly, 287–288

Gantt, Ruth, 102

German Americans, as "enemy aliens," 58

German measles, 220–221

Germany, surrender of, 4, 6, 28, 91, 142, 222

ghosts, 56–57

Gilbert Islands, invasion of, 280

Gill, Tom, 378

giri (duty and obligation), 84, 92

Gomes (a janitor at Central Intermediate School), 41

Goshima, Robert, 156

Gothic line, 100th/442nd RCT at, 4, 6, 221–222

Green, Edith, 377

Griggs, Helen, 102

Griner, Maj. Gen. George W., 280

Guadalcanal: 81st Infantry Division at, 129; POWs captured at, 179

Guam: American occupation of, 312; invasion of, 8; Japanese surrender of, 182–184

Gustav line, 100th Infantry Battalion at, 74–75

Hachiya, Sgt. Frank, 398

haji (shame), 92–93, 367

Hall, Jack, 376

Hamada, Margaret, 306, 307

Harano, Kenneth, 54

Hardy, Col. Robert, 332, 333, 334

Hashimoto, Sidney, 378

Hatanaka, Masao, 156

Hawaii: "English Standard" schools in, 82–83; ethnic diversity of, xii–xiii, 364–365, 371; martial law declared in, xi, 37, 308; statehood for, xii, 228, 360, 377, 410; Tendai Buddhist mission in, 409

Hawaiian Provisional Infantry Battalion, 3, 21, 278, 397

Hawaii Government Employees Association (HGEA), 376–377

Hawaii Japanese Immigrant History Center, 409

Hawaii National Guard, 396; 298th

Regiment, 3, 19, 20, 23, 55,
151–152, 178, 189, 278; 299th
Regiment, 3, 22, 23, 46, 178,
189, 278, 372; postwar service
in, 222; recruitment for, 115
Hawaii Political History Documen-
tation Project, 370
Hawaii Territorial Guard (HTG),
xii, 43, 86, 95–96, 336–337
Hazard, Lt. Ben, 280, 281, 282
Headquarters Company, 4th Ma-
rine Division, 180–182
Hemenway, Charles R., 39,
351–358
HGEA (Hawaii Government Em-
ployees Association), 376–377
Higa, Takejiro, 341; frontline expe-
rience of, 291–302
Higa, Warren, 291, 292, 293, 294,
295, 299
Higa, Yuriko, 291, 292, 293–294
Higashi, Roy, 279
Higgins, Lt. Col., 134
Higuchi, Chaplain Hiro, 258;
frontline experience of,
232–254; influence on Ernest
Uno, 145
Higuchi, Hisako ("Mom"): letters
to, 232–254
Hill, Capt. Joe, 224
Hill C (France), 204
Hill D (France), 100th Infantry
Battalion at, 194, 195
Hill 600 (Italy), 100th Infantry
Battalion at, 27, 61, 108
Hino, Sadayuki, 390, 391
Hirahara, Tomosu, 392–394
Hiraoka, Isami, 258
Hirasuna, Noboru, 156
Hirata, Jesse Masao: on military
training, 54–68

Hirohito (emperor of Japan), 332;
K. Tagami's meeting with,
318–320; surrender message
of, 327
Hiroshima, bombing of, 91, 100,
182, 299, 342
Hirotsu, Nobuo, 249
Hisaoka, Sgt. Gary, 385–387
Hite, Charles M., 39
Hitler, Adolph, 85, 236
Hodai, Tadao, 156
Honda, Richard, 190
Honma, Gen. Masaharu, 332
Honolulu Bible Training School
(HBTS), 36–37, 38
Honolulu Civil Defense Fire
Engine Unit, 97
Honolulu Civil Defense First Aid
Corps, 219
Honolulu Major Disaster Council,
35
Honouliuli (Hawaii) relocation
camp, 220
Horio, Don, 379
Hyer, Gardner, 229, 230

Ichiyama, Edward: at liberation of
Dachau, 285–288; on patrio-
tism, 401–402; recollections
of Henry Tetsuo Kobayashi,
403–404
Inada, Kenneth: frontline experi-
ence of, 321–323
Inouye, Daniel K., xi–xiii, 145,
148, 267, 376
Iowa National Guard, 79
Ishii, Herbert, 156
Ishitani, Sgt. Saburo, 205
Ishizuka, Karen, 186
Ishizuka, Sakae, 21
Isobe, Kosaku, 32, 33

issei: Americanization of, 15; connections to Japanese culture and society, 14, 15, 17, 47, 78, 84, 122, 165, 168, 267, 304–305, 336; deportation of, 142; as "enemy aliens," 37, 38, 39, 96–97, 107, 123–124, 137; oral history of, 409–410; as parents of American soldiers, 107–109, 115, 116

Itagaki, Joseph, 376; letters to Charles Hemenway, 351–358

Ito, Hachiro, 61–62

Iwai, Warren: on nisei loyalty, 103–104

Iwasa, James, 56–57

Iwashita, Masami, 156

Iwo Jima, invasion of, 8, 180–182, 337

Jackson, Archie, 102

Jameson, Maj. Malcolm M., 280

Japan: Allied Occupation of, 132–133, 184–185, 309, 312–314, 316–320, 331–334; constitution of, 317; surrender of, 91, 100, 132, 142, 182, 316, 327; War Crimes Commission in, 167–168

Japanese American Citizens League (JACL), 147, 148

Japanese Americans: and antialien land laws, 121; apology and reparations for internment of, 147–148; citizenship of, xv, 85, 187, 261, 279, 375, 380–381; as "enemy aliens," xi–xii, 37, 38, 39, 87, 96–97, 107, 123–124, 137, 139; government policy toward, 39; internment of, 57–58, 68, 96–97, 98, 124–126, 137, 138–139, 142–143, 157, 220, 307, 351, 398. *See also* issei; nisei; sansei

Joint Intelligence Center, Pacific Ocean Area (JICPOA), 130, 180, 279

"jungle rot," 175–176

Junior ROTC (Reserve Officers' Training Corps) training, 19, 83, 279

jus sanguinis (law of blood), 85

jus soli (law of land), 85

Kagawa, Toyohiko, 267

kagezen, 111

Kahanamoku, Anna, 376

Kaholokula, Eddie, 59

Kai, Ernest, 39

Kai, Sgt. James, 131, 132

Kamishita, Seiso: on Pearl Harbor attack, 45–48

Kaneko, Ken, 63

Kanemura, Fred, 156

Kanemura, Harold, 67

Kaneohe Naval Air Station (Oahu), 16

Kashiwaeda, Goro, 258

Katayama, Bob: on military training, 51–53

Kato, Terumi, 68

Kawahara, Sgt. Edwin, 97

Kawano, Pvt. Yasuo, 398

Kawasaki, Duke, 230

Kempeitai, 165, 168

Kendall, Charlie, 377

kibei (Americans educated in Japan), 128, 177

kibei senpai (mentor), 21

Kido, Marquis Koichi, 332
Kido, Mitsuyuki ("Mits"), 96, 365
Kihara, John, 156
Kihara, Shig, 330
Kim, Lt. Young Oak, 63
Kimoto, Sanji, 344–345
Kimura, Lefty, 386
Kishaba, Choyei, 114, 115, 116
Kishaba, Minoru: on issei parents'
    attitudes, 113–117
Kishaba, Susumu, 115, 116
Kishaba, Uto, 114, 115, 116
Kishiue, Dick, 279, 280, 281
Kitahara, Sgt. Kei, 131, 132
Kobayashi, Bert, 362, 363
Kobayashi, Henry Tetsuo, 403–404
Koiso, Kuniaki, 332
Koizumi, 1st Lt. Shoichi ("Pops"),
    262
Koizumi, Masao, 156
Komatsu, James, 156
Kometani, Carol, 276–277
Kometani, Franklin, 275–276
Kometani, James, 276
Kometani, Katsumi ("Doc"), 23,
    58, 269–270, 346; frontline
    experience of, 270, 273–277
Kometani, Yaeko, 273–275
Kono, Hideto, xv–xvii, 341, 411; on
    military training, 69–70
Kono, Russell, 376
Konoye, Prince Fumimaro
    ("Butch"), 332–333
kotonk (mainland Japanese Ameri-
    can), 65, 121–134, 135–148,
    200, 201, 355
Kuahane, Charlie, 376
Kubo, Hoichi: frontline experience
    of, 278–282
Kubota, Sadaichi, 116

Kuniyuki, Aisuke, 219–220, 221
Kuniyuki, Henry S.: frontline expe-
    rience of, 219–222
Kwajalein, 8

La Houssiere (France), liberation
    of, 338
La Junta (New Mexico) relocation
    camp, 220
Lashio (Burma), 316
Lemke, Herman, 377
Leyte Island (Philippines), 132,
    294, 295
Lihue Armory (Kauai), 46
Logan-Smith, Erma (a school-
    teacher), 102
Lovell, Maj. James, 23, 80, 152,
    156, 385–386
Lum, Herman, 376
Lurline, SS, 87, 144

MacArthur, Gen. Douglas, 8, 10,
    163, 164, 167, 230, 294, 309,
    312, 316–320, 332, 334
MacNaughton, Malcolm, 378
Maeda, Katsumi, 156
Majuro Island, invasion of, 8, 280
Makin Island. See Gilbert Islands
Manchuria Mongolia Development
    Young People Service Corps
    (Man Mo Kaitaku Seishonen
    Gyudan), 292
Marshall, Gen. George C., 329
Marshall Islands. See Majuro Island
Mars Task Force (Myitkina), 316
Marumoto, Masaji, 309
Maruo, Tsuneshi, 403
Marzano, Lt. Rocco, 156
Masuda, Sgt. Dick, 223
Matsuda, Pvt., 398

Matsumoto, Koyei, 156
Matsunaga, Spark M., 145, 148,
257, 376; essay on peace,
407–408; Memorial Day
address by, 395–400
Matsuo, Shiro, 230
Matsuoka (chairman of Japanese
lower Diet), 316–317
Matsuoka, Yosuke (Japanese dele-
gate to the UN), 95
Maui, SS (troopship), 21–22, 74,
153, 178, 268, 278
Mayeda, Thomas, 289–290
McCloy, John, 255
McCollum, Bernice (a school-
teacher), 122
McCone, Col., 134
McCrae, John, 339
McGuire Army General Hospital,
389
Meacham, Larry, 370
Medical Detachment, of 442nd
RCT, 5, 89
Meritorious Service Award, for
1399th Engineer Construction
Battalion, 10, 231
Messerschmidts (German air-
planes), 196
Miake, Rev. Eimu, 102
Middlesworth, Vance, 378
Midway Island, U.S. victory at,
128, 278, 396
Military Air Transport Service
(MATS) planes, 101
Military Intelligence Hall of Fame
(Fort Huachuca, Arizona), 169
Military Intelligence Service (MIS):
commendations awarded, 99,
169, 282; deployment of,
74, 128, 228; description of,
7–8; frontline experience of,
128–134, 163; Japanese

American service in, xii, xvi,
70, 97, 127, 139–140, 269,
309, 338; recruitment for,
125–126, 279, 293; training
of, 7, 59, 97–98, 99, 126–127,
142, 178, 293, 309, 312,
315–316, 329, 337
Military Intelligence Training Unit,
99
Mink, Patsy, 376
MIS. *See* Military Intelligence
Service (MIS)
Mitchell, Lt. Norman, 386
Miyao, Richard, 386
Miyashiro, Lt. "Chicken," 206
Miyatake, Michael: frontline experi-
ence of, 170–176
Mizuno, Tom: on Pearl Harbor
attack, 32–33
Mizusawa, Toshio, 156
Moir, John T., Jr., 371–372
Monte Cassino (Italy), 100th
Infantry Battalion at, 4, 27–28,
74–75, 80, 108, 162, 188,
189–190, 374, 385–386
Mori, Frank, 279
Moriguchi, Walter ("Biffa"):
injuries of, 346–347
Morikawa, Yoshito, 386
Morisako, Henry, 171, 174–175,
176
Moritsugu, Richard, 279
Moulin, Max Henri, 195
Mount Folgorito (Italy), 442nd
RCT at, 6, 222
Mueller, Maj. Gen. Paul, 128, 132
Munich, conditions in, 214–215
Muntinglupa Prison (Philippines),
167

Nagasaki, bombing of, 91, 182,
185, 299

Nagata, Tsutomu Tom: frontline experience of, 158–159
Nakaeda, Elizabeth, 69
Nakahara, Richard, 190
Nakamura, Robert, 186
Nakamura, Shunsho, 296–297, 298, 299, 300
Nakano, Taneyoshi, 156
Nanbara, Masaru, 386
Naples (Italy), American forces at, 88, 238
National Guard. *See* Hawaii National Guard
New Caledonia, R & R in, 131
New Guinea, 8, 87; 112th RCT in, 170–176
New York National Guard, 27th Infantry Division, 188, 279, 280
96th Infantry Division, 294, 299, 301
IXth Corps, Military Intelligence, 133, 134
nisei: Americanization of, 14, 15, 20–21, 78, 83, 84, 95, 168, 335; biculturalism of, 335–339, 340–342; as bridge between U.S. and Japan, 320; generation gap with parents, 15; loyalty of, 47–48, 53, 74, 78–79, 85, 86, 92, 95, 102, 139, 174, 187, 188, 260, 267, 336, 397–398; oral history of, 411–412; political participation by, 145, 359–369, 375–379; in V-J Day observances, 401–402
Nishimi, Gilbert, 403
Nishimoto, Lily, 263–264
Nishimoto, Pvt. Tom T., 263–264
Norikane, Minoru, 205
Nosaka, Raymond: on dog-bait training, 155–157; frontline experience of, 190
Nuno, William, 279
Nuuanu Congregational Church, 38

Oahu: military defense installations on, 9; sugar plantations on, 13–14
Oba, Ronald: frontline experience of, 223–226
Officer Candidate School (OCS), recruitment for, 131
Ohama, Sgt. Abraham, 194
ohana (family), spirit of, 20
okage sama de, 305–310, 369
Okamitsu, Takao, 371
Okamura, Kazuto, 331, 332
Okinawa, battle of, 8, 291, 294–302, 337
Okuma, Seiei, 156
"Old Taro Patch Division," 152
Omata, Shiro, 316
on (obligation, duty, debt of gratitude), 24, 84, 92, 94–95, 164–165
105th Infantry Regiment, 280–281
141st Battalion, 36th Division. *See* Texas "Lost Battalion"
100th Infantry Battalion (Separate): battalion flag of, 74, 103; commendations awarded, 4, 65, 74, 76, 159, 373, 397; deployment of, 26, 73, 74, 103, 153, 158, 228, 278–279, 373; description of, 3–4, 73, 74, 186–188, 266–269; dog-bait training in, 155–157; as First Battalion of 442nd RCT, 4, 5, 65, 75, 110, 269, 386; formation of, xii, 3, 265, 266, 372–373; frontline

experience of, 153, 158–159, 161–162; motto of, 74; nickname of, 4; training of, 4, 16, 17, 18–21, 22–26, 57–60, 79, 103, 153, 155, 178, 279, 373, 397. *See also* Club 100

133rd Infantry Regiment, 26, 386

112th Regimental Combat Team, 170–176

124th Cavalry regiment, 316

O'Neill, Eugene, 290

Ono, Tokuji, 156; on Pearl Harbor attack, 29–31

Operation Forager, 280

Operation Iceberg, 295

Oran (North Africa), 100th Infantry Battalion in, 4, 26, 60, 79, 103, 158, 373

Oshima, Hiroshi, 333

Oshiro, Bill, 388

Oshiro, Bob, 378, 379

Oshiro, Cynthia, 370

P-38 (American airplanes), 210

Pacific Club, racial policy of, 368

Pacific Military Intelligence Research Section (PACMIRS), 99, 101

Palau Islands, 81st Infantry Division at, 129–130, 131

peace, Matsunaga's essay on, 407–408

Pearl Harbor: Japanese attack on, xi, 11–48 passim, 54–55, 57, 78, 85–86, 107, 108, 136, 137, 219, 308, 311, 315, 336, 337, 396; restricted access to, 331

Pearson, Drew, 377

Pelelieu Island. *See* Palau Islands

Pence, Col. Charles W., 257

Petrie, Lester, 39

Peyre, 1st Lt. Roger, 281, 282

Philippines: military successes in, 87, 167; MIS in, 8, 163–164

Plutarch, 77

Poindexter, Joseph B. (governor of Hawaii), 39

Porter, Lt. Col. Paul, 152

Porteus, Hebden, 376

Poston relocation camps, 124–125

Potane, Antonicceo, 190

Prather, Nelson, 362

Presidential Unit Citations: for 100th Infantry Battalion, 4, 65, 397; for 442nd RCT, 6, 397

Presidio (San Francisco), 7, 178, 390

prisoners of war (POWs), nisei soldiers as, 165–167, 203–218

Purple Heart Medals: for 100th Infantry Battalion, 4; for 442nd RCT, 6, 389

Pye, Lt. William, 205

Quinn, William, 377

Rasmussen, Col. Kai, 126, 127, 181

Reagan, Ronald, 148

relocation centers: at Amache (Colorado), 138, 142, 220; Crystal City (Texas), 142–143; Honouliuli (Hawaii), 220; La Junta (New Mexico), 220; Poston, 124–125

Reserve Officers' Training Corps (ROTC) program, 23, 43. *See also* Junior ROTC training; University of Hawaii, ROTC program at

Robinson (a Caucasian deed holder), 122

Rodarme, Capt. Jack Woodrow, 225

Rome (Italy), 100th Infantry Battalion at, 61, 75

Roosevelt, Franklin D.: on Bill of Rights Day, 43; on declaration of national emergency, 34; on declaration of war with Japan, 38, 40; and internment of Japanese Americans, 137; issei support for, 372; on peacetime draft, 77

ROTC. *See* Reserve Officers' Training Corps (ROTC) program

Royal T. Frank (transport), 372

Ryder, Maj. Gen. Charles W., 26, 268

Saipan, invasion of, 8, 280–281, 337

Saito, Larry, 279

Saito, Miwa, 300

Sakai, Robert K., 411; on mainland nisei experiences, 121–134

Sakai, Sady Kitaoka, 125, 126, 127

Sakakida, Richard M.: frontline experience of, 163–169

Sakamaki, Ben, 179

Sakamaki, George, 179

Sakata, Harold, 230

Sakomizu, Shukichi, 313

Salerno (Italy), 100th Infantry Battalion in, 4, 26–27, 60–61, 74, 79–80, 153, 158–159, 266, 373–374

sansei: career opportunities for, 145; questioning of received history by, 411–412

Santa Anita Assembly Center, 138

Sasai, Kazu Uno, 81, 82

Sasai, Sam: on 442nd RCT, 81–93

Sasai, Tamaki, 81, 82

Sasaki, "Happy," 56–57

Sasebo (Japan), 183, 184–185

Sato, Robert: on citizenship for issei, 380–381; frontline experience of, 189–190; on issei parents' attitudes, 110–111, 112

SAWPAC (Southwest Pacific Command), 174

SCAP (Supreme Commander, Allied Powers), 133

Schofield Barracks (Oahu), 9, 279, 396; military training at, 15, 17–21, 30, 46, 51–53, 55–57, 78, 95, 152, 178, 189, 231, 278, 372–373; Officers Club at, 152

Sea Tiger, 67

2nd Marine Division, 280

Seki, Don: injuries of, 388–391

7th Infantry Division, 6th Army, 315

Seventh Army, U.S.: and 442nd RCT, 357; 522nd Field Artillery Battalion assigned to, 6

shell shock, 260

Shepardson, Anita, 125

Shigemori, Tairo no, 282

Shimamura, Joe: recollections of Sanji Kimoto, 343–345

Shimatsu, Hisa, 47–48

shinbo (endurance), 84

Shinoda, Minoru, 330

Shintaku, Jimmy, 58–59

Shioi, Stanley, 230–231

Ship Island (Gulf of Mexico), dog-bait training on, 155–157

Shiratori, Toshio, 333

Short, Lt. Gen. Walter C., 39

shunshin (ethics, moral training), 24, 84, 95

Siegfried line, 209
Silver Star Medals: for 100th Infantry Battalion, 4, 397; for 442nd RCT, 6, 397
Sinatra, Frank, 60
6th Army, 315
Smith, Capt. Nolle, 96
Smith, Elsie (a schoolteacher), 122
Smyser, A. A. ("Bud"): speech by, 227–231
Solomon Islands invasion, 8
Sonoda, Lt. George, 331
Southwest Pacific Command (SWAPAC), 174
Spaulding, Ethel, 102
Stalag VIIA (German POW camp), 212–218
Stettinius, Edward Reilly, 375
Stilwell, Gen. Joseph, 315
Sugai, Robert, 289–290
Sugamo Prison (Japan), 331–334
Sugawara, Shin, 258
Sugihara, Senpo, 287, 288
Supreme Commander, Allied Powers (SCAP), 133
Suvereto (Italy): 100th Infantry Battalion at, 257; 442nd RCT at, 5–6
Suzuki, William, 40

Tagami, Kan: meeting with Japanese emperor, 315–320
Takaezu, William, 156
Takahashi, Capt. Sakae, 66, 257; frontline experience of, 186–188
Takahashi, Sgt. Hiroki "Chico," 129
Takaki, Fujio: on tree-planting in Maizuru City, 311–314
Takaki, Hideo, 312–313

Takamori, Saigo, 78
Takashige, Robert, 156
Takata, Sgt. Shigeo Joe, 74, 158–159, 274
Takata, Yasuo, 156
Takeshi, Peter, 239, 241, 245
tamashi, 20
Tamashiro, Aiko, 160, 161
Tamashiro, Ben: on 100th Infantry Battalion's reputation, 77–80; frontline experience of, 160–162; recollections of Tomosu Hirahara, 392–394
Tanaka, Charlie, 62–63
Tanaka, Douglas, 61
Tanaka, Lt. Ernest, 156
Tanaka, Keichi, 59
Tanaka, Takeshi, 156
Tanigawa, Seiji, 156
Tanimoto, Jack, 279, 280
Tarawa, invasion of, 8, 337
Tawada, Toyo, 300
Taylor, Harry, 371
Tennessee National Guard, 128
10th Army Air Force, 337
Texas "Lost Battalion" (141st Battalion, 36th Division), rescue of, 4, 6, 27, 75, 90, 259, 321, 393
3rd Battalion, 195
1399th Engineer Construction Battalion: commendations awarded, 10, 230, 231; description of, 9–10; nickname of, 10; wartime experience of, 227–231
38th Evac. (Evacuation) Hospital, 257
34th Construction Engineer Regiment, 96. See also Varsity Victory Volunteers (VVV)

34th "Red Bull" Infantry Division, 4, 36, 79, 266, 373

32nd Division Headquarters Language Team, 172

36th Infantry Division, 4, 6, 75

395th Quartermaster Battalion, 9

370th Engineer Battalion, 9, 229

300th General Hospital, 66

321st Regiment, 129

322nd Regiment, 129

Thunderbirds (American airplanes), 210

Tojo, Gen. Hideki, 333–334, 338

Tojo, Tadashi: at liberation of Dachau, 289–290

Tokioka, Masayuki, 410

Tokunaga, Nobumi, 370

Tokunaga, Sgt. Mike, 205; interview with, 370–379

Tokushima, Patrick, 156

Toynbee, Arnold, 399

Trask, Arthur, 306

trench foot, 66, 114, 194. *See also* "jungle rot"

Tripler Army General Hospital, 391

Truman, Harry, 68, 222

Tsukano, John: frontline experience of, 191–202

Tsukayama, Conrad: on Pearl Harbor attack, 13–28

Tsukiyama, Seinosuke, 335

Tsukiyama, Ted, 309; on nisei biculturalism, 335–339

Tsukiyama, Wilfred, 376

Tsukiyama, Yoshiko Kagawa, 335

Turner, Albert ("Bert"), 151–154

Turner, Col. Farrant L. ("Old Man"), 23, 151–154, 159, 268

Tuttle, Daniel W., Jr., 370

206th Army Ground Forces Band, 5

232nd Combat Engineers Company, 5

Ulithi Island. *See* Palau Islands

United Japanese Society of Hawaii (UJSH), 387

United Nations, 374

University of Hawaii, ROTC program at, 23, 86, 95, 177–178, 279, 336

Uno, Edison, 143, 147, 148

Uno, Ernest: on mainland nisei experiences, 135–148

Uno, Grace, 144

Uno, Kanemitsu, 82

Uno, Kay, 143

Uno, Kumemaro, 135–136, 137, 142, 143

Uno, Riki Kita, 135, 143, 146

Ushiro, Doc, 242, 243

Varsity Victory Volunteers (VVV), xii, 96, 337

V-J Day observances, 401–402

Vosges Mountain campaign (in France), 100th/442nd RCT in, 4, 6, 27, 90, 91, 114, 191–202, 204–206, 322–323, 338–339, 388

Waihee, John, 377, 379

Wainwright, Gen. Jonathan, 164, 165

Wakukawa, Ernest, 102

Walter-McCarran Act of 1952, 310, 380–381

Walter Reed Army Hospital, 347

War Crimes Commission, U.S., 167–168

Washington (D.C.) Document Center, 101

West, Chaplain Thomas Eugene, 234

Wheeler Air Force Base (Honolulu), 312

Wheeler Field (Honolulu), attack on, 32–33

White, Bruce E., 375

Whitney, Gen., 317

Willoughby, Gen. Charles, 8

Wilson, Johnny, 375

Women Army Corps (WACs), 99

Wood, Col. Stuart, 164

Yamada, Chaplain Masao, 234, 250; frontline experience of, 255–264

Yamagata, Clarence, 164, 165

Yamamoto, Ben I.: frontline experience of, 177–185

Yamamoto, Sgt. Mas, 172

Yamasaki, Eddy, 258

Yamasato, Rev. Jikai, 102

Yamate, Sohei: frontline experience of, 328–334

Yamato damashii (spirit of Japan), 23, 102, 140, 168, 337, 412

Yap Island, American success at, 294

Yasui, Sgt. Kanji, 329–330

Yasutake, "Pistol," 98–99

Yazawa, Mack, 156

Yempuku, Ralph, 97, 309

YMCA (Young Men's Christian Association), 143–146

Yokooji, Iwao, 401

Yokoto, Yukio, 156

Yokoyama (aunt of Y. Fujitani), 100

Yokoyama, Masayuki, 100–101

Yonezawa, Kaoru: recollections of Gary Hisaoka, 385–387

Yosemori, Rev. Chiro, 102

Yoshida, Jimmy, 373

Yoshida, Mas, 226

Yoshida, Shigeo, 96

Yoshida, Shigeru (Japanese prime minister), 317

Yoshida, Tatsuki, 231

Yoshimura, Akiji, 331

Yoshinaga, Nadao, 145

Yost, Chaplain Israel: recollection of, 265–272

Young Men's Christian Association (YMCA), 143–146

Zeros (Japanese airplanes), 16, 30, 32–33, 54, 5